CHABOUTÉ

D1296936

BASED ON THE NOVEL BY BENOIT COHEN

Batavia Public Library
Batavia, Illinois

WITHDRAWN

Facebook: **facebook.com/idwpublishing**
Twitter: **@idwpublishing**
YouTube: **youtube.com/idwpublishing**
Instagram: **@idwpublishing**

ISBN: 978-1-68405-892-1   25 24 23 22   1 2 3 4

Translation by
Edward Gauvin

Letters by
Nathan Widick

Edits by
Alonzo Simon and
Zac Boone

YELLOW CAB. MAY 2022. FIRST PRINTING. © Editions Glénat 2021 by Chabouté – ALL RIGHTS RESERVED. Based on the original Work by Benoit Cohen. © 2022 Idea and Design Works, LLC. The IDW Logo is registered in the U.S. Patent and Trademark Office. IDW Publishing, a division of Idea and Design Works, LLC. Editorial offices: 2765 Truxtun Road, San Diego, CA 92106. Any similarities to persons living or dead are purely coincidental. With the exception of artwork used for review purposes, none of the contents of this publication may be reprinted without permission of Idea and Design Works, LLC. IDW Publishing does not read or accept unsolicited submissions of ideas, stories, or artwork. Printed in Korea.

Nachie Marsham, Publisher
Blake Kobashigawa, VP of Sales
Tara McCrillis, VP Publishing Operations
John Barber, Editor-in-Chief
Mark Doyle, Editorial Director, Originals
Scott Dunbier, Director, Special Projects
Lauren LePera, Managing Editor
Joe Hughes, Director, Talent Relations
Anna Morrow, Sr. Marketing Director
Alexandra Hargett, Book & Mass Market Sales Director
Keith Davidsen, Director, Marketing & PR
Topher Alford, Sr. Digital Marketing Manager
Shauna Monteforte, Sr. Director of Manufacturing Operations
Jamie Miller, Sr. Operations Manager
Nathan Widick, Sr. Art Director, Head of Design
Neil Uyetake, Sr. Art Director, Design & Production
Shawn Lee, Art Director, Design & Production
Jack Rivera, Art Director, Marketing

Ted Adams and Robbie Robbins, IDW Founders

TO ALL THESE MUSES, WHO CARRY US ...

WEDNESDAY, JUNE 3, 2015

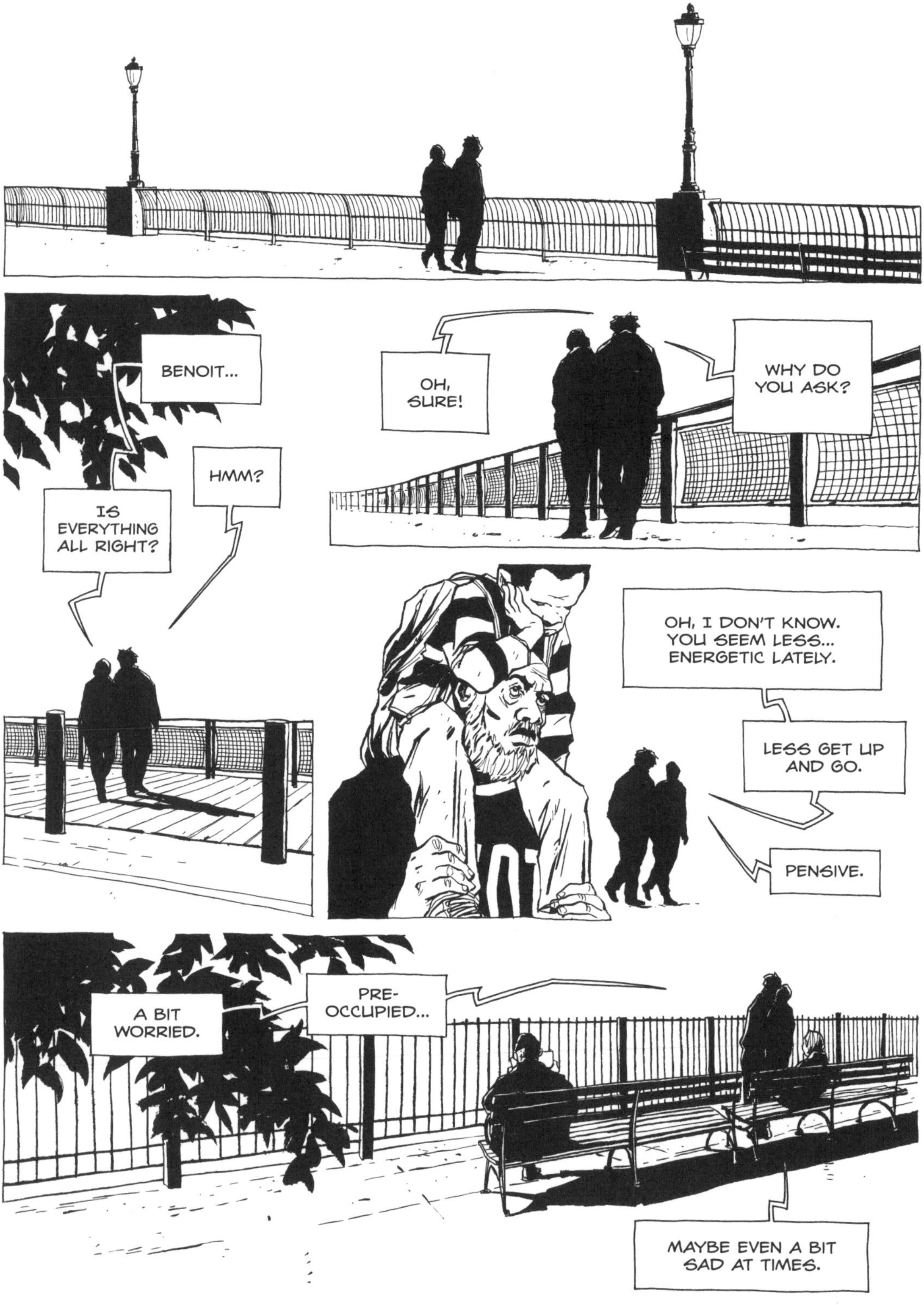
BENOIT...
IS EVERYTHING ALL RIGHT?
HMM?
OH, SURE!
WHY DO YOU ASK?
OH, I DON'T KNOW. YOU SEEM LESS... ENERGETIC LATELY.
LESS GET UP AND GO.
PENSIVE.
A BIT WORRIED.
PRE-OCCUPIED...
MAYBE EVEN A BIT SAD AT TIMES.

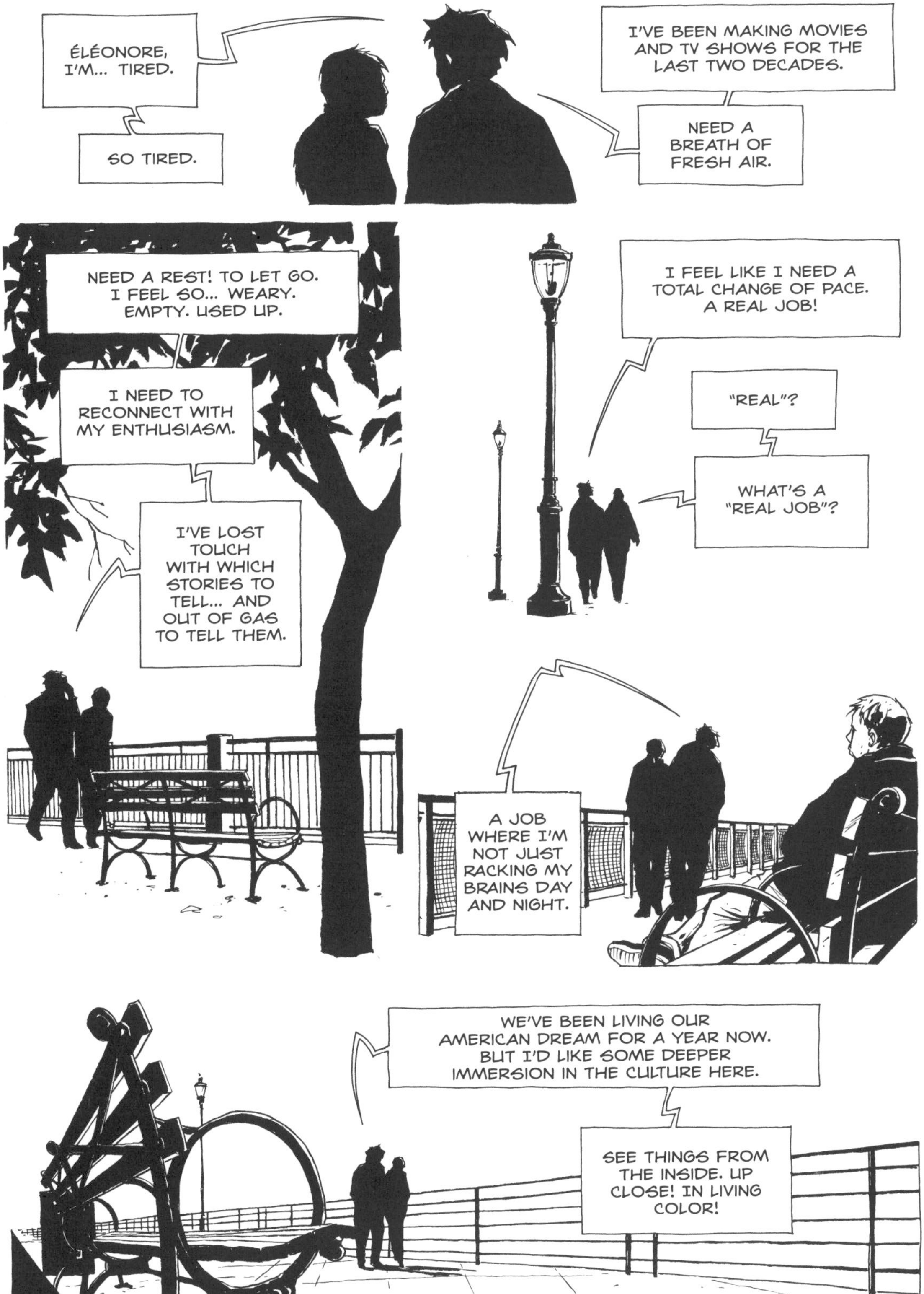
ÉLÉONORE, I'M... TIRED.
SO TIRED.
I'VE BEEN MAKING MOVIES AND TV SHOWS FOR THE LAST TWO DECADES.
NEED A BREATH OF FRESH AIR.
NEED A REST! TO LET GO. I FEEL SO... WEARY. EMPTY. USED UP.
I NEED TO RECONNECT WITH MY ENTHUSIASM.
I'VE LOST TOUCH WITH WHICH STORIES TO TELL... AND OUT OF GAS TO TELL THEM.
I FEEL LIKE I NEED A TOTAL CHANGE OF PACE. A REAL JOB!
"REAL"?
WHAT'S A "REAL JOB"?
A JOB WHERE I'M NOT JUST RACKING MY BRAINS DAY AND NIGHT.
WE'VE BEEN LIVING OUR AMERICAN DREAM FOR A YEAR NOW. BUT I'D LIKE SOME DEEPER IMMERSION IN THE CULTURE HERE.
SEE THINGS FROM THE INSIDE. UP CLOSE! IN LIVING COLOR!

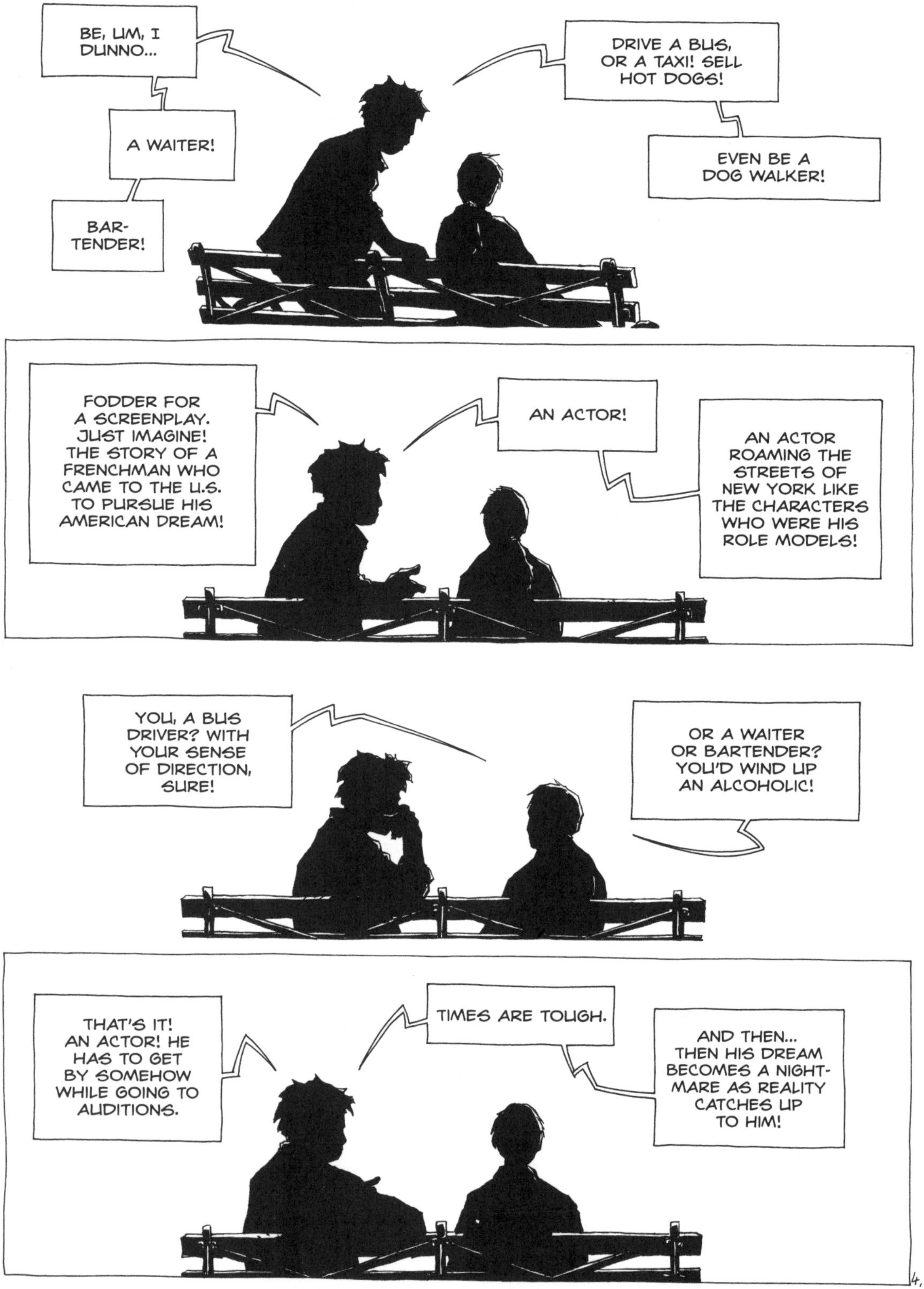
BE, UM, I DUNNO...
A WAITER!
BAR-TENDER!
DRIVE A BUS, OR A TAXI! SELL HOT DOGS!
EVEN BE A DOG WALKER!
FODDER FOR A SCREENPLAY. JUST IMAGINE! THE STORY OF A FRENCHMAN WHO CAME TO THE U.S. TO PURSUE HIS AMERICAN DREAM!
AN ACTOR!
AN ACTOR ROAMING THE STREETS OF NEW YORK LIKE THE CHARACTERS WHO WERE HIS ROLE MODELS!
YOU, A BUS DRIVER? WITH YOUR SENSE OF DIRECTION, SURE!
OR A WAITER OR BARTENDER? YOU'D WIND UP AN ALCOHOLIC!
THAT'S IT! AN ACTOR! HE HAS TO GET BY SOMEHOW WHILE GOING TO AUDITIONS.
TIMES ARE TOUGH.
AND THEN... THEN HIS DREAM BECOMES A NIGHT-MARE AS REALITY CATCHES UP TO HIM!

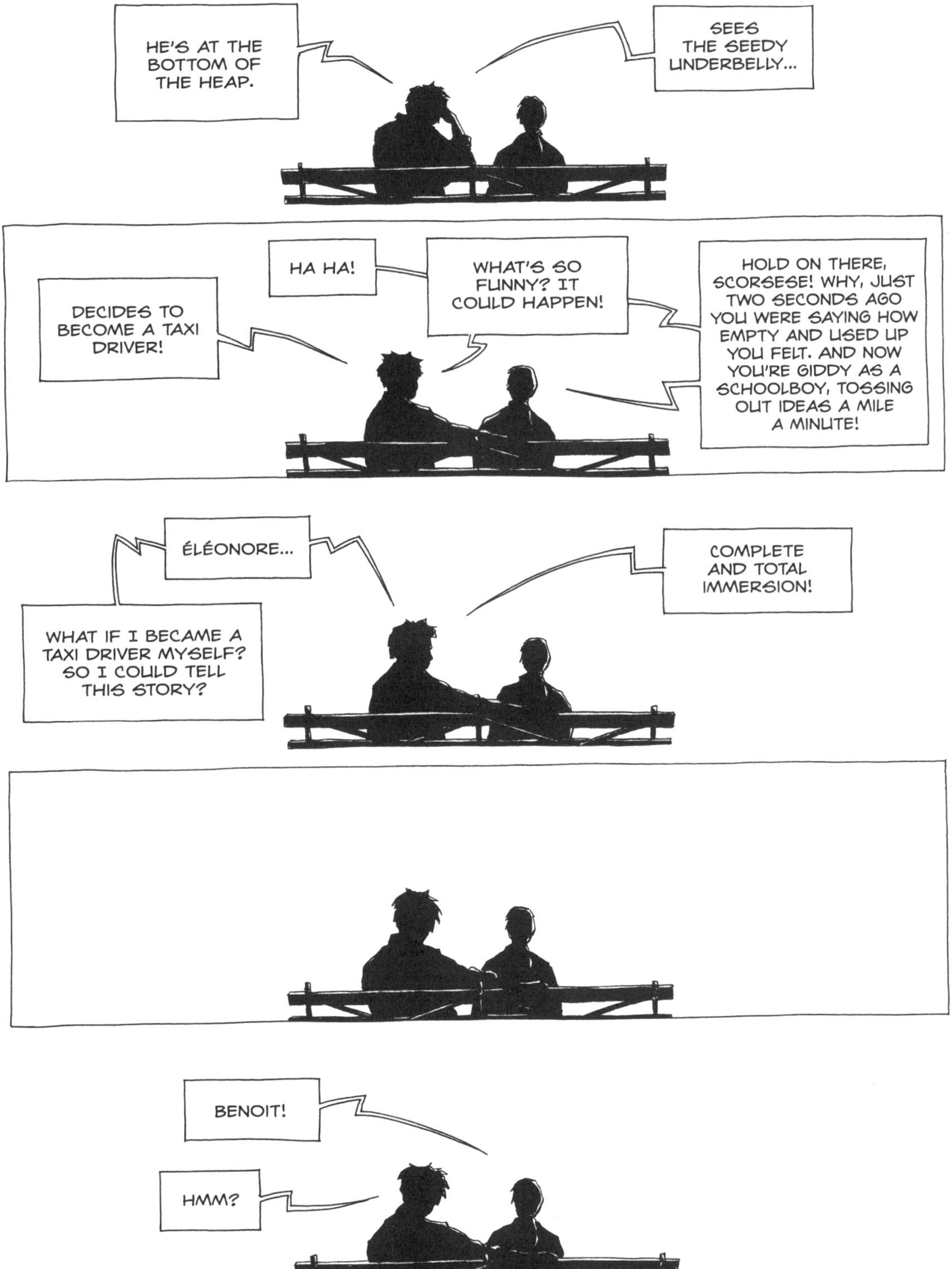
HE'S AT THE BOTTOM OF THE HEAP.
SEES THE SEEDY UNDERBELLY...
DECIDES TO BECOME A TAXI DRIVER!
HA HA!
WHAT'S SO FUNNY? IT COULD HAPPEN!
HOLD ON THERE, SCORSESE! WHY, JUST TWO SECONDS AGO YOU WERE SAYING HOW EMPTY AND USED UP YOU FELT. AND NOW YOU'RE GIDDY AS A SCHOOLBOY, TOSSING OUT IDEAS A MILE A MINUTE!
ÉLÉONORE...
WHAT IF I BECAME A TAXI DRIVER MYSELF? SO I COULD TELL THIS STORY?
COMPLETE AND TOTAL IMMERSION!
BENOIT!
HMM?

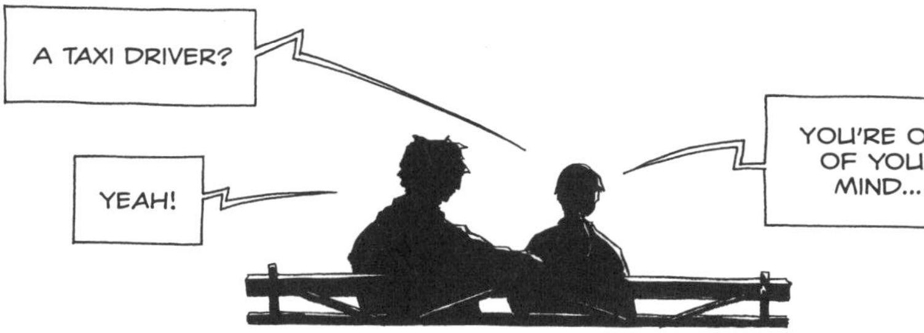
A TAXI DRIVER?
YEAH!
YOU'RE OUT OF YOUR MIND...

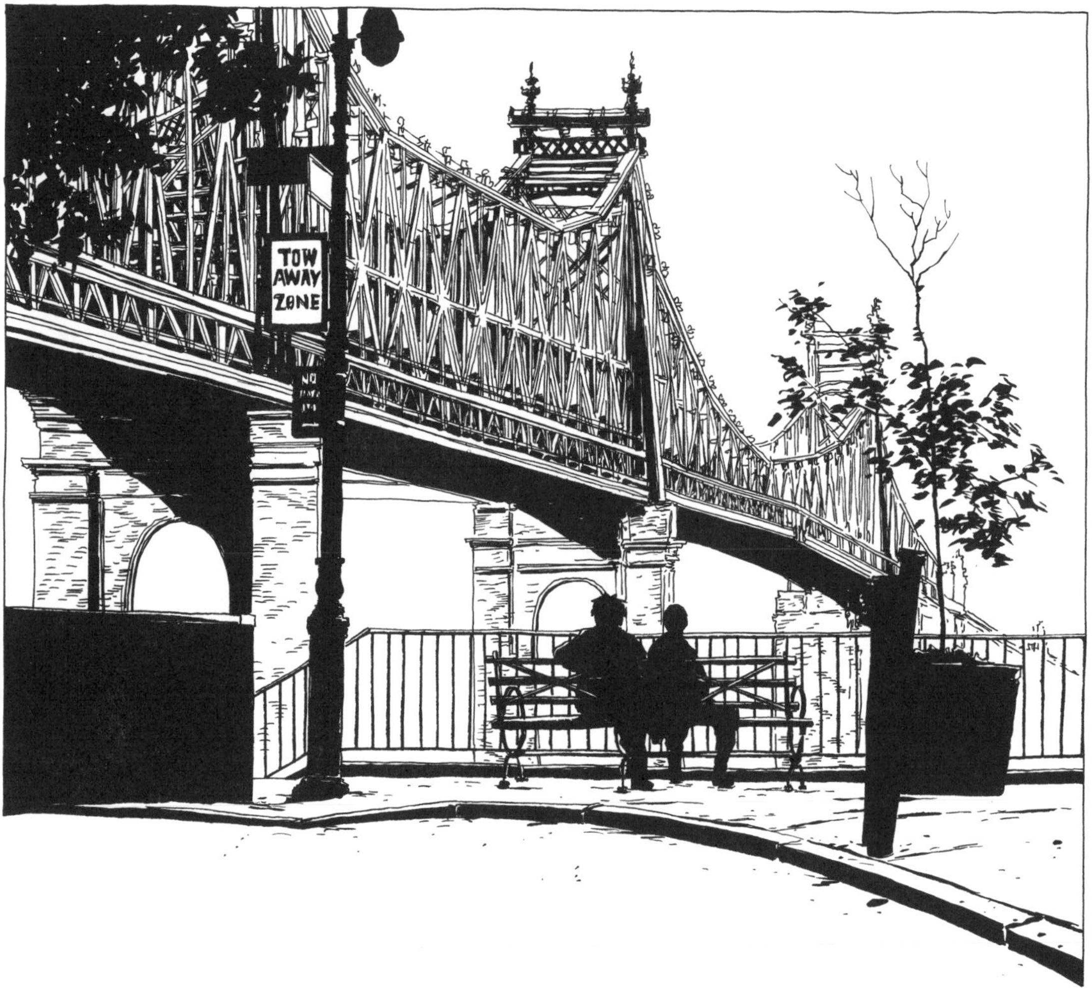
TOW AWAY ZONE

THURSDAY, JUNE 4, 2015

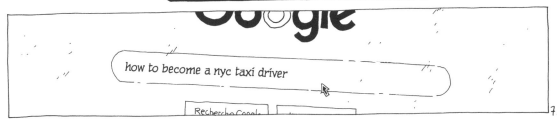

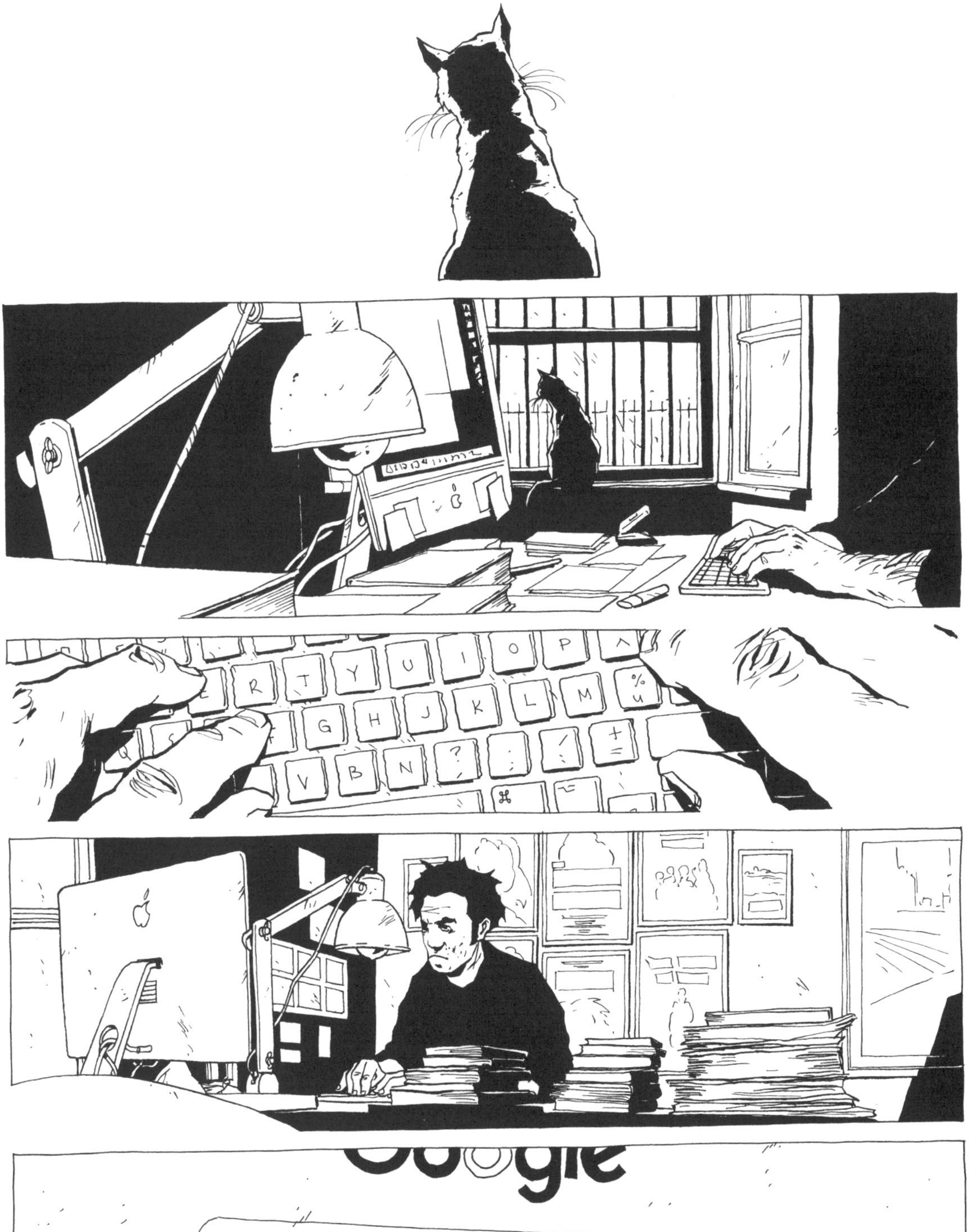
how to become a nyc taxi driver

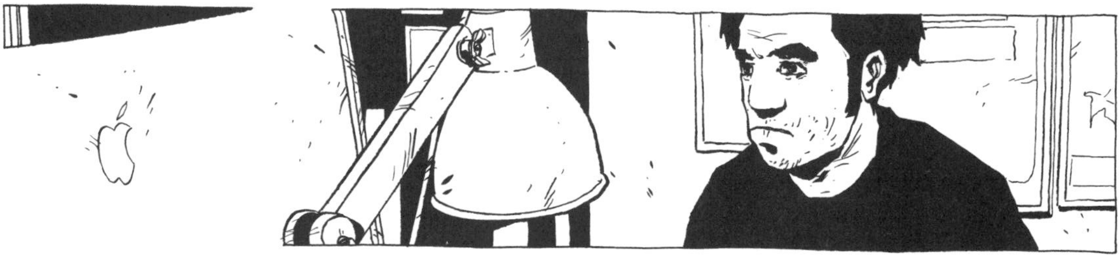

A YELLOW CAB DRIVER! YELLOW CABS ARE THE VERY ESSENCE OF NEW YORK. THEY'RE MOVIES: *TAXI DRIVER*, DE NIRO, SCORSESE, JARMUSCH, *BREAKFAST AT TIFFANY'S*, FINCHER'S *THE GAME*, BRANDO IN *ON THE WATERFRONT*, JAMES CAGNEY, AUDREY HEPBURN, BEN GAZZARA, BENNY THE CAB...

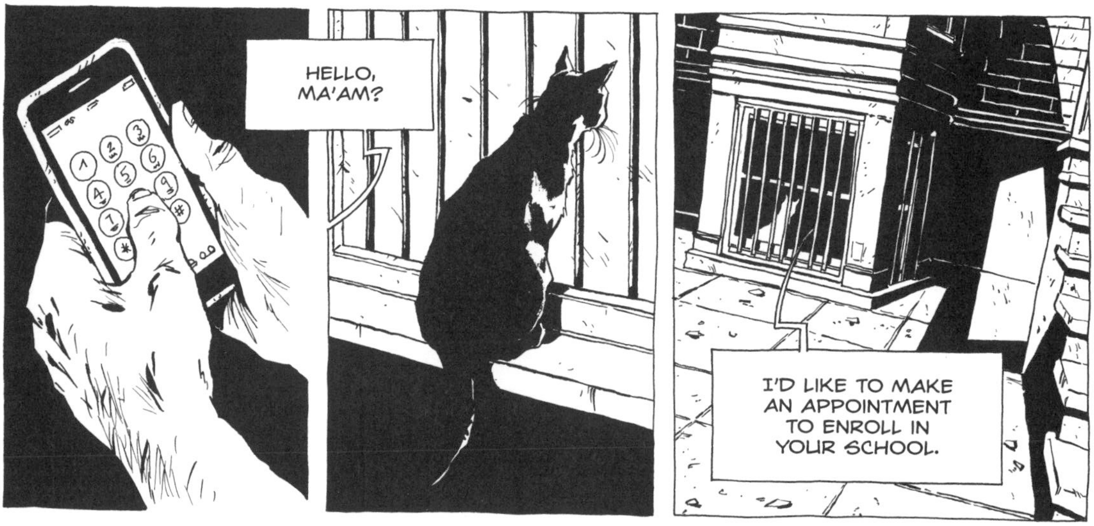
HELLO, MA'AM?
I'D LIKE TO MAKE AN APPOINTMENT TO ENROLL IN YOUR SCHOOL.

IT'S A WINDOW ON THE MADNESS, ENERGY, DIVERSITY, AND VIOLENCE OF THIS CITY.

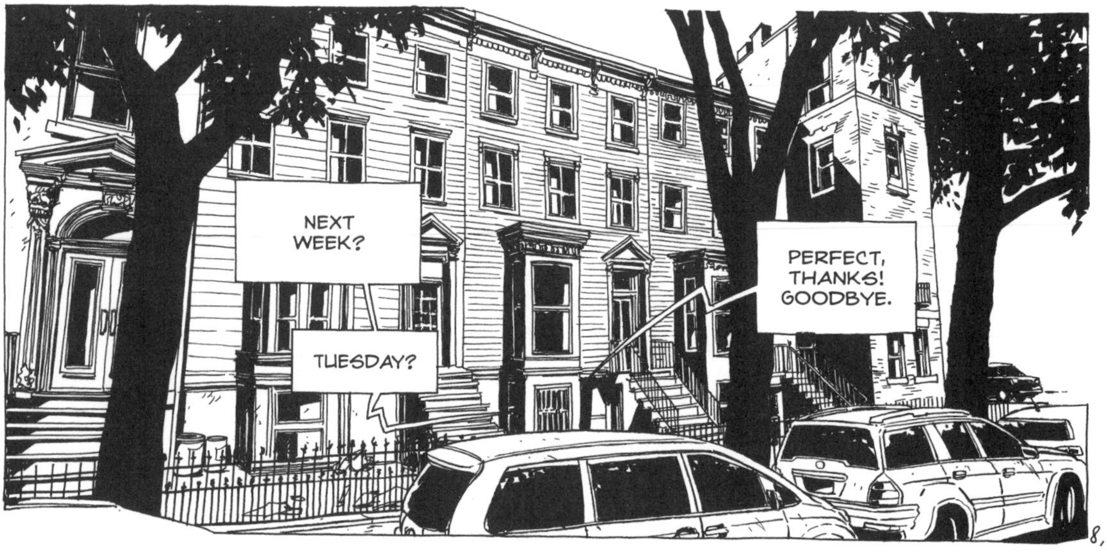
NEXT WEEK?
TUESDAY?
PERFECT, THANKS! GOODBYE.

TUESDAY, JUNE 9, 2015

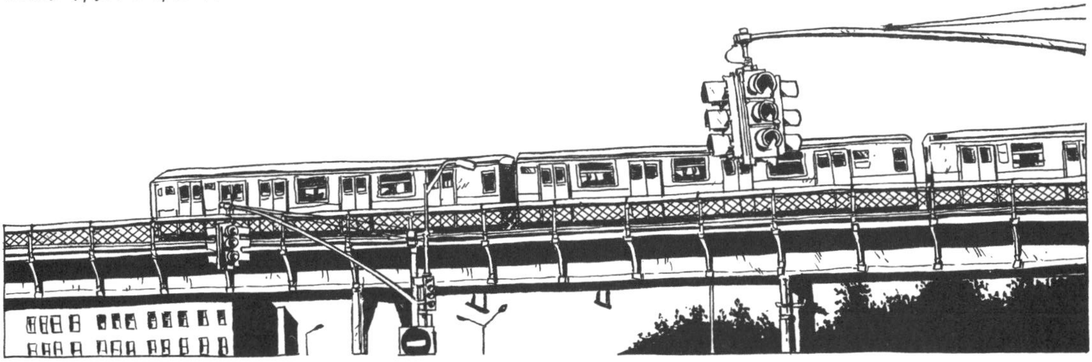

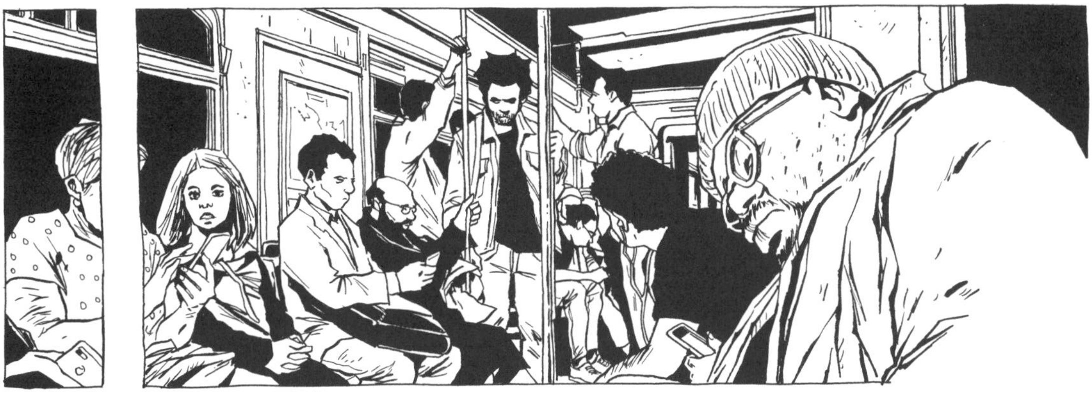

ONSCREEN, IT SEEMED SO SIMPLE. I HAD TO ENROLL IN A SPECIALIZED SCHOOL, LOG AT LEAST TWENTY-FOUR HOURS OF CLASSES, TAKE A WRITTEN EXAM, AND PASS A DRUG TEST. AVERAGE COST: $500!

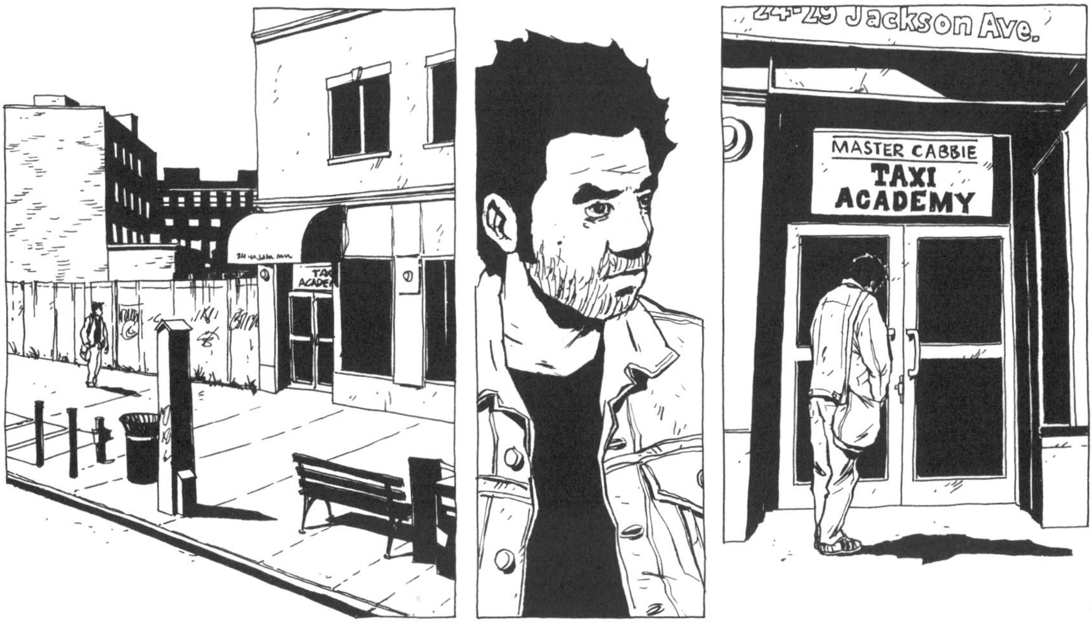
24-29 Jackson Ave.
MASTER CABBIE
TAXI ACADEMY

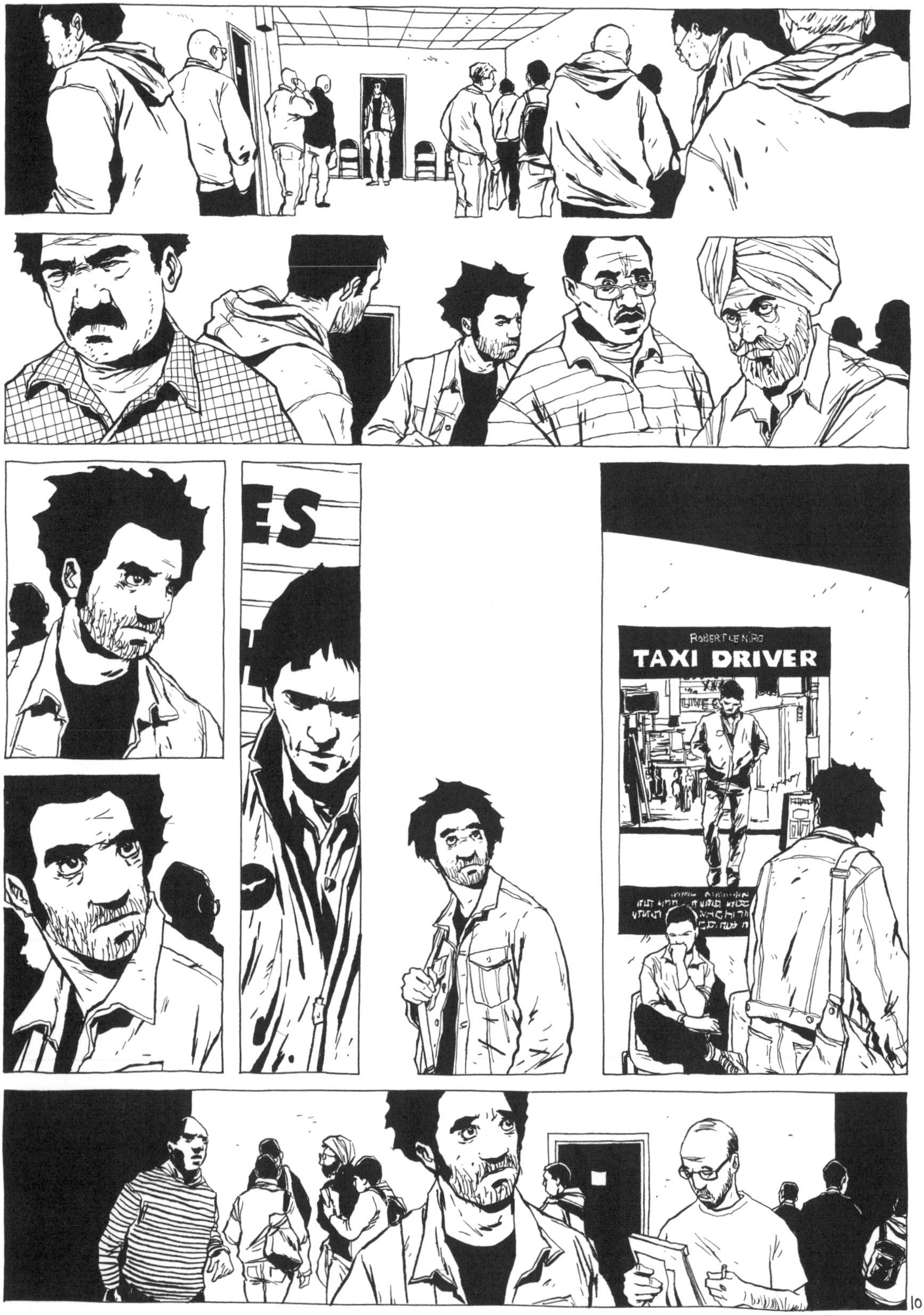
ES
ROBERT DE NIRO
TAXI DRIVER

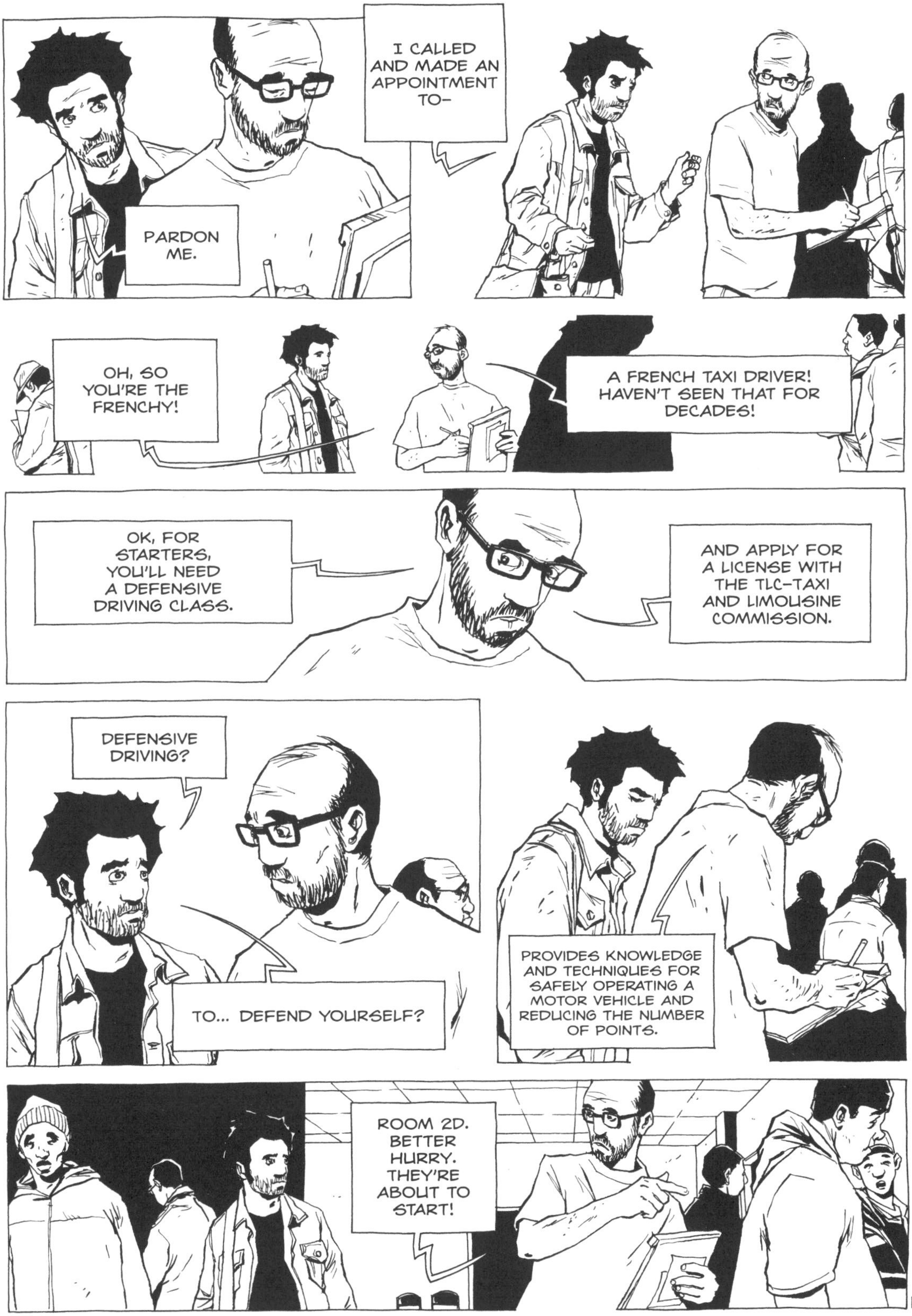
PARDON ME.
I CALLED AND MADE AN APPOINTMENT TO–
OH, SO YOU'RE THE FRENCHY!
A FRENCH TAXI DRIVER! HAVEN'T SEEN THAT FOR DECADES!
OK, FOR STARTERS, YOU'LL NEED A DEFENSIVE DRIVING CLASS.
AND APPLY FOR A LICENSE WITH THE TLC–TAXI AND LIMOUSINE COMMISSION.
DEFENSIVE DRIVING?
TO... DEFEND YOURSELF?
PROVIDES KNOWLEDGE AND TECHNIQUES FOR SAFELY OPERATING A MOTOR VEHICLE AND REDUCING THE NUMBER OF POINTS.
ROOM 2D. BETTER HURRY. THEY'RE ABOUT TO START!

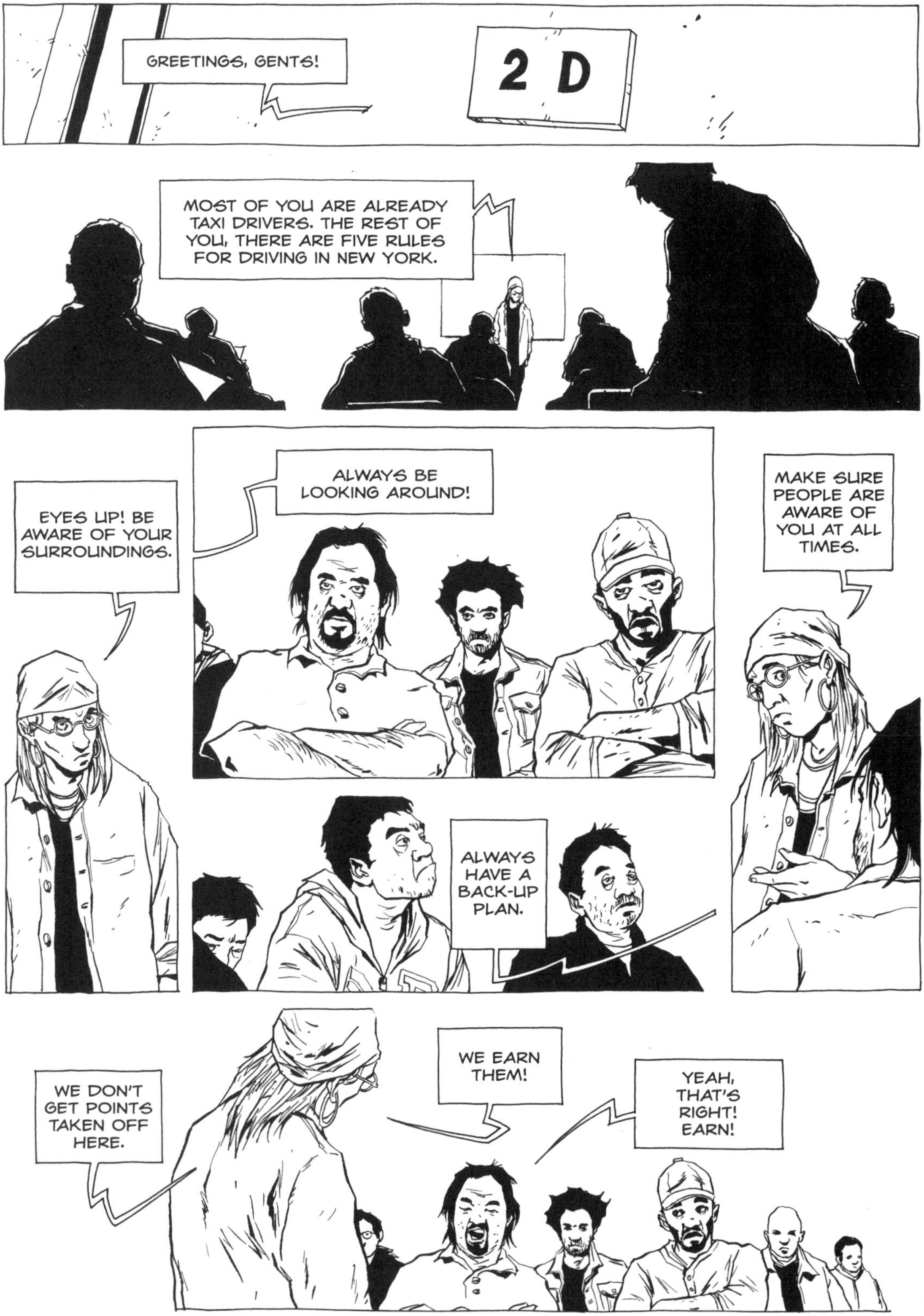
GREETINGS, GENTS!
2 D
MOST OF YOU ARE ALREADY TAXI DRIVERS. THE REST OF YOU, THERE ARE FIVE RULES FOR DRIVING IN NEW YORK.
EYES UP! BE AWARE OF YOUR SURROUNDINGS.
ALWAYS BE LOOKING AROUND!
MAKE SURE PEOPLE ARE AWARE OF YOU AT ALL TIMES.
ALWAYS HAVE A BACK-UP PLAN.
WE DON'T GET POINTS TAKEN OFF HERE.
WE EARN THEM!
YEAH, THAT'S RIGHT! EARN!

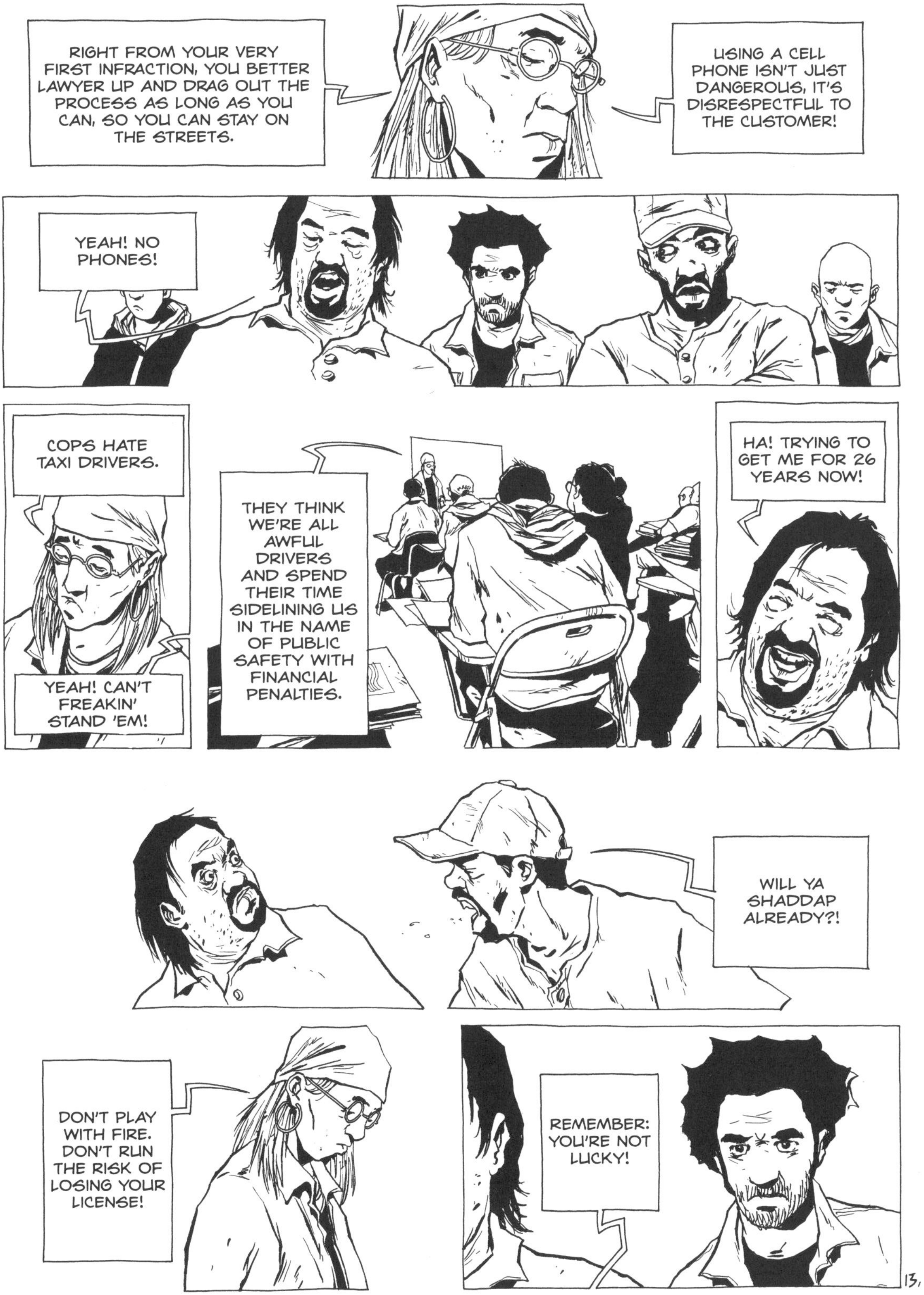
RIGHT FROM YOUR VERY FIRST INFRACTION, YOU BETTER LAWYER UP AND DRAG OUT THE PROCESS AS LONG AS YOU CAN, SO YOU CAN STAY ON THE STREETS.
USING A CELL PHONE ISN'T JUST DANGEROUS, IT'S DISRESPECTFUL TO THE CUSTOMER!
YEAH! NO PHONES!
COPS HATE TAXI DRIVERS.
YEAH! CAN'T FREAKIN' STAND 'EM!
THEY THINK WE'RE ALL AWFUL DRIVERS AND SPEND THEIR TIME SIDELINING US IN THE NAME OF PUBLIC SAFETY WITH FINANCIAL PENALTIES.
HA! TRYING TO GET ME FOR 26 YEARS NOW!
WILL YA SHADDAP ALREADY?!
DON'T PLAY WITH FIRE. DON'T RUN THE RISK OF LOSING YOUR LICENSE!
REMEMBER: YOU'RE NOT LUCKY!
13.

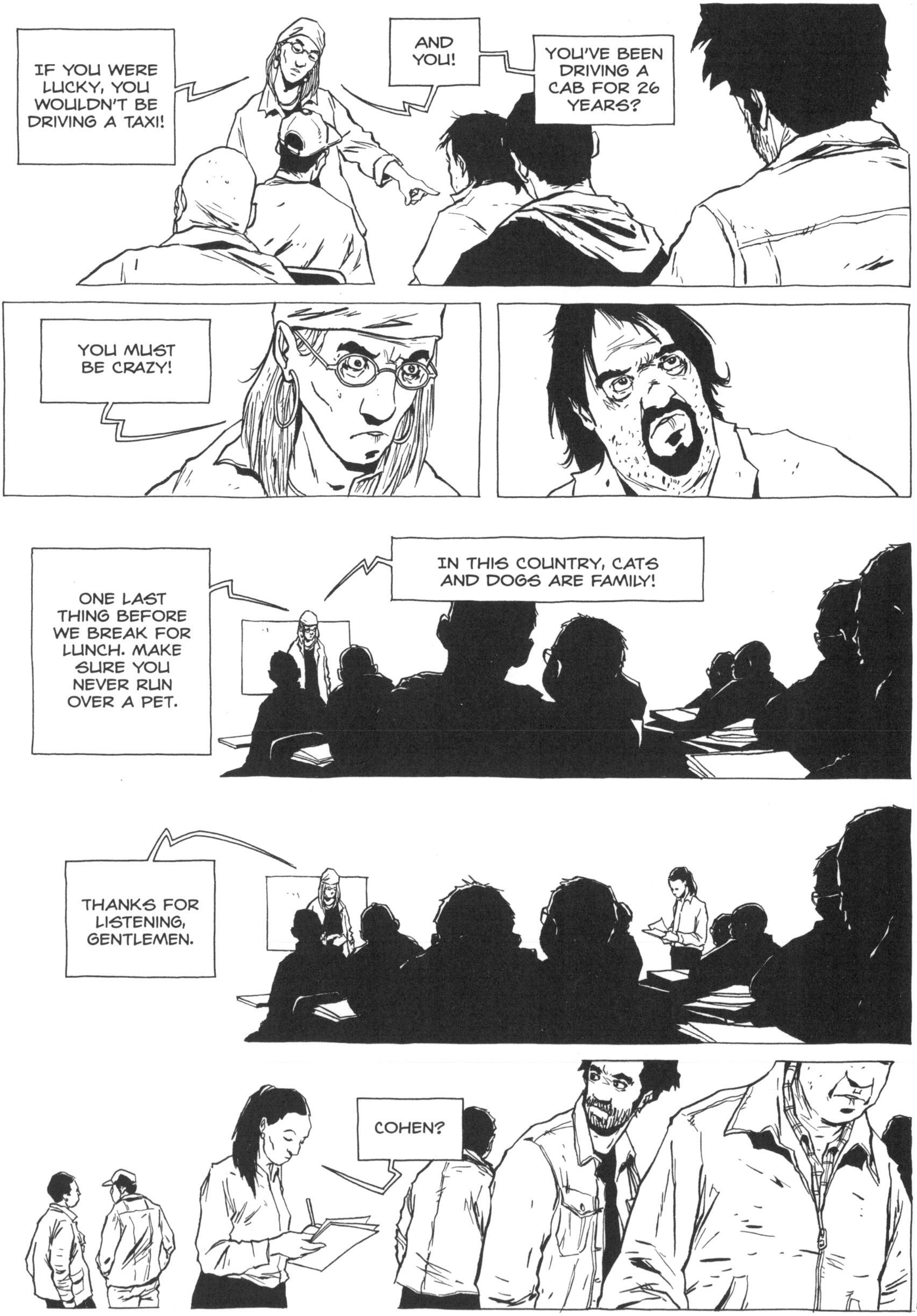
IF YOU WERE LUCKY, YOU WOULDN'T BE DRIVING A TAXI!
AND YOU!
YOU'VE BEEN DRIVING A CAB FOR 26 YEARS?
YOU MUST BE CRAZY!
ONE LAST THING BEFORE WE BREAK FOR LUNCH. MAKE SURE YOU NEVER RUN OVER A PET.
IN THIS COUNTRY, CATS AND DOGS ARE FAMILY!
THANKS FOR LISTENING, GENTLEMEN.
COHEN?

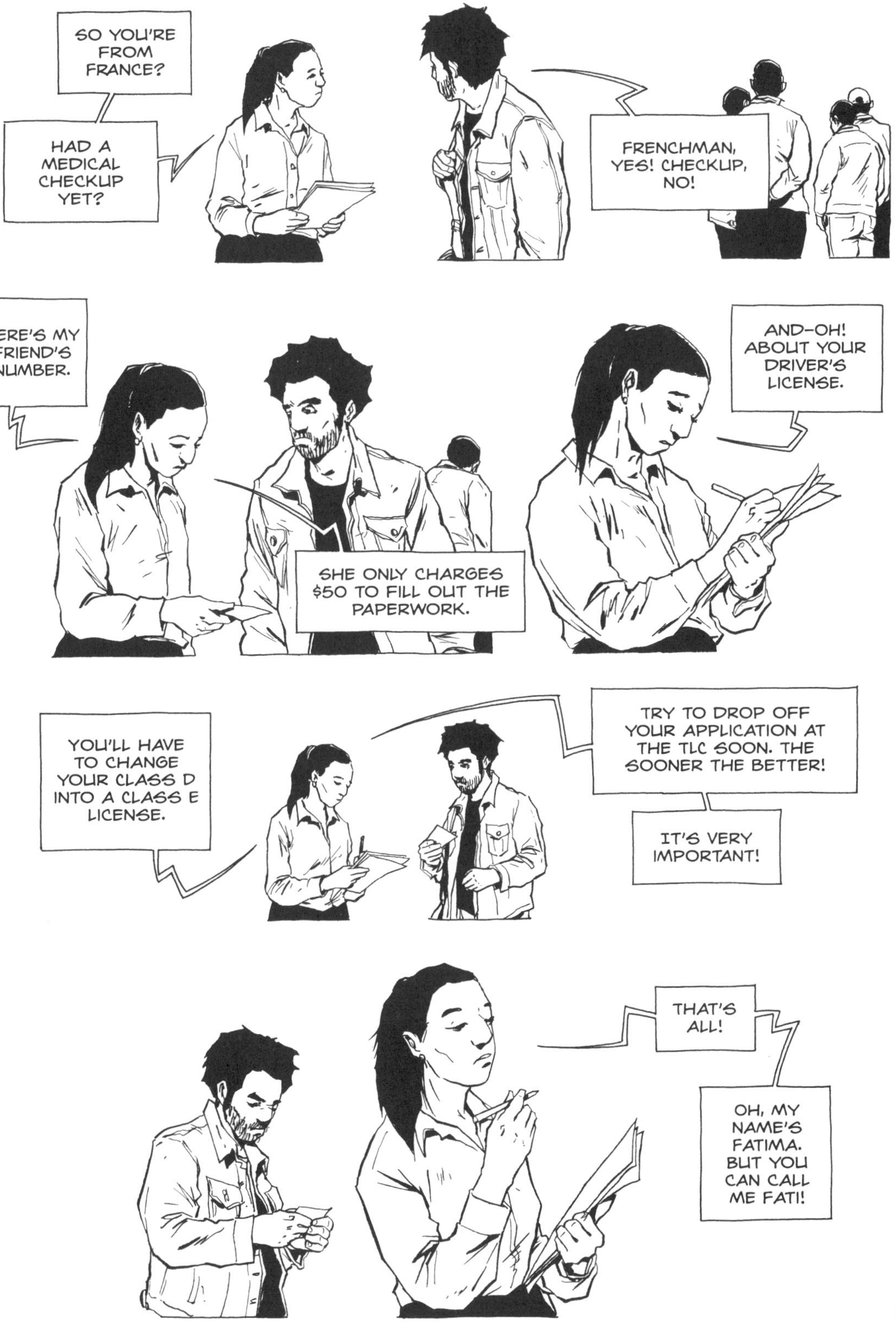
SO YOU'RE FROM FRANCE?
HAD A MEDICAL CHECKUP YET?
FRENCHMAN, YES! CHECKUP, NO!
HERE'S MY FRIEND'S NUMBER.
SHE ONLY CHARGES $50 TO FILL OUT THE PAPERWORK.
AND-OH! ABOUT YOUR DRIVER'S LICENSE.
YOU'LL HAVE TO CHANGE YOUR CLASS D INTO A CLASS E LICENSE.
TRY TO DROP OFF YOUR APPLICATION AT THE TLC SOON. THE SOONER THE BETTER!
IT'S VERY IMPORTANT!
THAT'S ALL!
OH, MY NAME'S FATIMA. BUT YOU CAN CALL ME FATI!

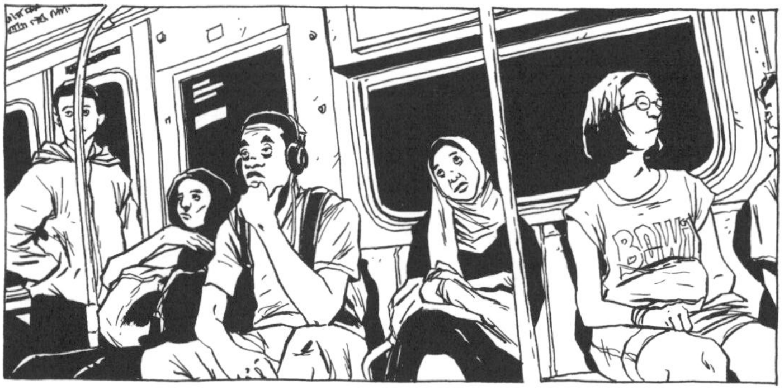

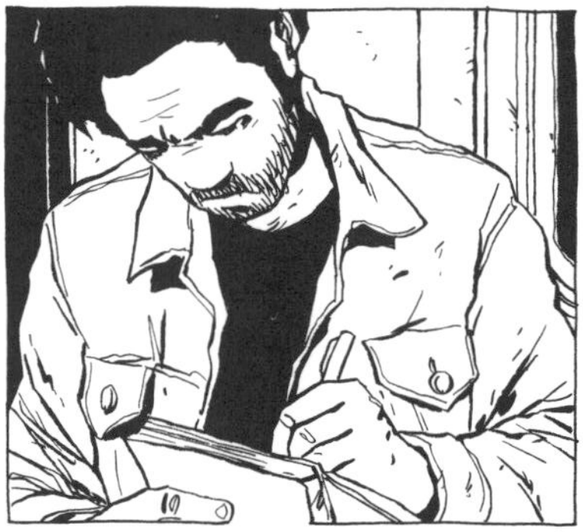

HEADING BACK HOME TO MY GENTRIFIED NEIGHBORHOOD WHILE MY FELLOW DRIVERS HEAD OFF IN THE OPPOSITE DIRECTION, TOWARD JACKSON HEIGHTS IN NORTHERN QUEENS. MOST DRIVERS LIVE IN THAT PART OF THE CITY WHERE 167 LANGUAGES ARE SPOKEN.

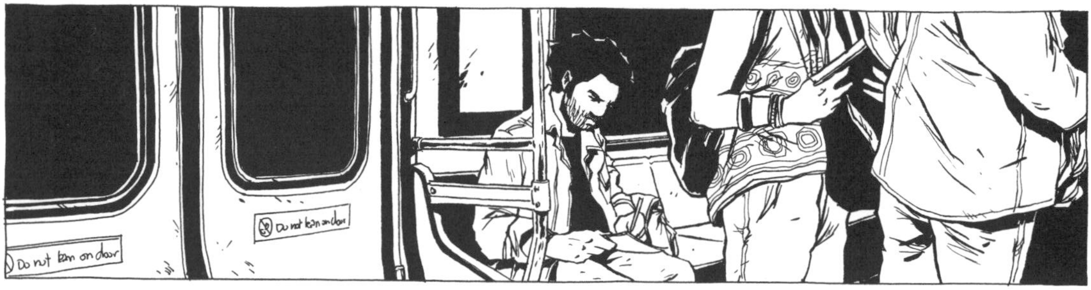
Do not lean on door
Do not lean on door

ALL MEN, NOT A SINGLE WOMAN. WHAT IF I MADE MY PROTAGONIST A WOMAN? A WHITE WOMAN AMONG PAKISTANIS, INDIANS, AFRICANS, A STRANGER IN A STRANGE LAND. HMM... KEEP THINKING. A PERFECT ROLE FOR ÉLÉONORE?

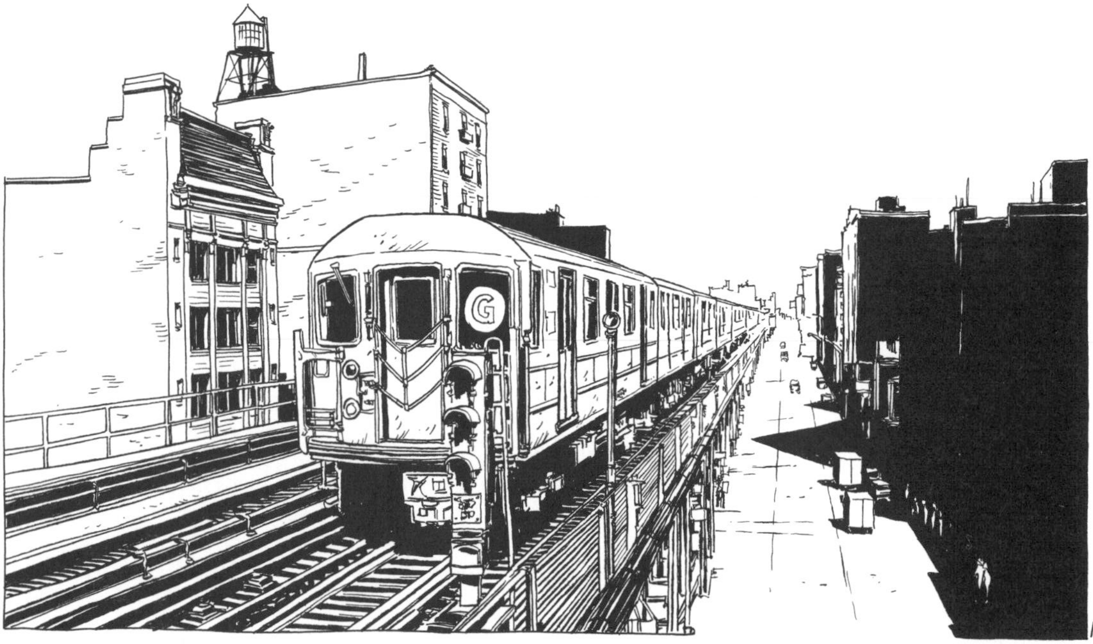
G

THURSDAY, JUNE 11, 2015

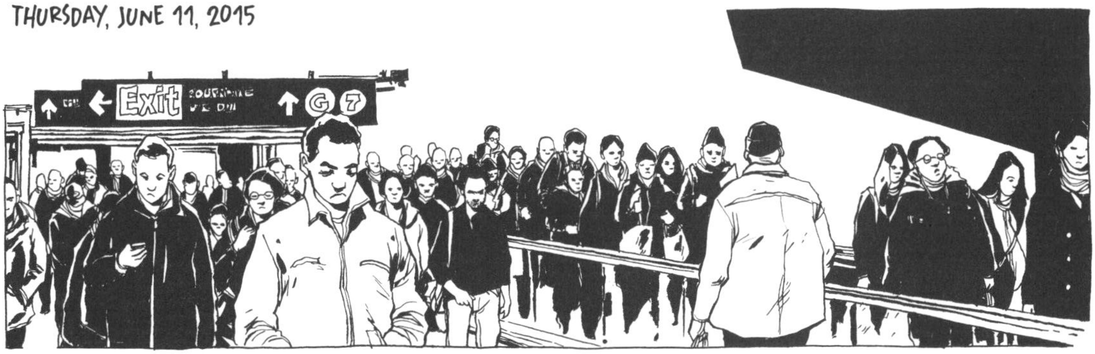
Exit
G
7

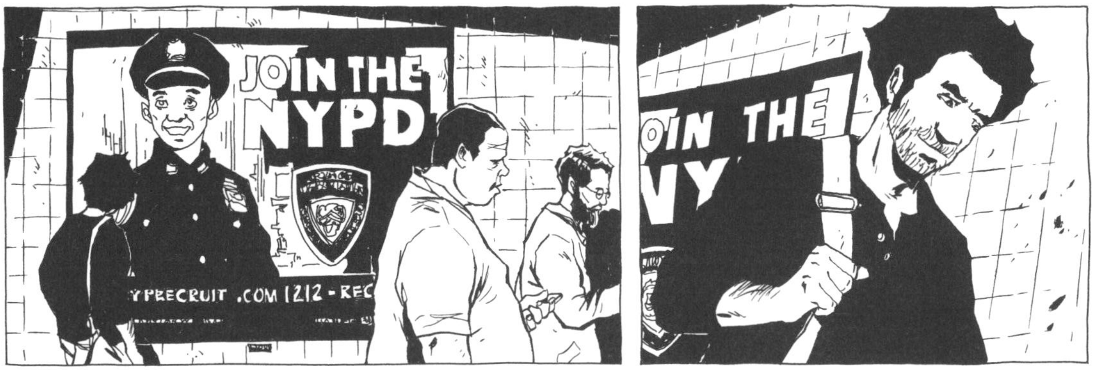
JOIN THE
NYPD
YPRECRUIT .COM 1212-REC
OIN THE
NY

JOIN THE NYPD? ANOTHER IDEA? ANOTHER LIFE?

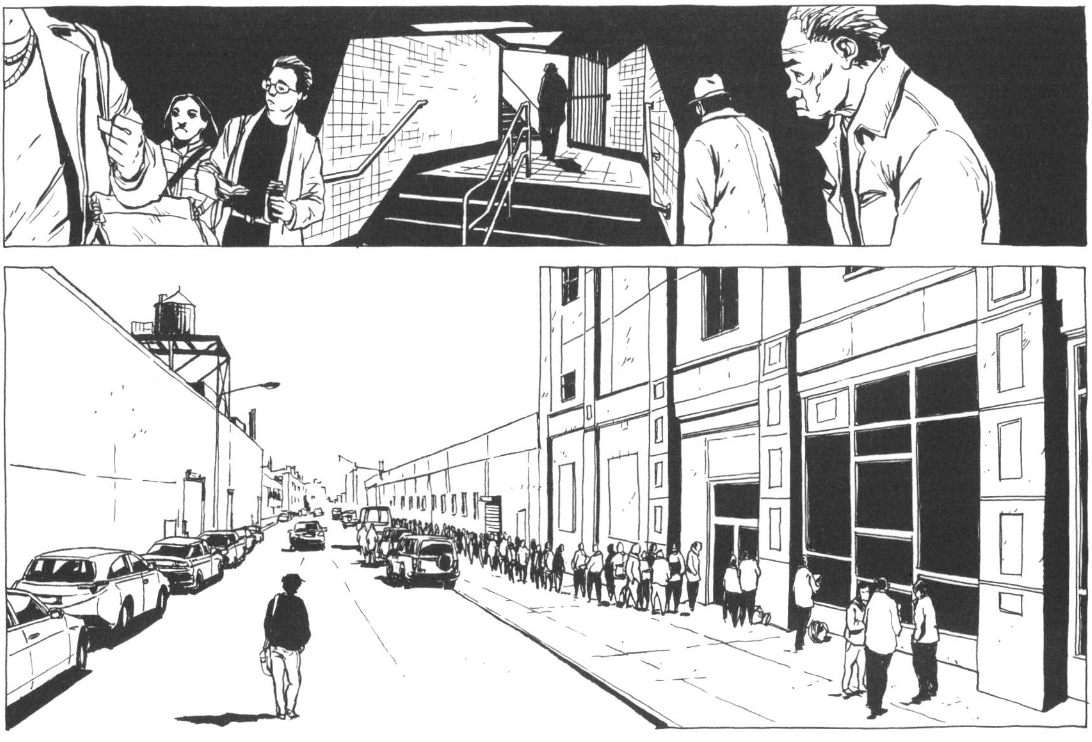

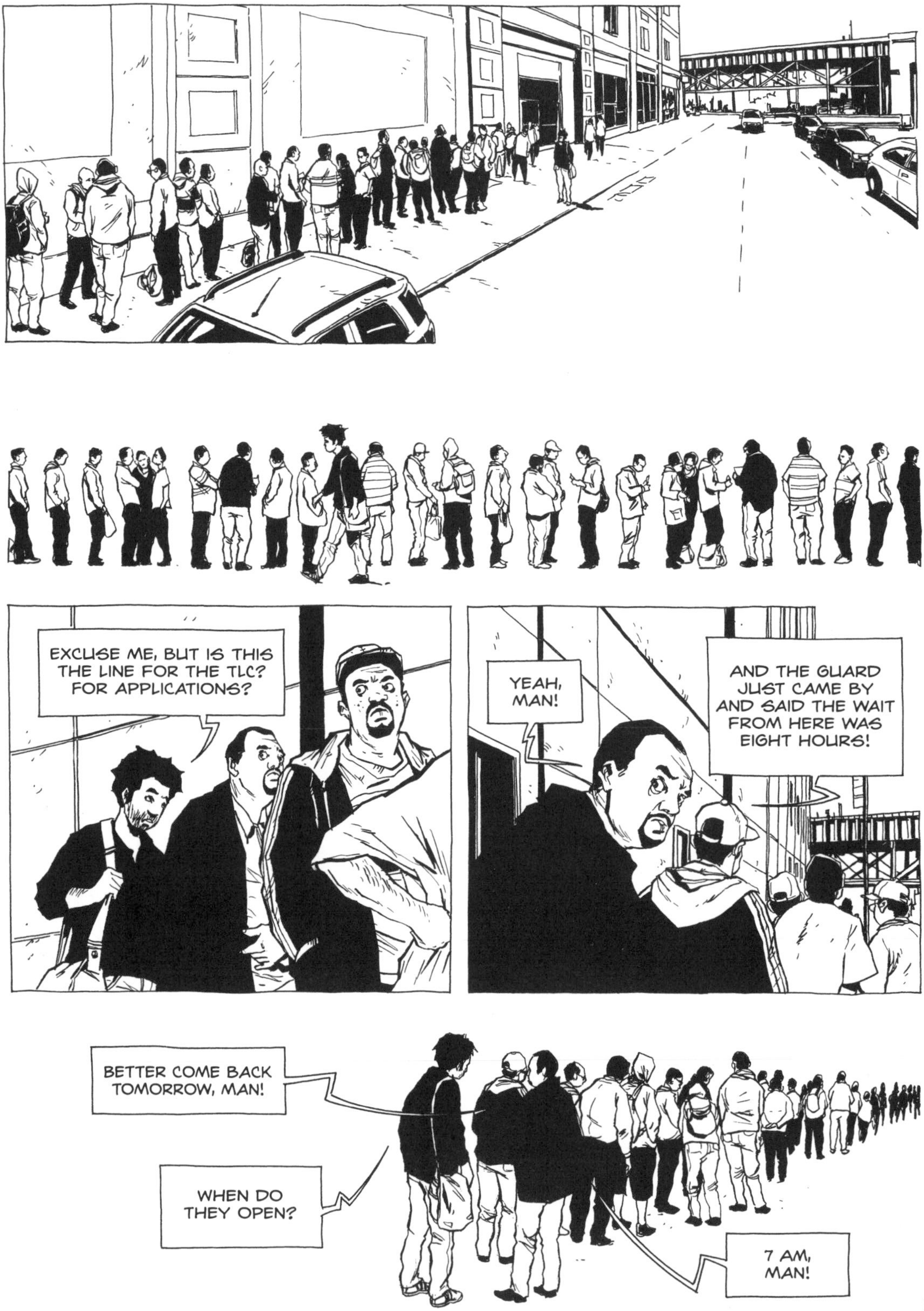

EXCUSE ME, BUT IS THIS THE LINE FOR THE TLC? FOR APPLICATIONS?
YEAH, MAN!
AND THE GUARD JUST CAME BY AND SAID THE WAIT FROM HERE WAS EIGHT HOURS!
BETTER COME BACK TOMORROW, MAN!
WHEN DO THEY OPEN?
7 AM, MAN!

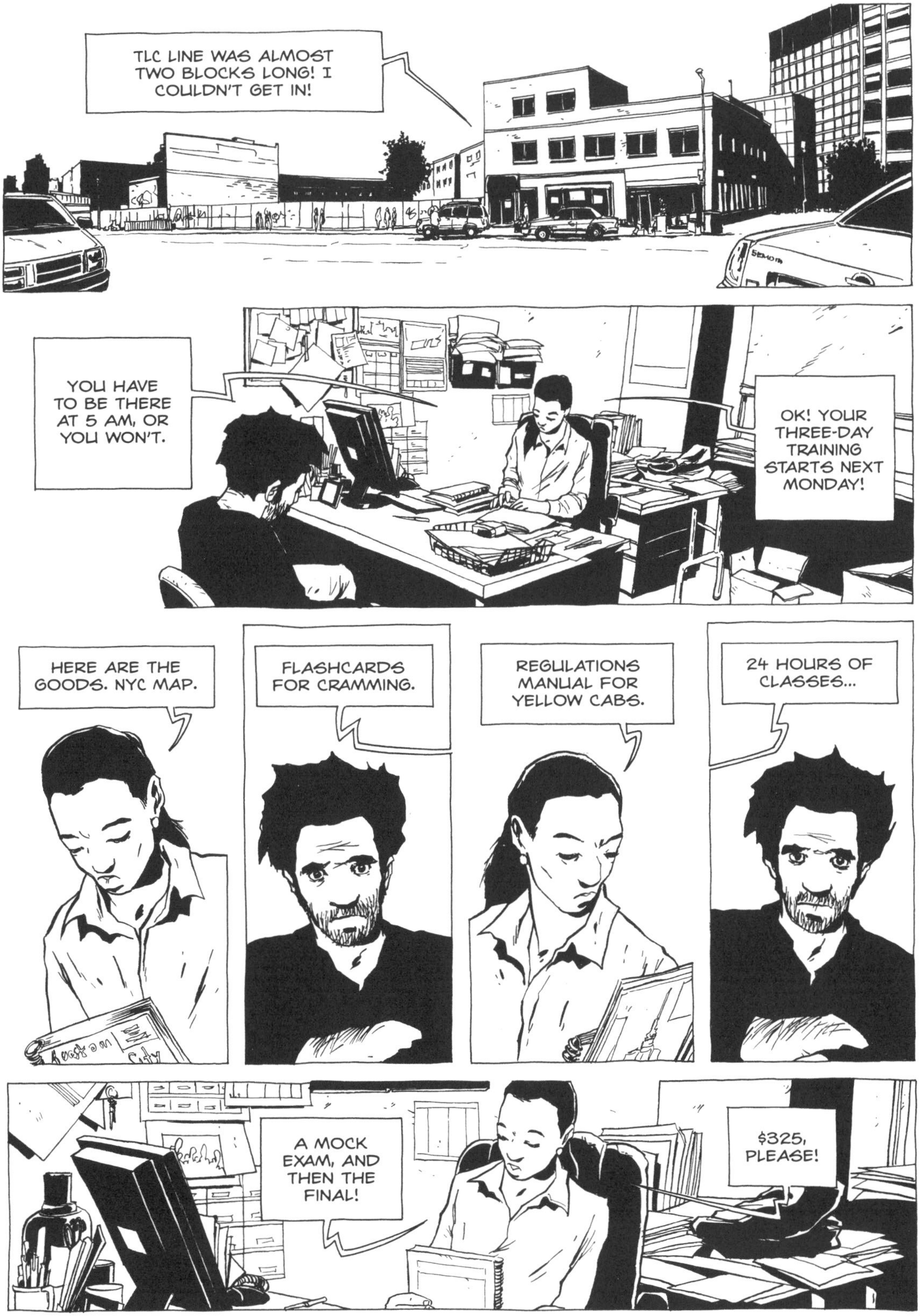
TLC LINE WAS ALMOST TWO BLOCKS LONG! I COULDN'T GET IN!
YOU HAVE TO BE THERE AT 5 AM, OR YOU WON'T.
OK! YOUR THREE-DAY TRAINING STARTS NEXT MONDAY!
HERE ARE THE GOODS. NYC MAP.
FLASHCARDS FOR CRAMMING.
REGULATIONS MANUAL FOR YELLOW CABS.
24 HOURS OF CLASSES...
A MOCK EXAM, AND THEN THE FINAL!
$325, PLEASE!

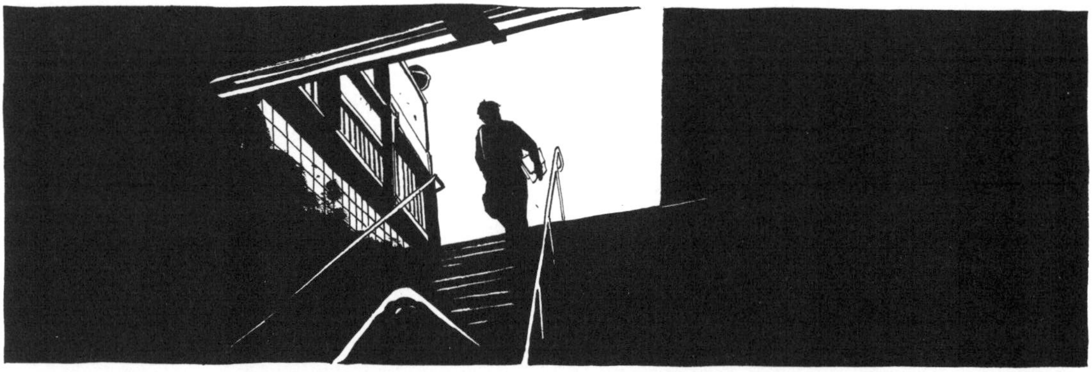

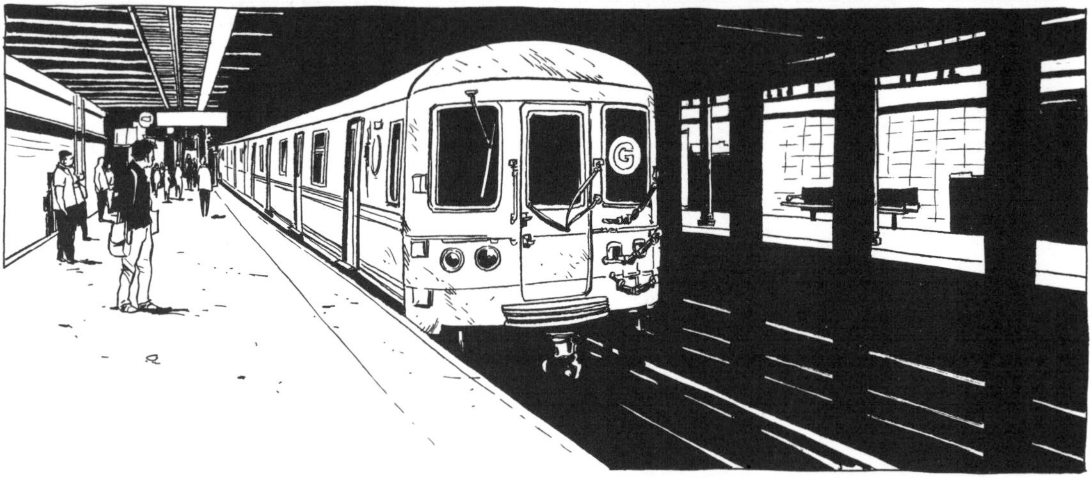
G

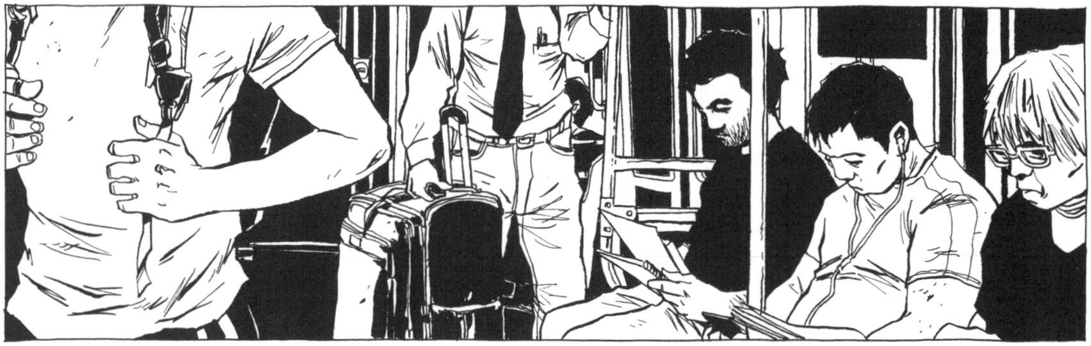

DEFENSIVE DRIVING: $60. NEW LICENSE: $40. MEDICAL CHECKUP: $50. WHEELCHAIR TRAINING: $60. 24 HOURS OF CLASS PLUS TEST: $325. SO I'LL NEED TO MAKE $535 BEFORE I START SEEING A CENT OF PROFIT...

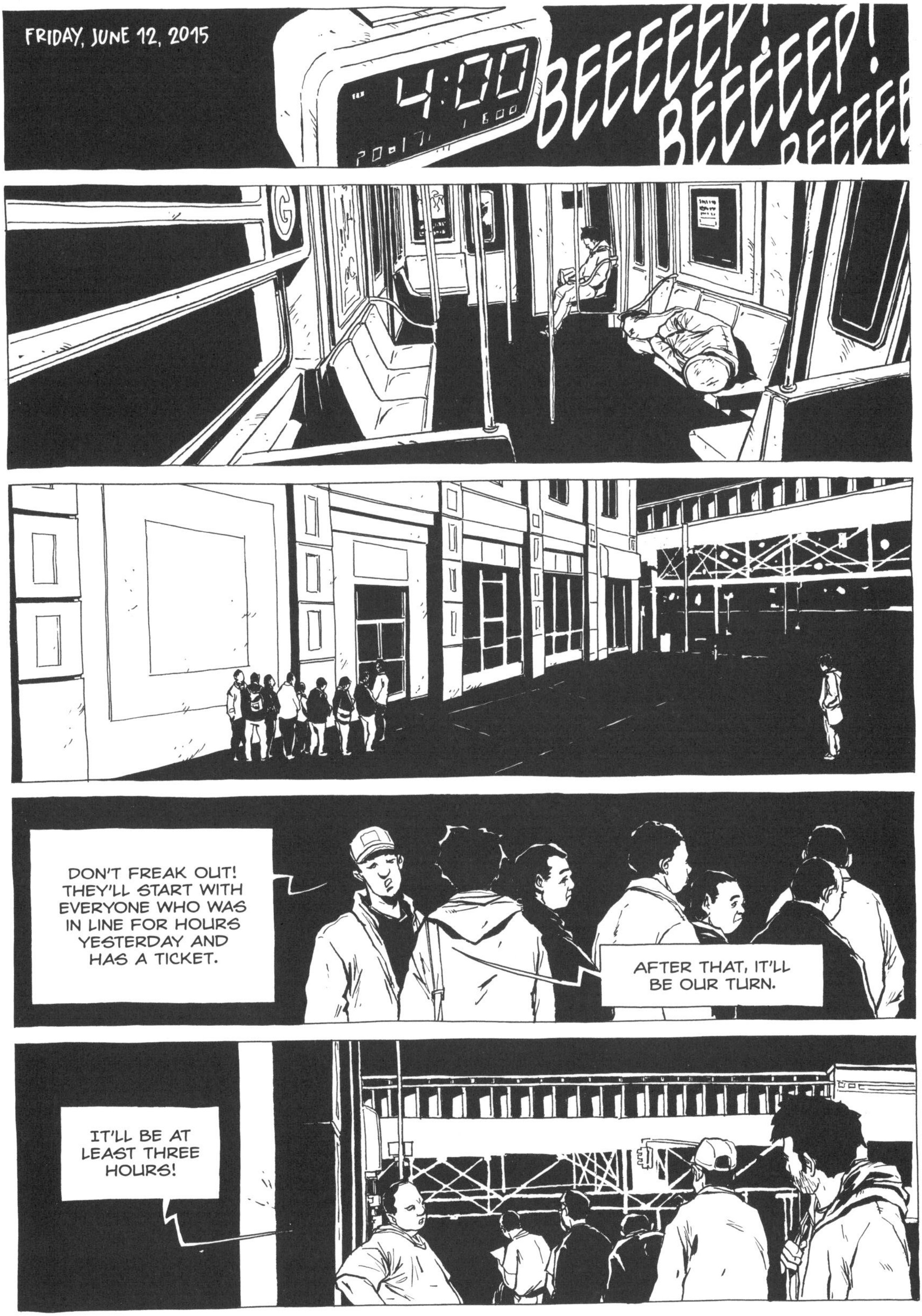
FRIDAY, JUNE 12, 2015
4:00
BEEEEEP! BEEEEEP!
DON'T FREAK OUT! THEY'LL START WITH EVERYONE WHO WAS IN LINE FOR HOURS YESTERDAY AND HAS A TICKET.
AFTER THAT, IT'LL BE OUR TURN.
IT'LL BE AT LEAST THREE HOURS!

COME BACK IN SEPTEMBER.
WHAT?!
SEPTEMBER? WHY SEPTEMBER?
YOU'VE STILL GOT A PROBATIONARY LICENSE.
COME BACK IN SEPTEMBER.
LOOK, MAYBE I GOT MY U.S. LICENSE IN MARCH, BUT I'VE BEEN DRIVING IN FRANCE FOR OVER 20 YEARS.
DOESN'T MATTER. COME BACK IN SEPTEMBER!
2091
Boarding
HELLO? FATIMA? YEAH, GOT A PROBLEM WITH MY PROBATIONARY LICENSE.
CLASS ON MONDAY? TO GET AN IDEA OF THE EXAM?
UH, SURE!
OK! MONDAY!

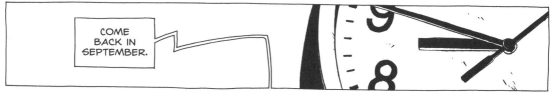

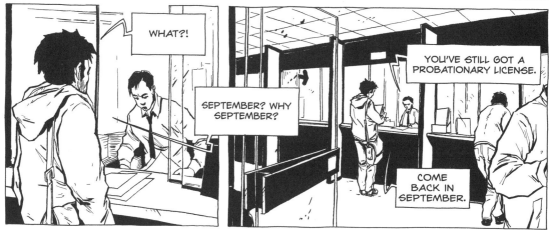

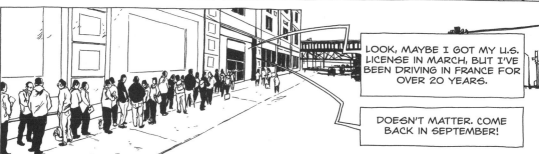

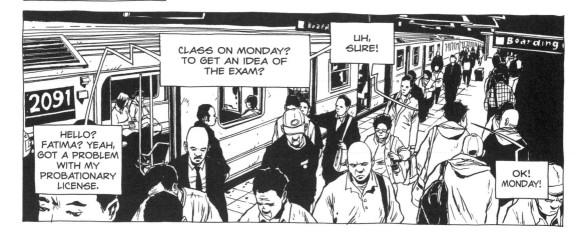

MEDICAL CHECKUP ONLY VALID FOR A MONTH, SO $50 DOWN THE DRAIN, AND ANOTHER $50 OUT THE DOOR SOON. MY LEADING LADY BETTER FIND A GIG IN THE MEANTIME, OR SHE'LL BE EATING $2 HOT DOGS FOR A FEW WEEKS...

MONDAY, JUNE 15, 2015

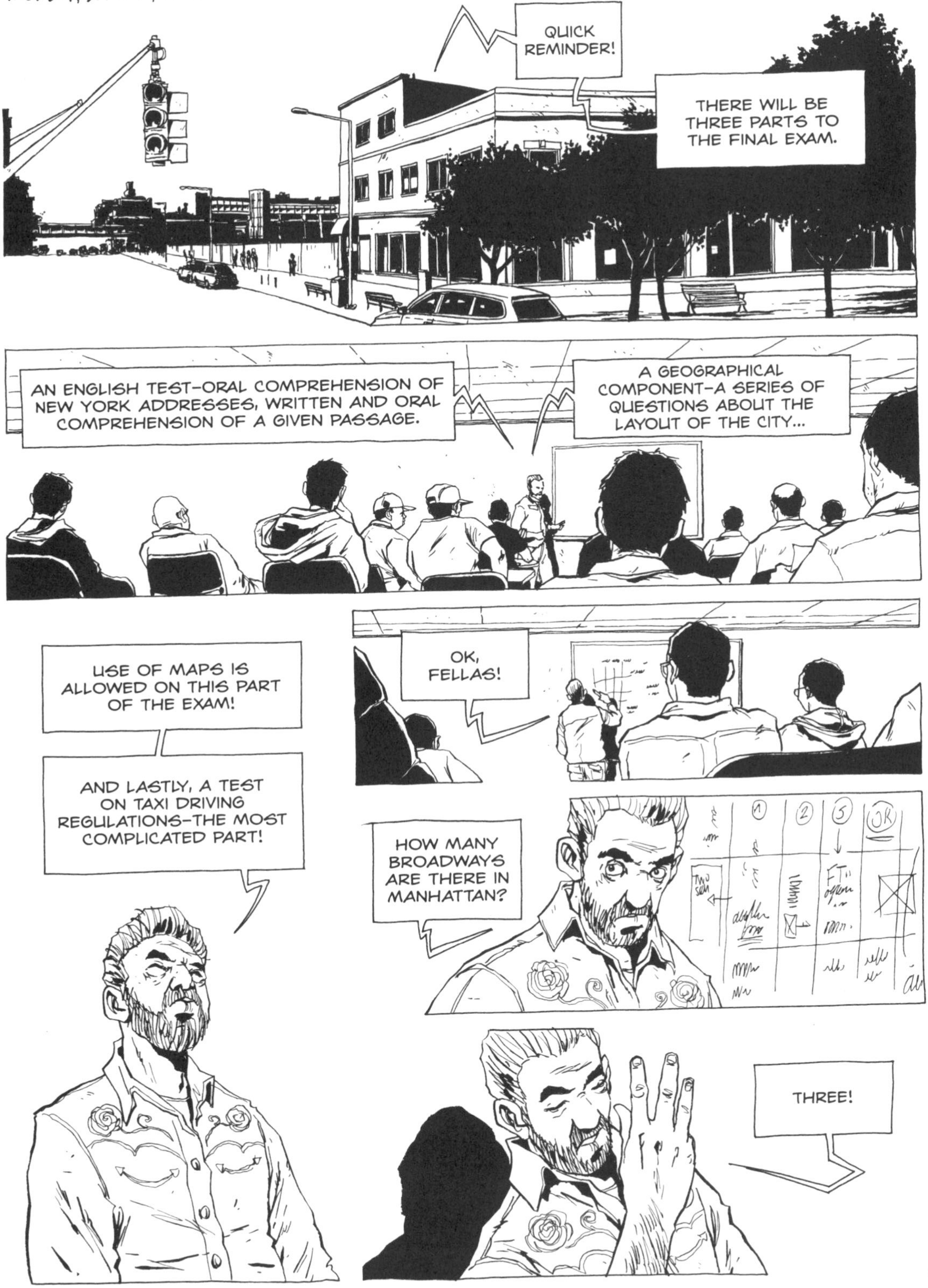

QUICK REMINDER!
THERE WILL BE THREE PARTS TO THE FINAL EXAM.
AN ENGLISH TEST–ORAL COMPREHENSION OF NEW YORK ADDRESSES, WRITTEN AND ORAL COMPREHENSION OF A GIVEN PASSAGE.
A GEOGRAPHICAL COMPONENT–A SERIES OF QUESTIONS ABOUT THE LAYOUT OF THE CITY...
USE OF MAPS IS ALLOWED ON THIS PART OF THE EXAM!
AND LASTLY, A TEST ON TAXI DRIVING REGULATIONS–THE MOST COMPLICATED PART!
OK, FELLAS!
HOW MANY BROADWAYS ARE THERE IN MANHATTAN?
THREE!

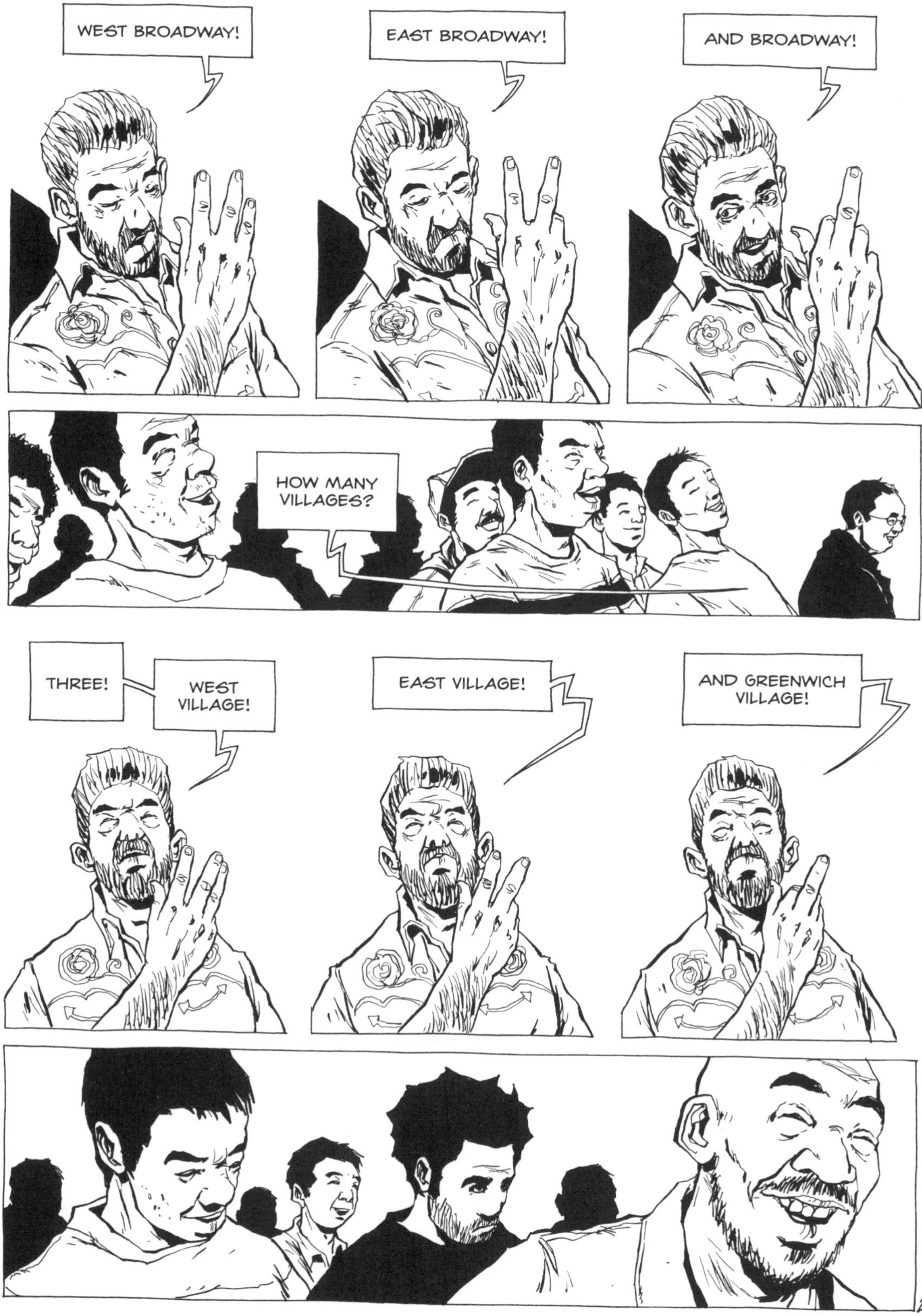
WEST BROADWAY!
EAST BROADWAY!
AND BROADWAY!
HOW MANY VILLAGES?
THREE!
WEST VILLAGE!
EAST VILLAGE!
AND GREENWICH VILLAGE!

FRIDAY, AUGUST 28, 2015

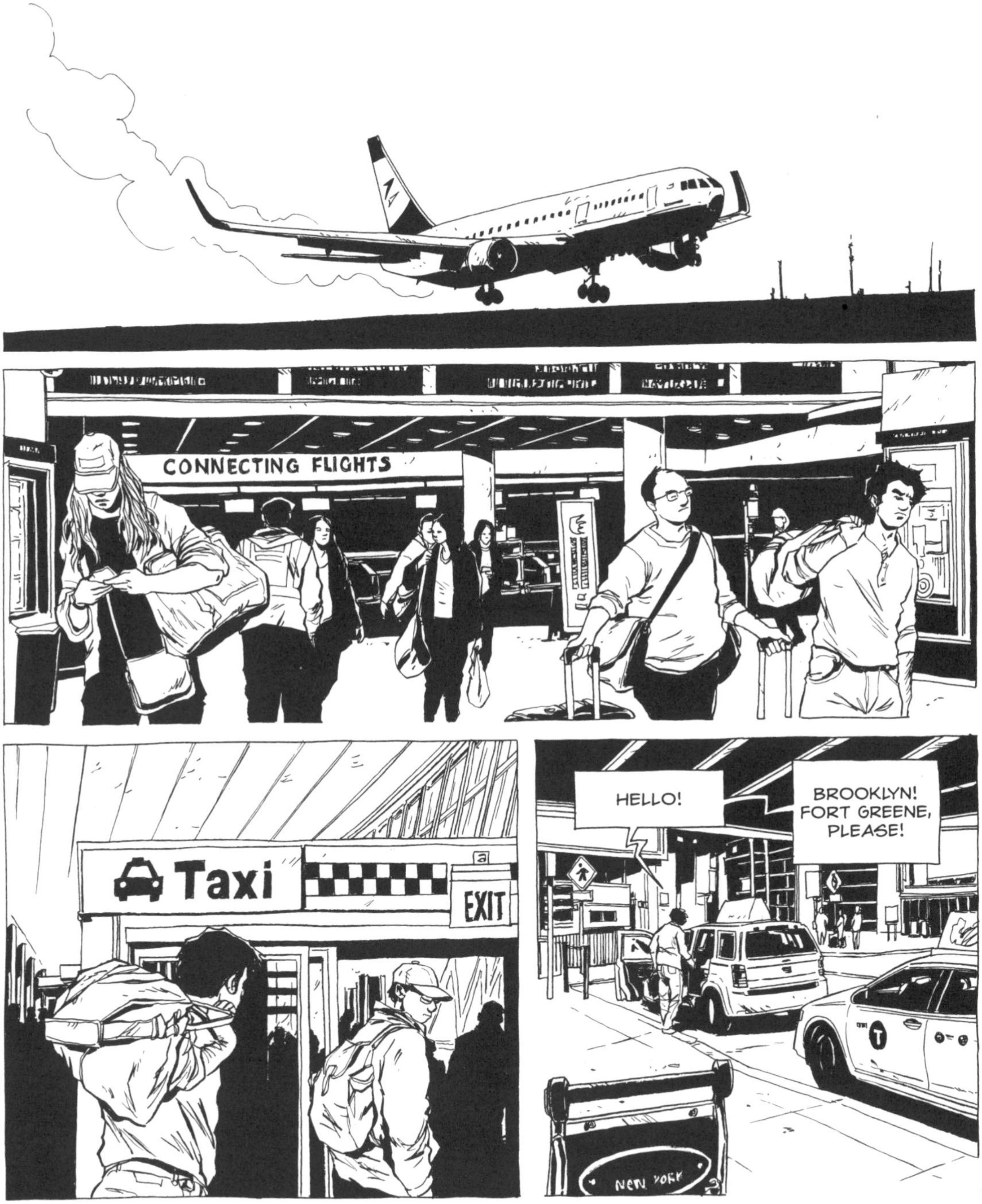
CONNECTING FLIGHTS
Taxi
EXIT
HELLO!
BROOKLYN! FORT GREENE, PLEASE!
NEW YORK

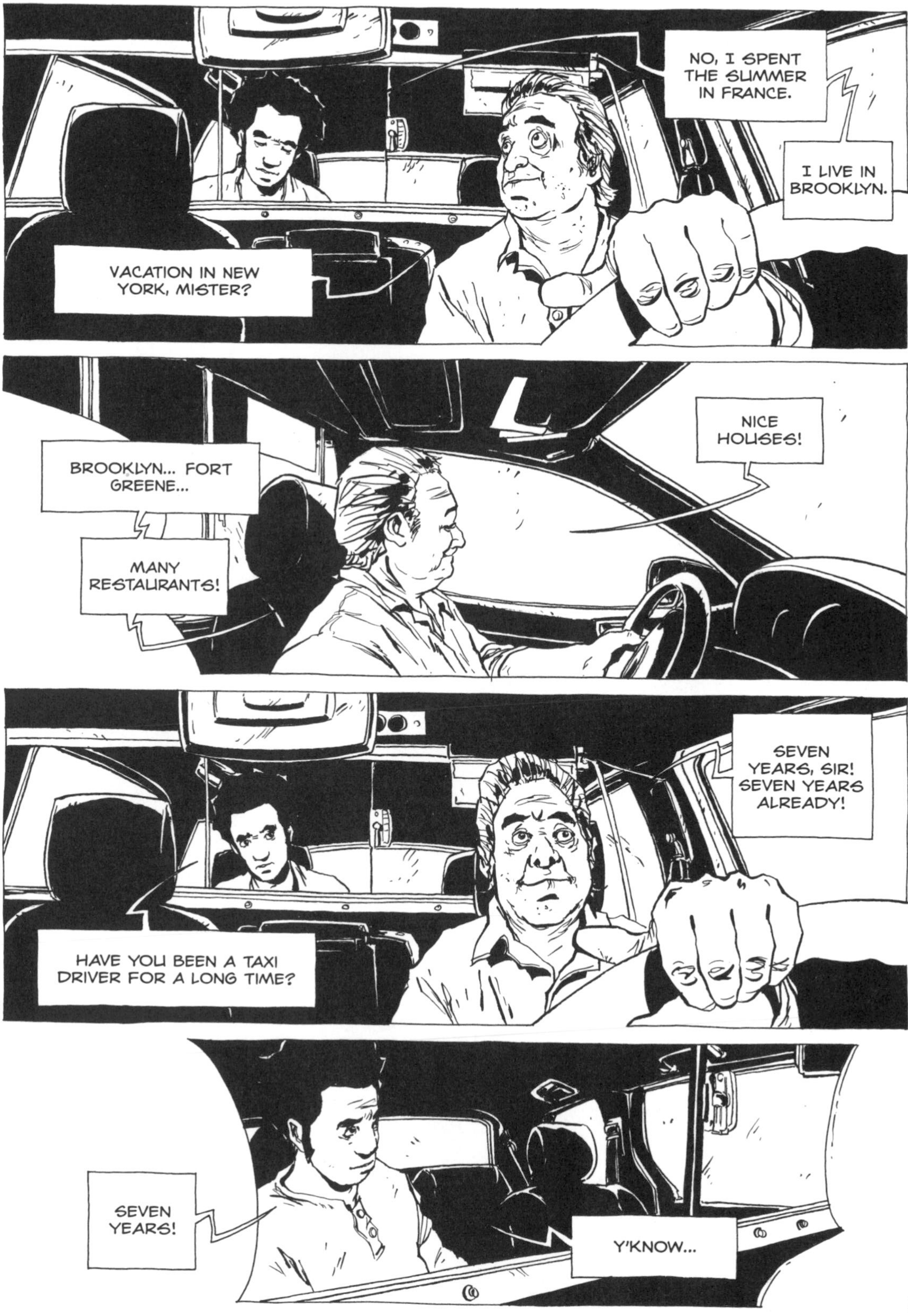
VACATION IN NEW YORK, MISTER?
NO, I SPENT THE SUMMER IN FRANCE.
I LIVE IN BROOKLYN.
BROOKLYN... FORT GREENE...
MANY RESTAURANTS!
NICE HOUSES!
HAVE YOU BEEN A TAXI DRIVER FOR A LONG TIME?
SEVEN YEARS, SIR! SEVEN YEARS ALREADY!
SEVEN YEARS!
Y'KNOW...

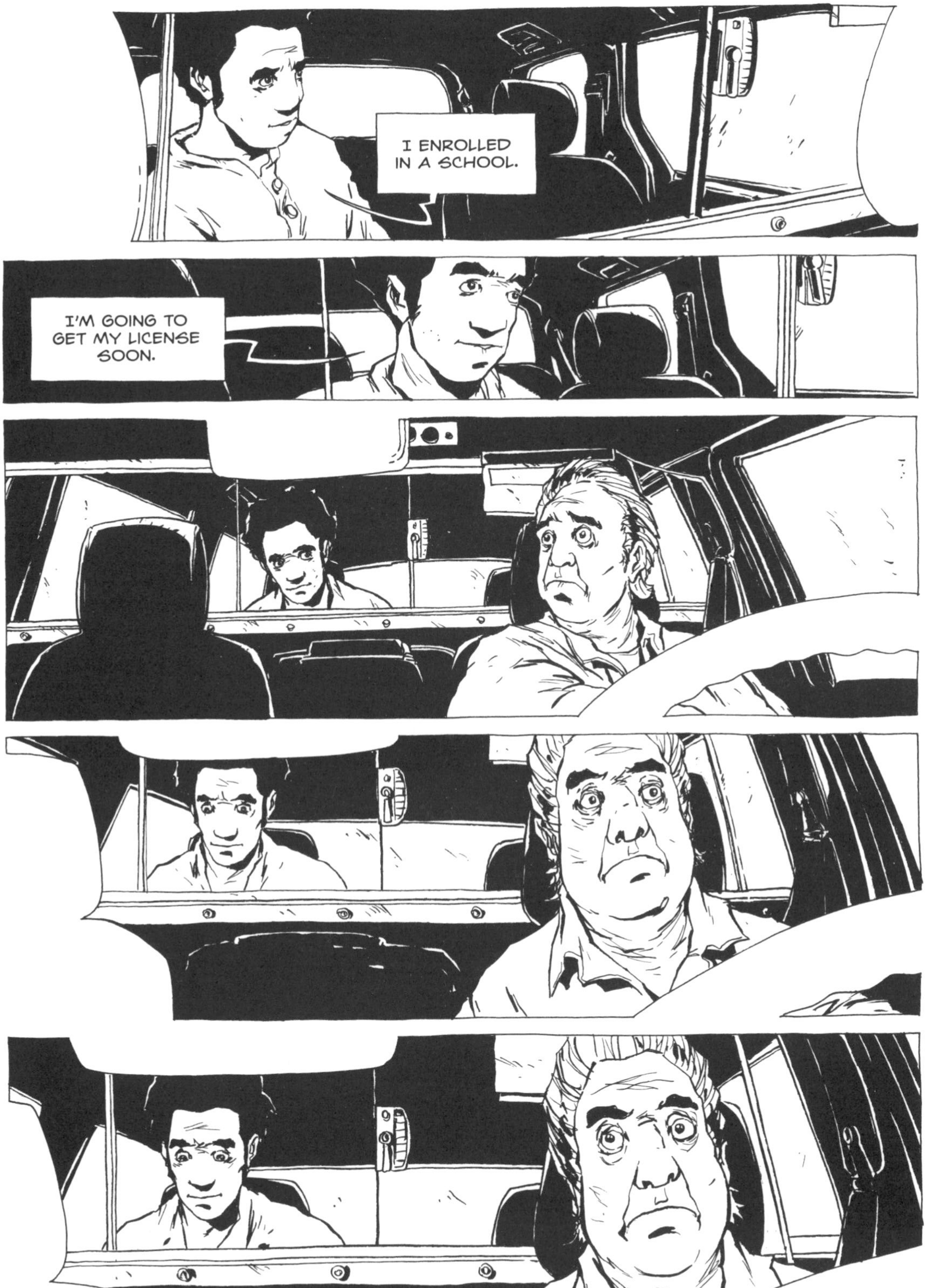
I ENROLLED IN A SCHOOL.
I'M GOING TO GET MY LICENSE SOON.

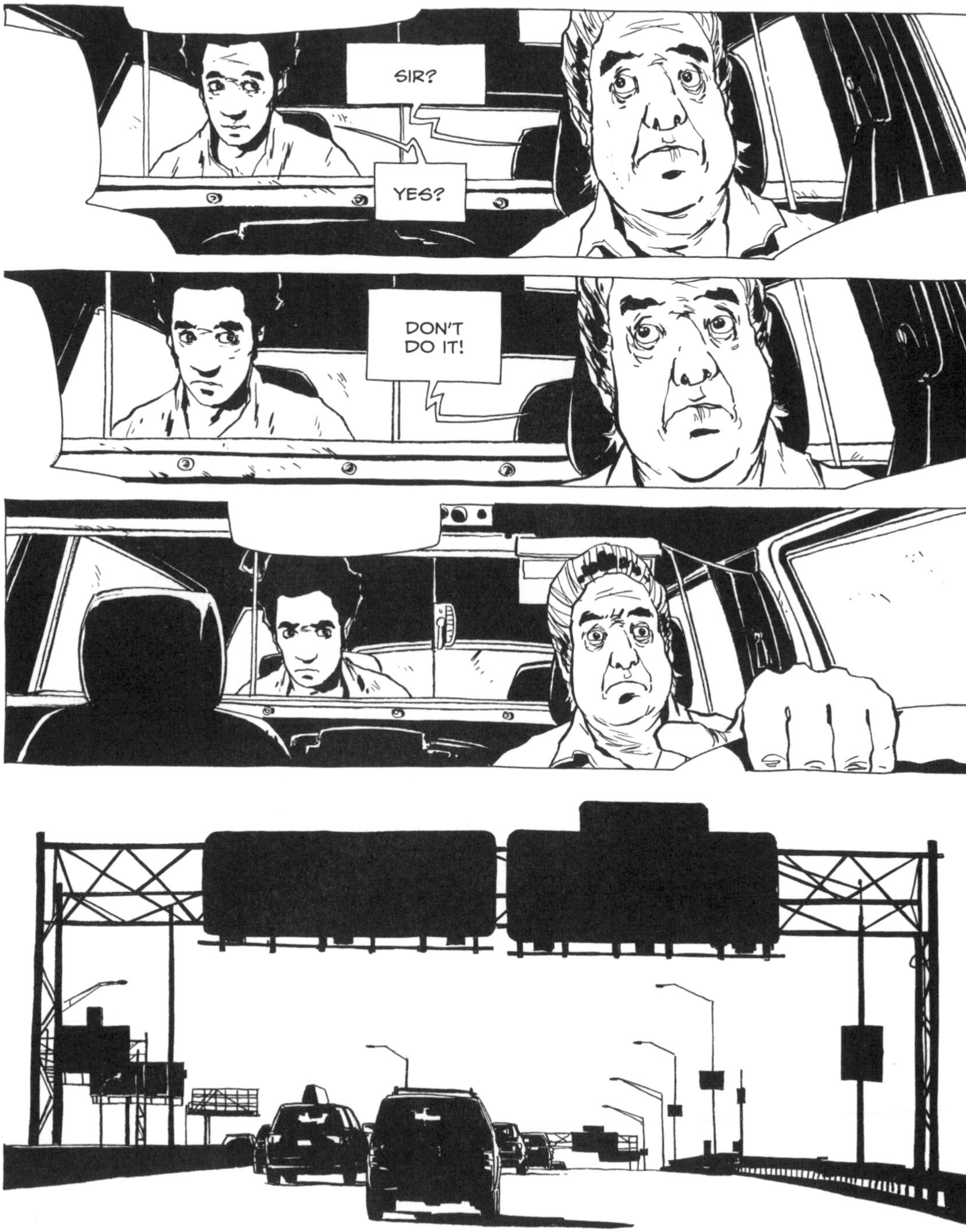
SIR?
YES?
DON'T DO IT!

TUESDAY, SEPTEMBER 15, 2015

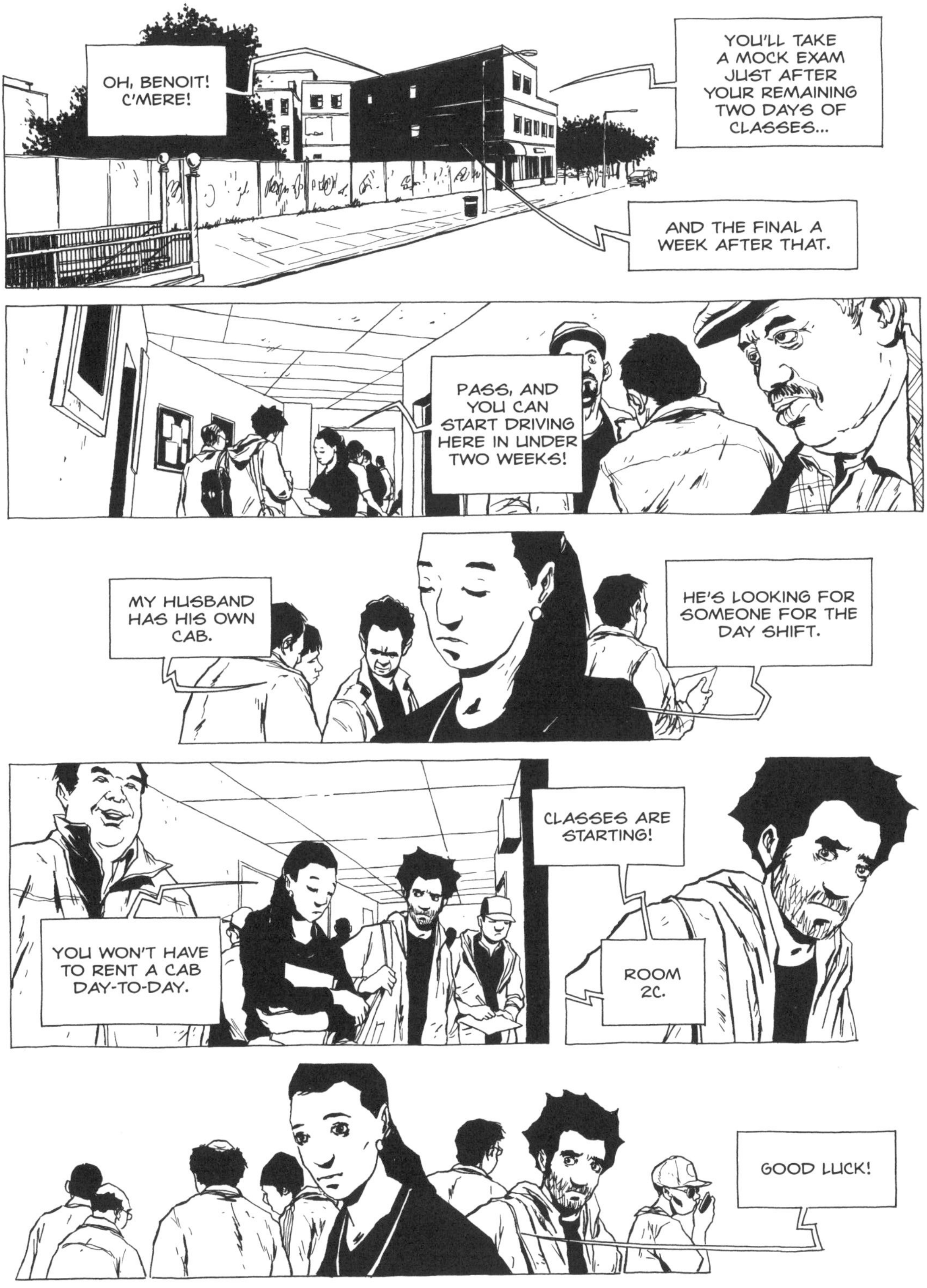

OH, BENOIT! C'MERE!
YOU'LL TAKE A MOCK EXAM JUST AFTER YOUR REMAINING TWO DAYS OF CLASSES...
AND THE FINAL A WEEK AFTER THAT.
PASS, AND YOU CAN START DRIVING HERE IN UNDER TWO WEEKS!
MY HUSBAND HAS HIS OWN CAB.
HE'S LOOKING FOR SOMEONE FOR THE DAY SHIFT.
YOU WON'T HAVE TO RENT A CAB DAY-TO-DAY.
CLASSES ARE STARTING!
ROOM 2C.
GOOD LUCK!

THE BETTER YOU KNOW THE RULES...

2 C

... THE MORE MONEY YOU'LL MAKE!

THE GOOD NEWS IS YOU'RE GONNA EARN MONEY.

THE BAD NEWS IS...

WENT TO THE WRONG ROOM!

OK! HAVE A SEAT.

THE BAD NEWS IS THAT YOU'RE GOING TO HAVE TO WORK HARD TO KEEP YOUR LICENSE.

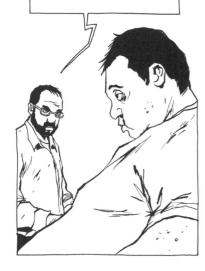

TO GET THE BEST TIPS, YOU HAVE TO CHARM YOUR FARES, LISTEN IF THEY FEEL LIKE TALKING.

BUT ALSO KNOW WHEN TO SHUT UP IF THEY'D RATHER BE READING THE PAPER OR TEXTING.

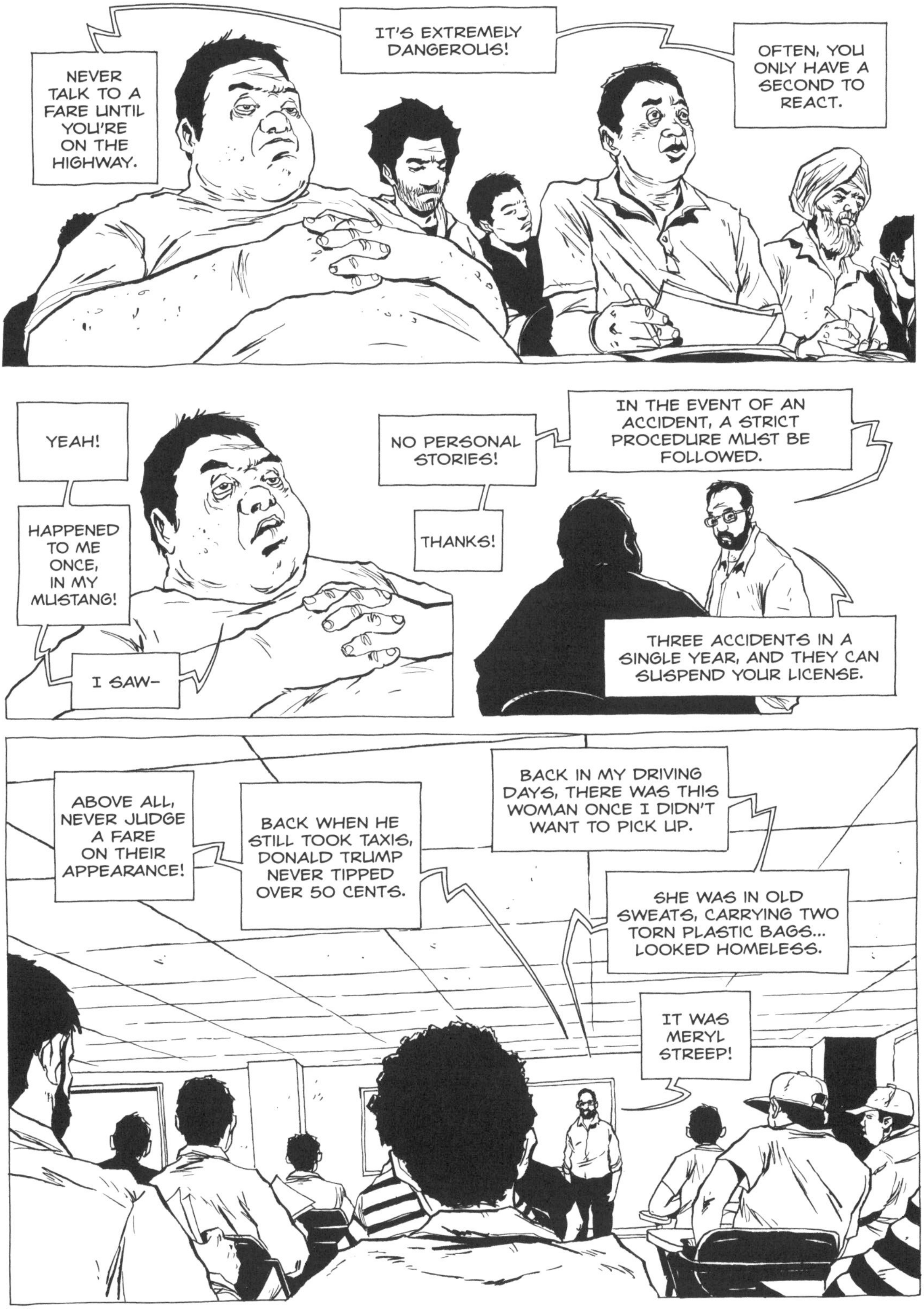
NEVER TALK TO A FARE UNTIL YOU'RE ON THE HIGHWAY.
IT'S EXTREMELY DANGEROUS!
OFTEN, YOU ONLY HAVE A SECOND TO REACT.
YEAH!
HAPPENED TO ME ONCE, IN MY MUSTANG!
I SAW–
NO PERSONAL STORIES!
THANKS!
IN THE EVENT OF AN ACCIDENT, A STRICT PROCEDURE MUST BE FOLLOWED.
THREE ACCIDENTS IN A SINGLE YEAR, AND THEY CAN SUSPEND YOUR LICENSE.
ABOVE ALL, NEVER JUDGE A FARE ON THEIR APPEARANCE!
BACK WHEN HE STILL TOOK TAXIS, DONALD TRUMP NEVER TIPPED OVER 50 CENTS.
BACK IN MY DRIVING DAYS, THERE WAS THIS WOMAN ONCE I DIDN'T WANT TO PICK UP.
SHE WAS IN OLD SWEATS, CARRYING TWO TORN PLASTIC BAGS... LOOKED HOMELESS.
IT WAS MERYL STREEP!

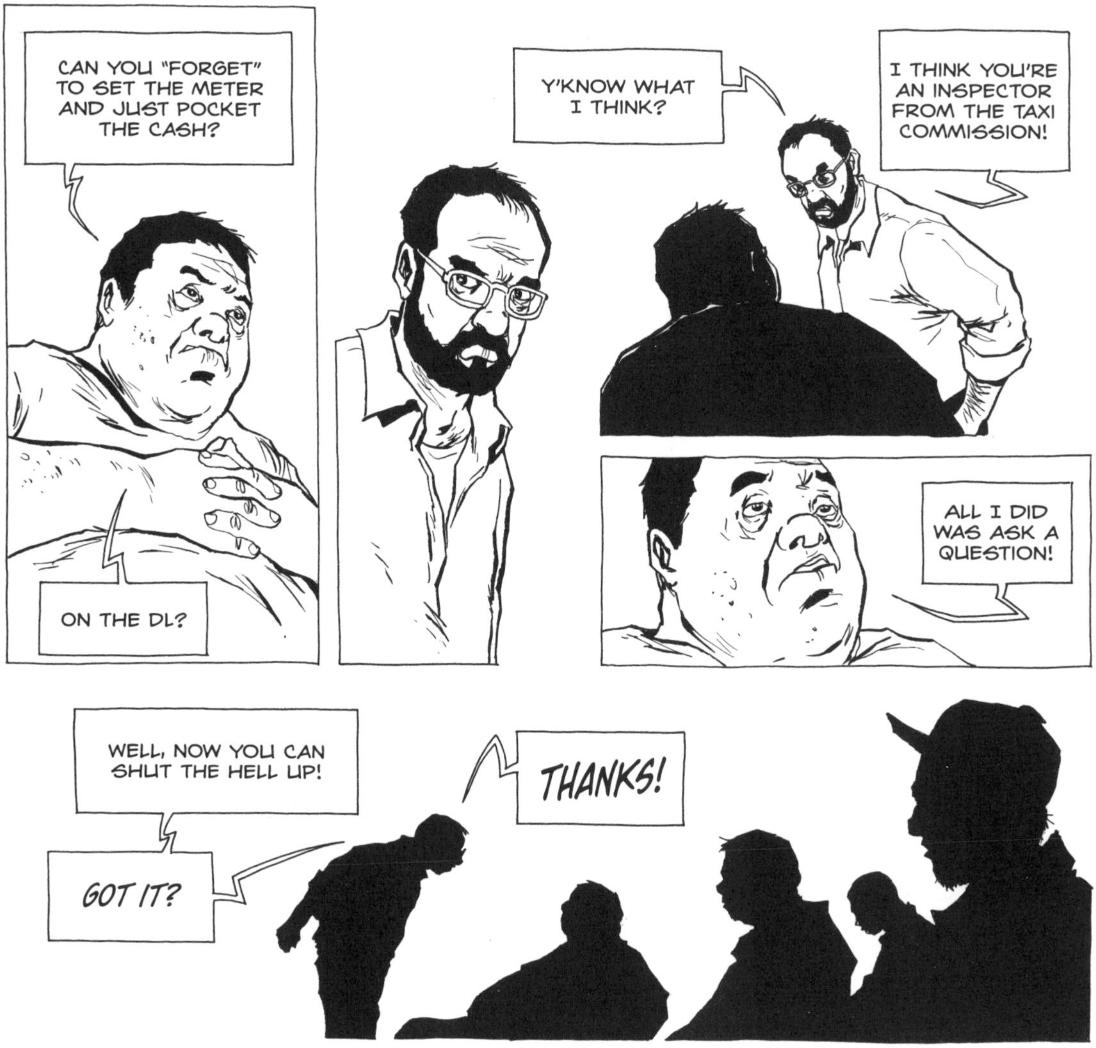
CAN YOU "FORGET" TO SET THE METER AND JUST POCKET THE CASH?
ON THE DL?
Y'KNOW WHAT I THINK?
I THINK YOU'RE AN INSPECTOR FROM THE TAXI COMMISSION!
ALL I DID WAS ASK A QUESTION!
WELL, NOW YOU CAN SHUT THE HELL UP!
GOT IT?
THANKS!

ANYONE WITH A FIVER IN THEIR POCKET CAN RAISE A HAND AND FLAG DOWN A CAB. DON'T NEED A BANK ACCOUNT OR A SMARTPHONE. THIS IS THE NEW YORK I WANT TO SHOW IN MY MOVIE.

I'LL HAVE TO THINK ABOUT MY CHARACTER'S MOTIVATIONS...

WHY DOESN'T SHE OPT FOR A RIDESHARE CLIENTELE, VERIFIED VIA AN ONLINE ACCOUNT, AND HENCE SAFER? WHY DOES THIS WOMAN TAKE ON THE RISK OF TRANSPORTING ANONYMOUS PASSENGERS?

WHERE'S SHE FROM?

WHAT HAS SHE LEFT BEHIND?

WEDNESDAY, SEPTEMBER 16, 2015

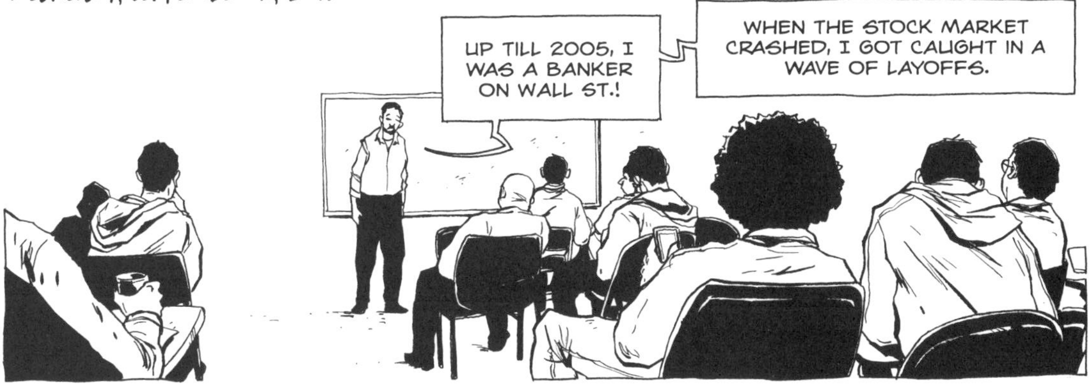
UP TILL 2005, I WAS A BANKER ON WALL ST.!
WHEN THE STOCK MARKET CRASHED, I GOT CAUGHT IN A WAVE OF LAYOFFS.

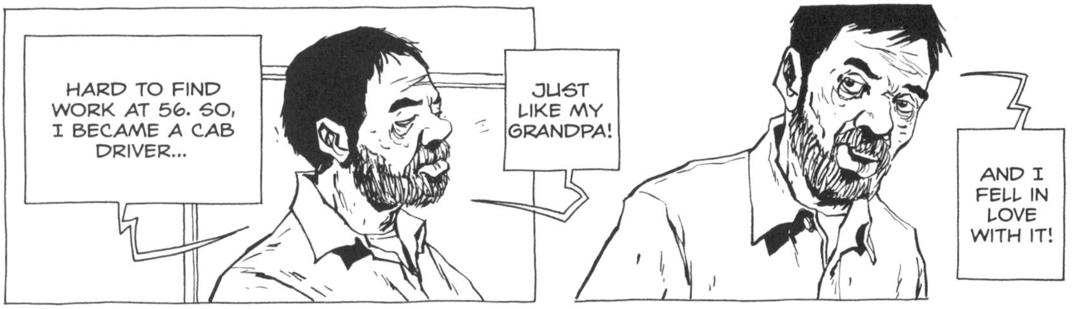
HARD TO FIND WORK AT 56. SO, I BECAME A CAB DRIVER...
JUST LIKE MY GRANDPA!
AND I FELL IN LOVE WITH IT!

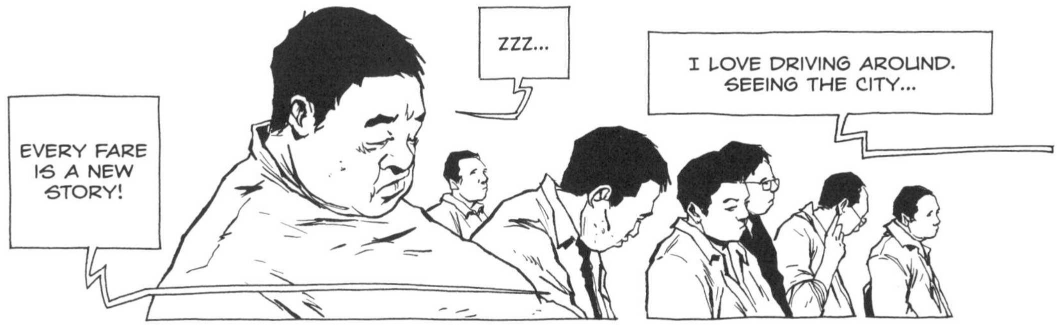
ZZZ...
I LOVE DRIVING AROUND. SEEING THE CITY...
EVERY FARE IS A NEW STORY!

WHAT IF THE SAME THING HAPPENS TO ME?
IF THIS EXPERIMENT TURNS INTO A REAL JOB?

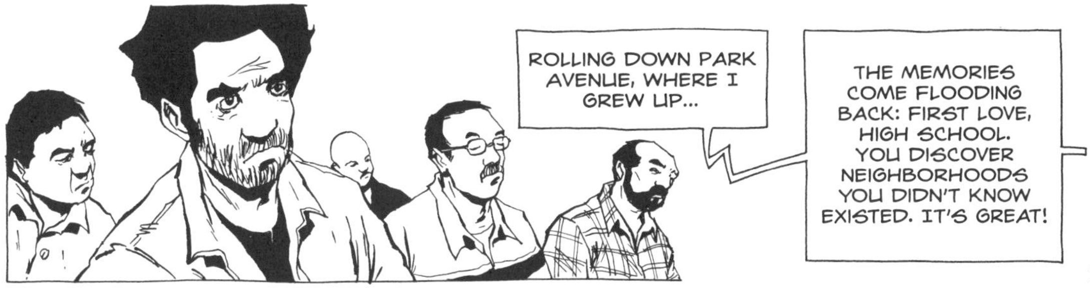
ROLLING DOWN PARK AVENUE, WHERE I GREW UP...
THE MEMORIES COME FLOODING BACK: FIRST LOVE, HIGH SCHOOL. YOU DISCOVER NEIGHBORHOODS YOU DIDN'T KNOW EXISTED. IT'S GREAT!

WHAT IF, INSTEAD OF WAITING MONTHS, SOMETIMES EVEN YEARS, FOR THE BLESSING OF ALL THOSE PEOPLE WHO DECIDE WHETHER I GET TO MAKE A MOVIE OR NOT—WHAT IF I JUST WORKED ANONYMOUSLY, TRANSPORTING ALL THESE PEOPLE AROUND TOWN?

A JOB THAT STOPS WHEN YOU PARK THE CAR AND DROP OFF THE KEYS. FINALLY, A CHANCE TO TURN THE MOTOR OFF NOW AND THEN...

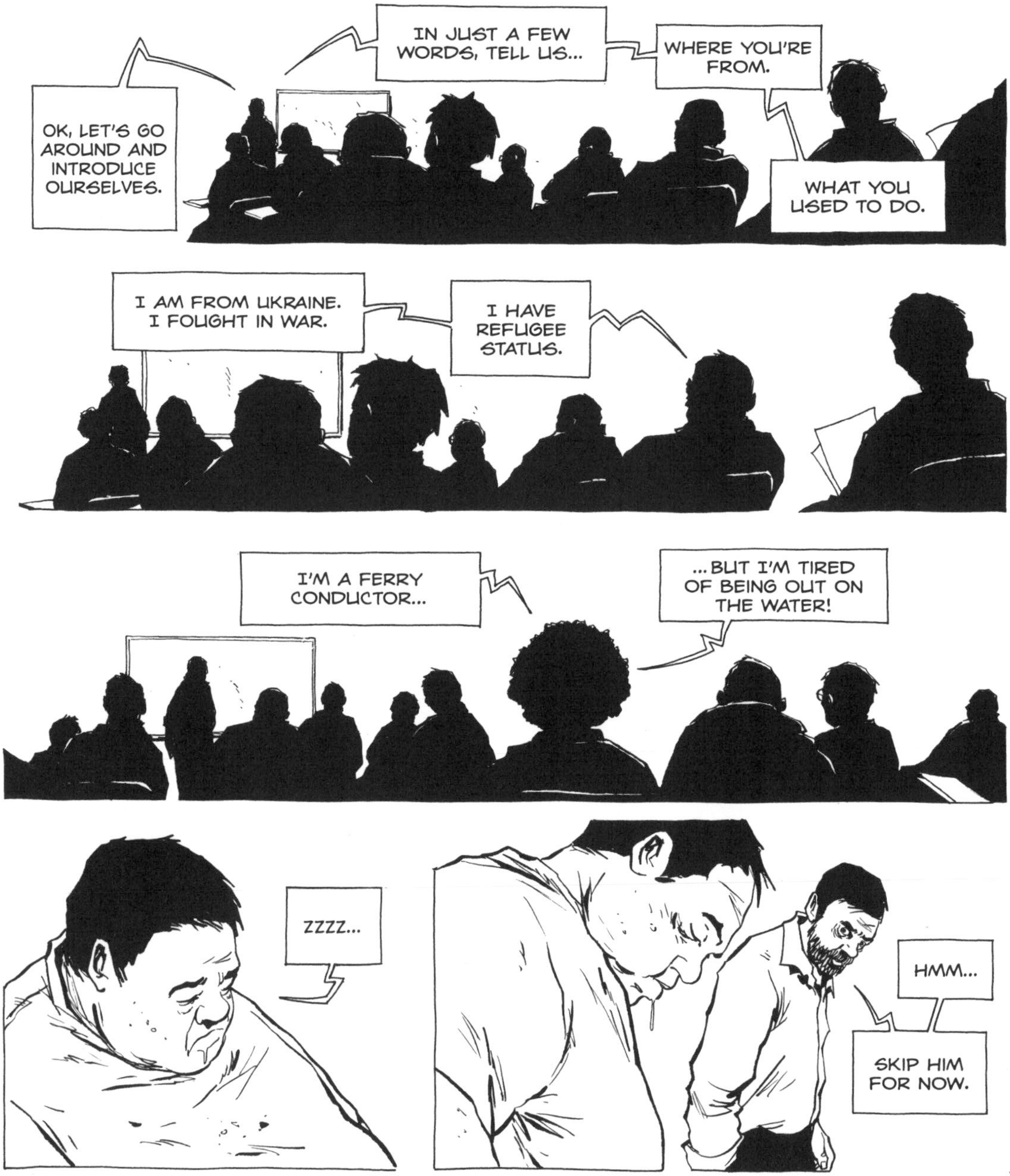
OK, LET'S GO AROUND AND INTRODUCE OURSELVES.
IN JUST A FEW WORDS, TELL US...
WHERE YOU'RE FROM.
WHAT YOU USED TO DO.
I AM FROM UKRAINE. I FOUGHT IN WAR.
I HAVE REFUGEE STATUS.
I'M A FERRY CONDUCTOR...
...BUT I'M TIRED OF BEING OUT ON THE WATER!
ZZZZ...
HMM...
SKIP HIM FOR NOW.

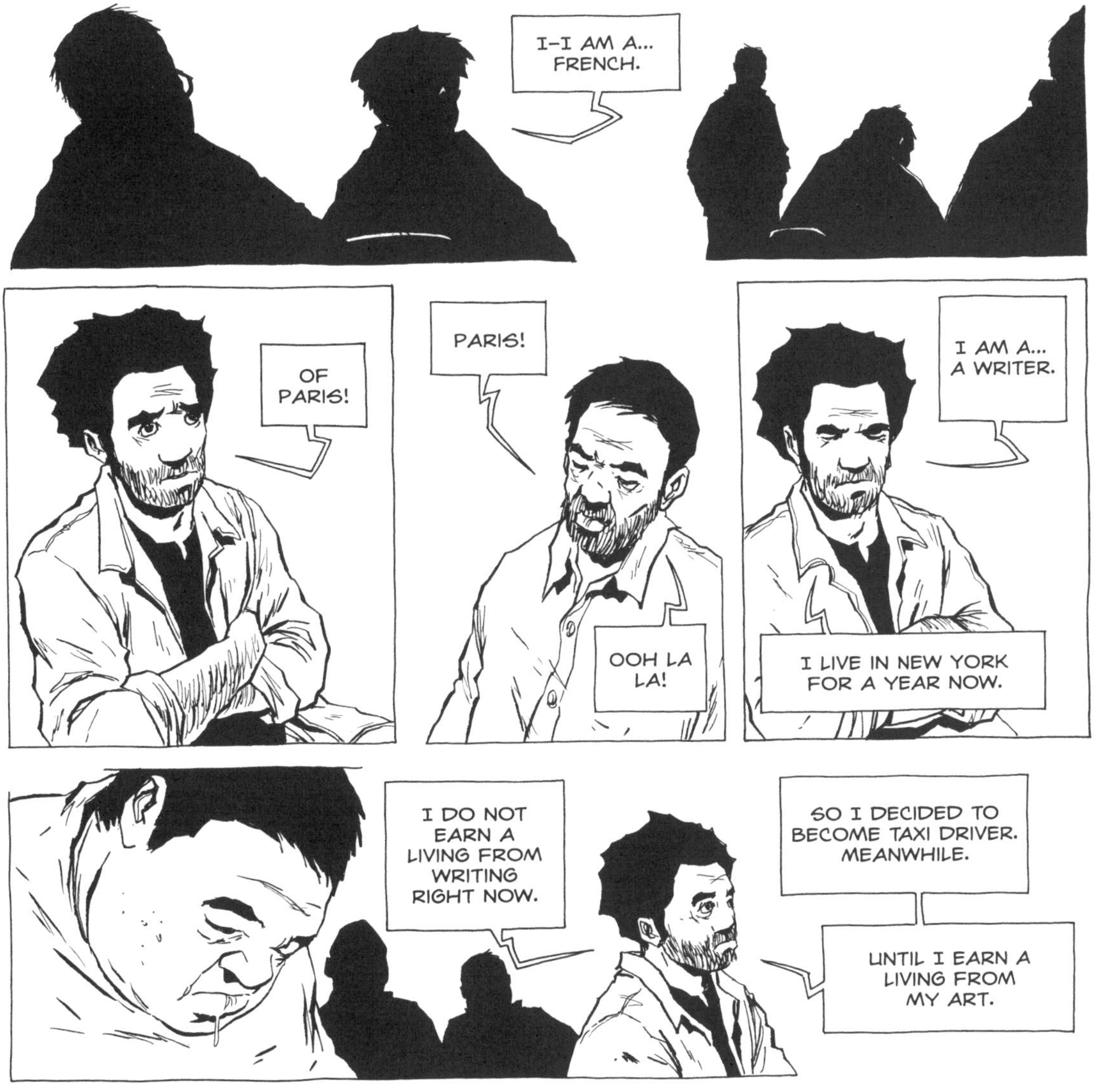
I-I AM A... FRENCH.
OF PARIS!
PARIS!
OOH LA LA!
I AM A... A WRITER.
I LIVE IN NEW YORK FOR A YEAR NOW.
I DO NOT EARN A LIVING FROM WRITING RIGHT NOW.
SO I DECIDED TO BECOME TAXI DRIVER. MEANWHILE.
UNTIL I EARN A LIVING FROM MY ART.

WHEN DO WE FIND OUT OUR MAIN CHARACTER'S AN ACTRESS? IN TAXI SCHOOL? LATER?
WHEN THE STORY BEGINS, WE DON'T KNOW ANYTHING ABOUT HER PAST, HER BACKGROUND...

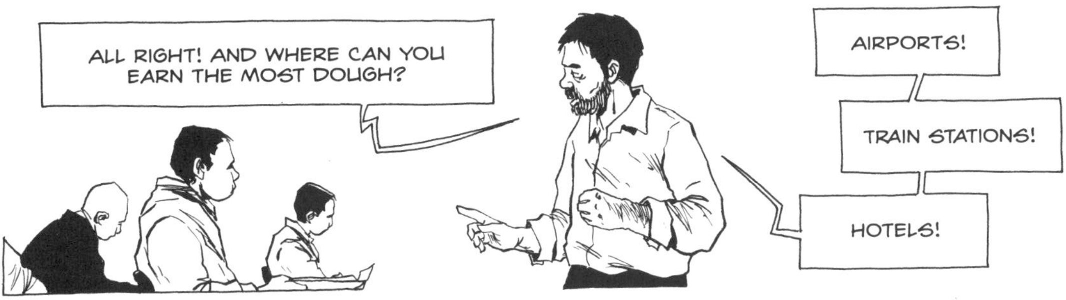
ALL RIGHT! AND WHERE CAN YOU EARN THE MOST DOUGH?
AIRPORTS!
TRAIN STATIONS!
HOTELS!

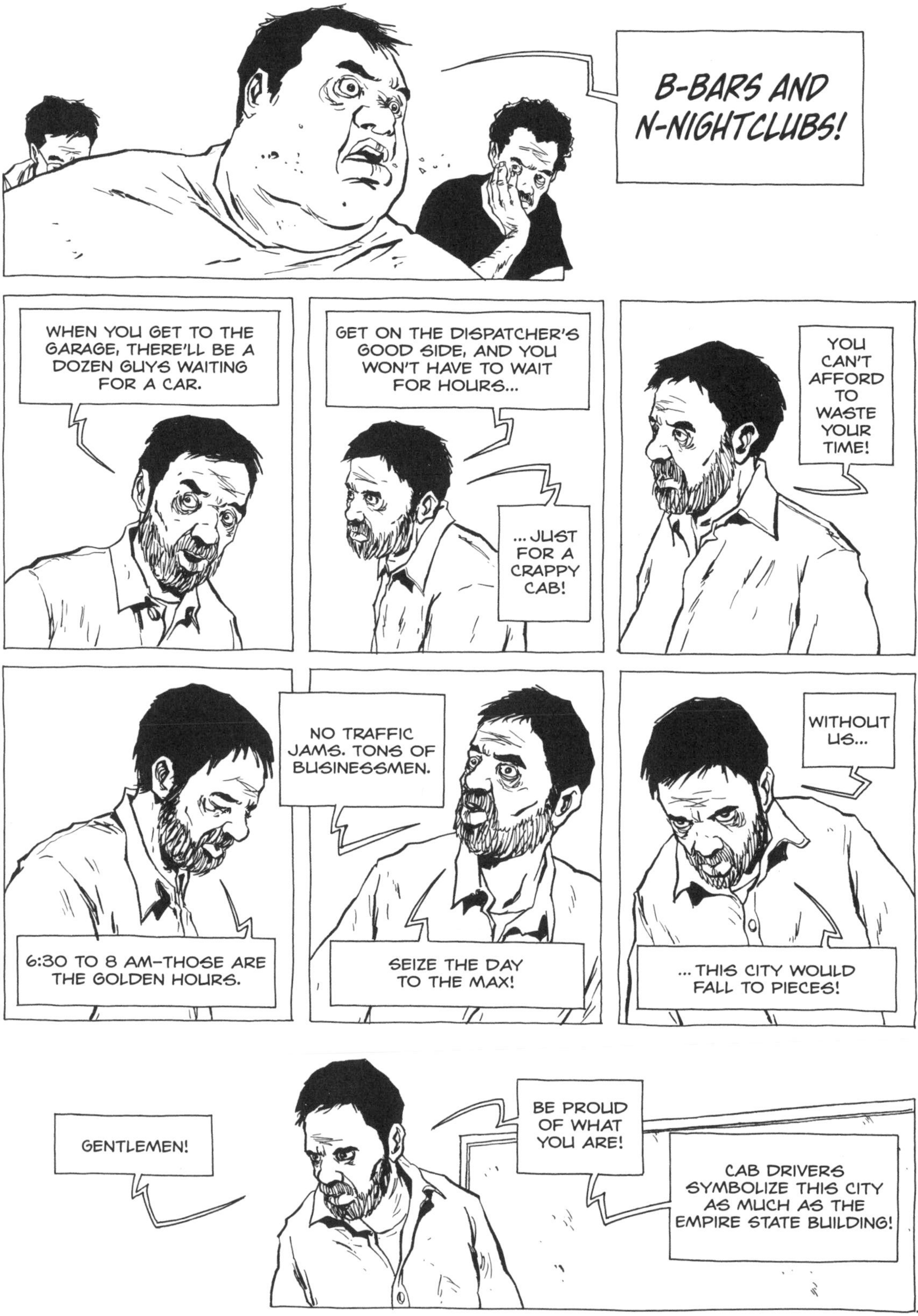
B-BARS AND N-NIGHTCLUBS!
WHEN YOU GET TO THE GARAGE, THERE'LL BE A DOZEN GUYS WAITING FOR A CAR.
GET ON THE DISPATCHER'S GOOD SIDE, AND YOU WON'T HAVE TO WAIT FOR HOURS...
...JUST FOR A CRAPPY CAB!
YOU CAN'T AFFORD TO WASTE YOUR TIME!
6:30 TO 8 AM—THOSE ARE THE GOLDEN HOURS.
NO TRAFFIC JAMS. TONS OF BUSINESSMEN.
SEIZE THE DAY TO THE MAX!
WITHOUT US...
...THIS CITY WOULD FALL TO PIECES!
GENTLEMEN!
BE PROUD OF WHAT YOU ARE!
CAB DRIVERS SYMBOLIZE THIS CITY AS MUCH AS THE EMPIRE STATE BUILDING!

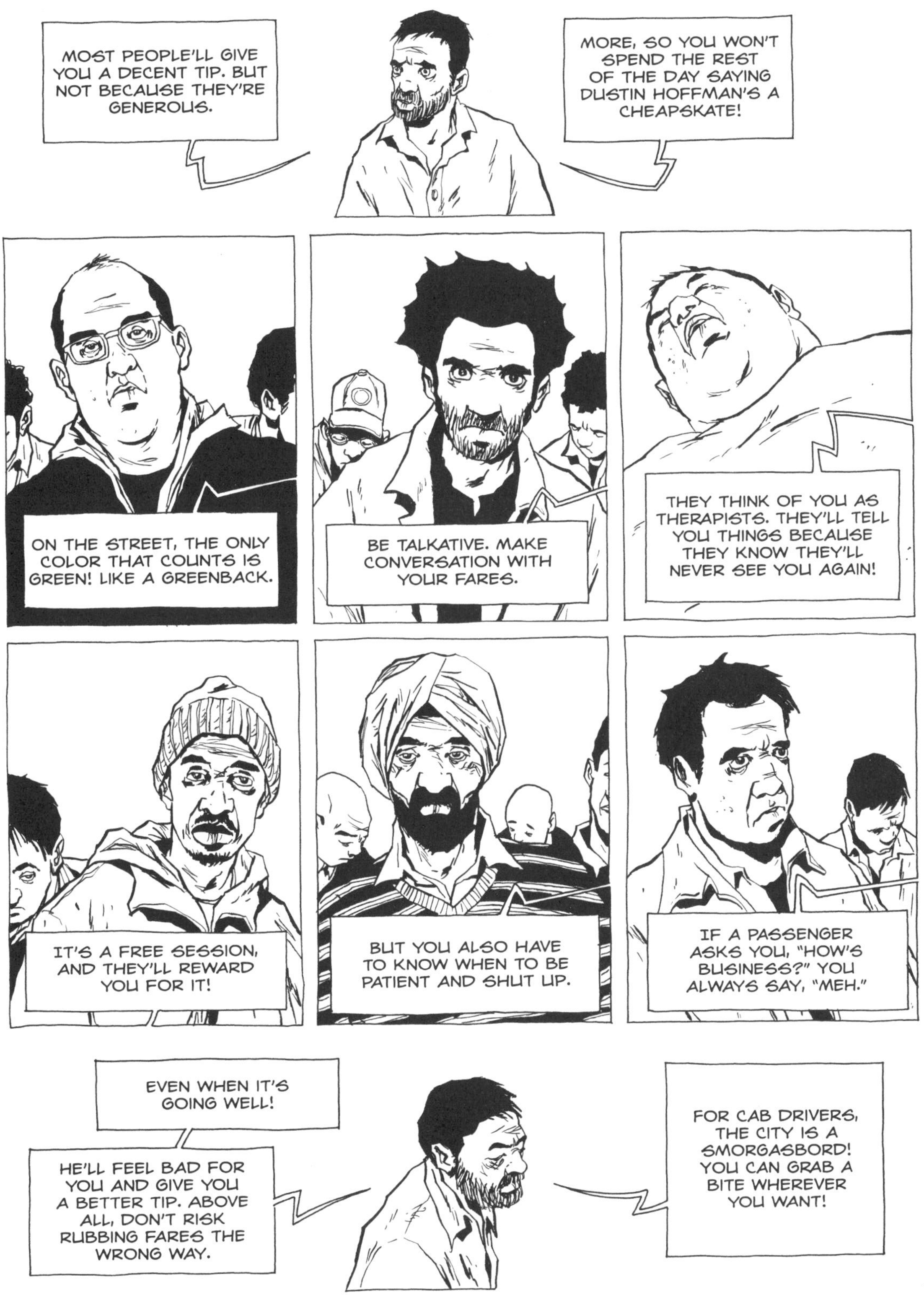
MOST PEOPLE'LL GIVE YOU A DECENT TIP. BUT NOT BECAUSE THEY'RE GENEROUS.
MORE, SO YOU WON'T SPEND THE REST OF THE DAY SAYING DUSTIN HOFFMAN'S A CHEAPSKATE!
ON THE STREET, THE ONLY COLOR THAT COUNTS IS GREEN! LIKE A GREENBACK.
BE TALKATIVE. MAKE CONVERSATION WITH YOUR FARES.
THEY THINK OF YOU AS THERAPISTS. THEY'LL TELL YOU THINGS BECAUSE THEY KNOW THEY'LL NEVER SEE YOU AGAIN!
IT'S A FREE SESSION, AND THEY'LL REWARD YOU FOR IT!
BUT YOU ALSO HAVE TO KNOW WHEN TO BE PATIENT AND SHUT UP.
IF A PASSENGER ASKS YOU, "HOW'S BUSINESS?" YOU ALWAYS SAY, "MEH."
EVEN WHEN IT'S GOING WELL!
HE'LL FEEL BAD FOR YOU AND GIVE YOU A BETTER TIP. ABOVE ALL, DON'T RISK RUBBING FARES THE WRONG WAY.
FOR CAB DRIVERS, THE CITY IS A SMORGASBORD! YOU CAN GRAB A BITE WHEREVER YOU WANT!

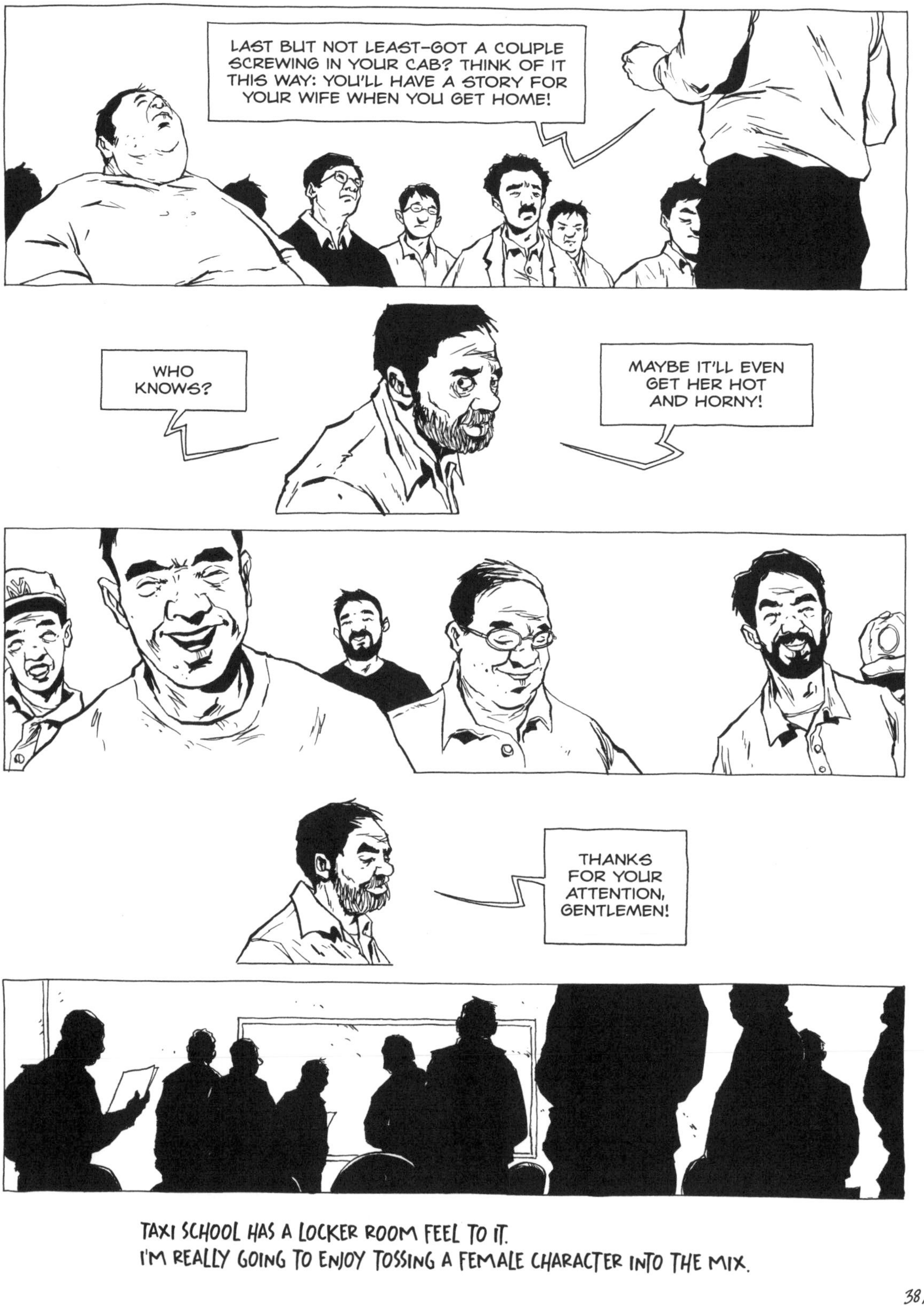
LAST BUT NOT LEAST–GOT A COUPLE SCREWING IN YOUR CAB? THINK OF IT THIS WAY: YOU'LL HAVE A STORY FOR YOUR WIFE WHEN YOU GET HOME!
WHO KNOWS?
MAYBE IT'LL EVEN GET HER HOT AND HORNY!
THANKS FOR YOUR ATTENTION, GENTLEMEN!

TAXI SCHOOL HAS A LOCKER ROOM FEEL TO IT.
I'M REALLY GOING TO ENJOY TOSSING A FEMALE CHARACTER INTO THE MIX.

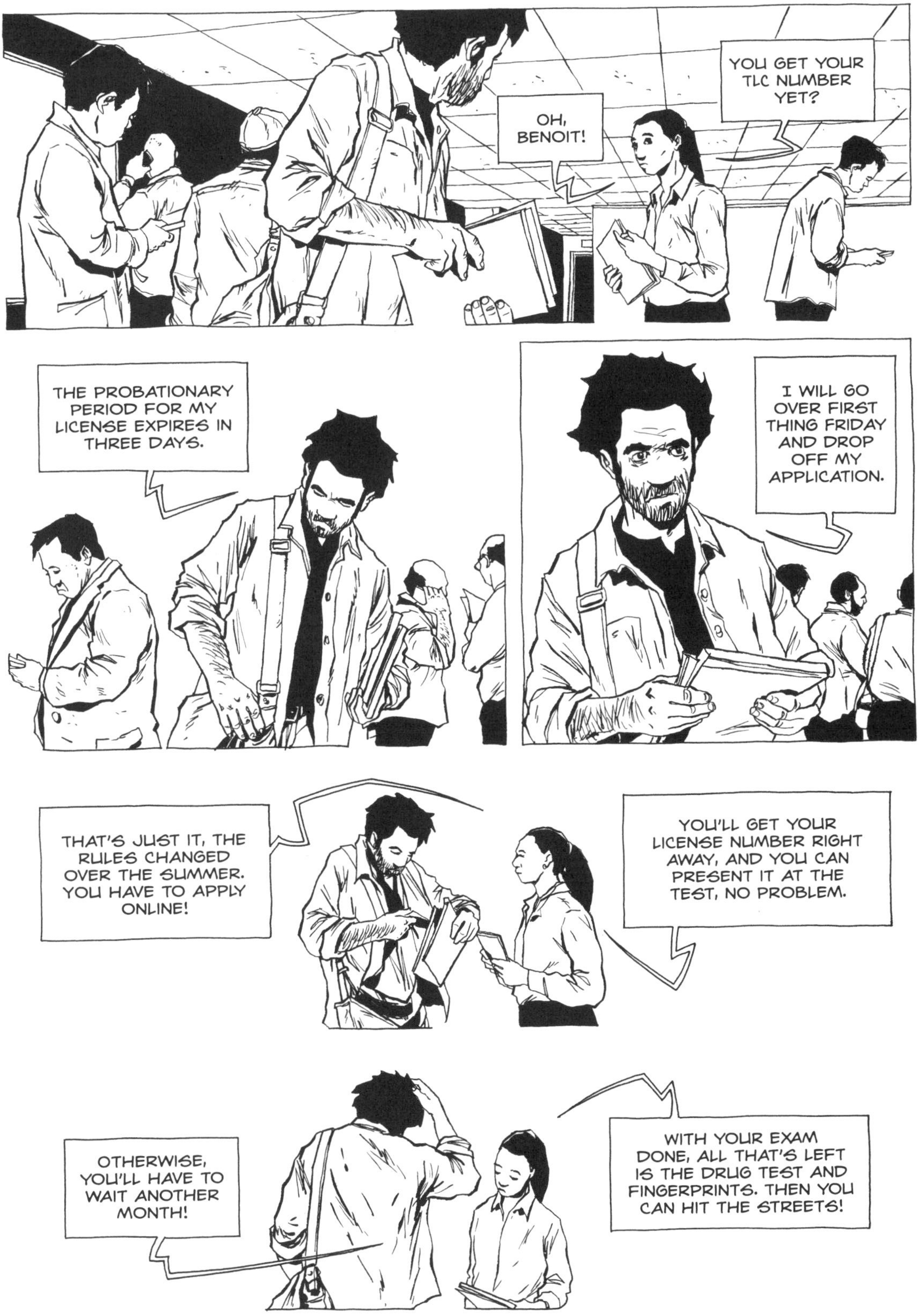
OH, BENOIT!
YOU GET YOUR TLC NUMBER YET?
THE PROBATIONARY PERIOD FOR MY LICENSE EXPIRES IN THREE DAYS.
I WILL GO OVER FIRST THING FRIDAY AND DROP OFF MY APPLICATION.
THAT'S JUST IT, THE RULES CHANGED OVER THE SUMMER. YOU HAVE TO APPLY ONLINE!
YOU'LL GET YOUR LICENSE NUMBER RIGHT AWAY, AND YOU CAN PRESENT IT AT THE TEST, NO PROBLEM.
OTHERWISE, YOU'LL HAVE TO WAIT ANOTHER MONTH!
WITH YOUR EXAM DONE, ALL THAT'S LEFT IS THE DRUG TEST AND FINGERPRINTS. THEN YOU CAN HIT THE STREETS!

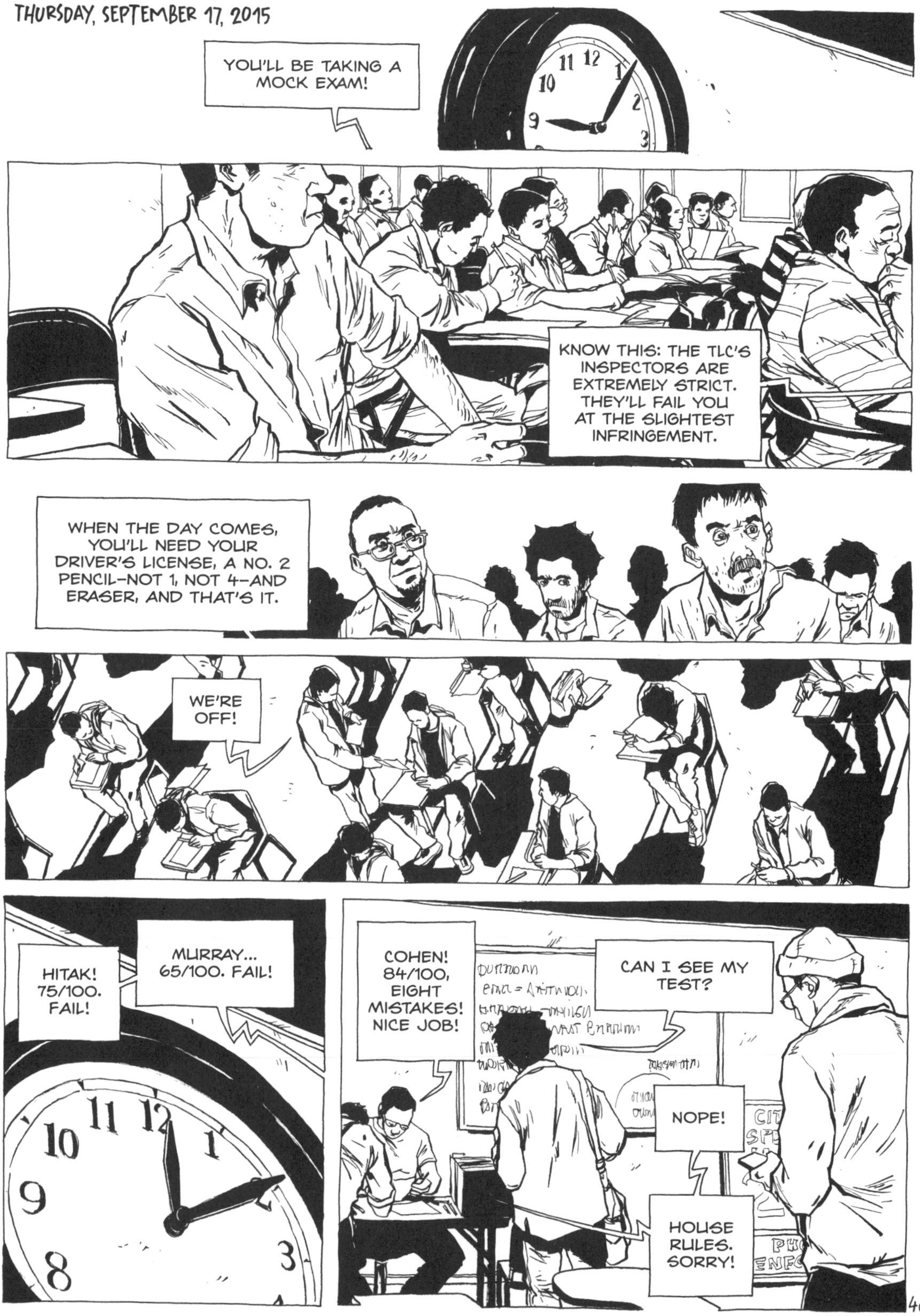
THURSDAY, SEPTEMBER 17, 2015
YOU'LL BE TAKING A MOCK EXAM!
KNOW THIS: THE TLC'S INSPECTORS ARE EXTREMELY STRICT. THEY'LL FAIL YOU AT THE SLIGHTEST INFRINGEMENT.
WHEN THE DAY COMES, YOU'LL NEED YOUR DRIVER'S LICENSE, A NO. 2 PENCIL–NOT 1, NOT 4–AND ERASER, AND THAT'S IT.
WE'RE OFF!
HITAK! 75/100. FAIL!
MURRAY... 65/100. FAIL!
COHEN! 84/100, EIGHT MISTAKES! NICE JOB!
CAN I SEE MY TEST?
NOPE!
HOUSE RULES. SORRY!

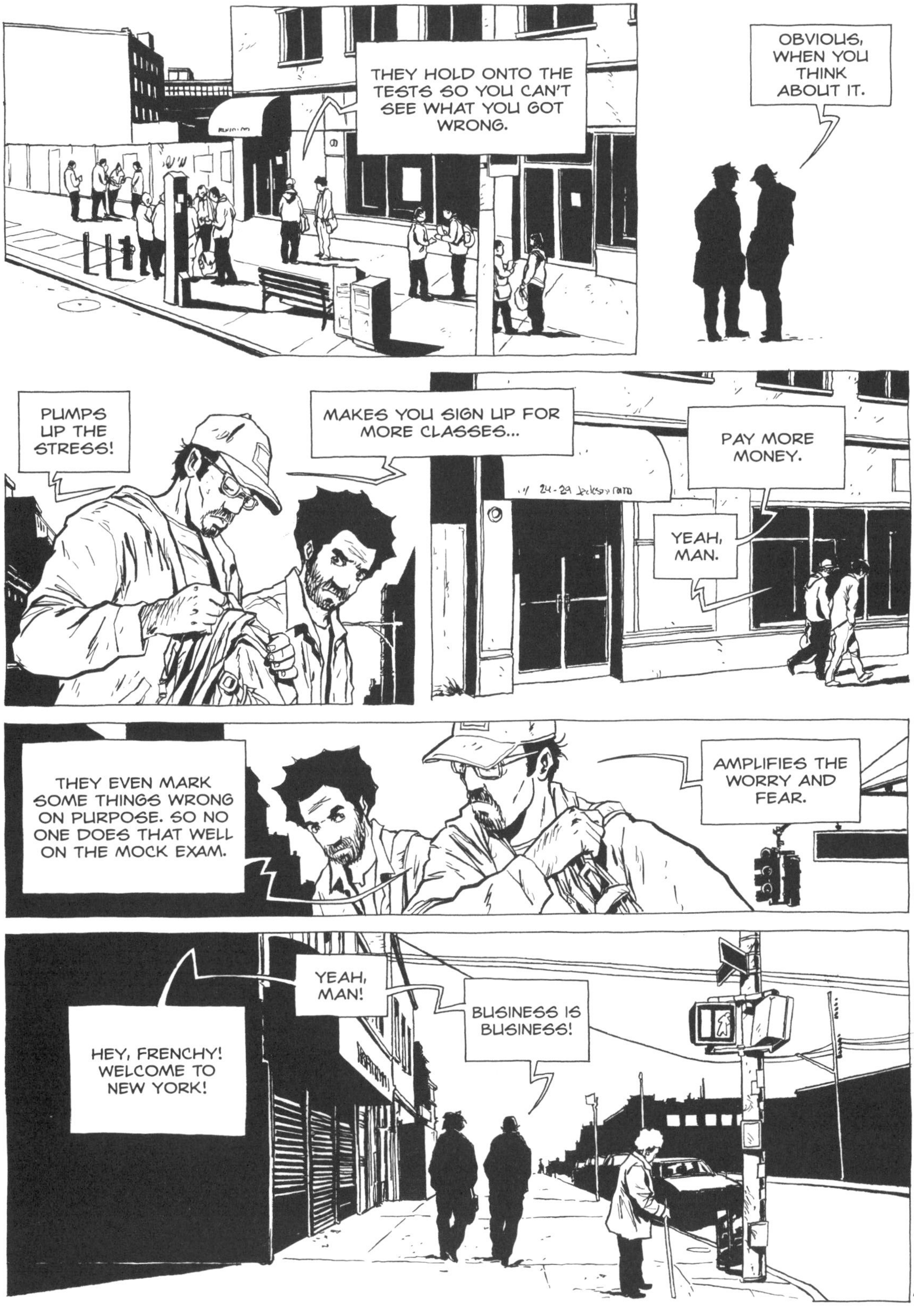
THEY HOLD ONTO THE TESTS SO YOU CAN'T SEE WHAT YOU GOT WRONG.
OBVIOUS, WHEN YOU THINK ABOUT IT.
PUMPS UP THE STRESS!
MAKES YOU SIGN UP FOR MORE CLASSES...
PAY MORE MONEY.
YEAH, MAN.
THEY EVEN MARK SOME THINGS WRONG ON PURPOSE. SO NO ONE DOES THAT WELL ON THE MOCK EXAM.
AMPLIFIES THE WORRY AND FEAR.
HEY, FRENCHY! WELCOME TO NEW YORK!
YEAH, MAN!
BUSINESS IS BUSINESS!

FRIDAY, SEPTEMBER 18, 2015

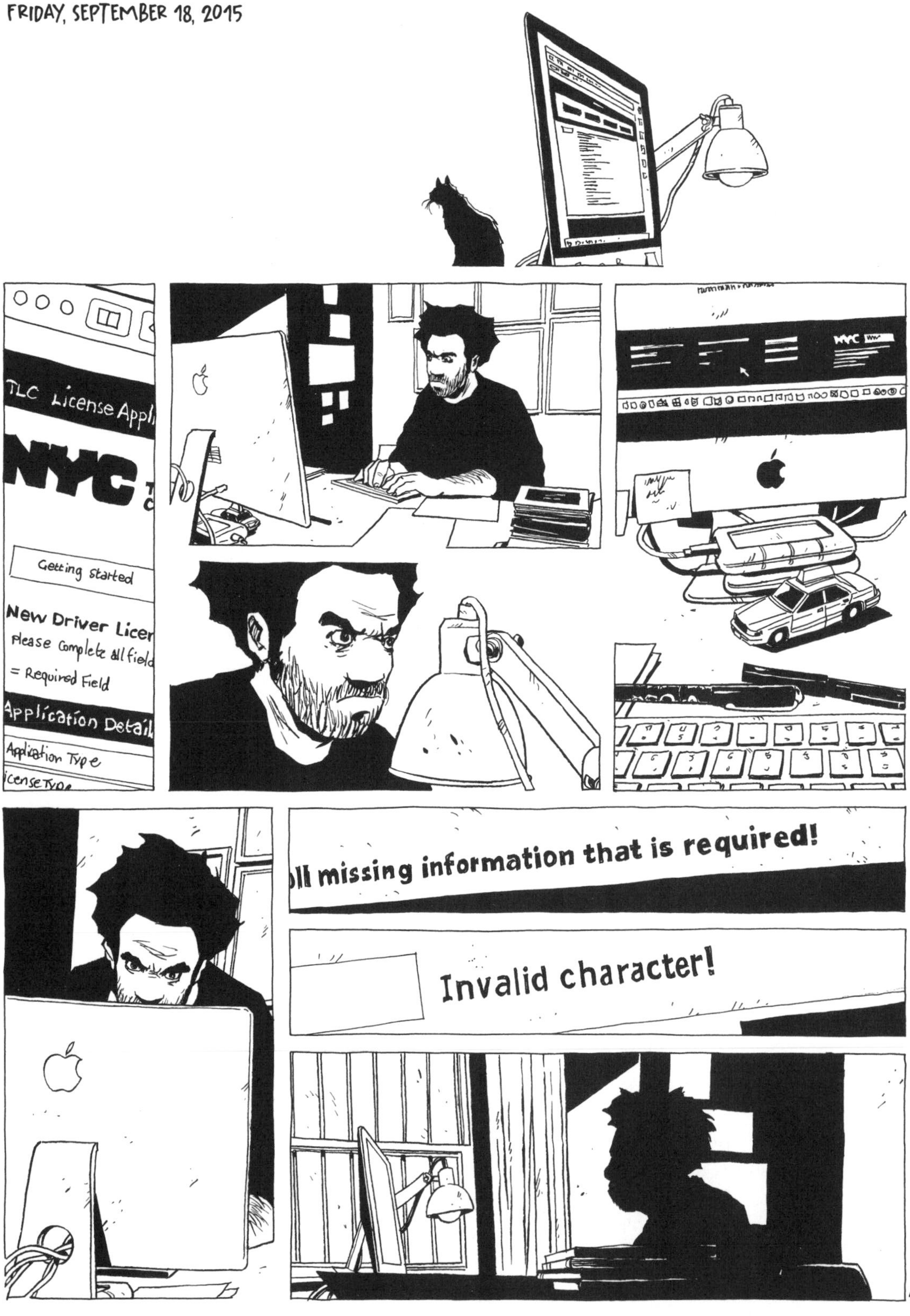

TLC License Appli
NYC
Getting started
New Driver Licer
Please Complete all field
= Required Field
Application Detail
Application Type
ll missing information that is required!
Invalid character!

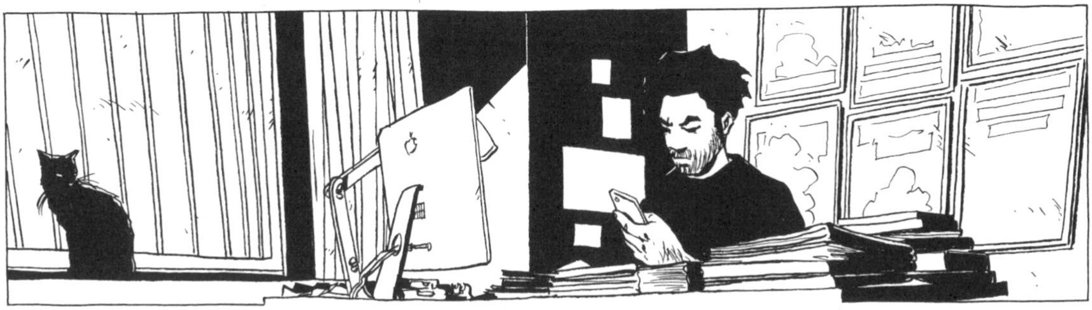

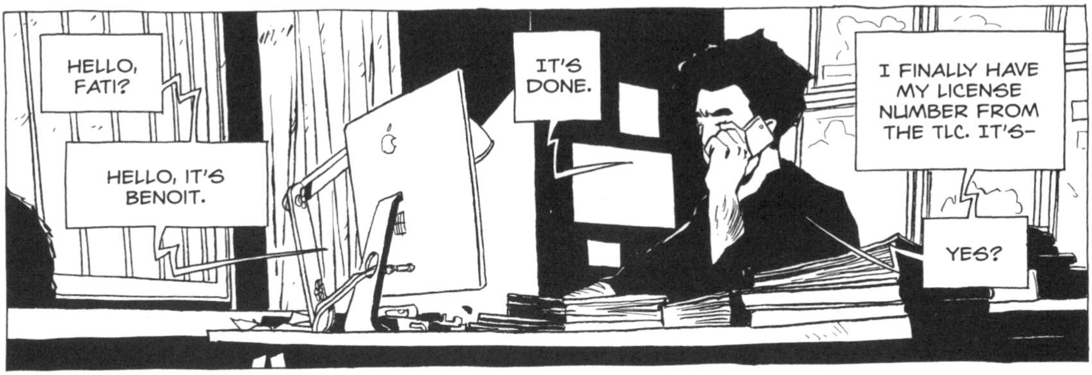
HELLO, FATI?
HELLO, IT'S BENOIT.
IT'S DONE.
I FINALLY HAVE MY LICENSE NUMBER FROM THE TLC. IT'S–
YES?

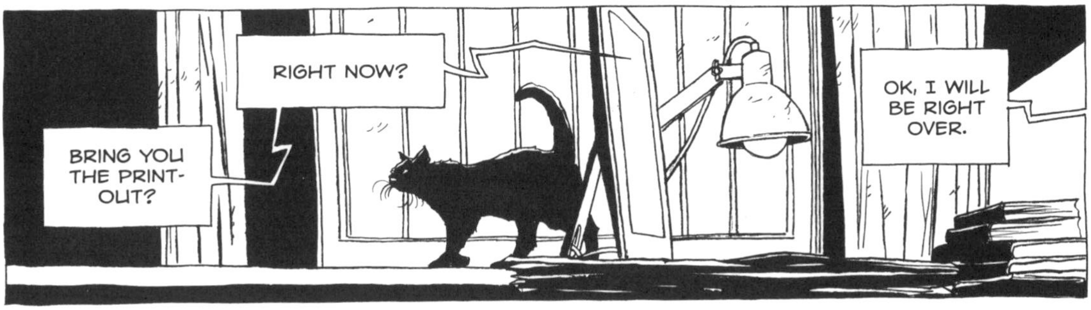
BRING YOU THE PRINT-OUT?
RIGHT NOW?
OK, I WILL BE RIGHT OVER.

OUR MAIN CHARACTER COULD GO TO AN AUDITION IN HER TAXI, DURING A WORKDAY...

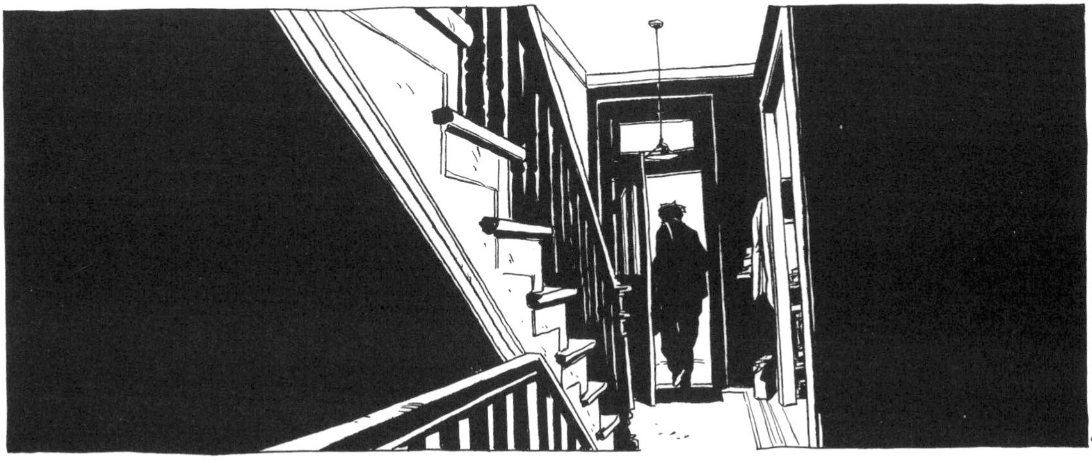

A GUY LIGHTS A CIGARETTE IN OUR MAIN CHARACTER'S CAB. SHE ASKS HIM TO PUT IT OUT, AND HE SAYS NO. SHE TELLS HIM TO GET OUT, HE PUTS UP A FIGHT AND THREATENS TO FILE A COMPLAINT WITH THE TLC, CLAIMS SHE INSULTED HIM. SURE, IT'S FALSE, BUT A DRIVER'S WORD AGAINST A FARE'S? THE CUSTOMER IS ALWAYS RIGHT.

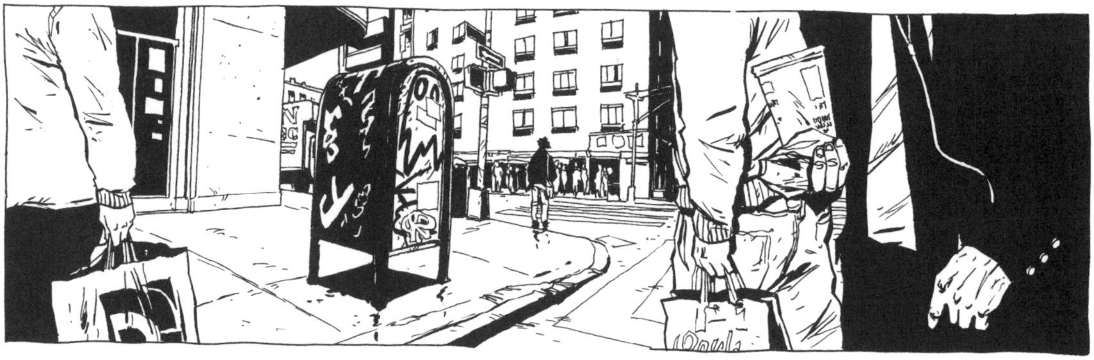

SHE FEELS POWERLESS.

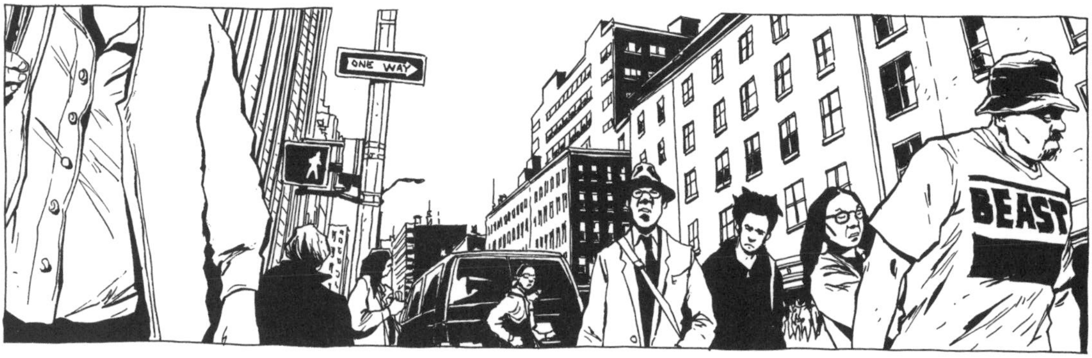
ONE WAY
BEAST

THE MANAGER OF HER TAXI SCHOOL COULD BE HER ANCHOR, HER ONLY POINT OF REFERENCE IN THE JUNGLE THAT IS GOTHAM.

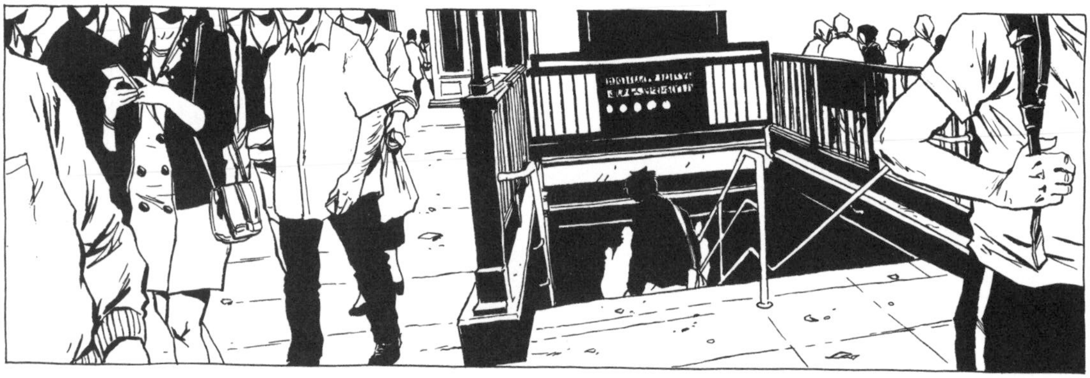

DON'T DICTATE THE STRUCTURE OF THE FILM. LET SCENES EMERGE AS YOU EXPERIENCE THEM, THEN RE-ARRANGE THEM LATER.

FRIDAY, SEPTEMBER 25, 2015

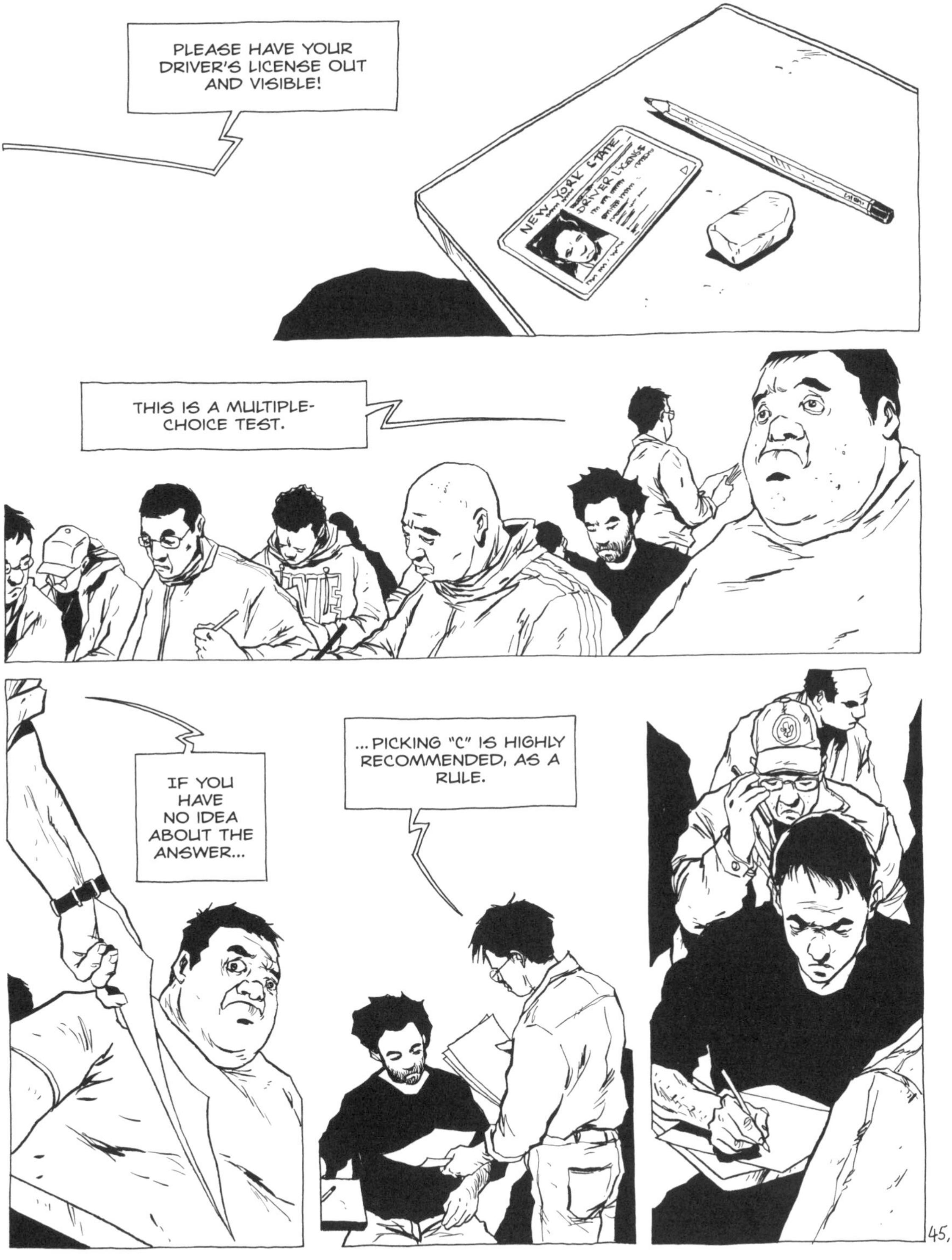
PLEASE HAVE YOUR DRIVER'S LICENSE OUT AND VISIBLE!
NEW YORK STATE
DRIVER LICENSE
THIS IS A MULTIPLE-CHOICE TEST.
IF YOU HAVE NO IDEA ABOUT THE ANSWER...
...PICKING "C" IS HIGHLY RECOMMENDED, AS A RULE.

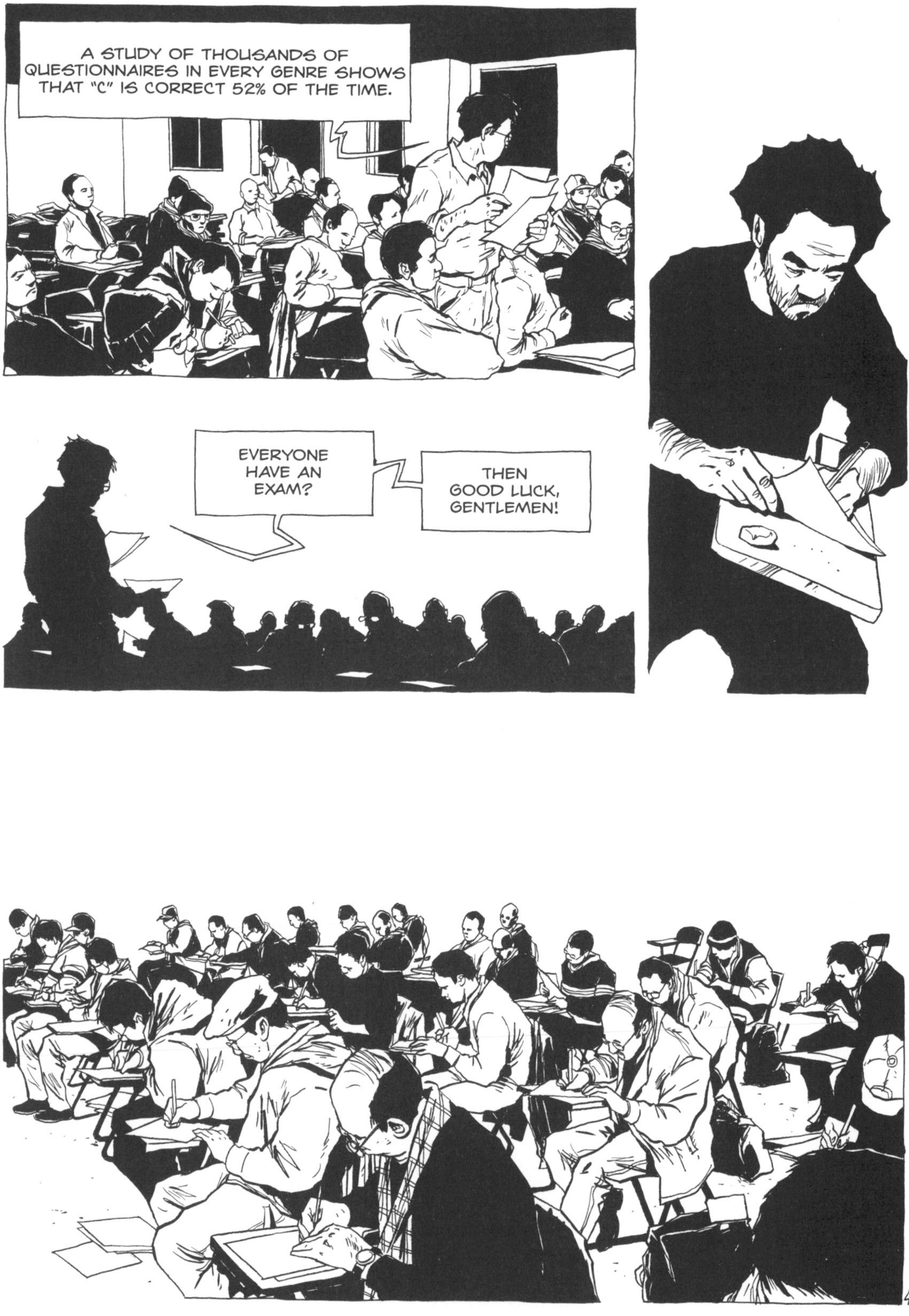
A STUDY OF THOUSANDS OF QUESTIONNAIRES IN EVERY GENRE SHOWS THAT "C" IS CORRECT 52% OF THE TIME.
EVERYONE HAVE AN EXAM?
THEN GOOD LUCK, GENTLEMEN!

MONDAY, SEPTEMBER 28, 2015

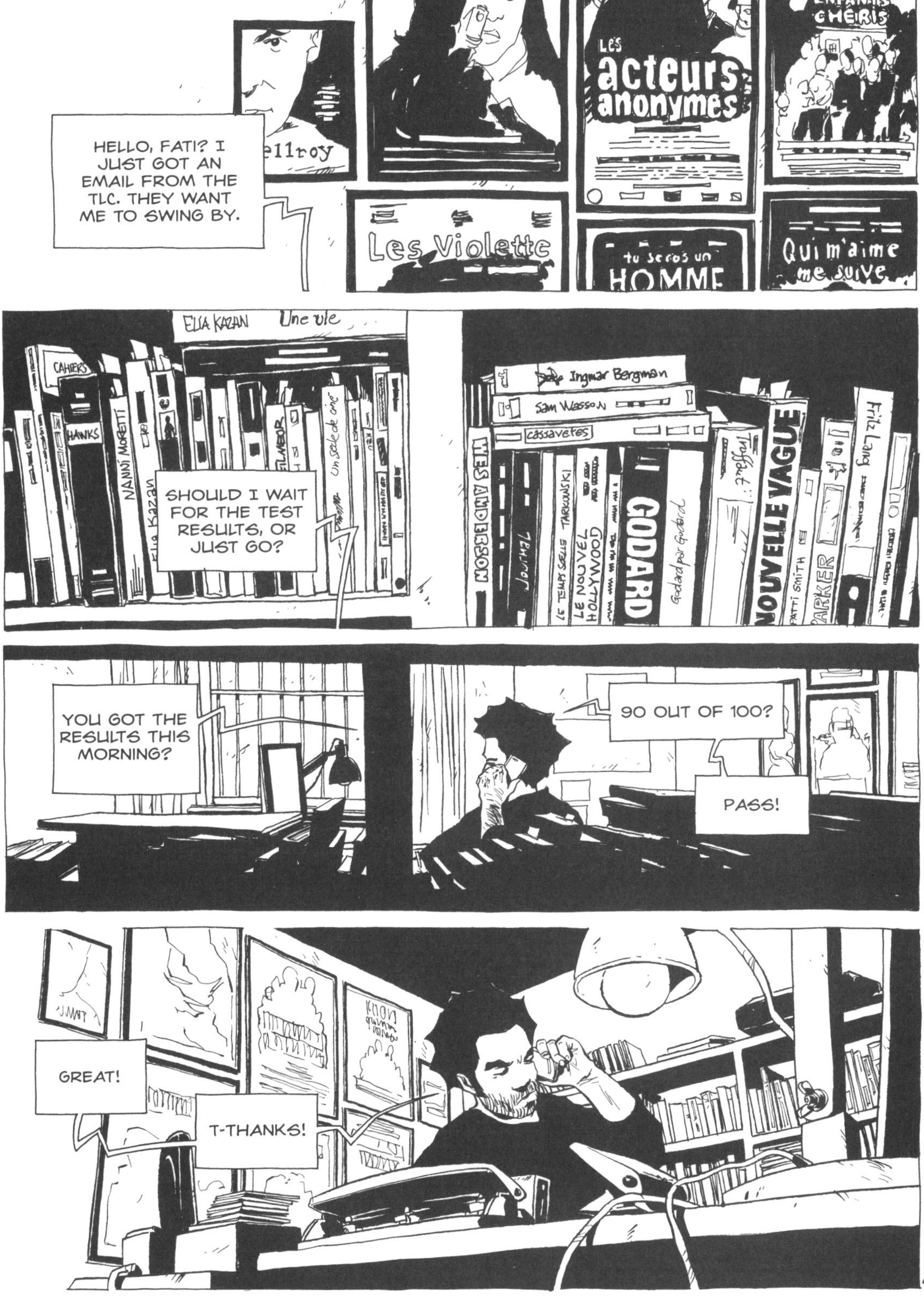

HELLO, FATI? I JUST GOT AN EMAIL FROM THE TLC. THEY WANT ME TO SWING BY.
Les acteurs anonymes
ENFANTS CHÉRIS
Les Violette
tu seras un HOMME
Qui m'aime me suive
ELIA KAZAN Une vie
CAHIERS
HAWKS
NANNI MORETTI
Elia Kazan
Un siècle de ciné
SHOULD I WAIT FOR THE TEST RESULTS, OR JUST GO?
Ingmar Bergman
Sam Wasson
cassavetes
WES ANDERSON
TARKOWSKI
LE TEMPS SCELLÉ
LE NOUVEL HOLLYWOOD
GODARD
Godard par Godard
Truffaut
NOUVELLE VAGUE
PATTI SMITH
PARKER
Fritz Lang
YOU GOT THE RESULTS THIS MORNING?
90 OUT OF 100?
PASS!
GREAT!
T-THANKS!

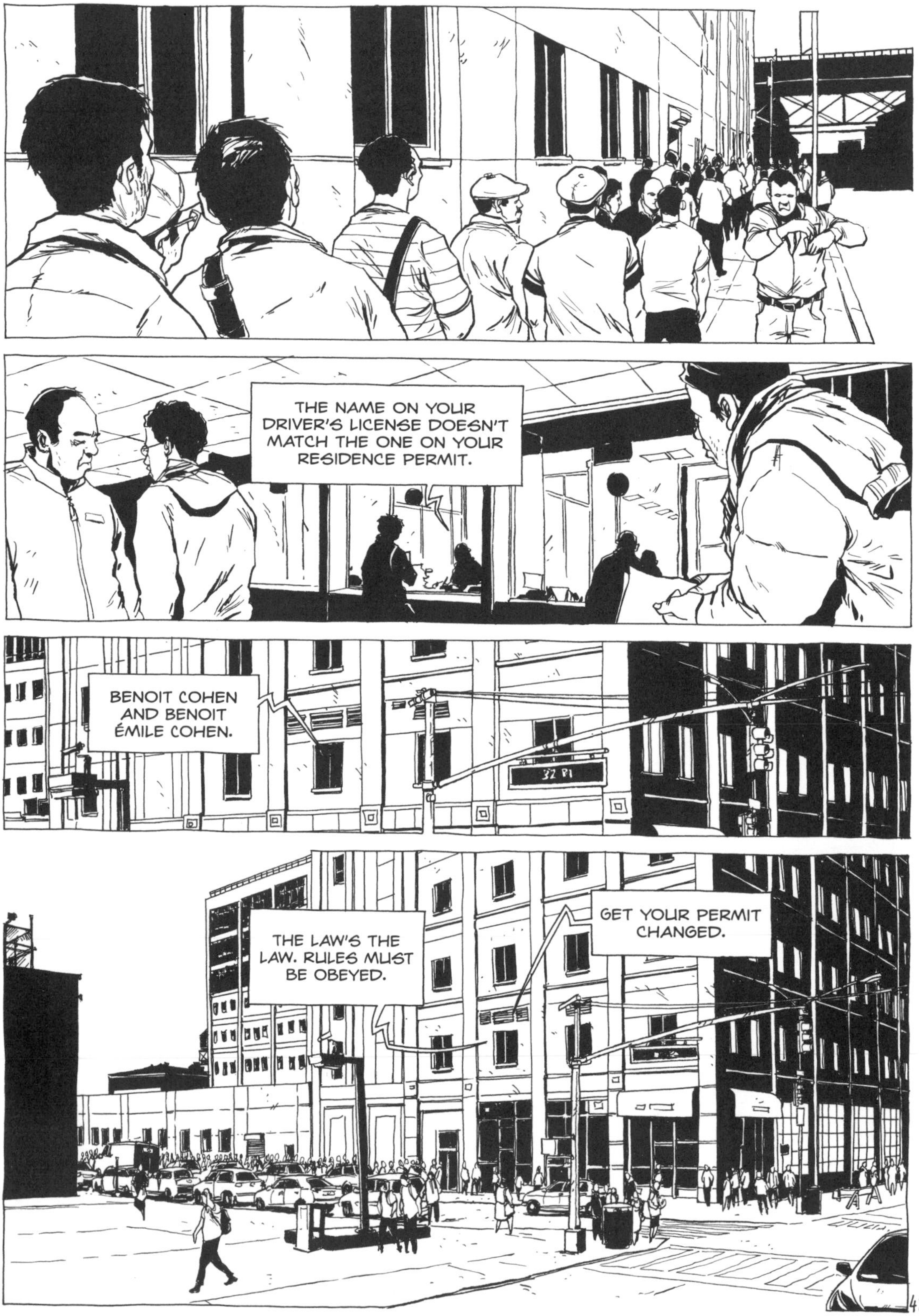
THE NAME ON YOUR DRIVER'S LICENSE DOESN'T MATCH THE ONE ON YOUR RESIDENCE PERMIT.
BENOIT COHEN AND BENOIT ÉMILE COHEN.
32 PI
THE LAW'S THE LAW. RULES MUST BE OBEYED.
GET YOUR PERMIT CHANGED.

TUESDAY, OCTOBER 6, 2015

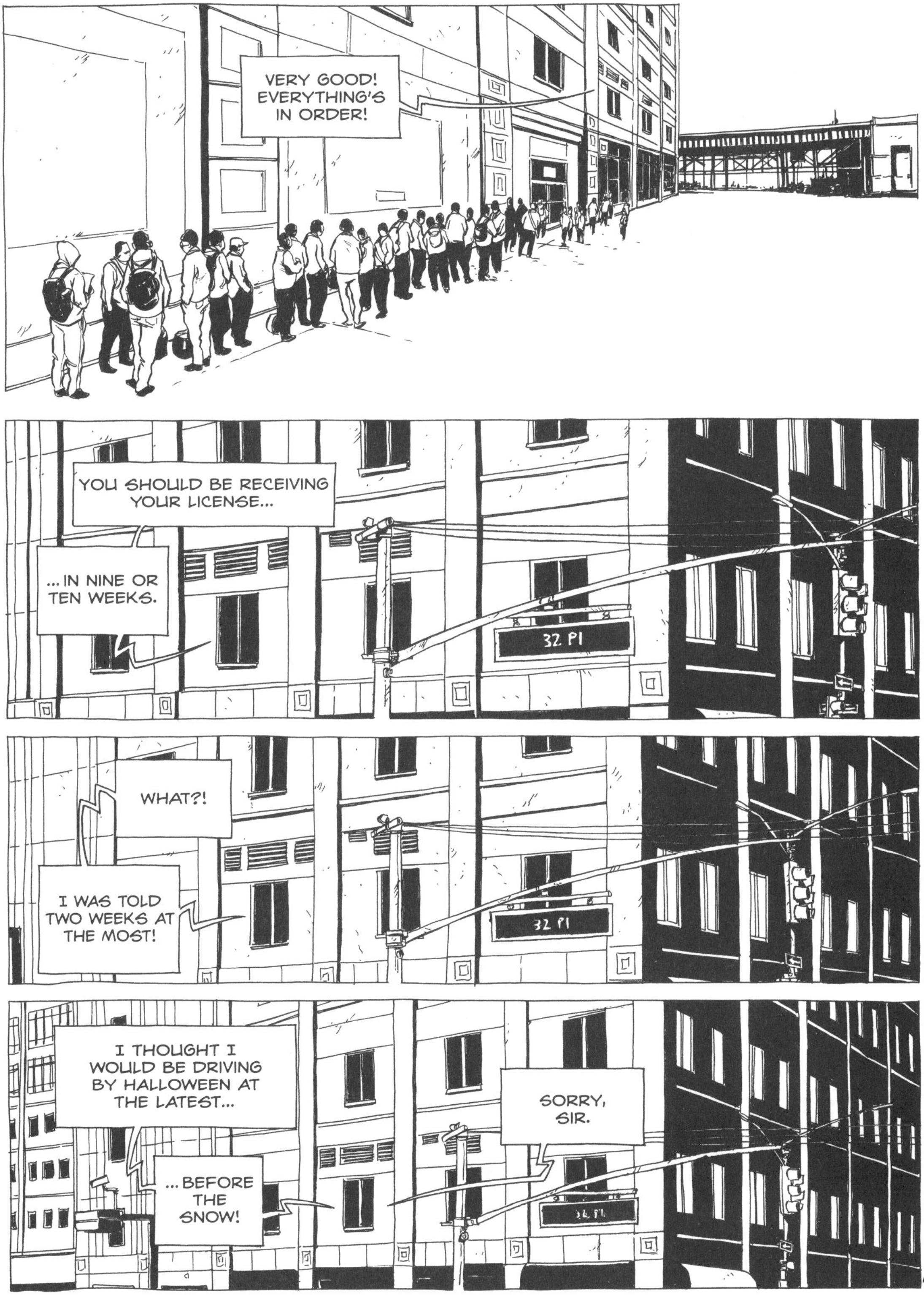

VERY GOOD! EVERYTHING'S IN ORDER!
YOU SHOULD BE RECEIVING YOUR LICENSE...
...IN NINE OR TEN WEEKS.
32 Pl
WHAT?!
I WAS TOLD TWO WEEKS AT THE MOST!
32 Pl
I THOUGHT I WOULD BE DRIVING BY HALLOWEEN AT THE LATEST...
...BEFORE THE SNOW!
SORRY, SIR.
32 Pl

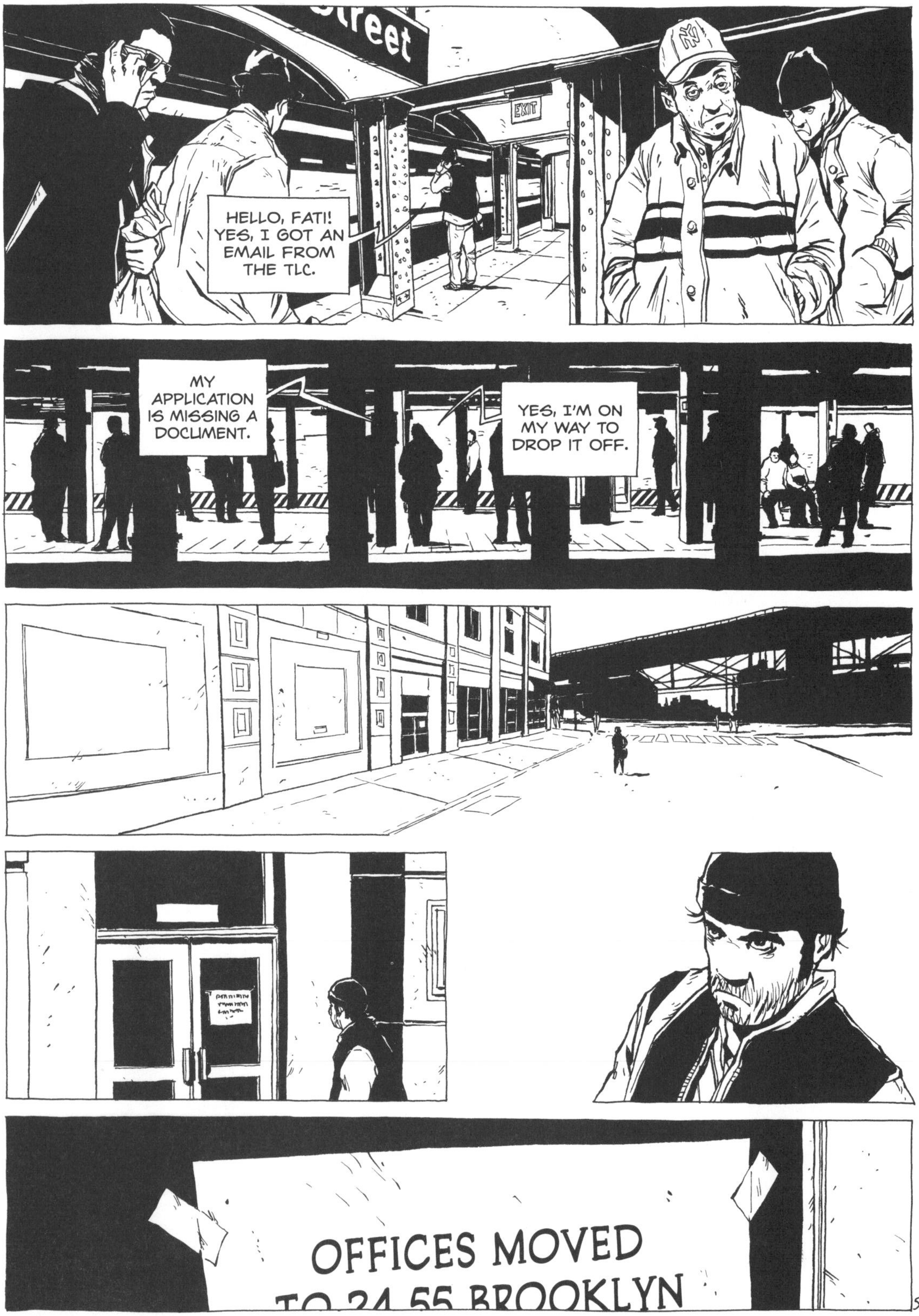
Street
EXIT
HELLO, FATI! YES, I GOT AN EMAIL FROM THE TLC.
MY APPLICATION IS MISSING A DOCUMENT.
YES, I'M ON MY WAY TO DROP IT OFF.
OFFICES MOVED
TO 24 55 BROOKLYN

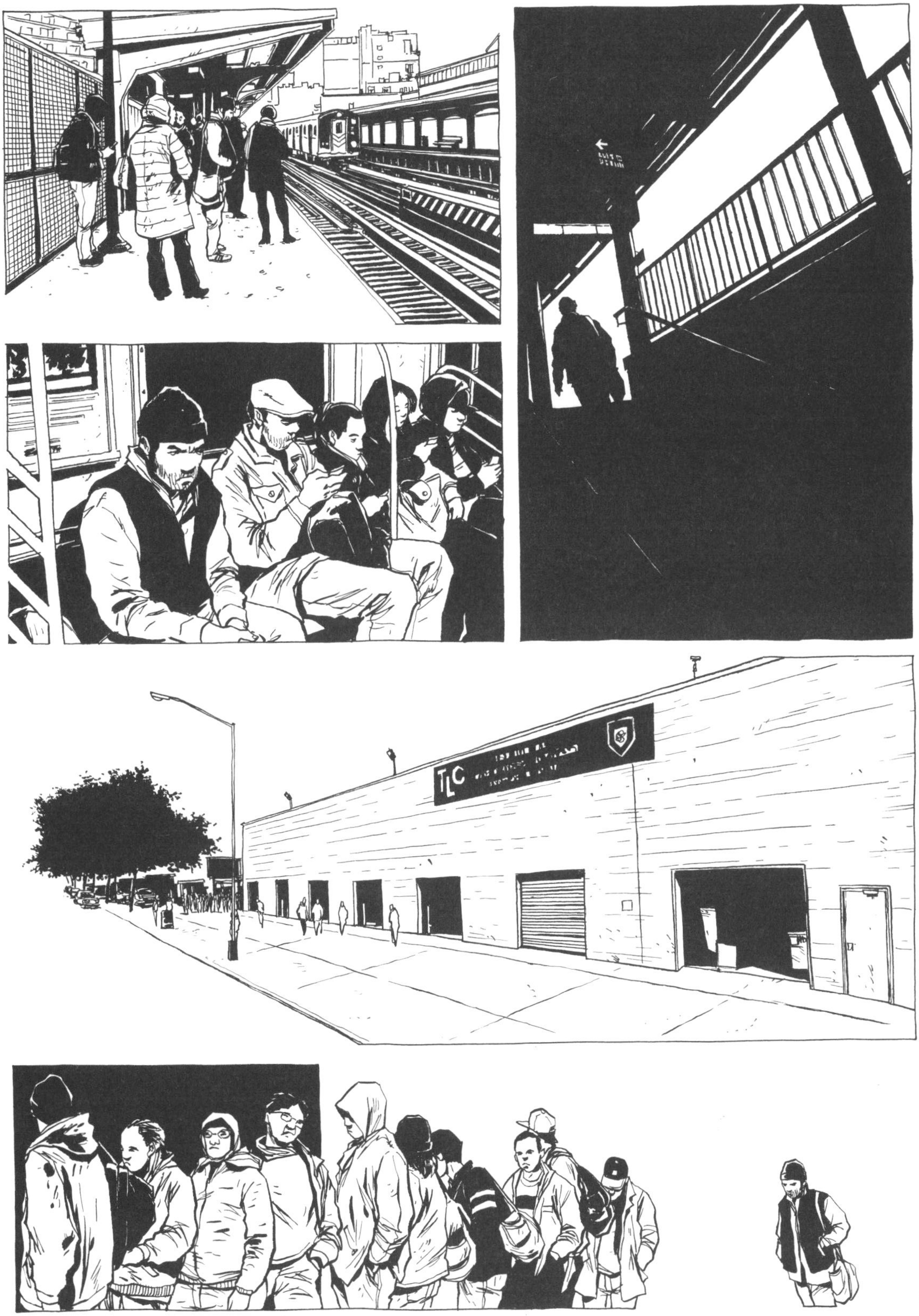
TLC

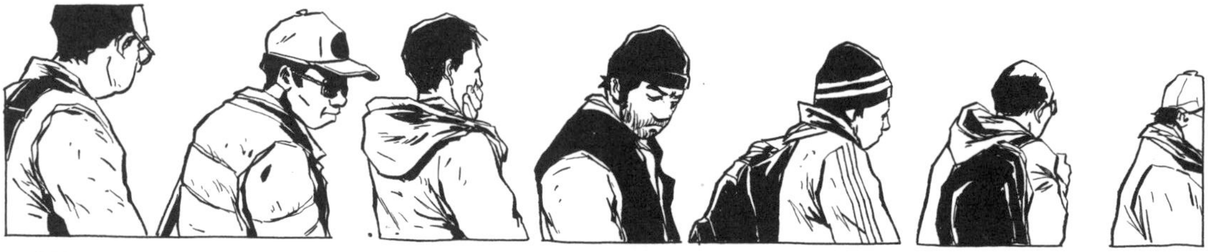

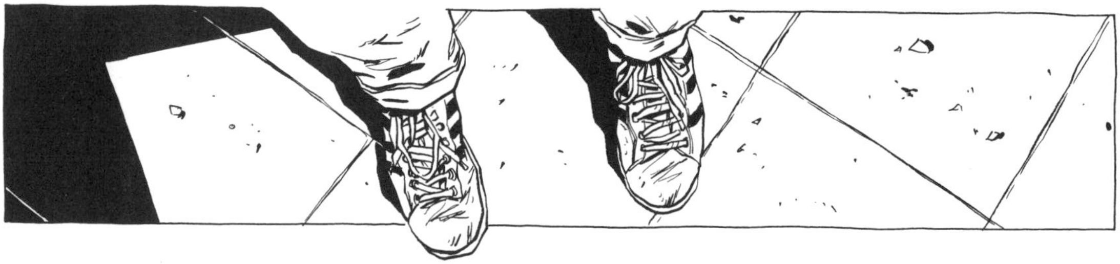

I BLEND INTO THE CROWD OF FUTURE DRIVERS WITH MY THREE-DAY SHADOW, SNEAKERS, AND OLD BLUE JEANS.

I'M ALWAYS WORRIED ABOUT FITTING IN, LOOKING AS MUCH LIKE MY "COWORKERS" AS I CAN, NOT DRAWING ATTENTION, NOT BEING FOUND OUT.

MY MAIN CHARACTER WILL ALSO BE TRYING TO FORGE A NEW IDENTITY FOR HERSELF, PLAY A PART. NOT BEING ON THE FRONT LINES WILL HELP HER PUT UP WITH THE TOUGHNESS OF HER NEW DAILY ROUTINE. EVERY TIME SHE GETS BEHIND THE WHEEL, SHE'LL FEEL LIKE SHE'S IN A MOVIE. THEN SHE'LL REMEMBER THAT NEW YORK IS THE CITY WHERE THE ACTORS STUDIO WAS FOUNDED, AND SHE'LL SUBMERGE HERSELF IN HER NEW ROLE.

LIKE DE NIRO, WHO GOT HIS LICENSE AND DROVE A TAXI FOR SEVERAL MONTHS BEFORE SHOOTING *TAXI DRIVER*.

BUT WHAT MOVIE IS MY MAIN CHARACTER PICTURING? A FANTASY? HER LIFE STORY?
I LIKE THE IDEA OF THE LINE BETWEEN FICTION AND REALITY BLURRING FOR HER.

NEW YORK LENDS ITSELF TO THAT KIND OF CONFUSION...

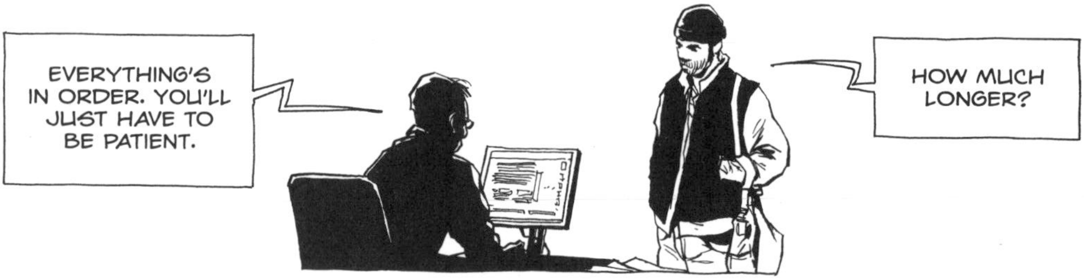
EVERYTHING'S IN ORDER. YOU'LL JUST HAVE TO BE PATIENT.
HOW MUCH LONGER?

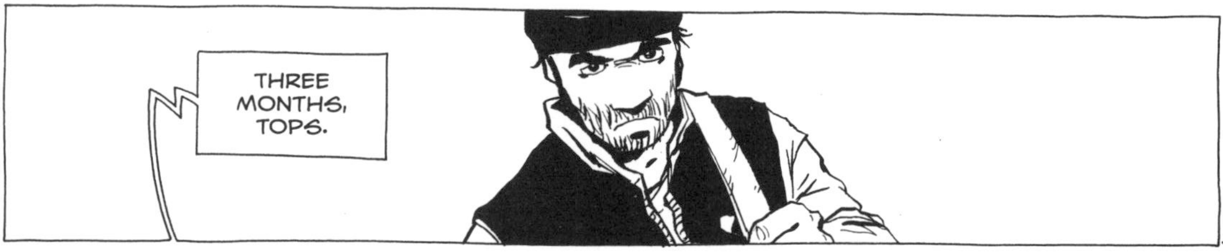
THREE MONTHS, TOPS.

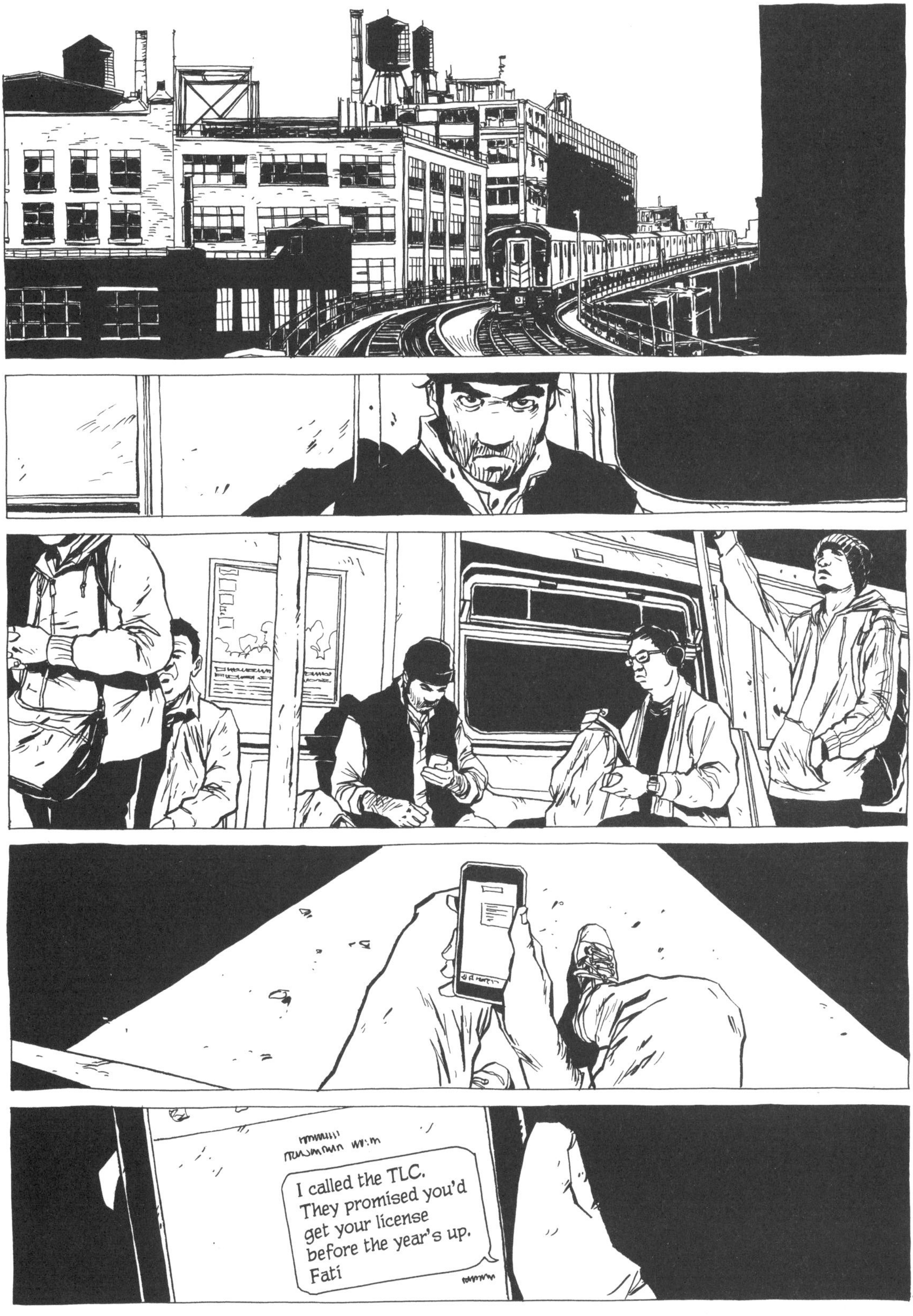
I called the TLC.
They promised you'd
get your license
before the year's up.
Fati

FRIDAY, JANUARY 1, 2016

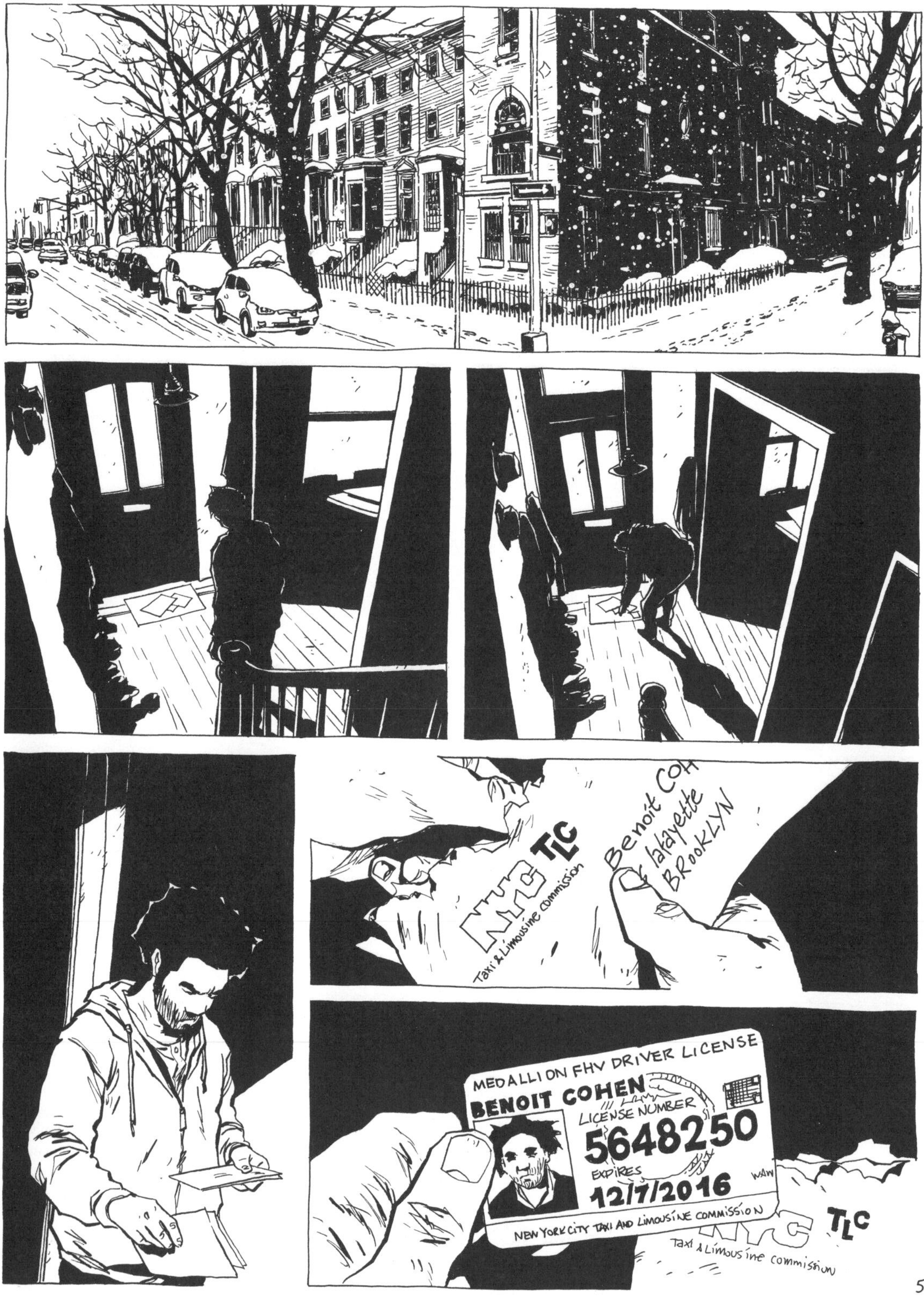
NYC TLC
Taxi & Limousine commission
Benoit COH
lafayette
BROOKLYN
MEDALLION FHV DRIVER LICENSE
BENOIT COHEN
LICENSE NUMBER
5648250
EXPIRES
12/7/2016
NEW YORK CITY TAXI AND LIMOUSINE COMMISSION
NYC TLC
Taxi & Limousine commission

MONDAY, JANUARY 4, 2016

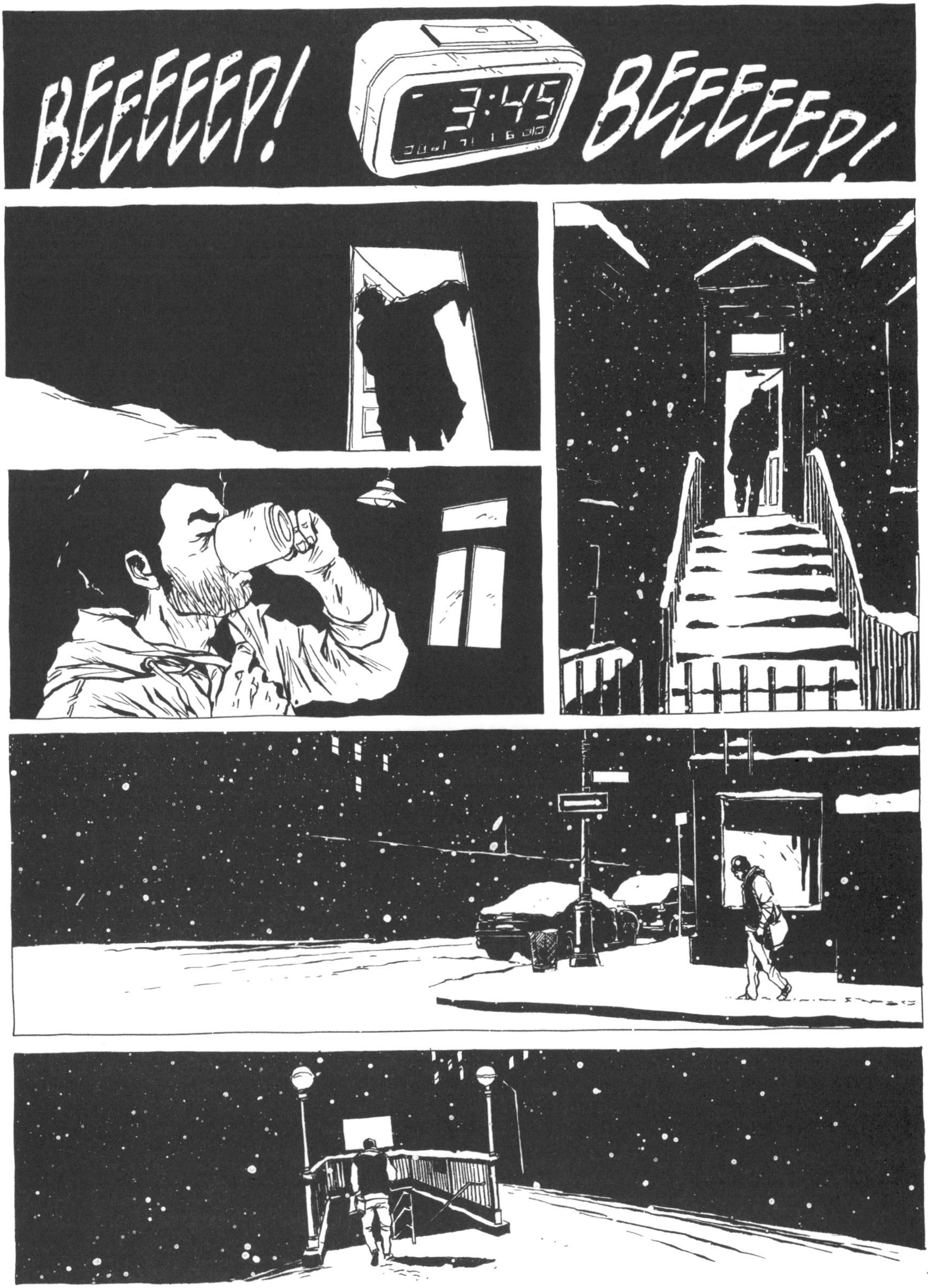
BEEEEEP!
3:45
BEEEEEP!

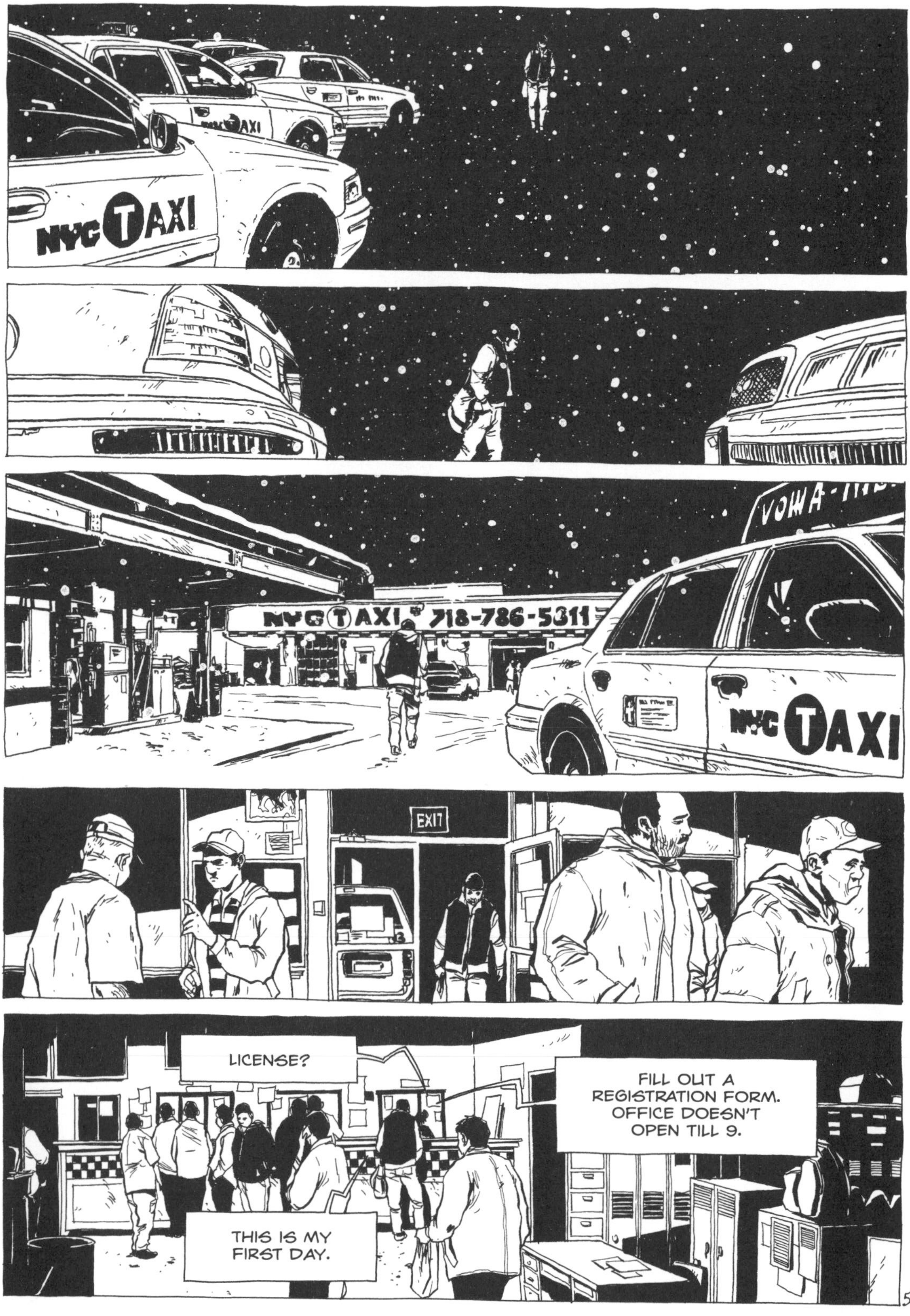
NYC TAXI
NYC TAXI 718-786-5311
NYC TAXI
EXIT
LICENSE?
FILL OUT A REGISTRATION FORM. OFFICE DOESN'T OPEN TILL 9.
THIS IS MY FIRST DAY.

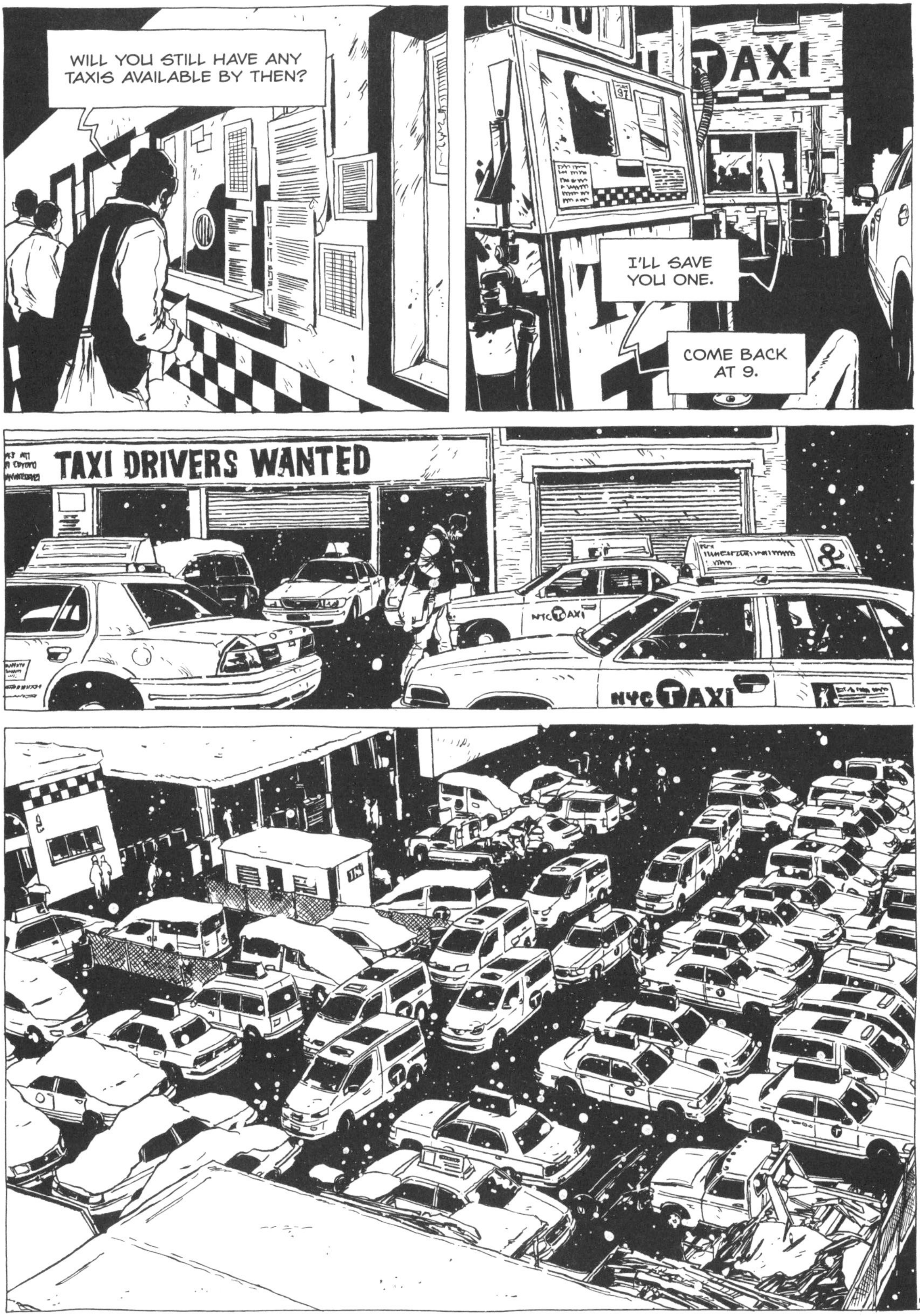
WILL YOU STILL HAVE ANY TAXIS AVAILABLE BY THEN?
TAXI
I'LL SAVE YOU ONE.
COME BACK AT 9.
TAXI DRIVERS WANTED
NYC TAXI
NYC TAXI

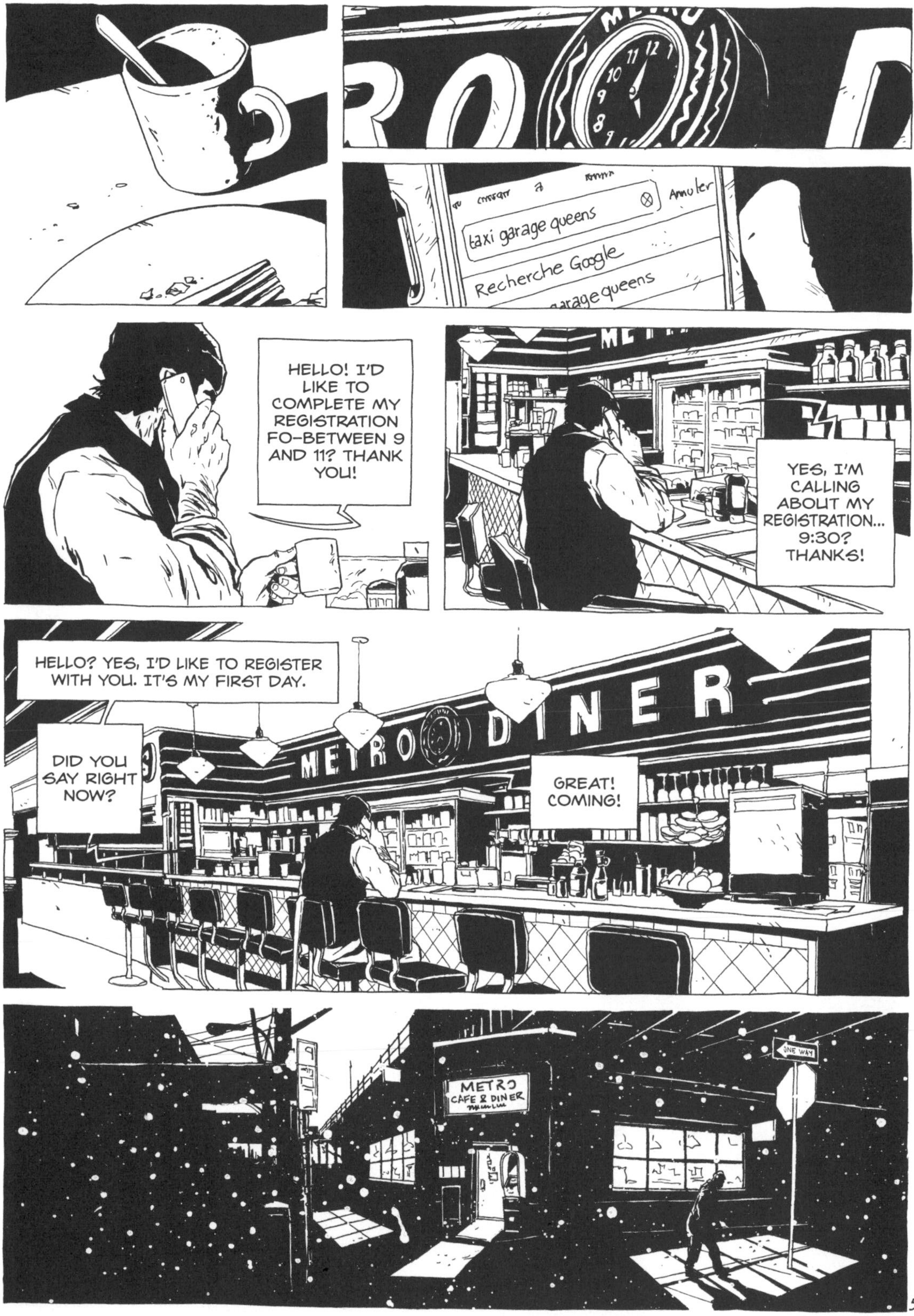
METRO
taxi garage queens
Annuler
Recherche Google
HELLO! I'D LIKE TO COMPLETE MY REGISTRATION FO–BETWEEN 9 AND 11? THANK YOU!
YES, I'M CALLING ABOUT MY REGISTRATION... 9:30? THANKS!
HELLO? YES, I'D LIKE TO REGISTER WITH YOU. IT'S MY FIRST DAY.
DID YOU SAY RIGHT NOW?
METRO DINER
GREAT! COMING!
METRO CAFE & DINER
ONE WAY

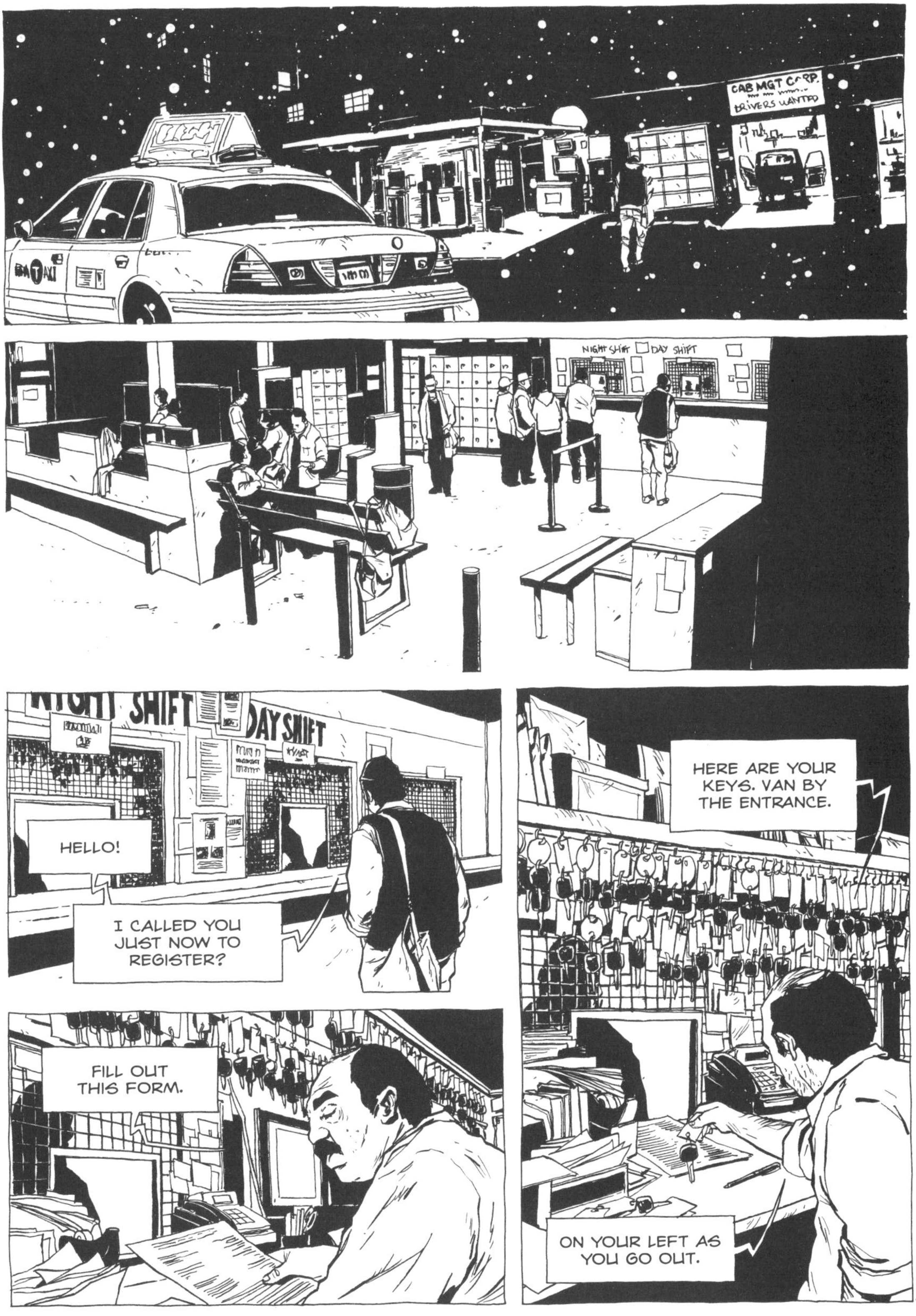
CAB MGT CORP.
DRIVERS WANTED
TAXI
NIGHT SHIFT
DAY SHIFT
NIGHT SHIFT
DAY SHIFT
HELLO!
I CALLED YOU JUST NOW TO REGISTER?
FILL OUT THIS FORM.
HERE ARE YOUR KEYS. VAN BY THE ENTRANCE.
ON YOUR LEFT AS YOU GO OUT.

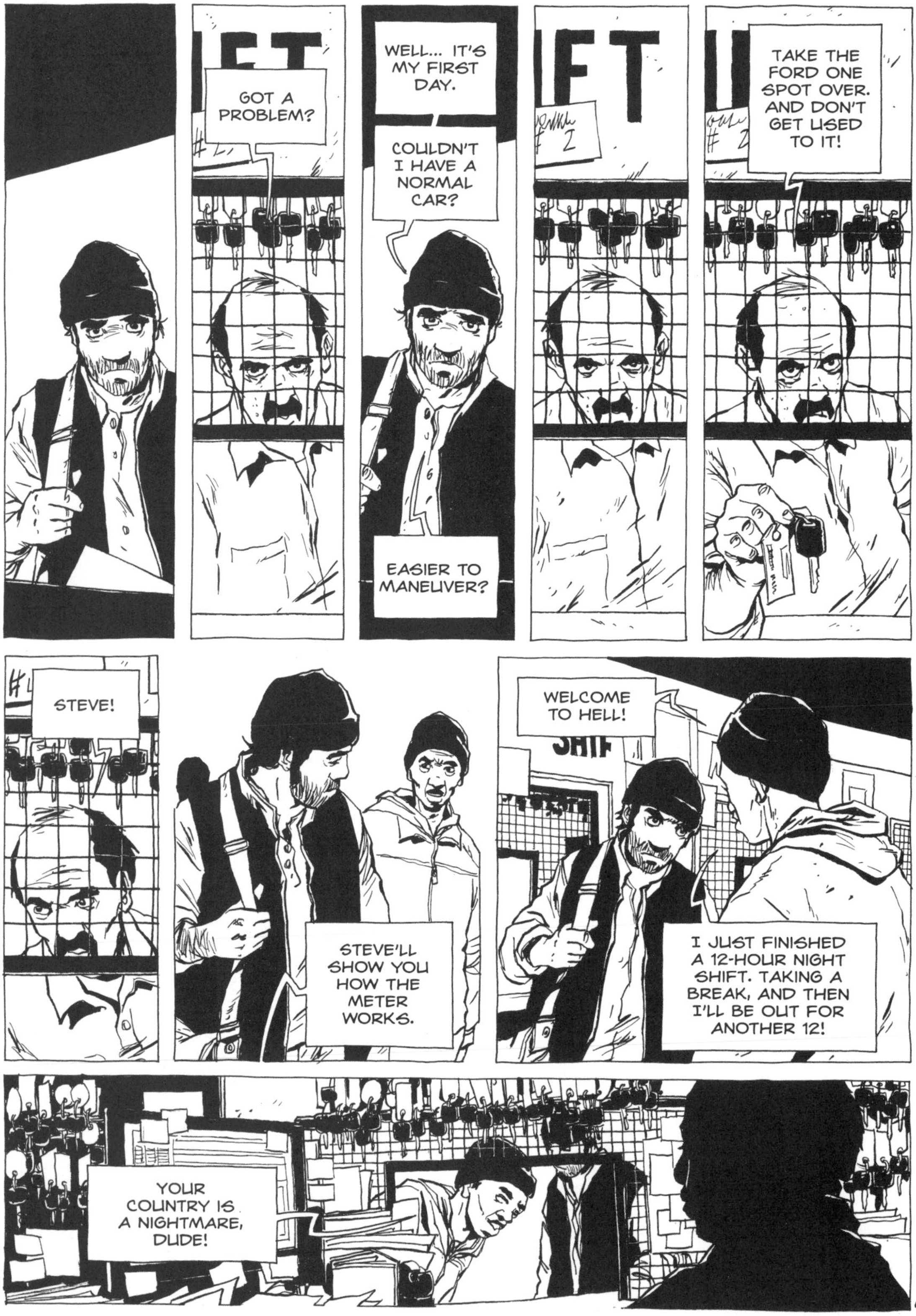
GOT A PROBLEM?
WELL... IT'S MY FIRST DAY.
COULDN'T I HAVE A NORMAL CAR?
EASIER TO MANEUVER?
TAKE THE FORD ONE SPOT OVER. AND DON'T GET USED TO IT!
STEVE!
STEVE'LL SHOW YOU HOW THE METER WORKS.
WELCOME TO HELL!
I JUST FINISHED A 12-HOUR NIGHT SHIFT. TAKING A BREAK, AND THEN I'LL BE OUT FOR ANOTHER 12!
YOUR COUNTRY IS A NIGHTMARE, DUDE!

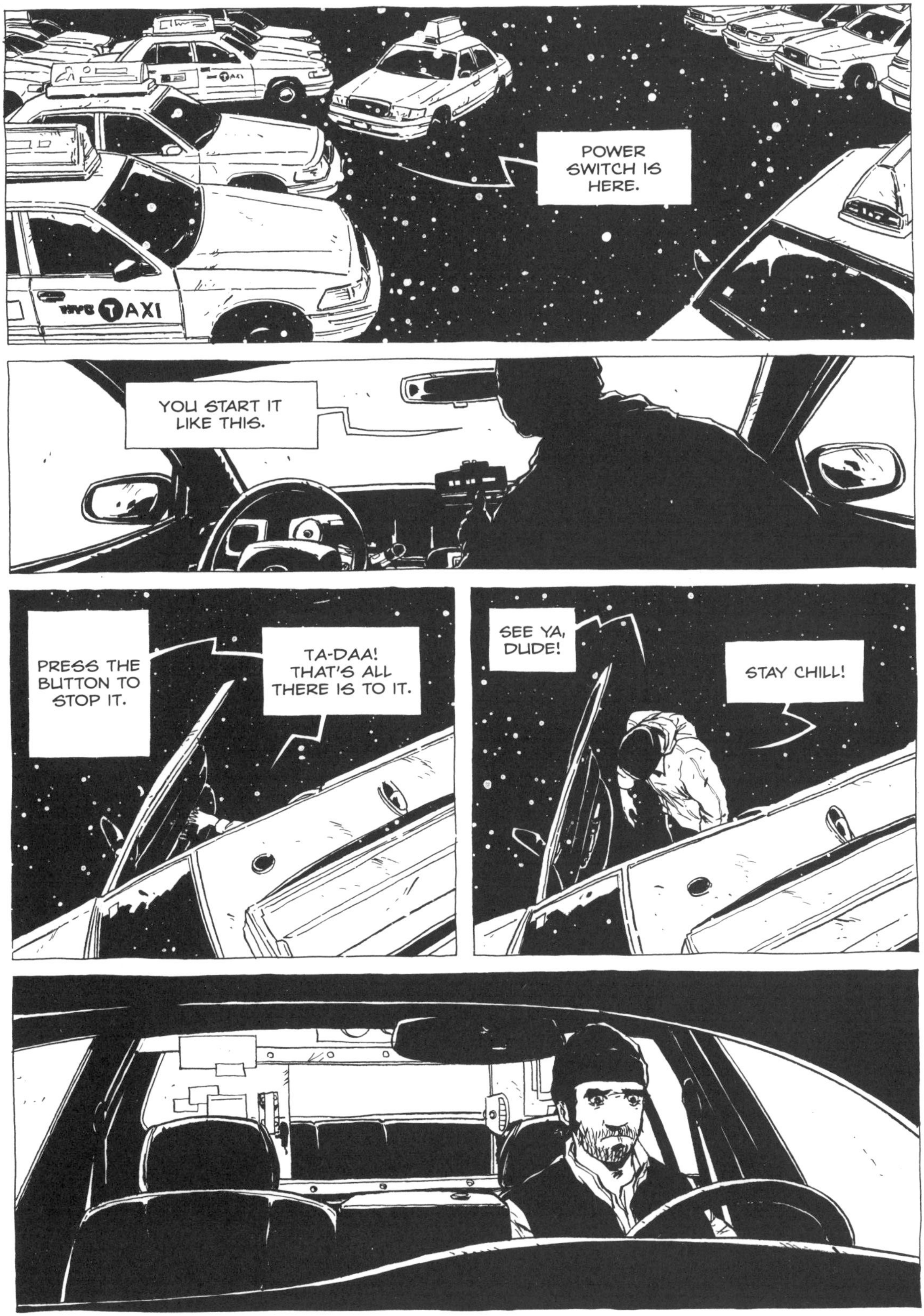
POWER SWITCH IS HERE.
NYC TAXI
YOU START IT LIKE THIS.
PRESS THE BUTTON TO STOP IT.
TA-DAA! THAT'S ALL THERE IS TO IT.
SEE YA, DUDE!
STAY CHILL!

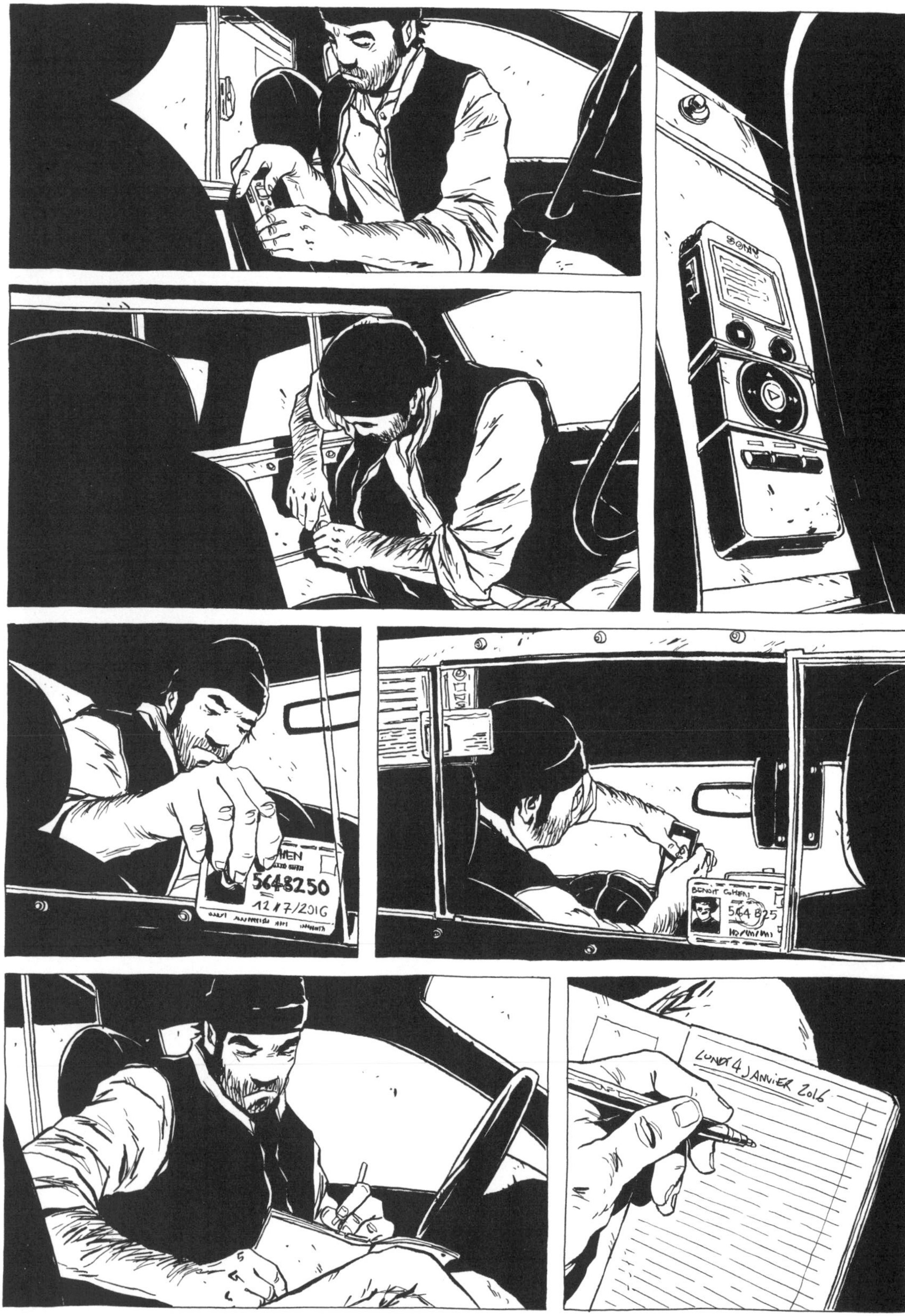
SONY
HEN
5648250
12/7/2016
BENOIT COHEN
564 825
LUNDI 4 JANVIER 2016

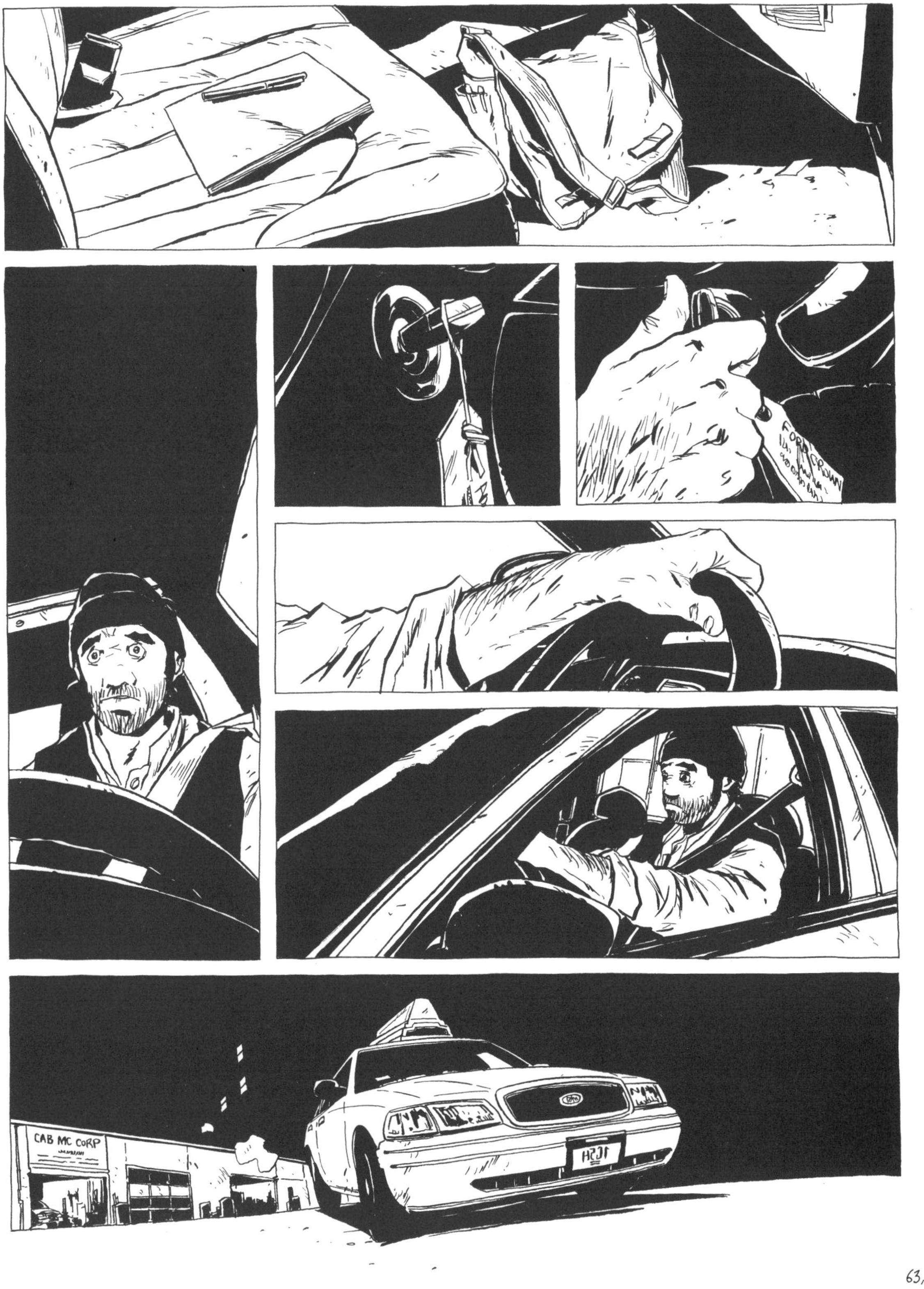
FORD CROWN
CAB MC CORP

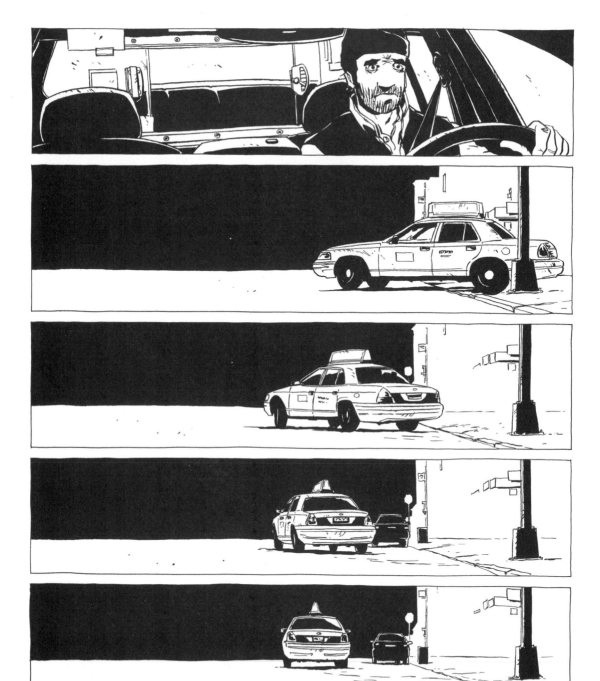

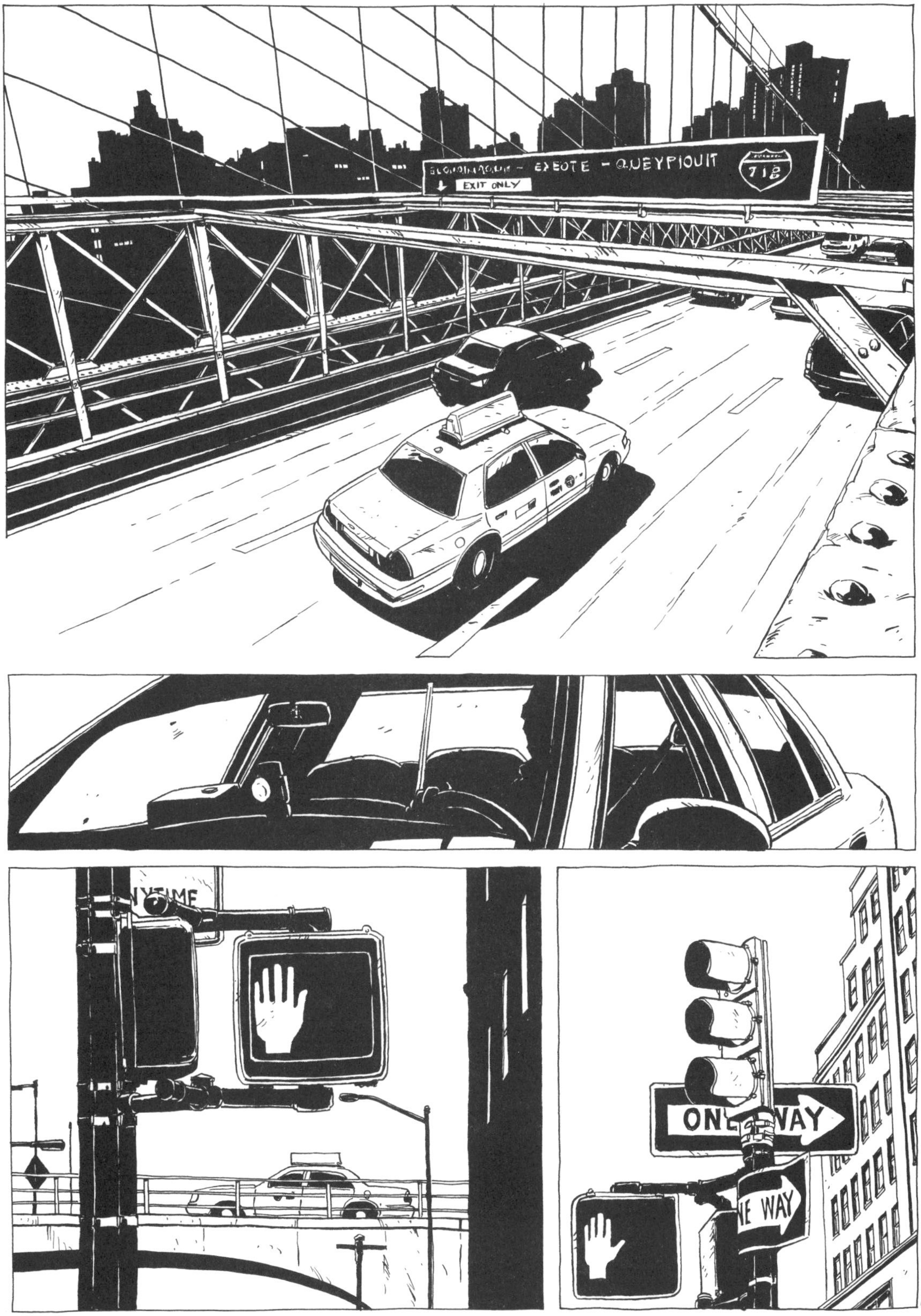
EXEOTE - QUEYPIOUIT
EXIT ONLY
718
NYTIME
ONE WAY
NE WAY

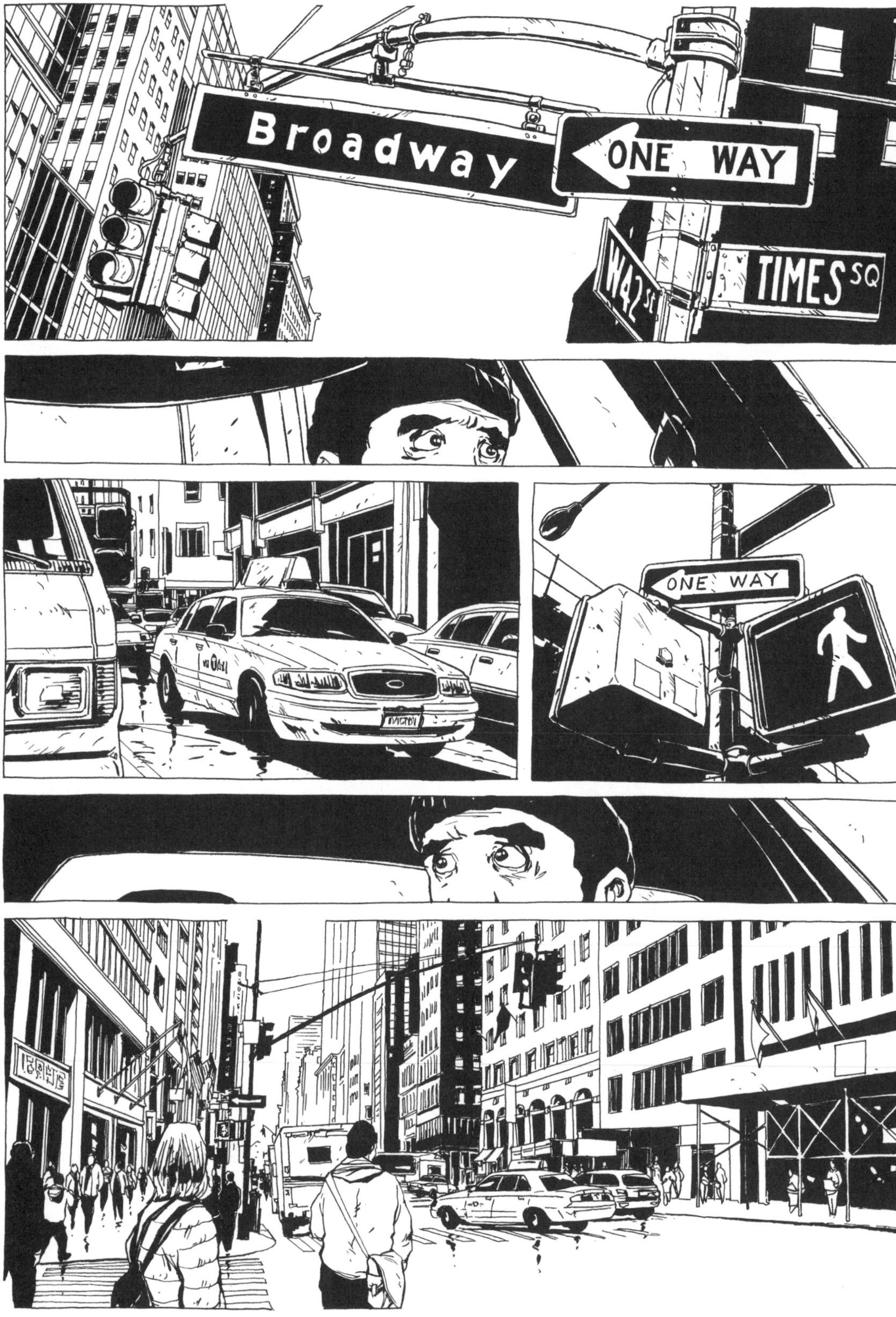
Broadway
ONE WAY
W42 St
TIMES SQ
ONE WAY

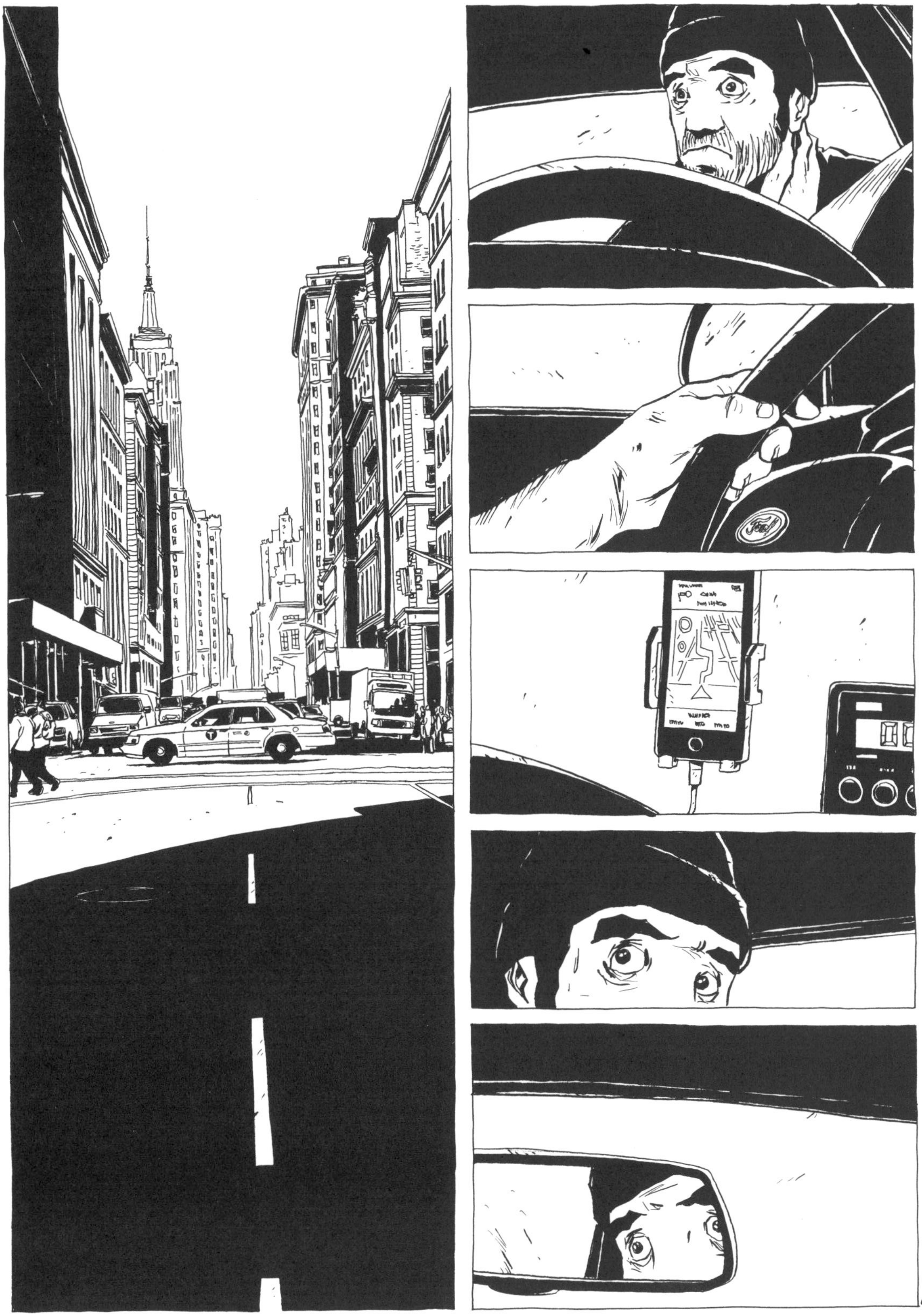

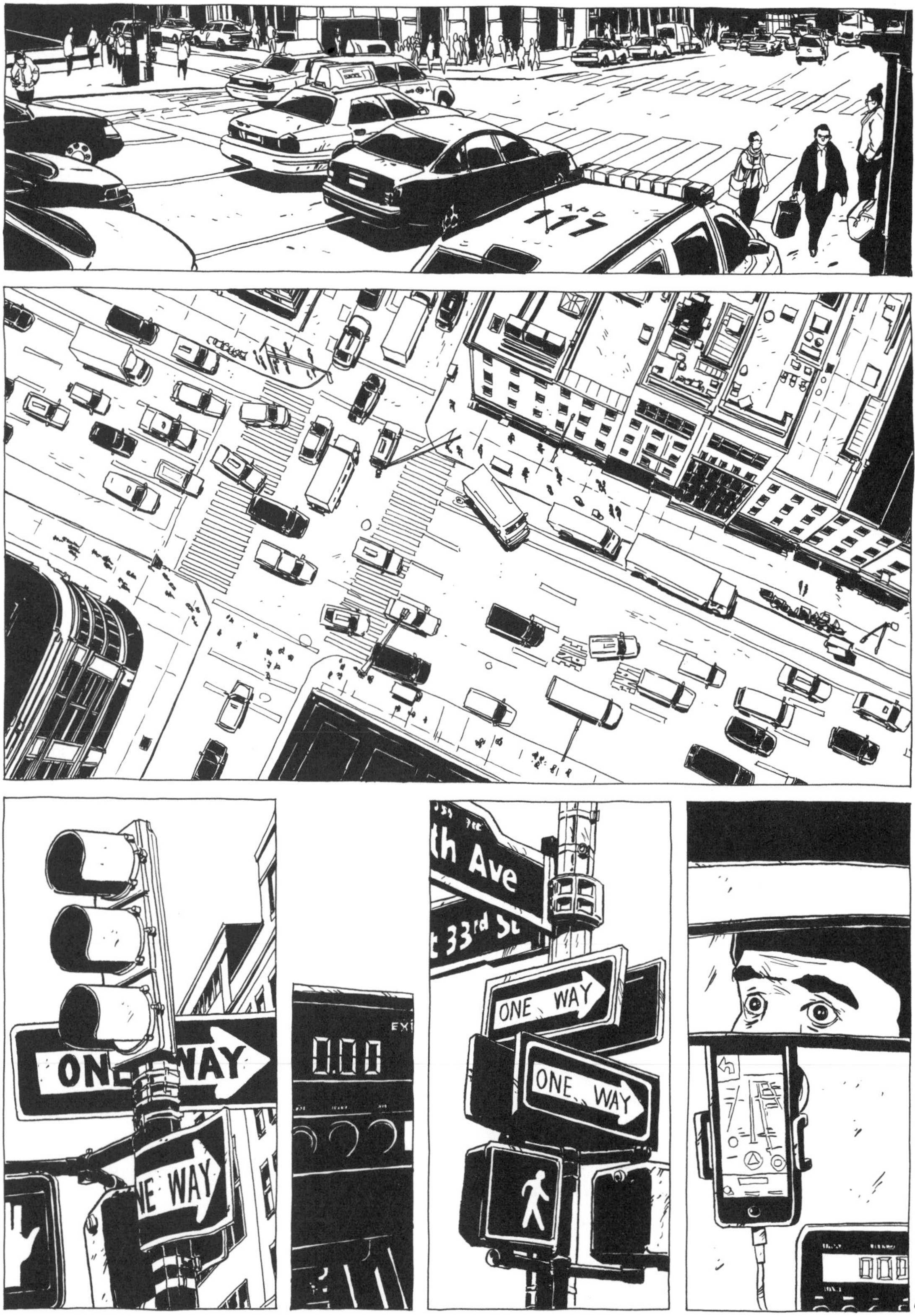
117
ONE WAY
0.00
th Ave
t 33rd St
ONE WAY
ONE WAY
ONE WAY

NO TURNS
ONE WAY
EXCHANGE PLACE

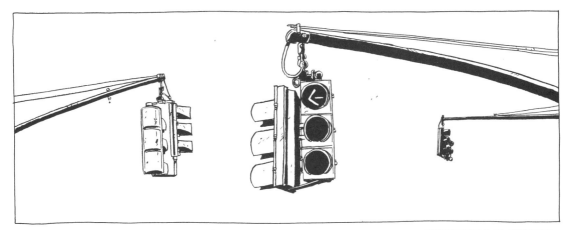

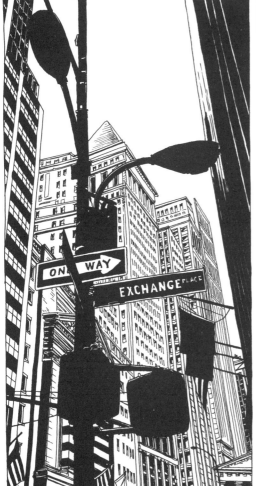

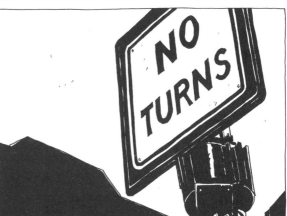

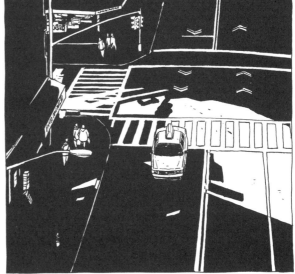

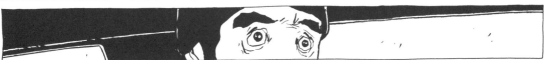

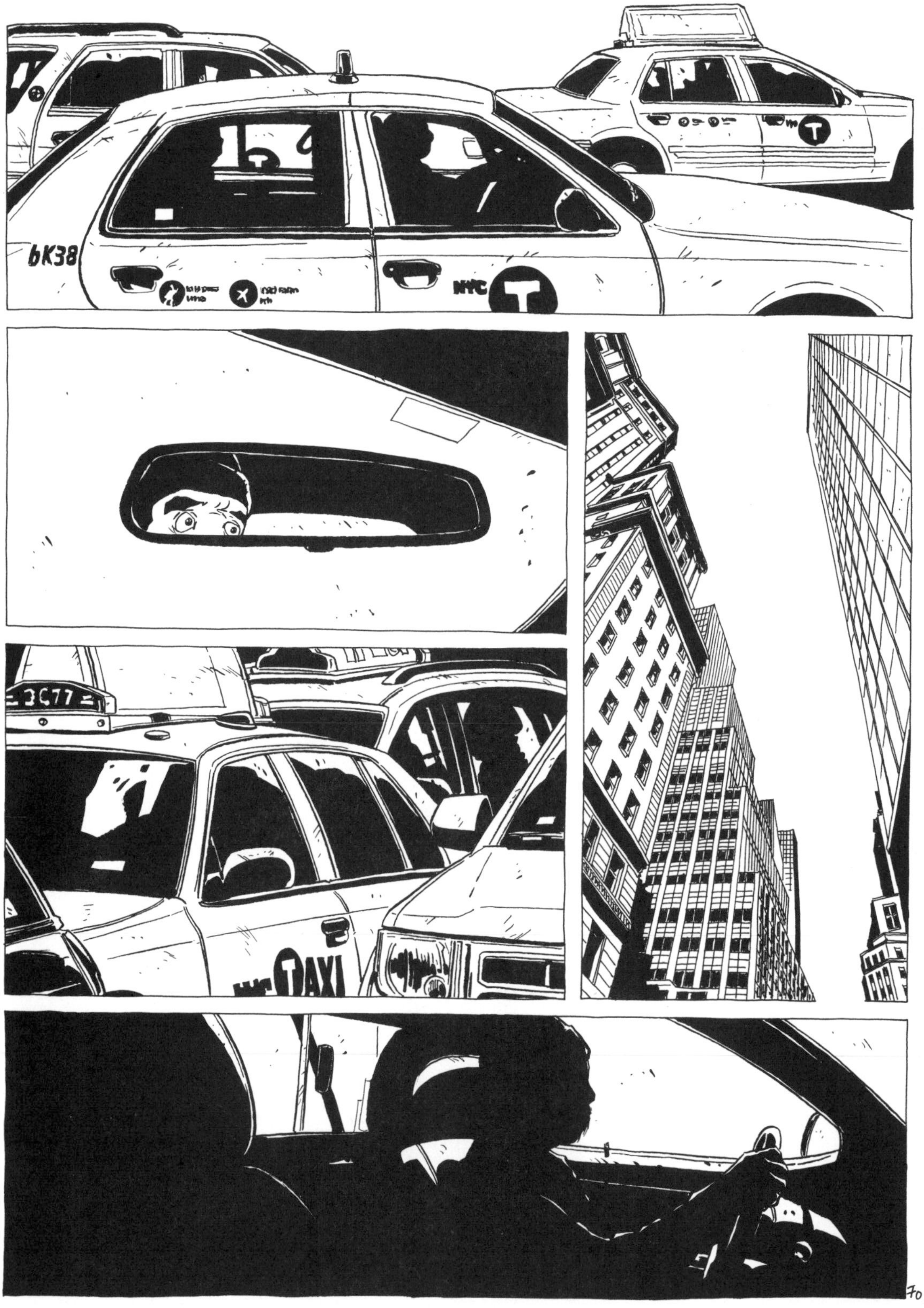
bK38
NYC
3C77
TAXI

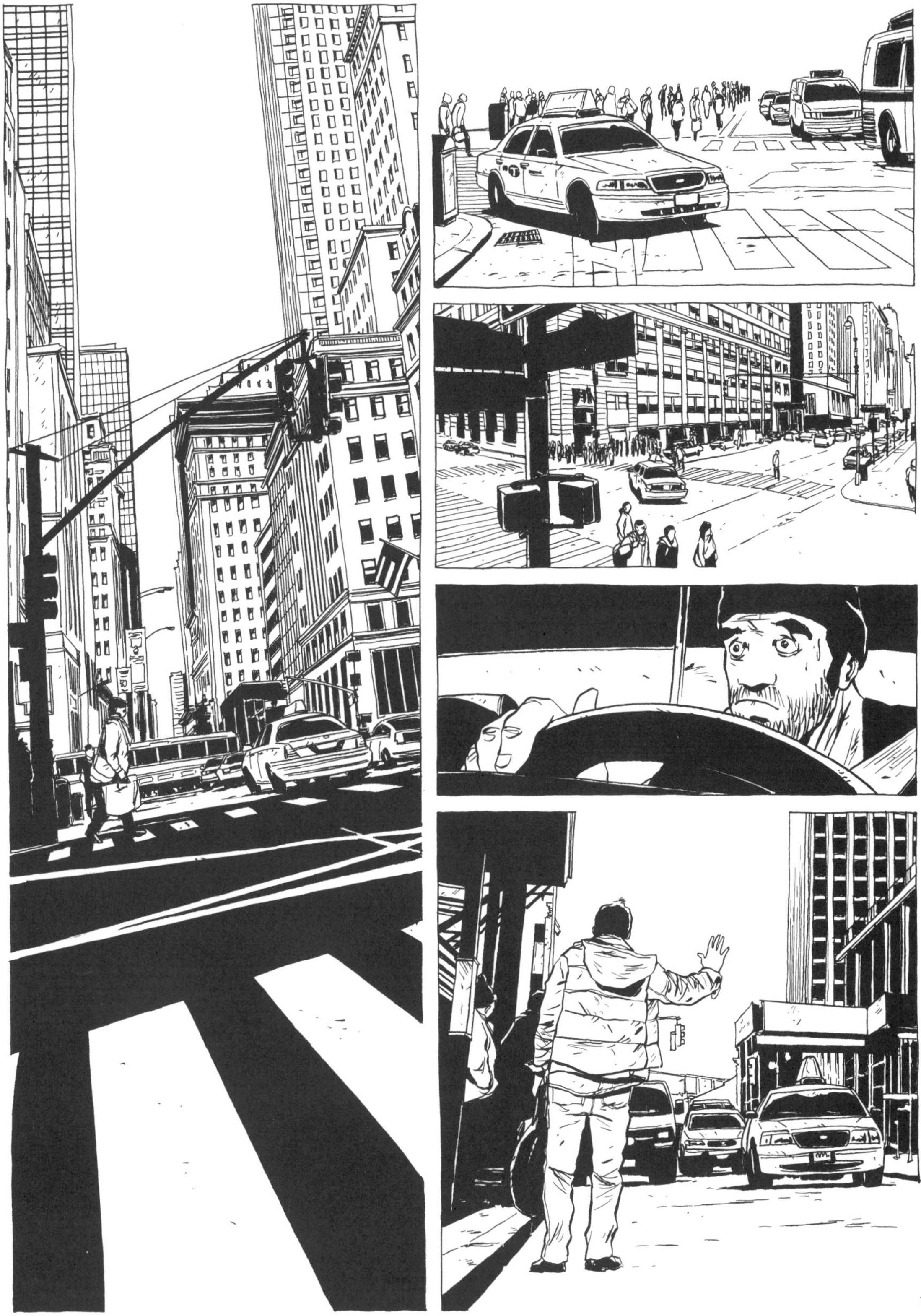

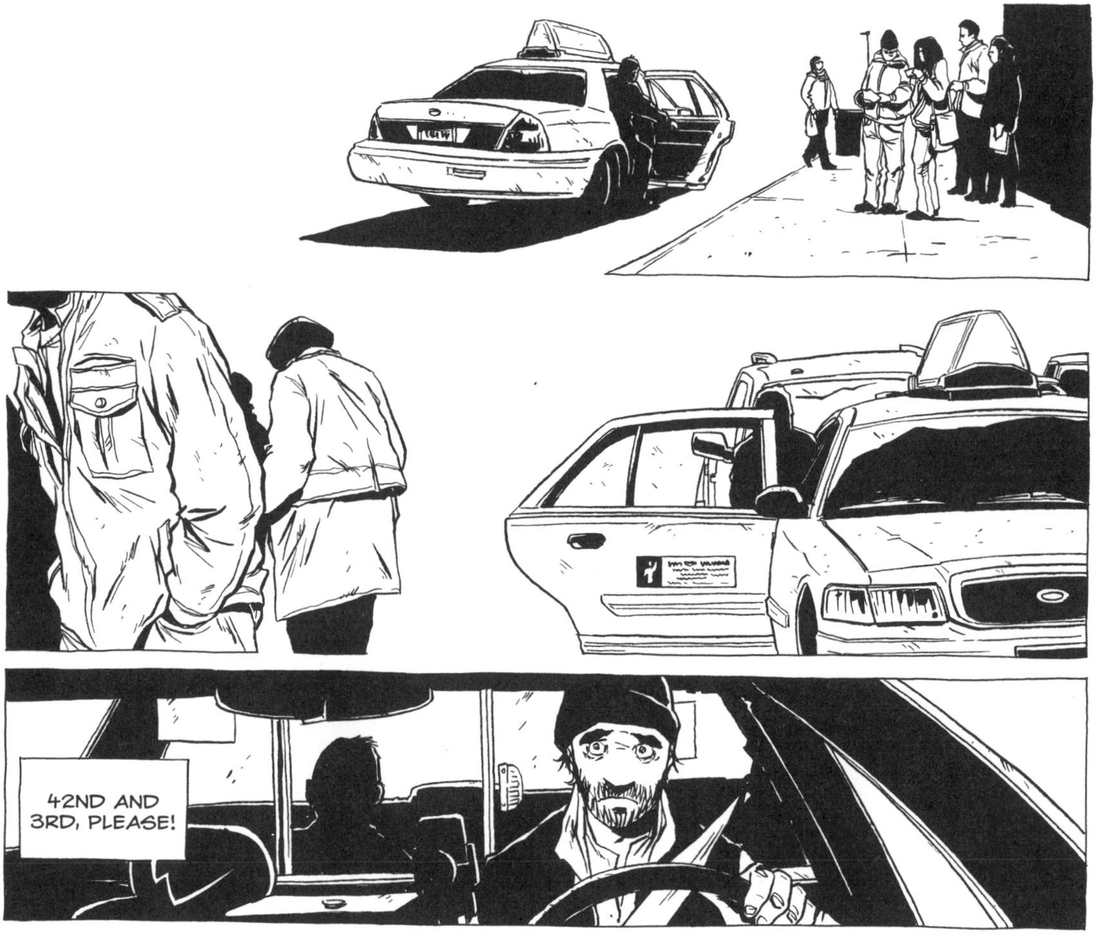
42ND AND
3RD, PLEASE!

IT'S MONDAY, JANUARY 4, 2016.

7:50 AM.
I'M 46 YEARS OLD...
...AND BEHIND THE WHEEL OF A NEW YORK YELLOW CAB.

57TH STREET AND 6TH AVENUE

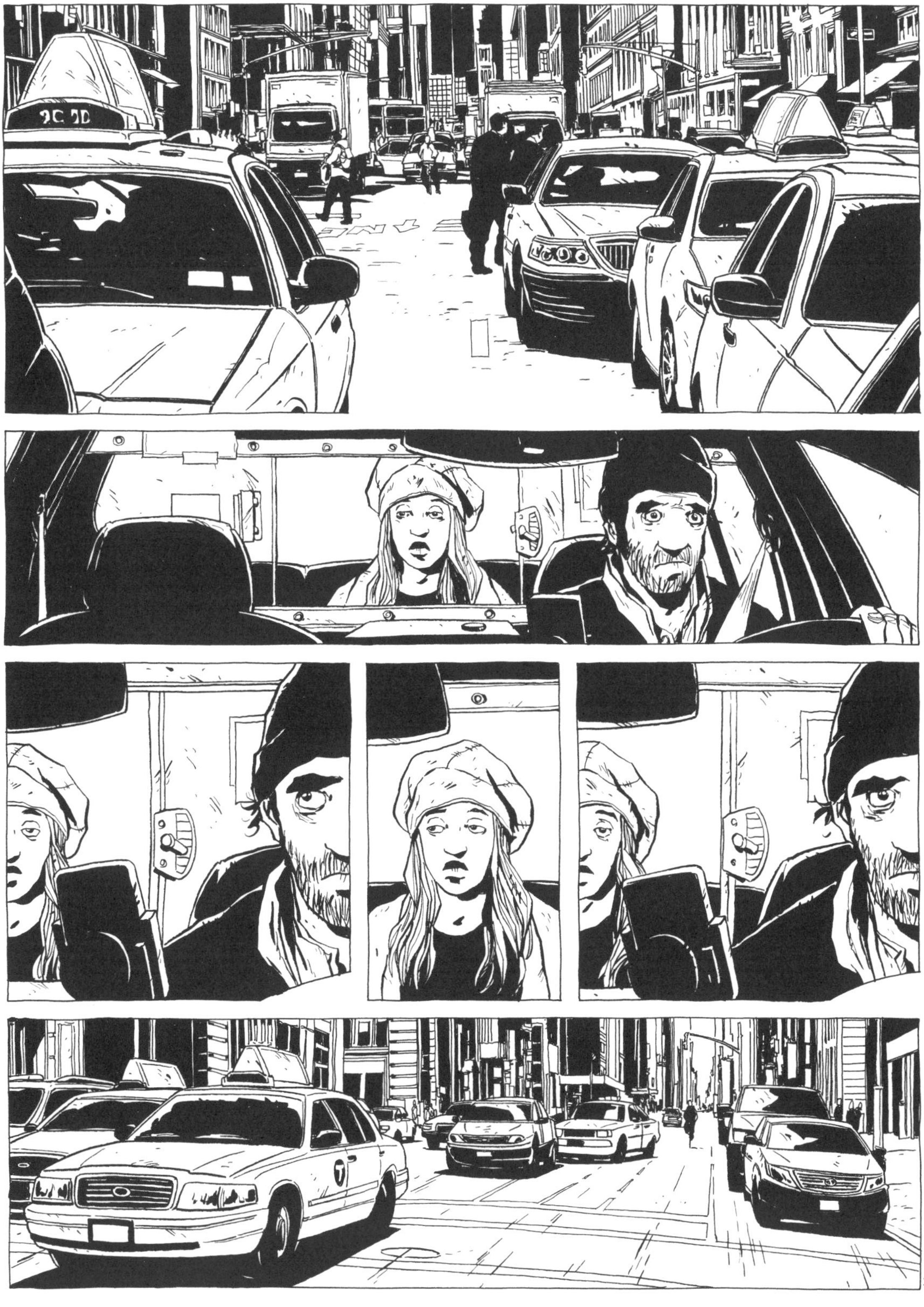

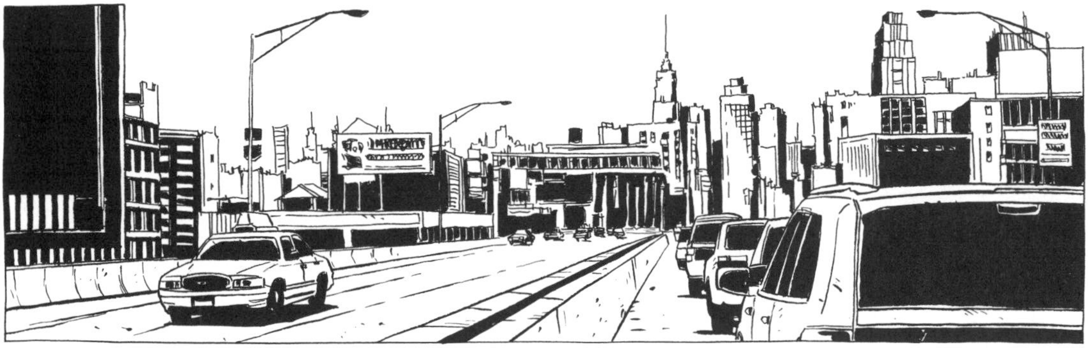

48TH STREET AND 5TH AVENUE

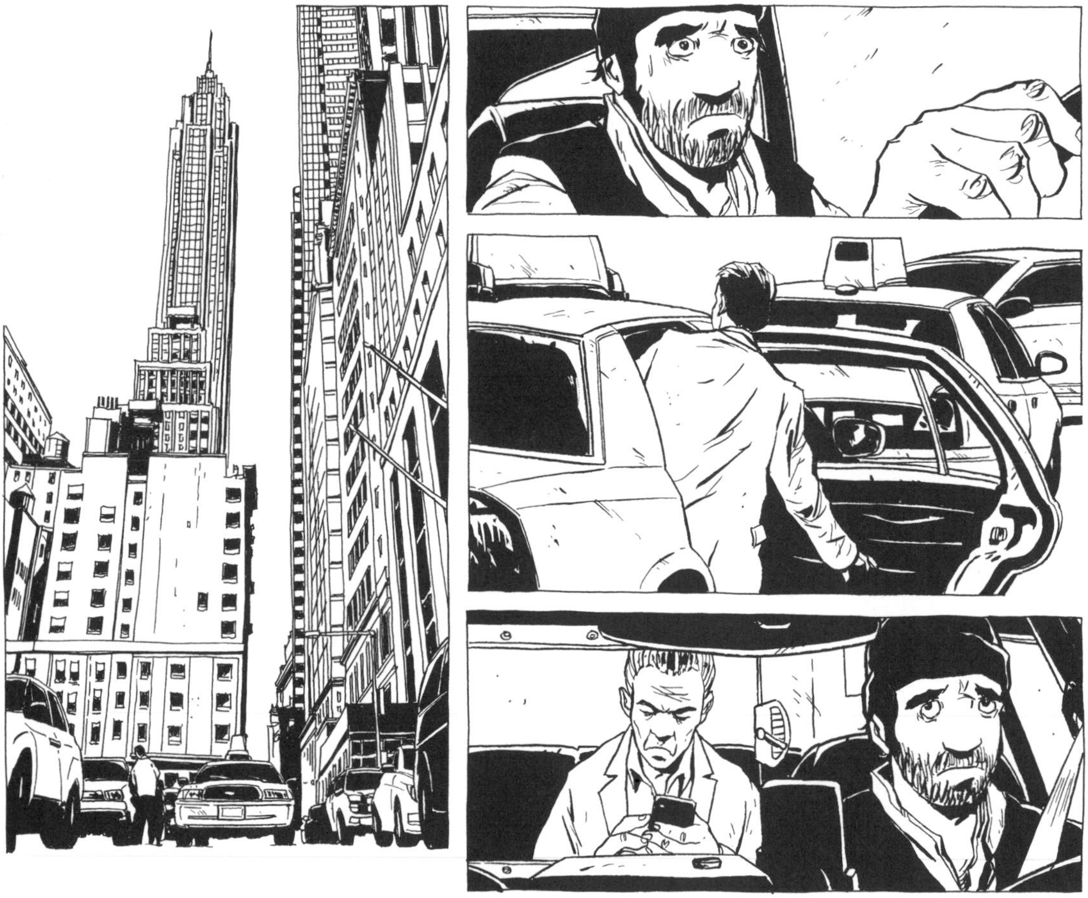

BROADWAY AND 57TH STREET

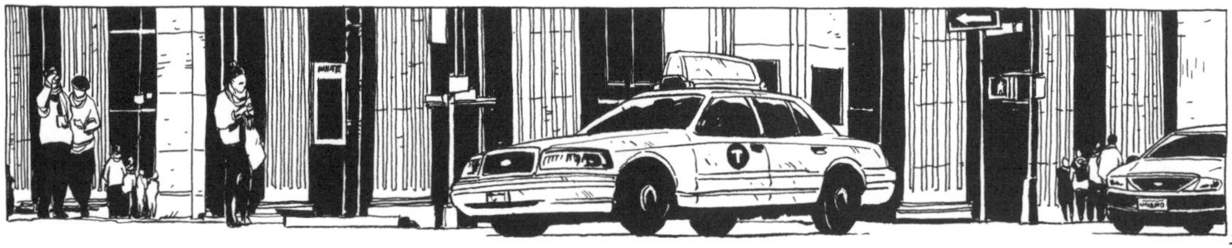

PENN STATION

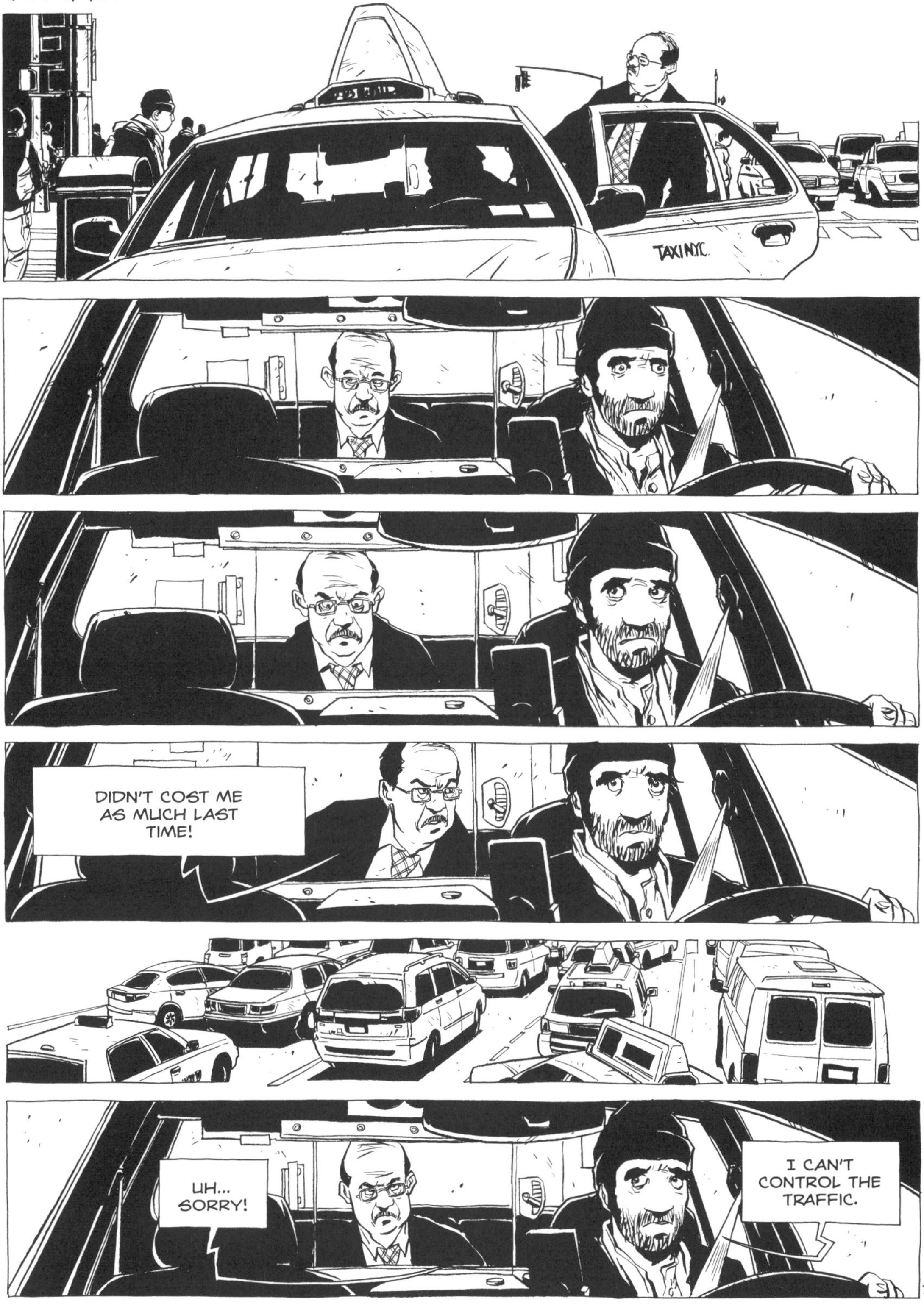

TAXI NYC
DIDN'T COST ME AS MUCH LAST TIME!
UH... SORRY!
I CAN'T CONTROL THE TRAFFIC.

22ND STREET AND 2ND AVENUE

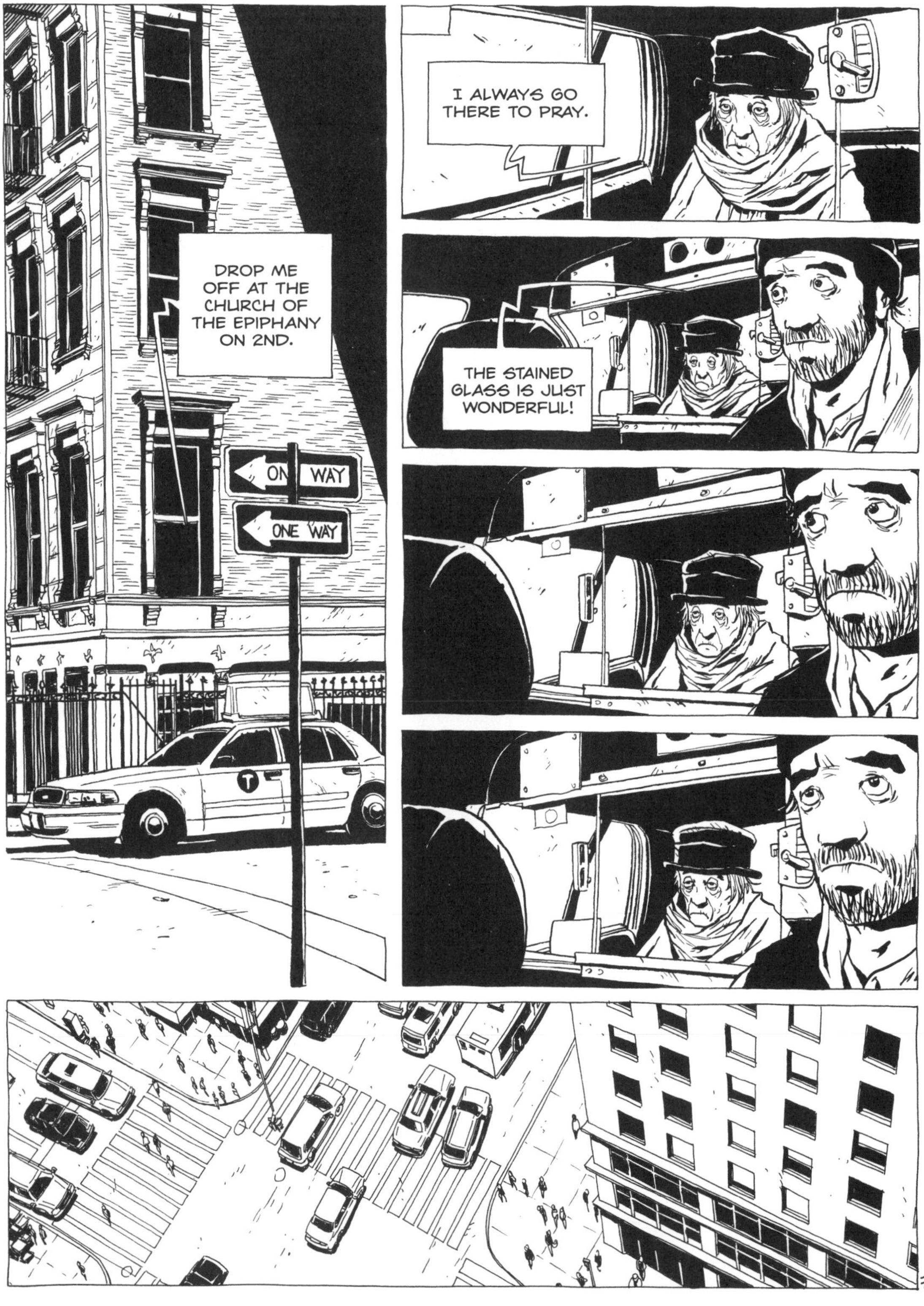
DROP ME OFF AT THE CHURCH OF THE EPIPHANY ON 2ND.
ONE WAY
I ALWAYS GO THERE TO PRAY.
THE STAINED GLASS IS JUST WONDERFUL!

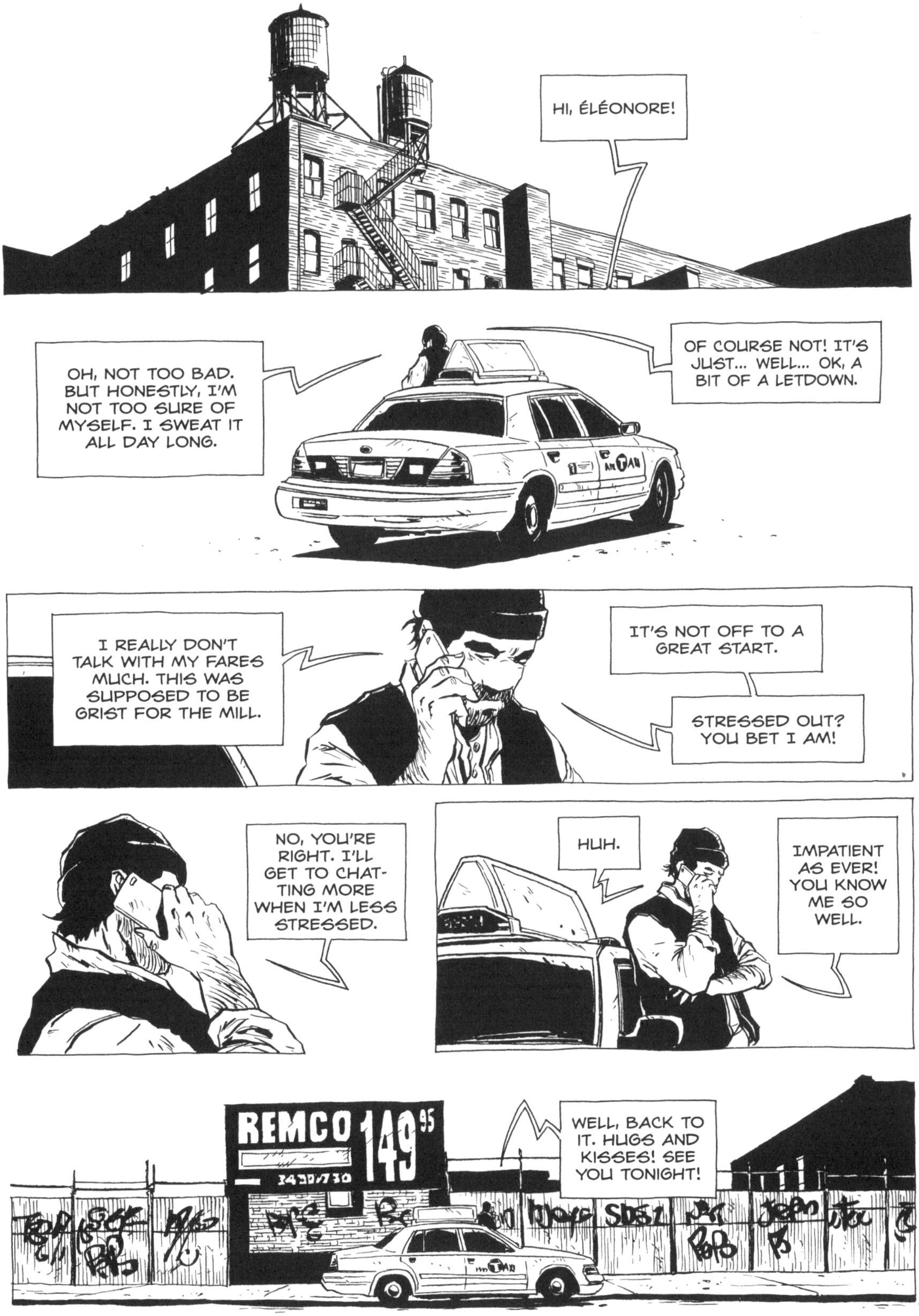
HI, ÉLÉONORE!
OH, NOT TOO BAD. BUT HONESTLY, I'M NOT TOO SURE OF MYSELF. I SWEAT IT ALL DAY LONG.
OF COURSE NOT! IT'S JUST... WELL... OK, A BIT OF A LETDOWN.
I REALLY DON'T TALK WITH MY FARES MUCH. THIS WAS SUPPOSED TO BE GRIST FOR THE MILL.
IT'S NOT OFF TO A GREAT START.
STRESSED OUT? YOU BET I AM!
NO, YOU'RE RIGHT. I'LL GET TO CHAT-TING MORE WHEN I'M LESS STRESSED.
HUH.
IMPATIENT AS EVER! YOU KNOW ME SO WELL.
REMCO 149.95
WELL, BACK TO IT. HUGS AND KISSES! SEE YOU TONIGHT!

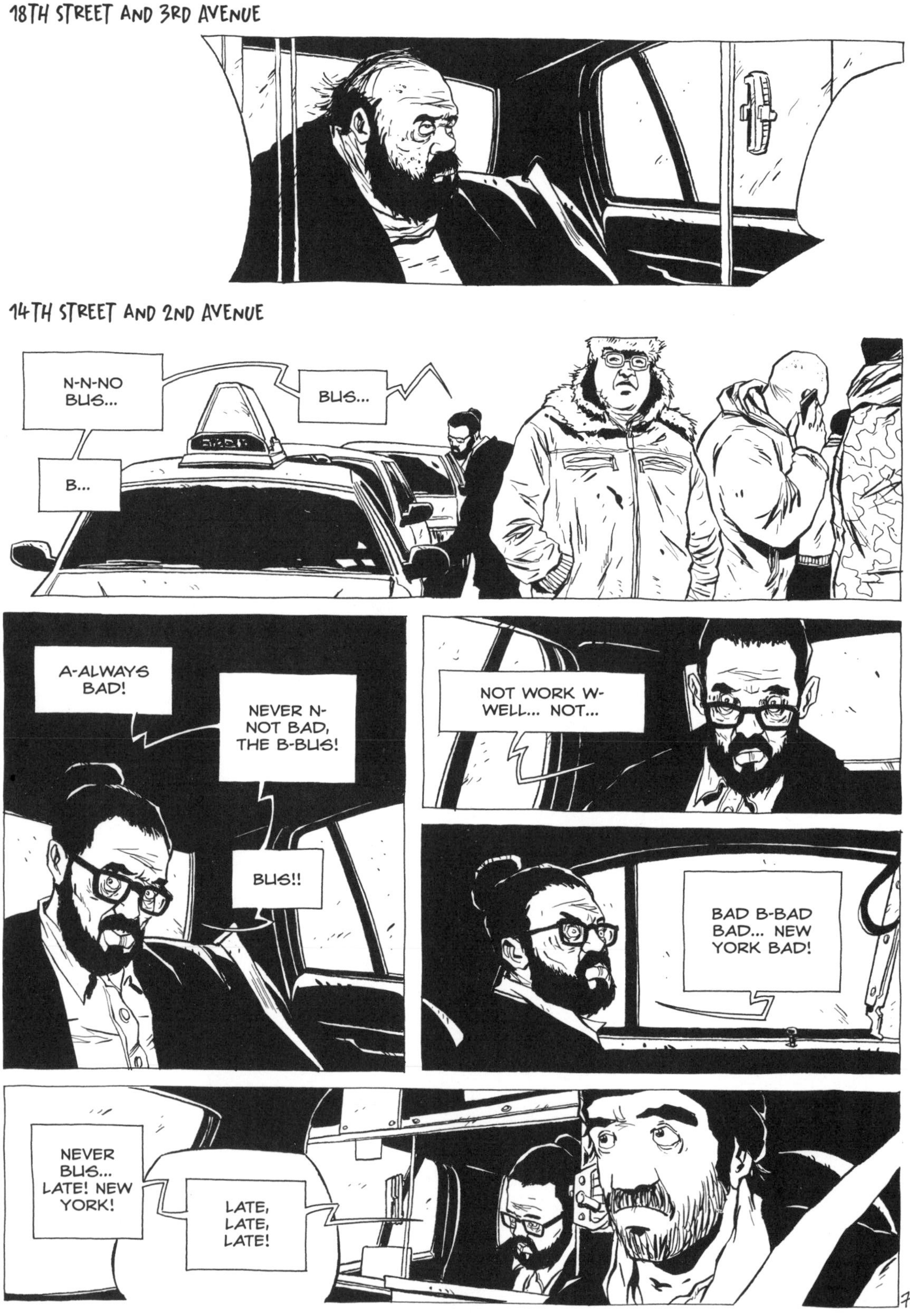
18TH STREET AND 3RD AVENUE
14TH STREET AND 2ND AVENUE
N-N-NO BUS...
BUS...
B...
A-ALWAYS BAD!
NEVER N-NOT BAD, THE B-BUS!
BUS!!
NOT WORK W-WELL... NOT...
BAD B-BAD BAD... NEW YORK BAD!
NEVER BUS... LATE! NEW YORK!
LATE, LATE, LATE!

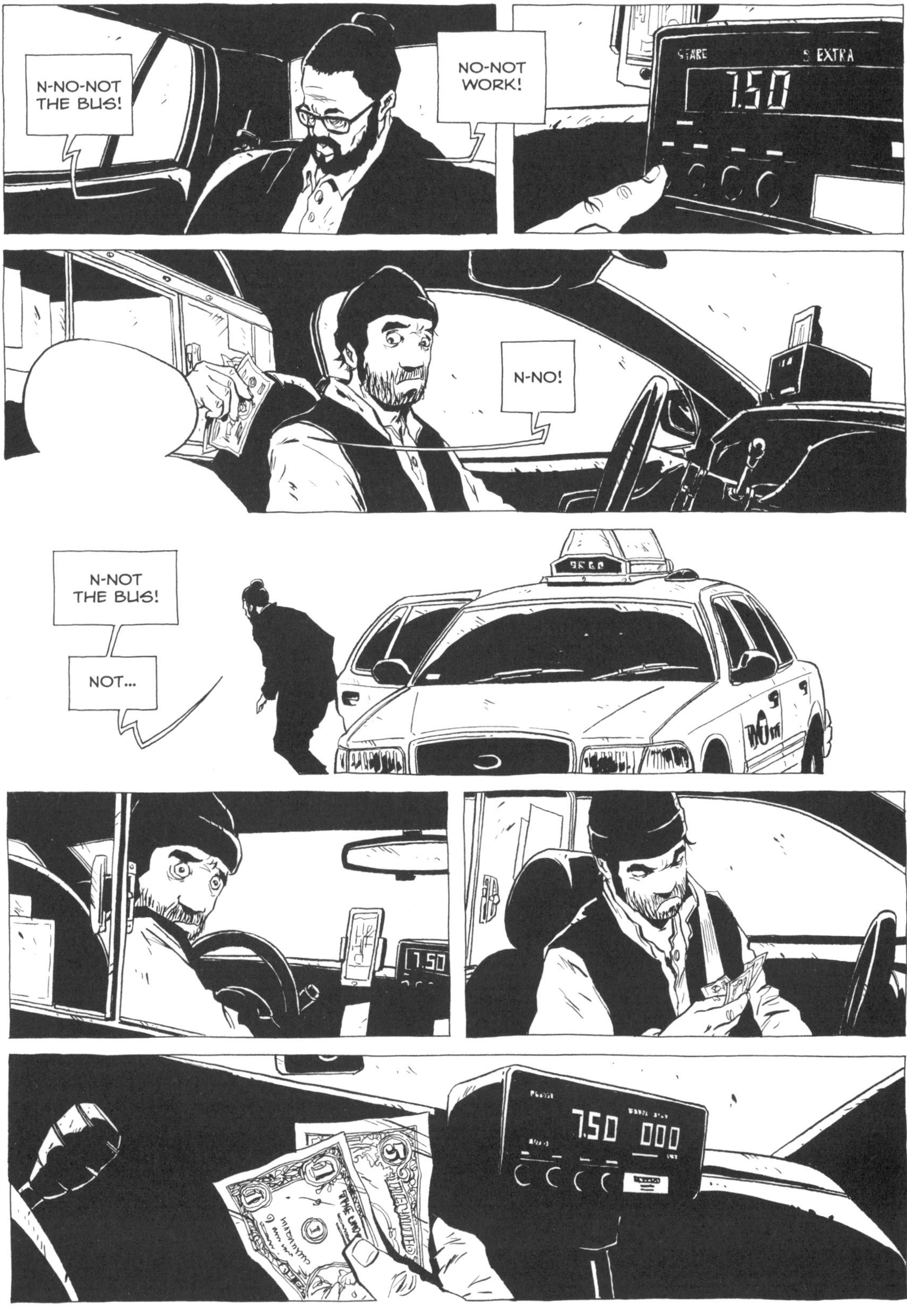
N-NO-NOT THE BUS!
NO-NOT WORK!
FARE
EXTRA
7.50
N-NO!
N-NOT THE BUS!
NOT...
7.50
7.50 000

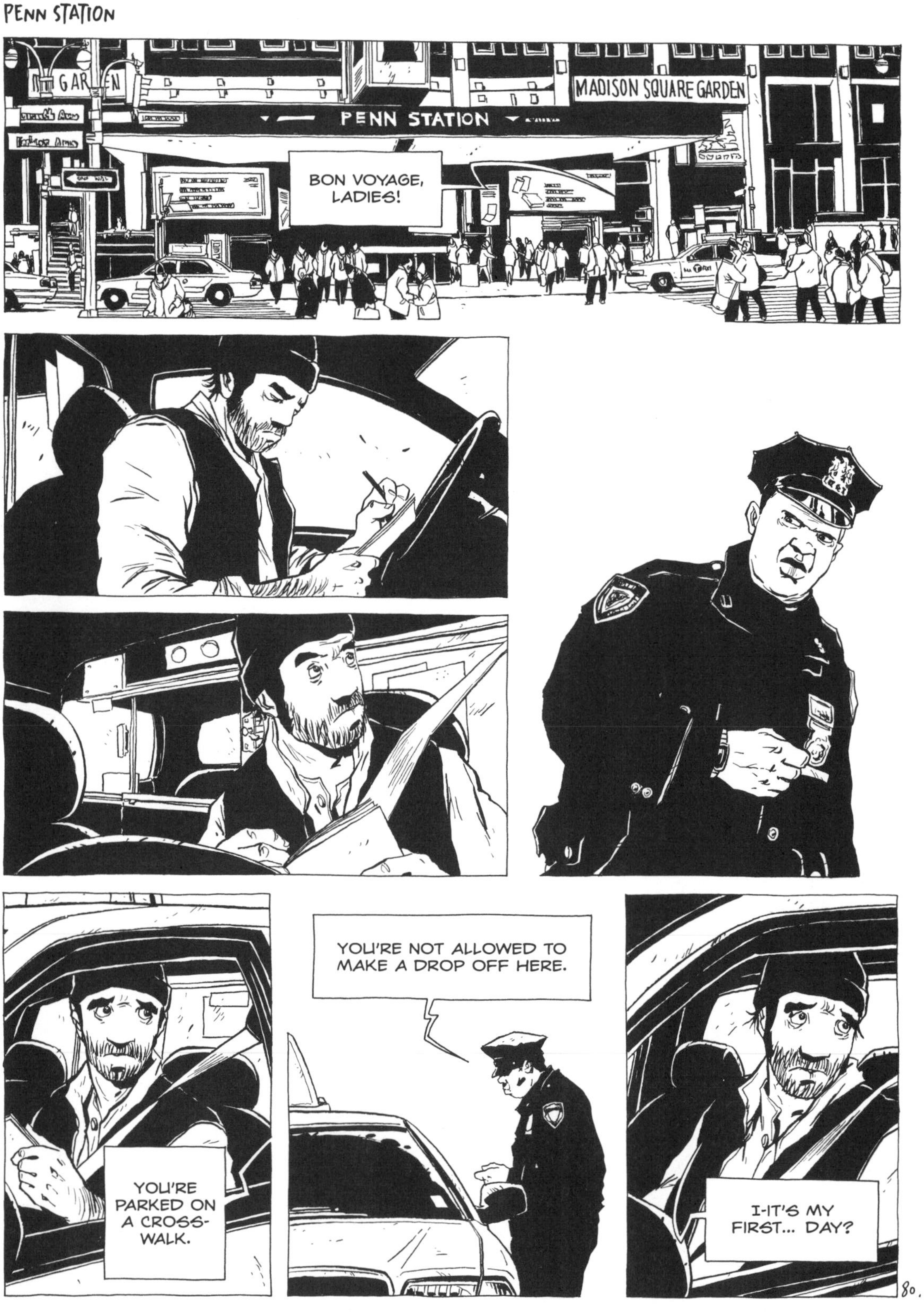
PENN STATION
GARDEN
MADISON SQUARE GARDEN
PENN STATION
BON VOYAGE, LADIES!
YOU'RE PARKED ON A CROSS-WALK.
YOU'RE NOT ALLOWED TO MAKE A DROP OFF HERE.
I-IT'S MY FIRST... DAY?

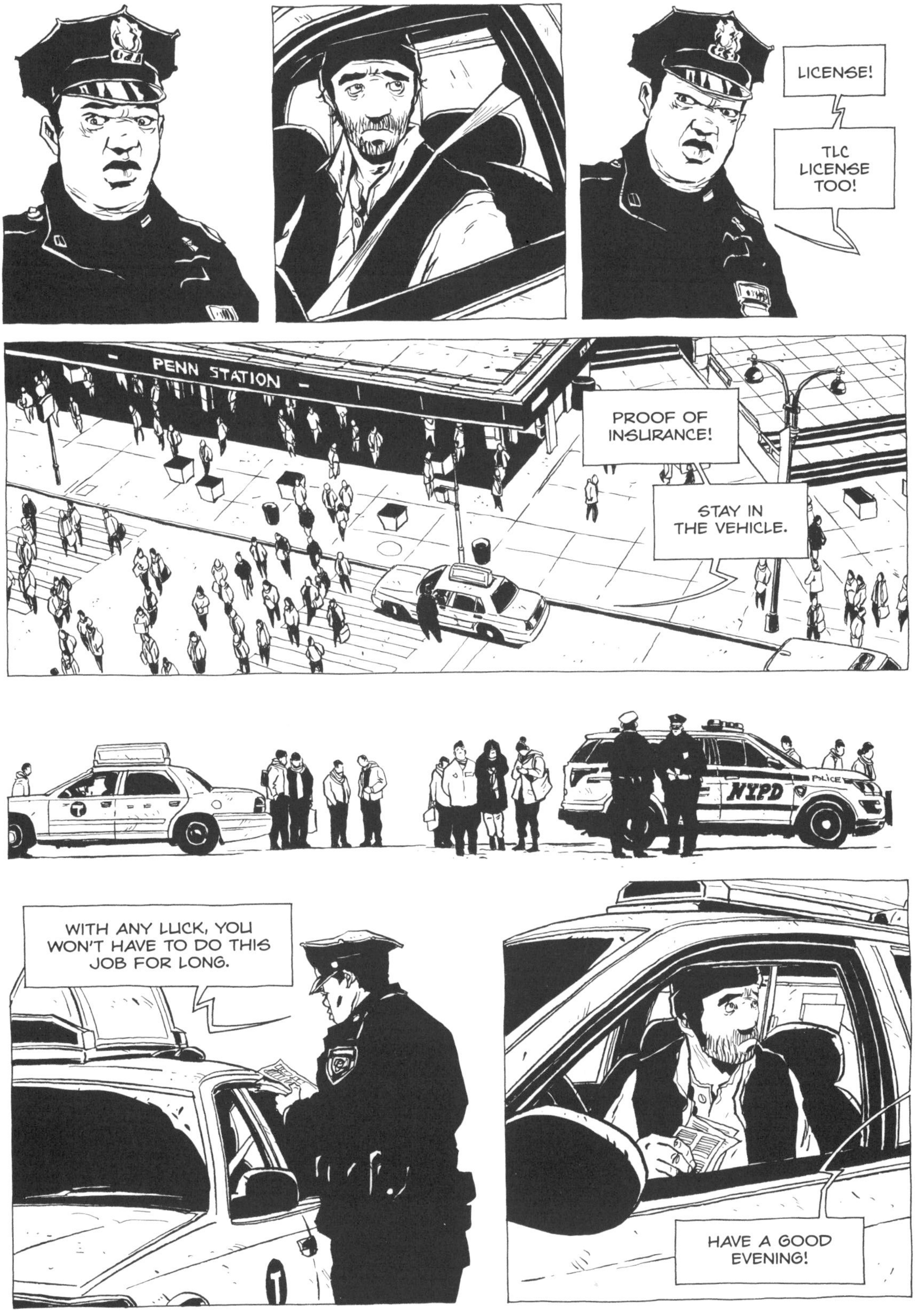
LICENSE!
TLC LICENSE TOO!
PENN STATION
PROOF OF INSURANCE!
STAY IN THE VEHICLE.
NYPD
POLICE
WITH ANY LUCK, YOU WON'T HAVE TO DO THIS JOB FOR LONG.
HAVE A GOOD EVENING!

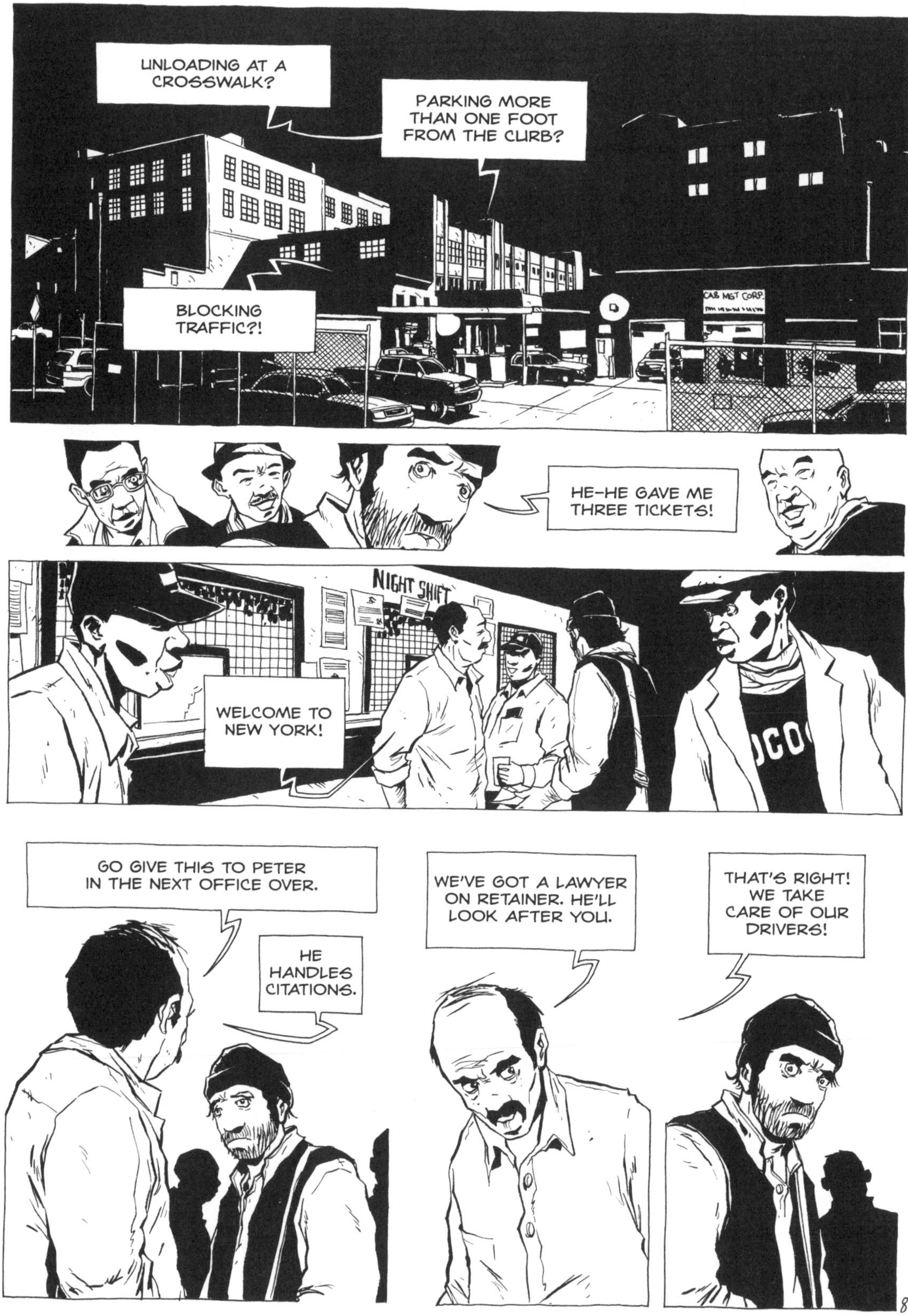
UNLOADING AT A CROSSWALK?
PARKING MORE THAN ONE FOOT FROM THE CURB?
BLOCKING TRAFFIC?!
CAB MGT CORP.
HE-HE GAVE ME THREE TICKETS!
NIGHT SHIFT
WELCOME TO NEW YORK!
GO GIVE THIS TO PETER IN THE NEXT OFFICE OVER.
HE HANDLES CITATIONS.
WE'VE GOT A LAWYER ON RETAINER. HE'LL LOOK AFTER YOU.
THAT'S RIGHT! WE TAKE CARE OF OUR DRIVERS!

TO SUM UP THE DAY: 18 FARES.
$206.45 MINUS $129.17 FOR TAXI RENTAL MINUS $150 IN FINES.

MINUS $72.72...

MY FIRST DAY I HAD A HARD TIME MAKING EVEN $80, AND IN THE END, IT'LL COST ME $70.

TO THINK I'D IMAGINED GETTING THE ADDRESS WRONG ON PURPOSE OR STIFFING A
CUSTOMER ON CHANGE SO I COULD GET MATERIAL FOR MY SCREENPLAY!

NOW I KNOW I WON'T HAVE TO. I'M NOT A DIRECTOR ANYMORE, ARRANGING EVENTS TO
SUIT MY FANCY.

I'M A CAB DRIVER. I HAVE TO FIND A WAY TO GET PEOPLE FROM POINT A TO POINT B SAFE
AND SOUND AND AS FAST AS POSSIBLE, WITHOUT GETTING LOST, OR INTO AN ACCIDENT, OR
STOPPED BY COPS, OR A BULLET TO THE HEAD.

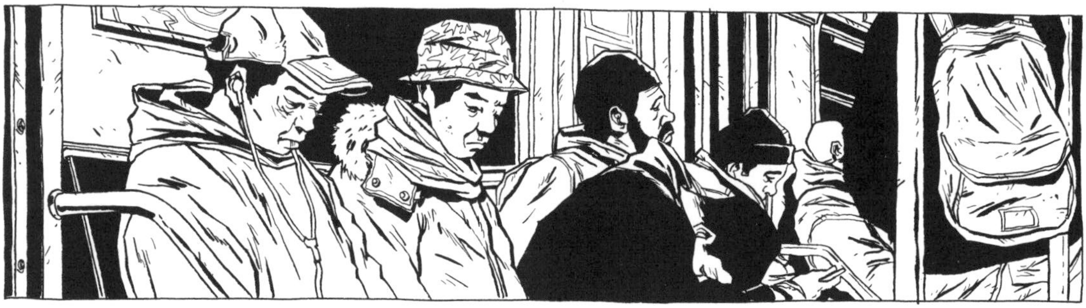

USUALLY WHEN YOU'RE WRITING A STORY, IT'S RARE TO HAVE SO MUCH RAW MATERIAL FROM DAILY LIFE AT YOUR DISPOSAL. RIGHT NOW, I'M WORKING CLOSER TO A DOCUMENTARY OR EVEN A SOCIOLOGICAL STUDY. I LIKE IT.

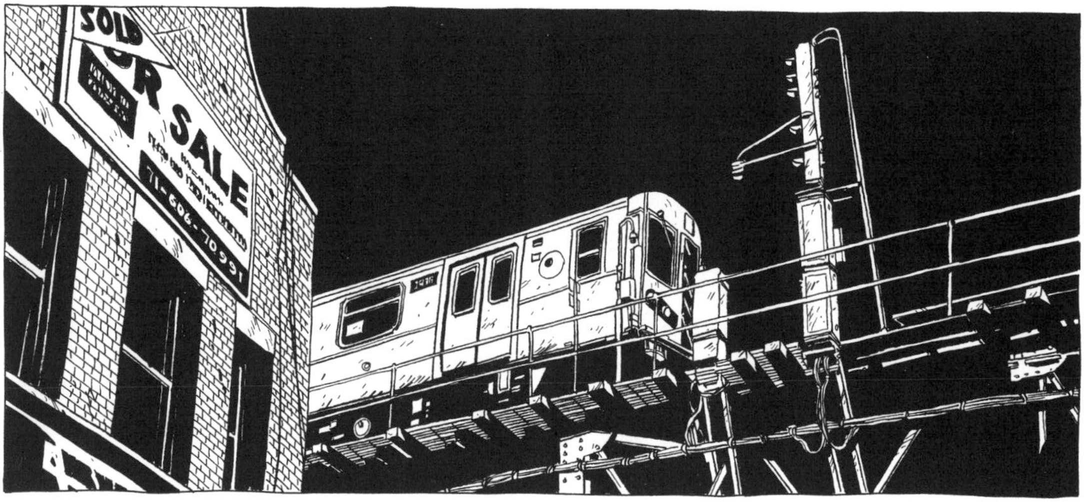
SOLD
SALE

WHENEVER SOMEONE GETS INTO MY CAB, ANYTHING CAN HAPPEN.

SURE, THERE'LL BE BORING STRETCHES, HOURS OF RUSHES I'LL NEVER USE, BUT ALSO EXTRAORDINARY SITUATIONS, I JUST KNOW IT. I FEEL THAT, AS WITH ACTING, I'LL SOAK UP THE JOB OVER TIME.

THOSE THREE TICKETS, FOR EXAMPLE. PERFECT FOR A COMEDY SCENE I'D PROBABLY NEVER HAVE DREAMED UP OTHERWISE.

000 000
NYC TAXI

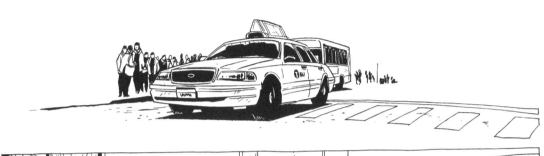

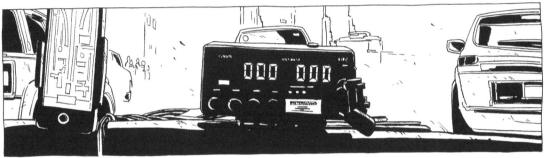

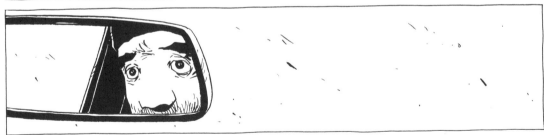

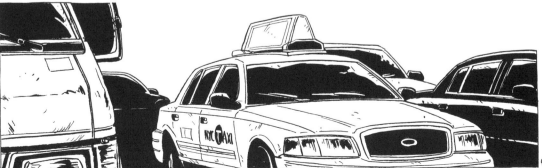

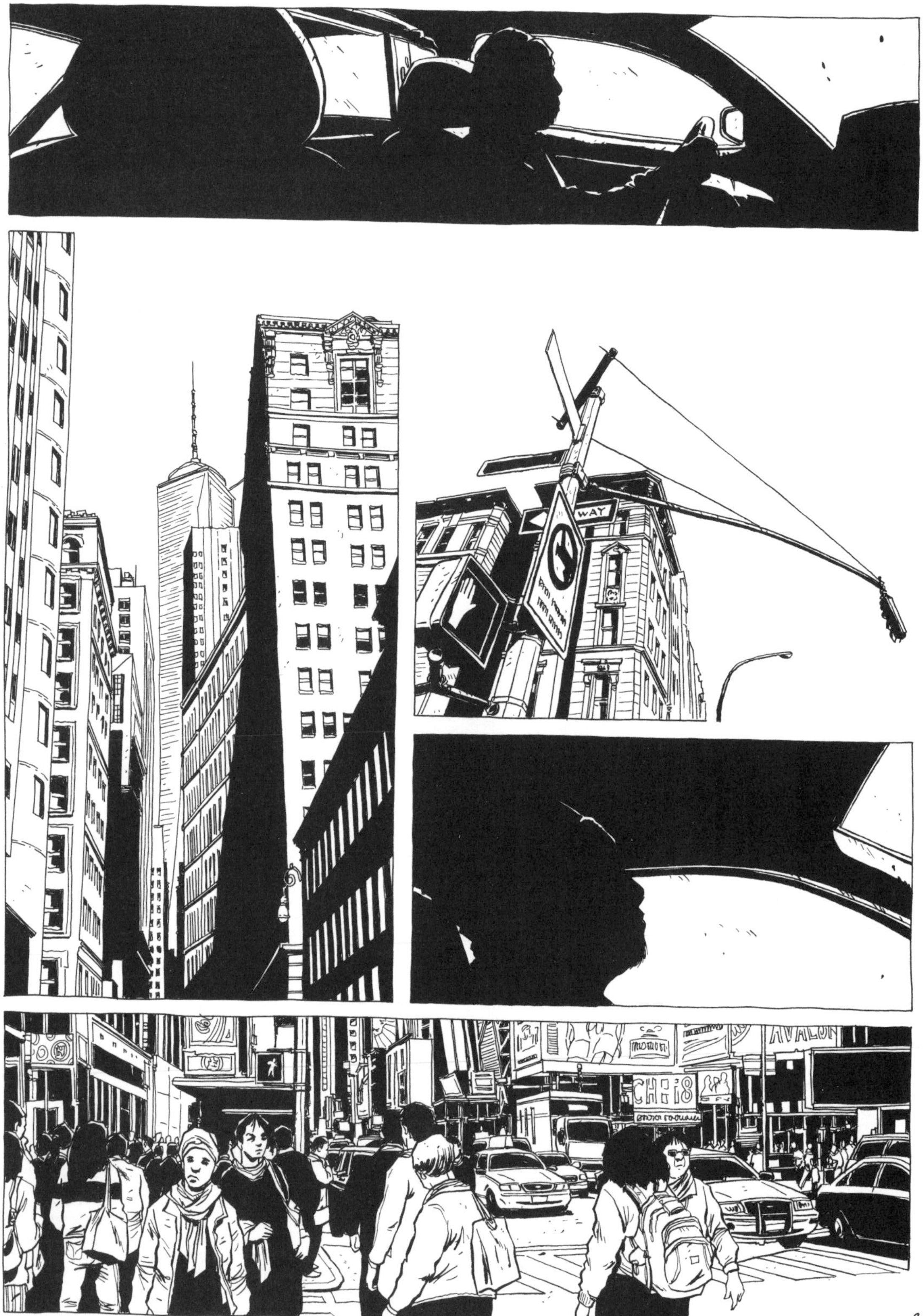
WAY

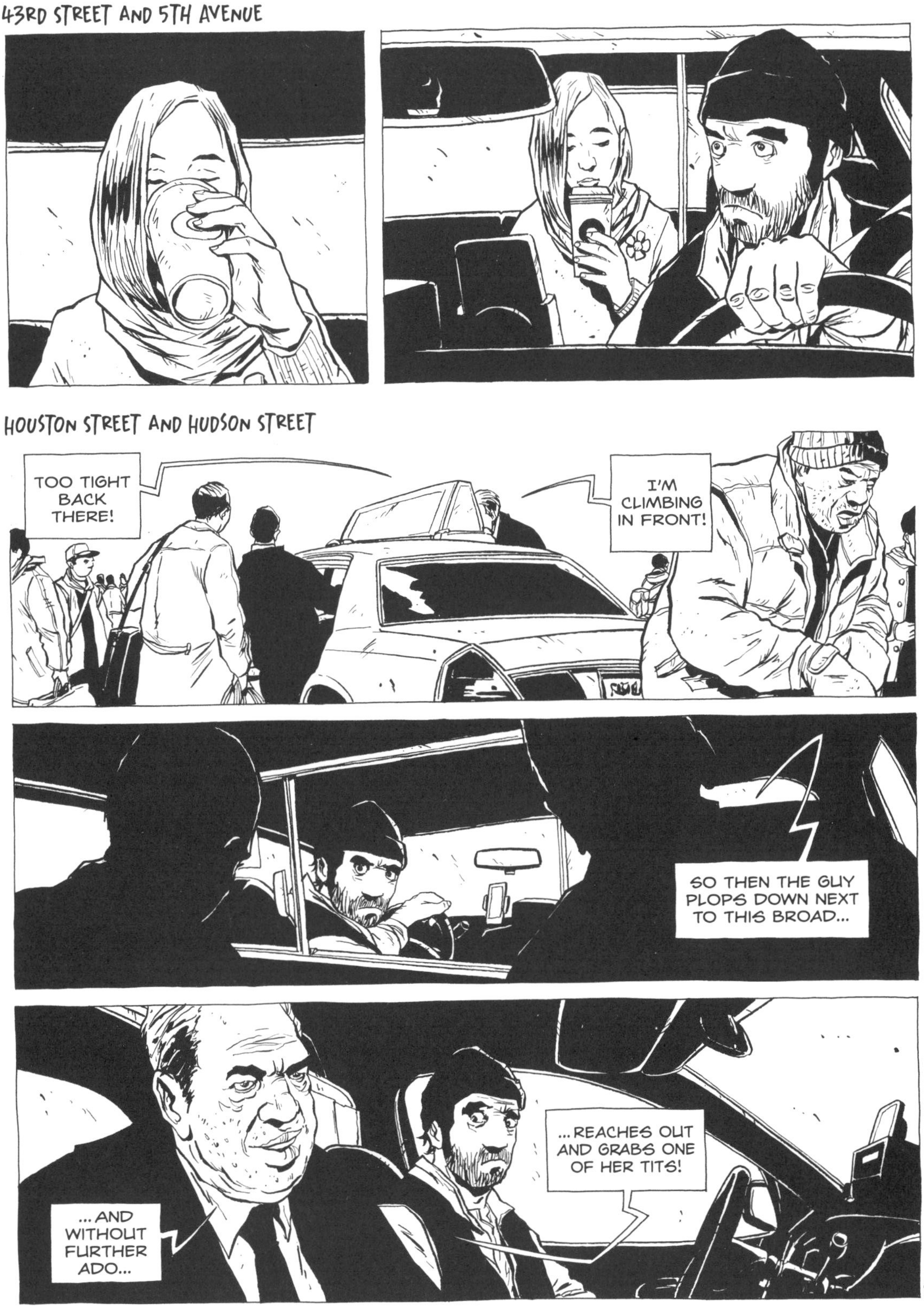
43RD STREET AND 5TH AVENUE
HOUSTON STREET AND HUDSON STREET
TOO TIGHT BACK THERE!
I'M CLIMBING IN FRONT!
SO THEN THE GUY PLOPS DOWN NEXT TO THIS BROAD...
...REACHES OUT AND GRABS ONE OF HER TITS!
...AND WITHOUT FURTHER ADO...

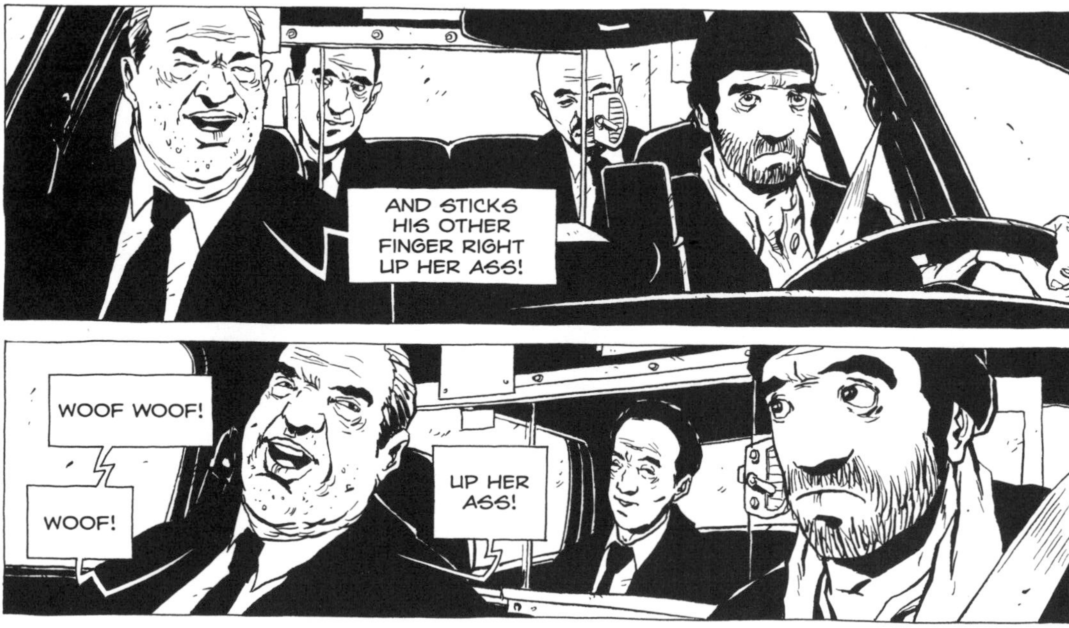
AND STICKS HIS OTHER FINGER RIGHT UP HER ASS!
WOOF WOOF!
WOOF!
UP HER ASS!

HOW WOULD THEY HAVE BEHAVED IF I WAS A WOMAN? WOULD THEY HAVE BEEN MORE DISCREET, MORE MISOGYNISTIC, TRIED TO PICK ME UP? WOULD THEY HAVE CALLED ME BY MY FIRST NAME, READ IT OFF MY LICENSE? AND MY MAIN CHARACTER: HOW WOULD SHE REACT? WOULD SHE TAKE THE TAXI SCHOOL'S ADVICE? NEVER RESPOND TO PROVOCATIONS, DON'T DISCUSS POLITICS OR OTHER TOUCHY SUBJECTS, REMEMBER YOU'LL NEVER SEE THESE PEOPLE AGAIN, NO MATTER IF THEY'RE NICE OR NASTY. IF SHE WANTS TO HANG ON TO HER JOB, SHE'S GOT NO CHOICE. SHE HAS TO KEEP A LOW PROFILE. SHE'S AN IMMIGRANT JUST LIKE THE REST OF THEM, IN A PRECARIOUS SITUATION. SHE SOON GETS A HANDLE ON HER NEW ROLE.

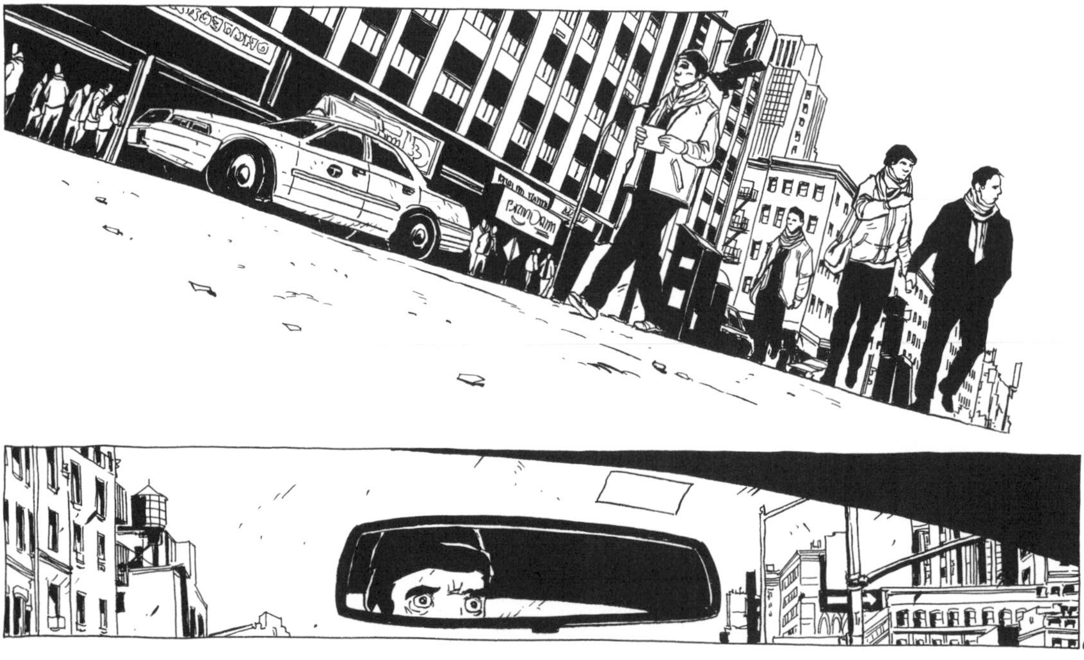

30TH STREET AND 1ST AVENUE

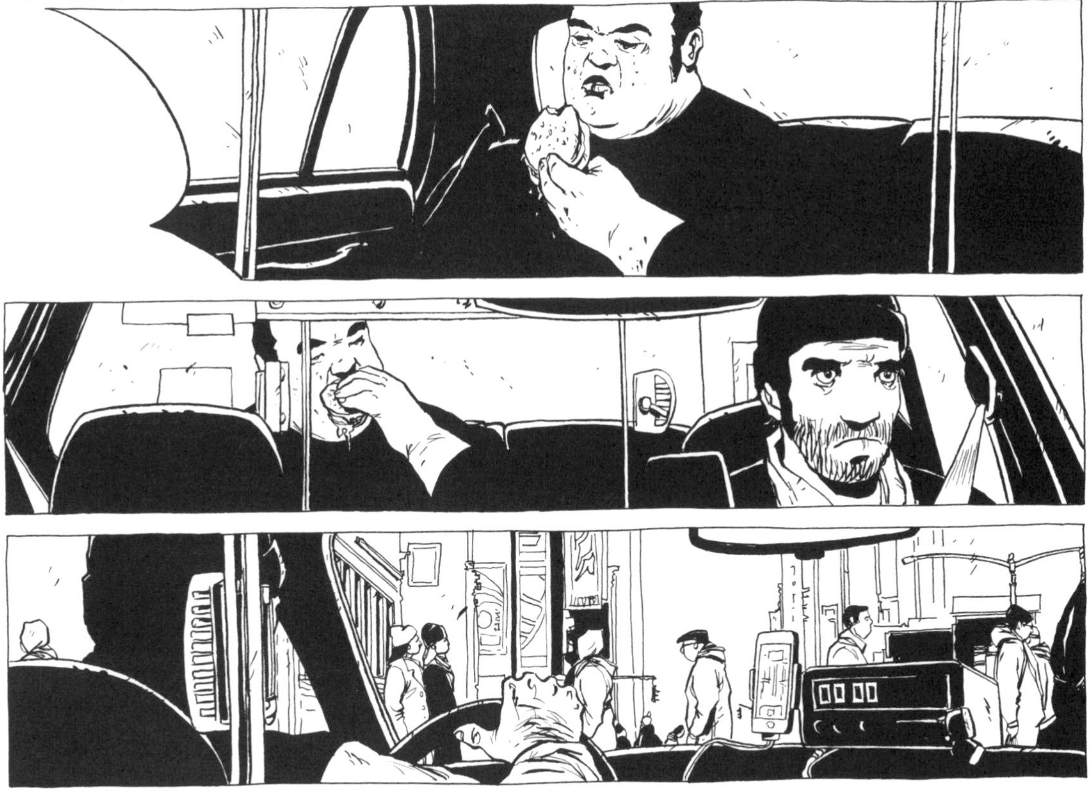

NOT MUCH CONVERSATION. WEIRD FEELING, FEELING INVISIBLE. A VERY INTERESTING IDEA, INVISIBILITY, TO MY ACTRESS CHARACTER. OTHER PEOPLE LOOKING RIGHT THROUGH YOU: WHAT COULD BE MORE AWFUL FOR AN ACTRESS? NOT SOMETHING SHE ANTICIPATED, GOING INTO THIS LINE OF WORK.

SHE TAKES THIS NEW DEAL HEAD ON, AND AT THE SAME TIME, THE FACT OF NOT DRAWING ATTENTION EITHER FOR HER GENDER OR HER BACKGROUND OR HER LOOKS (NOTE: DRESS HER LIKE YOURSELF) IS ALSO PROOF OF HER ASSIMILATION AND EMBRACE OF THE ROLE SHE'S CHOSEN FOR HERSELF: SHE'S NOT AN ACTRESS ANYMORE, SHE'S IN CHARACTER, A CAB DRIVER LIKE ANY OTHER, BELIEVABLE. LOOK AT IT LIKE THAT, AND IT'S A KIND OF VICTORY.

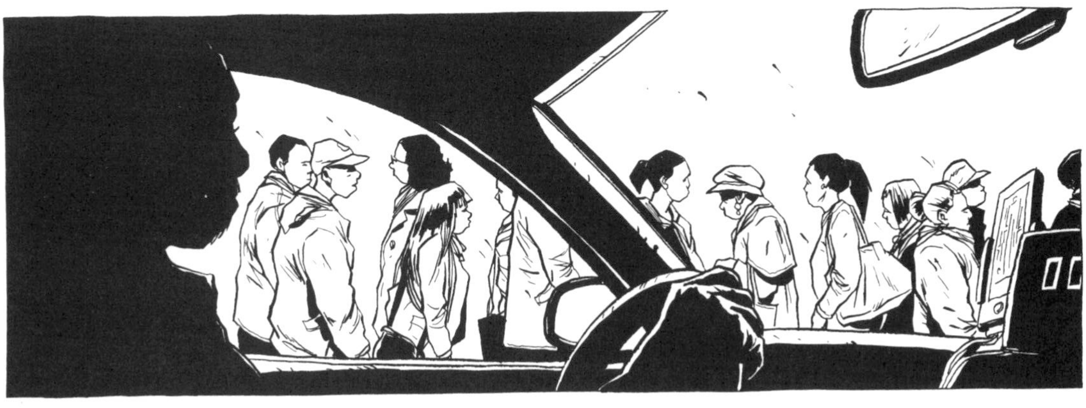

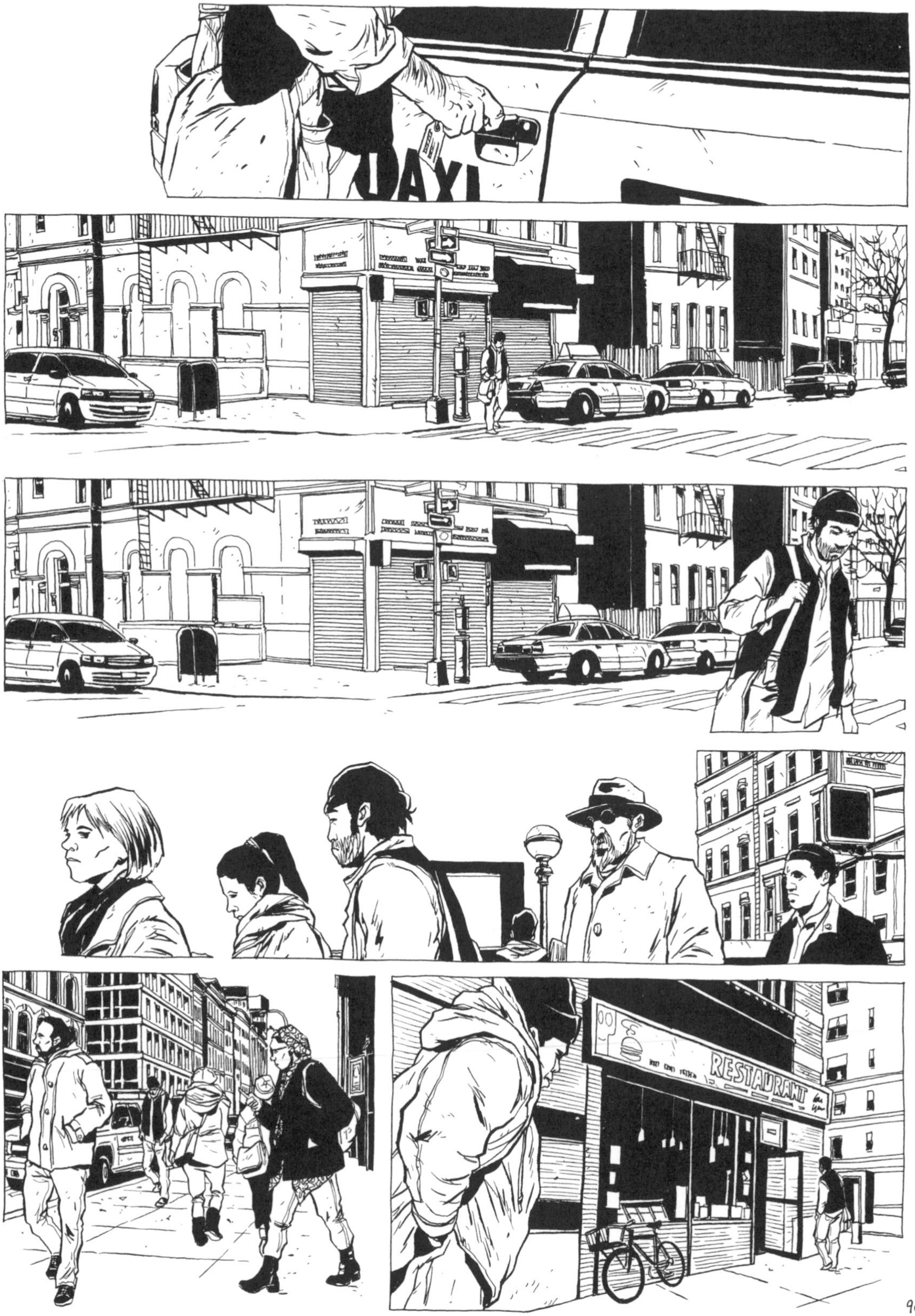
RESTAURANT

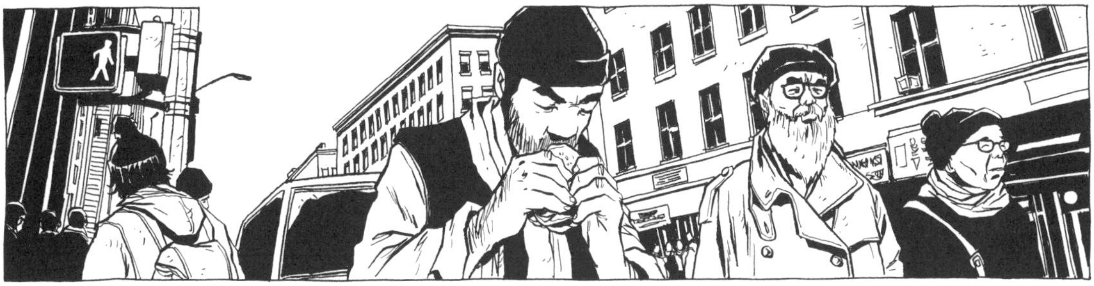

$12 FOR A BURGER, ONE OF THE BEST IN TOWN, A THIRD OF MY MORNING'S HARD-WON EARNINGS. I HAVE TROUBLE KEEPING MY TWO LIVES APART; I'M BRIMMING WITH GUILT. WHAT AM I DOING? ME, AN UPPER MIDDLE-CLASS BROOKLYNITE, DRIVING STRANGERS AROUND ALL DAY?

WEARING TOO MANY HATS...

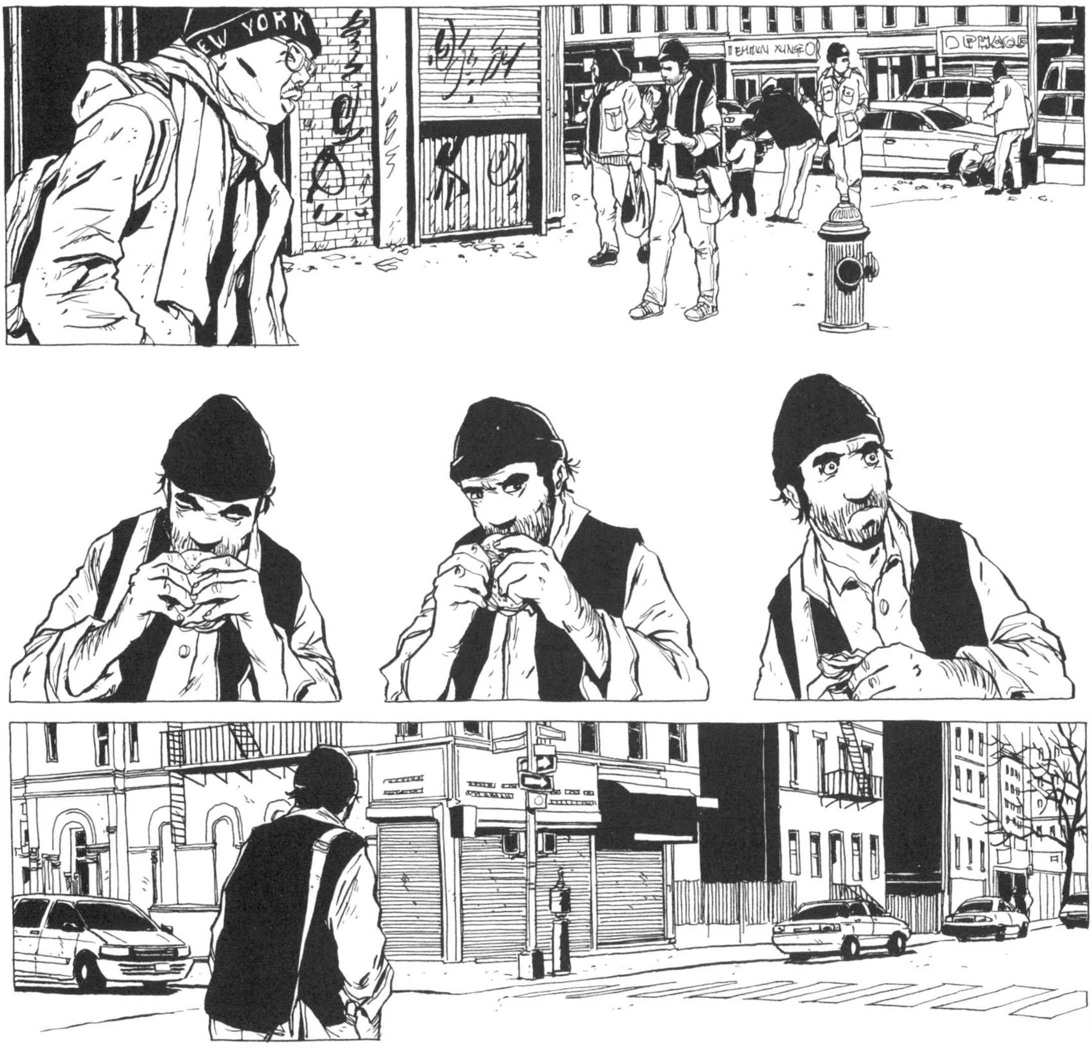
EW YORK

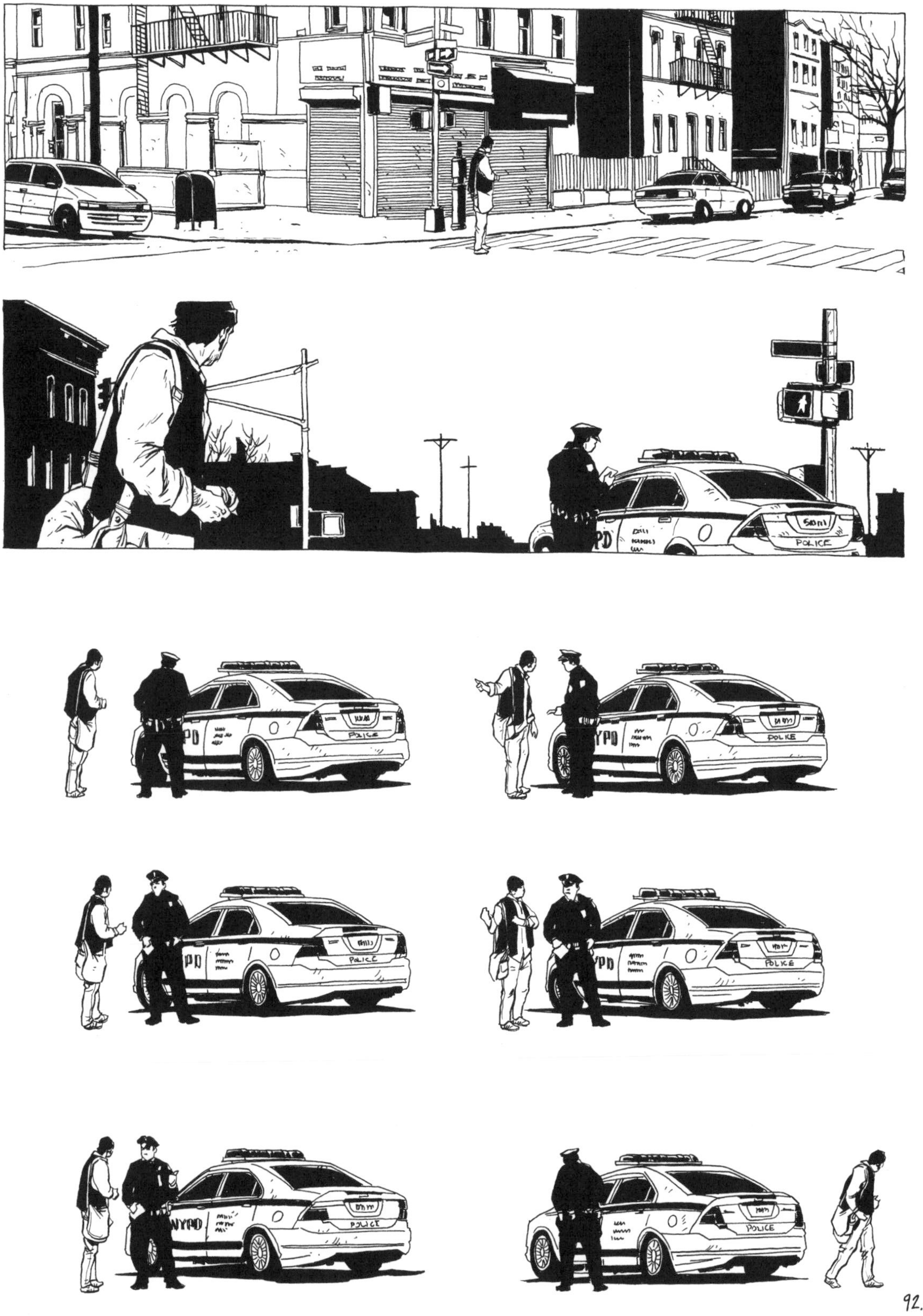
NYPD
POLICE

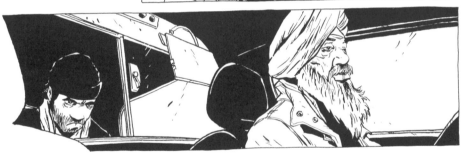

SO, HOW'D IT GO TODAY, BENOIT? NO TICKETS?

I GOT THE CAR BACK FROM THE IMPOUND. $55 FINE AND $185 FOR THE TOWING FEES.

CAB MGT CORP
DRIVERS WANTED

NICE BACKDROP FOR A DAYTIME SEQUENCE...

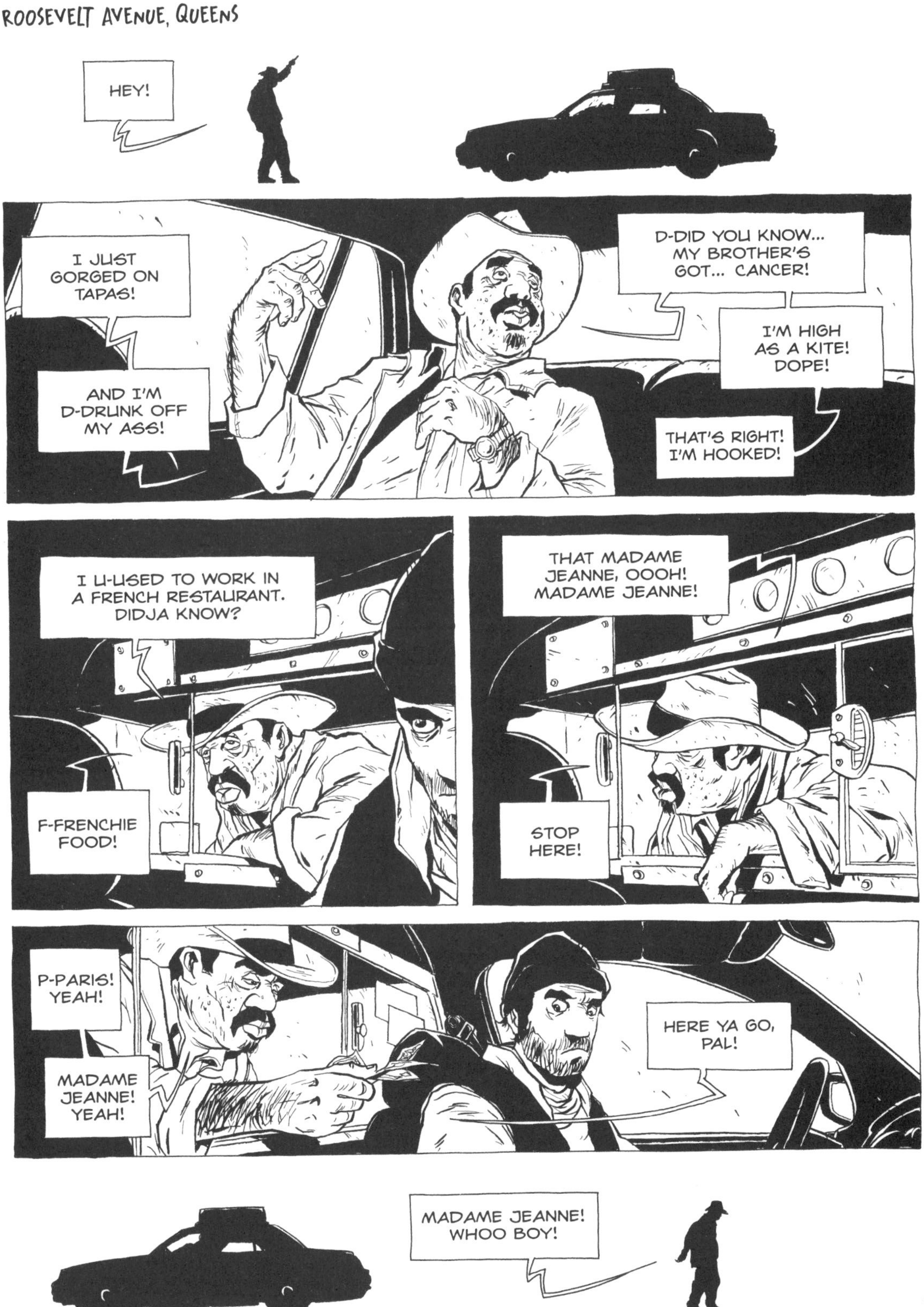
ROOSEVELT AVENUE, QUEENS
HEY!
I JUST GORGED ON TAPAS!
AND I'M D-DRUNK OFF MY ASS!
D-DID YOU KNOW... MY BROTHER'S GOT... CANCER!
I'M HIGH AS A KITE! DOPE!
THAT'S RIGHT! I'M HOOKED!
I U-USED TO WORK IN A FRENCH RESTAURANT. DIDJA KNOW?
F-FRENCHIE FOOD!
THAT MADAME JEANNE, OOOH! MADAME JEANNE!
STOP HERE!
P-PARIS! YEAH!
MADAME JEANNE! YEAH!
HERE YA GO, PAL!
MADAME JEANNE! WHOO BOY!

MANHATTAN...

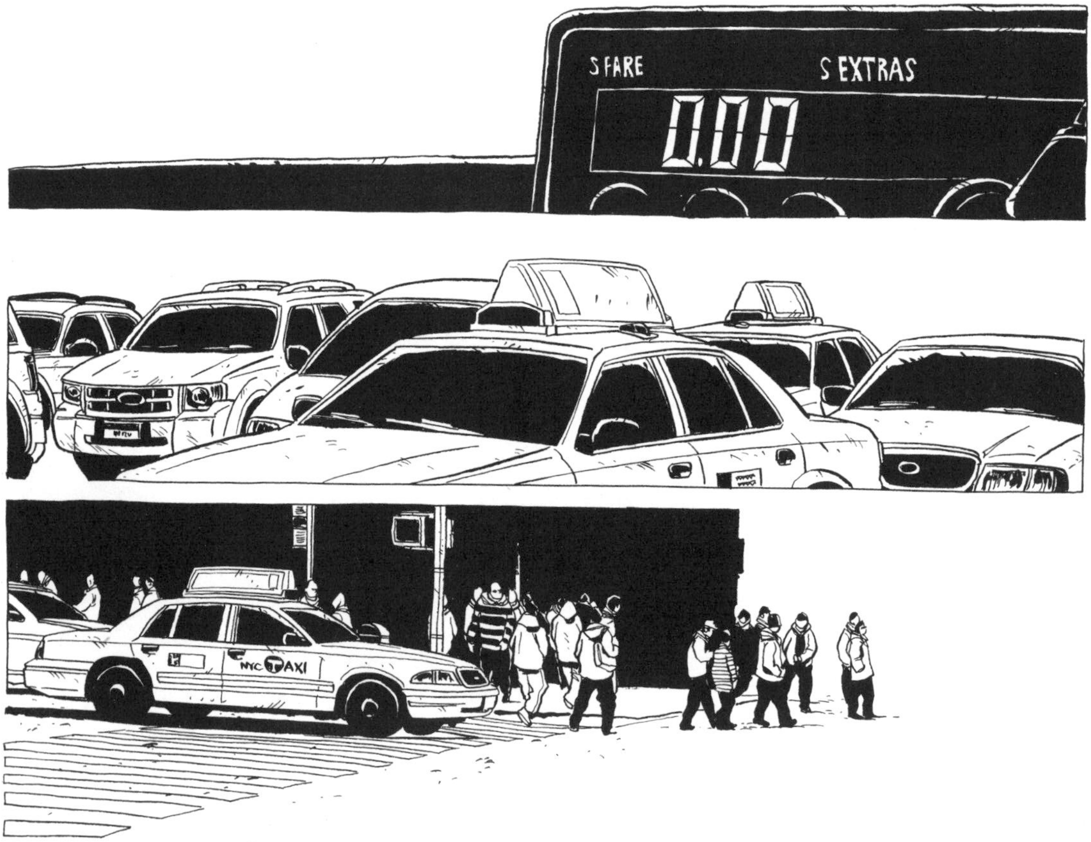
$ FARE
$ EXTRAS
0.00
NYC TAXI

IMPORTANT: SHOW THESE MOMENTS OF SOLITUDE AND WAITING IN THE MOVIE...

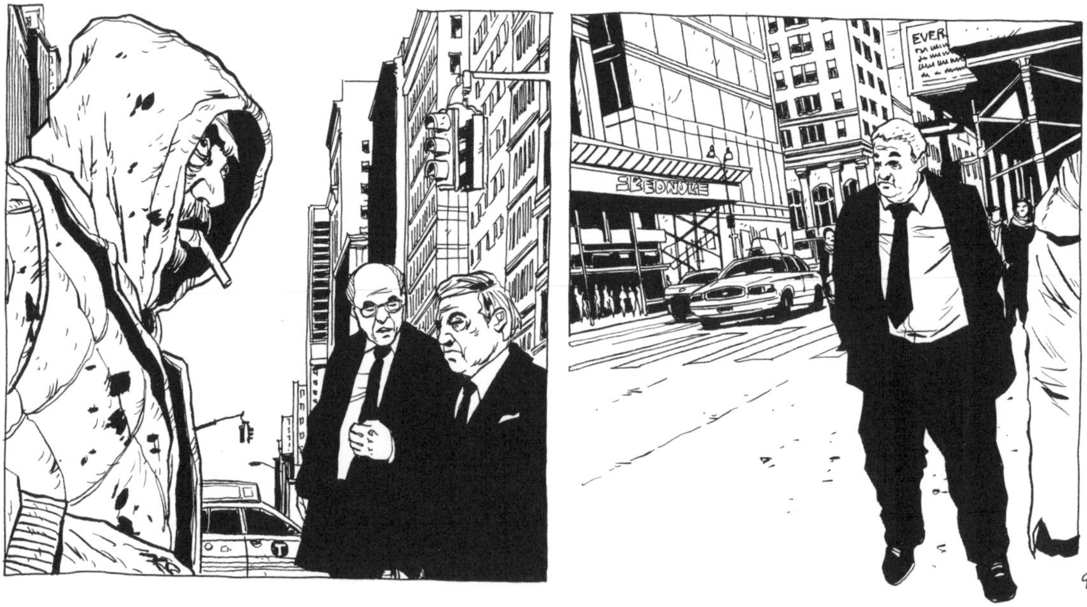
EVER

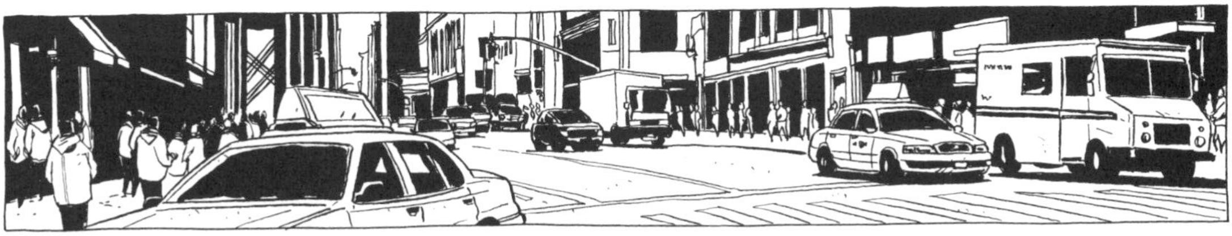

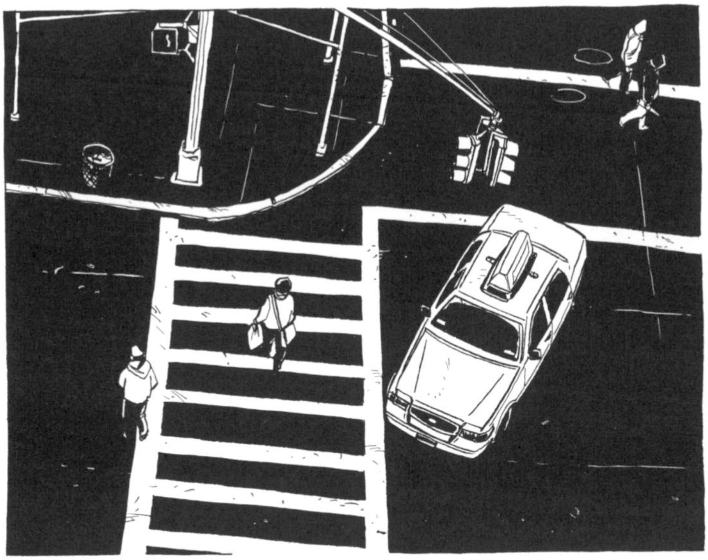

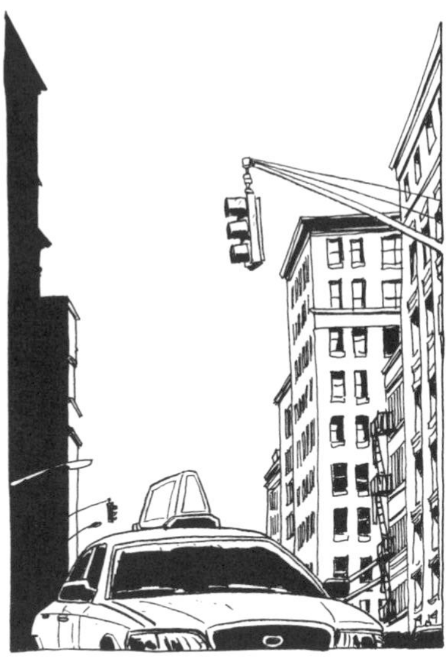

THESE MOMENTS WHEN THE HEROINE IS ALONE IN HER BUBBLE...

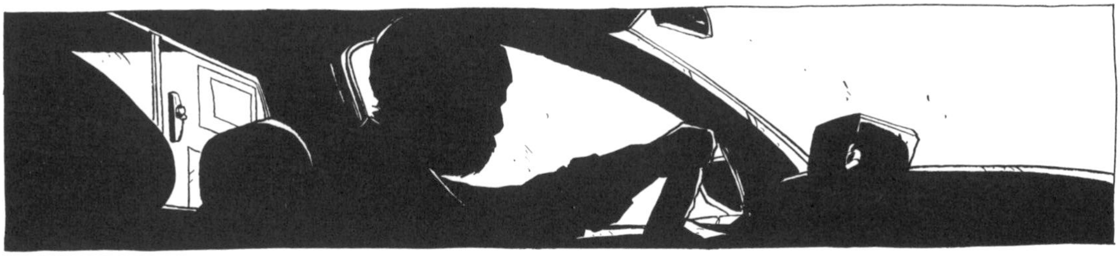

SAFE FROM THE WORLD, THE COLD, THE NOISE...

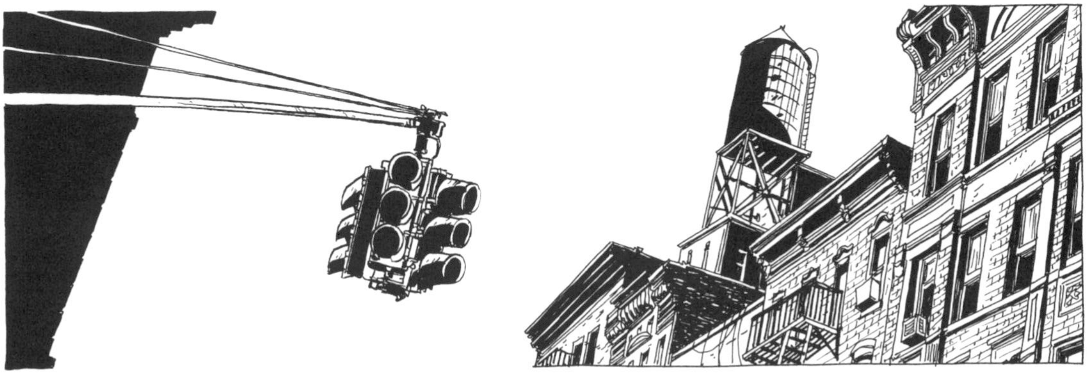

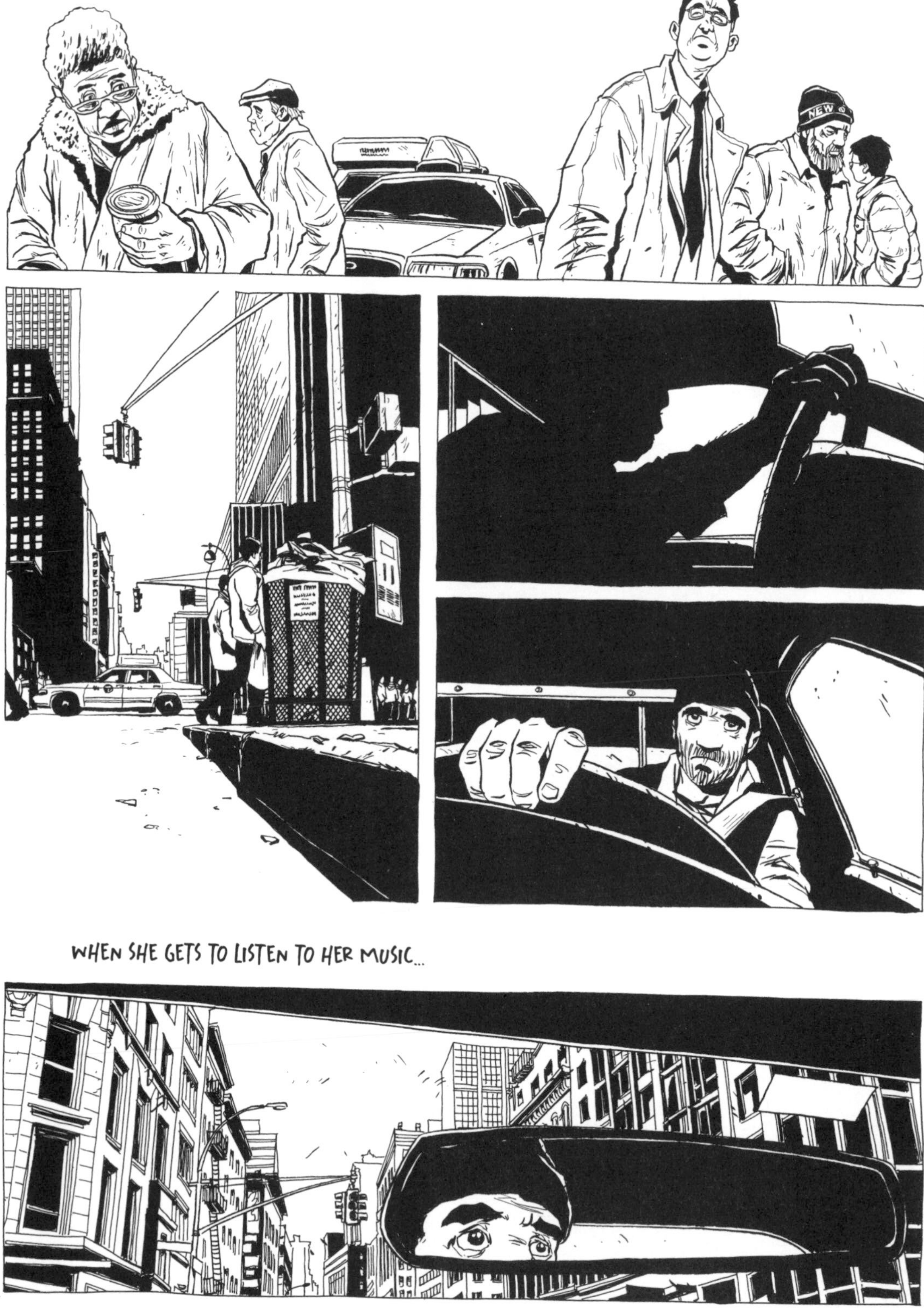
NEW
WHEN SHE GETS TO LISTEN TO HER MUSIC...

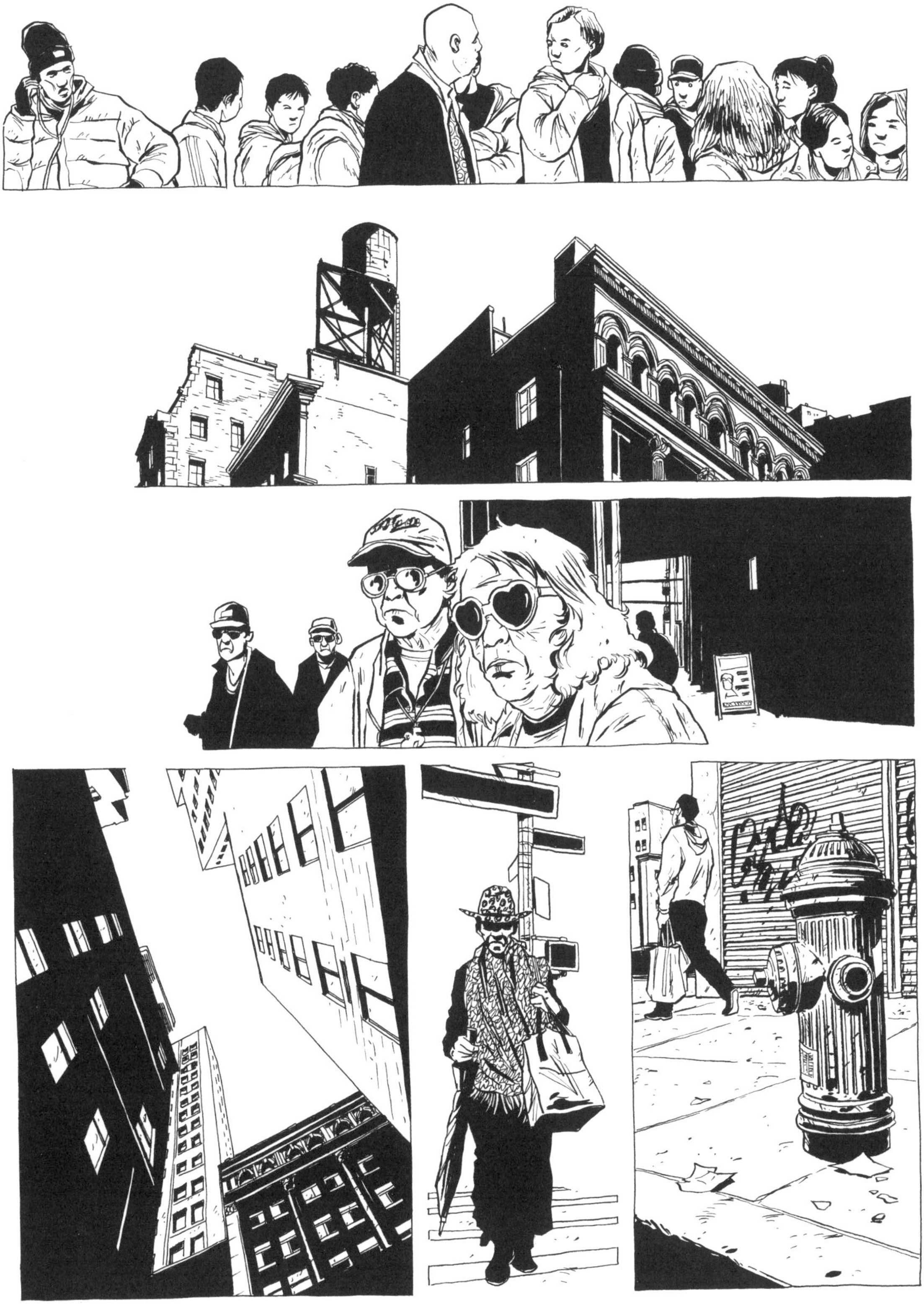

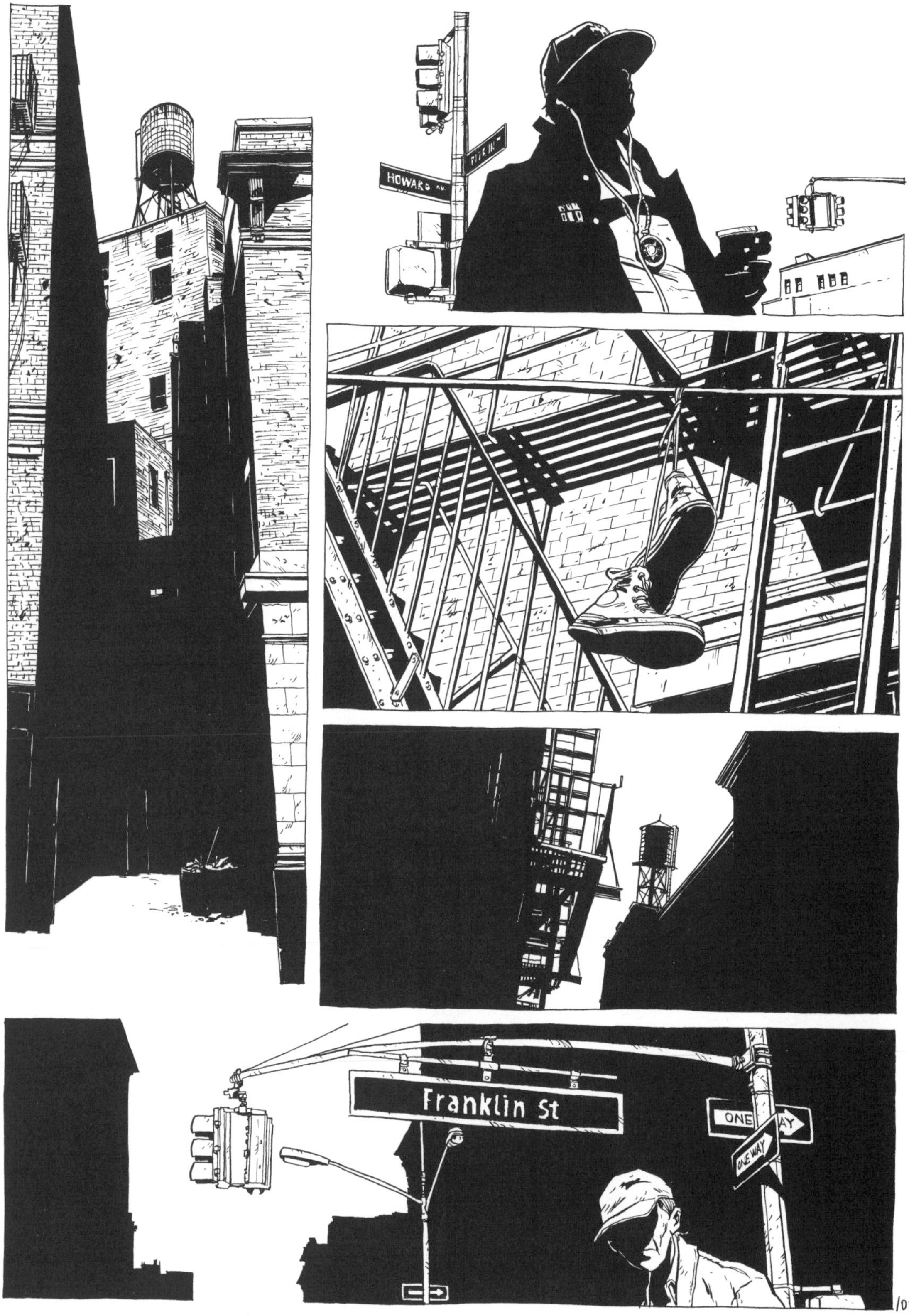
HOWARD
Franklin St
ONE WAY
ONE WAY

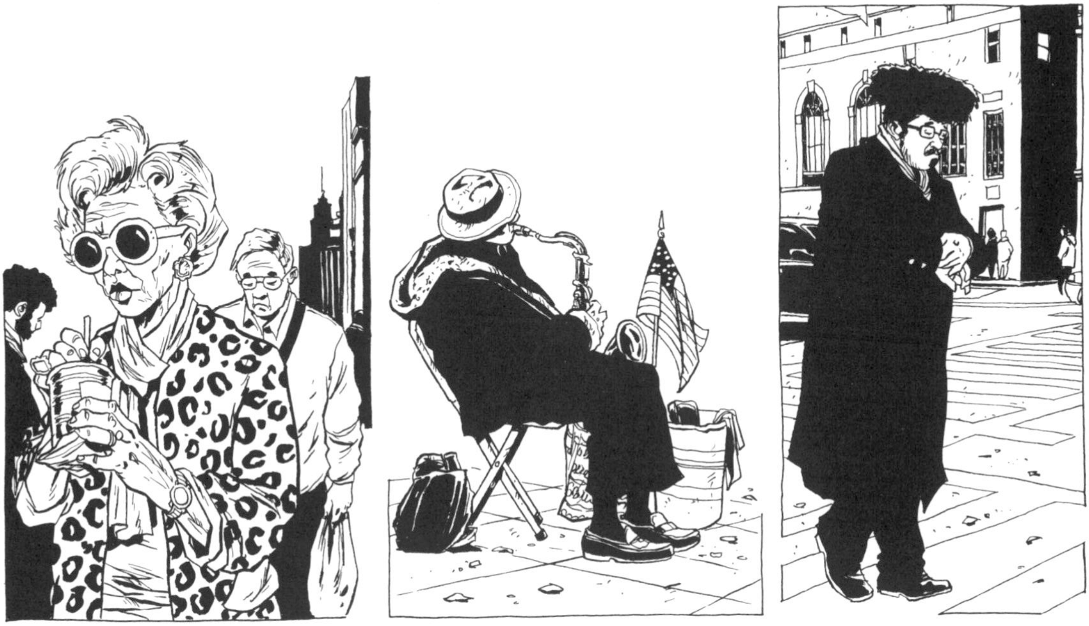

A PRIVILEGED SPECTATOR OF THE BALLET OF NEW YORK CITY STREETS...

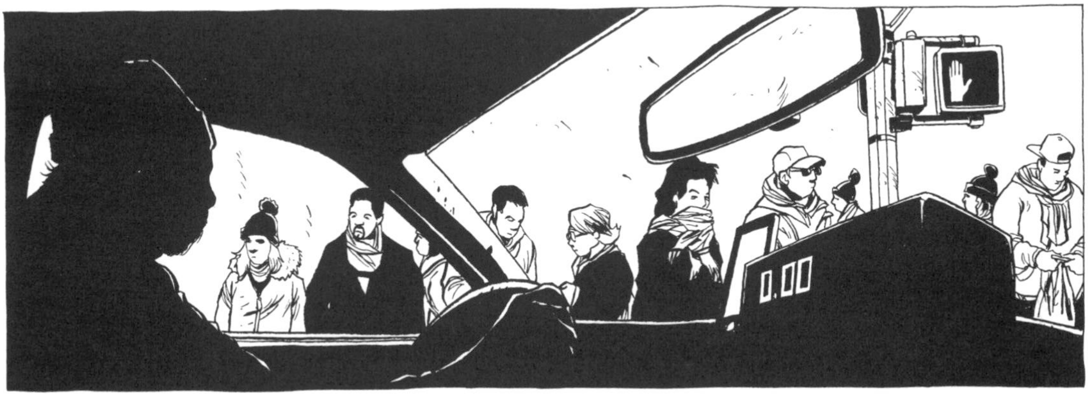
0.00

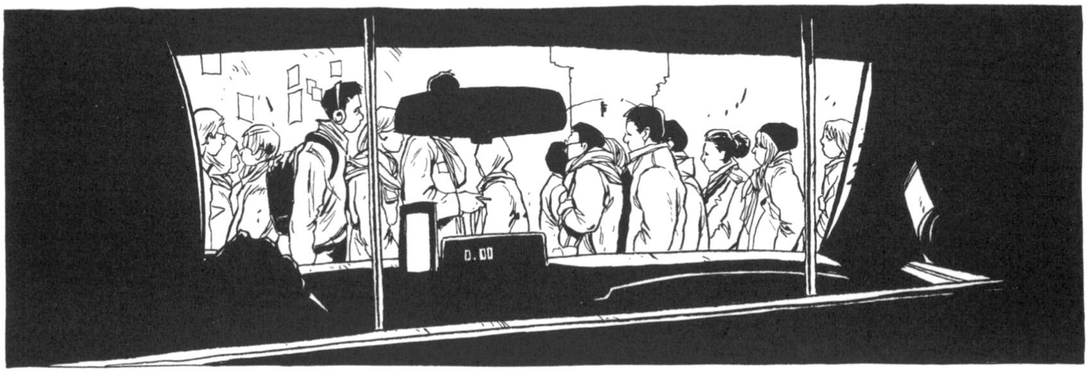
0.00

A "MOVIEGOER"...

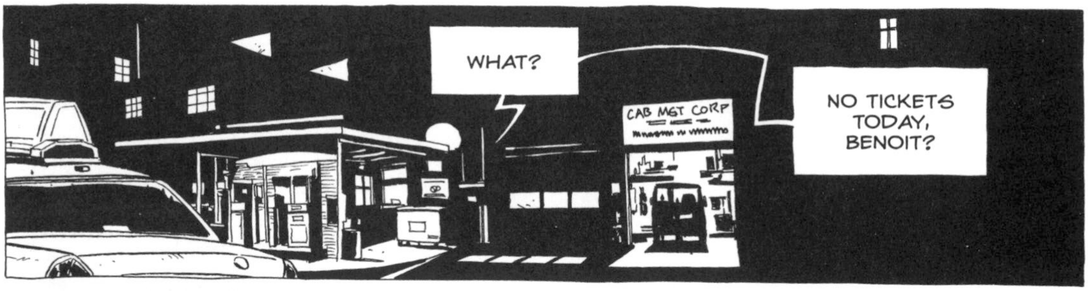
WHAT?
CAB MGT CORP
NO TICKETS TODAY, BENOIT?

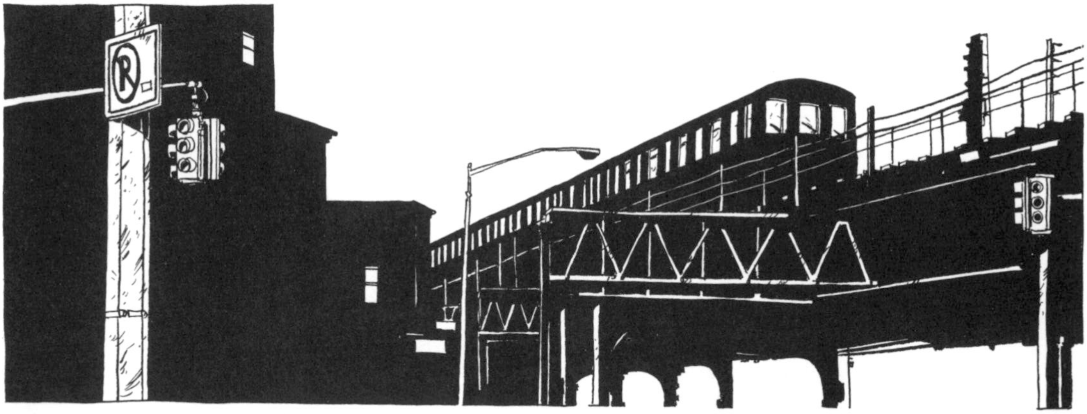

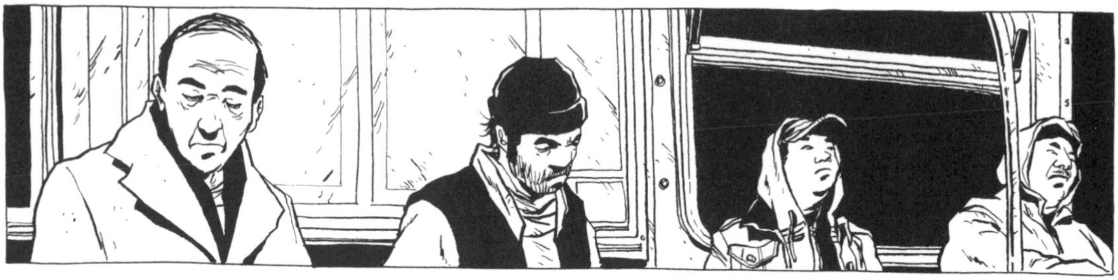

SHOULD MY MOVIE HAVE AN ASSAULT IN IT? IS MY MAIN CHARACTER SCARED WHEN SHE TAKES THE WHEEL? THE STREETS ARE A LOT SAFER THAN THEY WERE JUST A FEW YEARS AGO. THIRTY YEARS AGO, AN AVERAGE OF ONE TAXI DRIVER GOT MURDERED DAILY. DURING MY FIRST THREE DAYS ON THE JOB, I NEVER LEFT MANHATTAN EXCEPT FOR AN AIRPORT RUN, AND I HAVEN'T RUN INTO ANY WORRISOME OR THREATENING FARES.

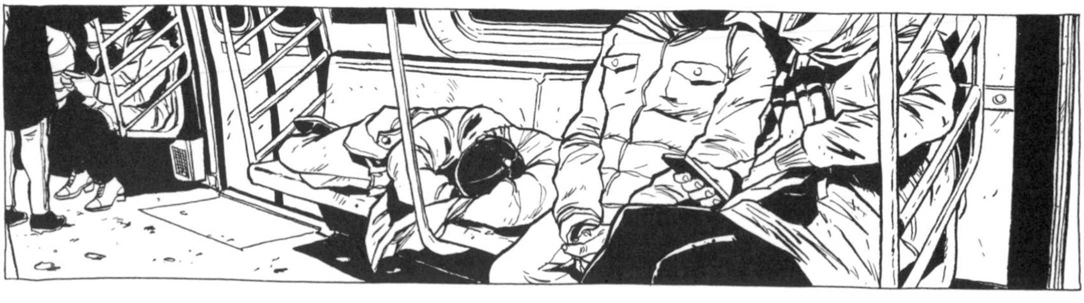

I MIGHT CHANGE MY MIND ONCE I START WORKING NIGHTS.

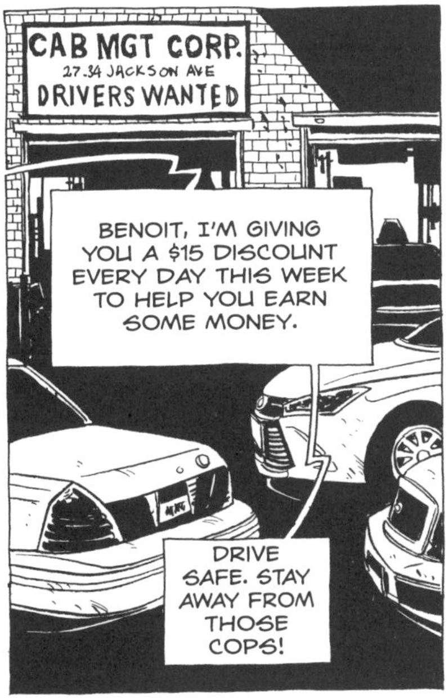
CAB MGT CORP.
27-34 JACKSON AVE
DRIVERS WANTED
BENOIT, I'M GIVING YOU A $15 DISCOUNT EVERY DAY THIS WEEK TO HELP YOU EARN SOME MONEY.
DRIVE SAFE. STAY AWAY FROM THOSE COPS!

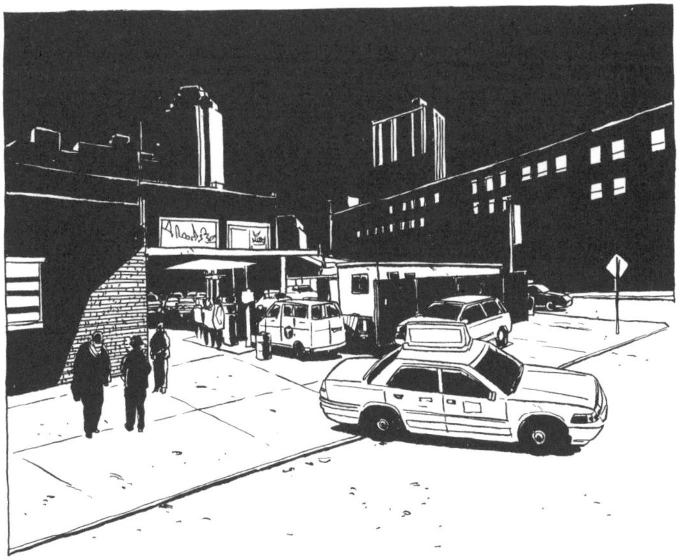

39TH STREET AND 7TH AVENUE

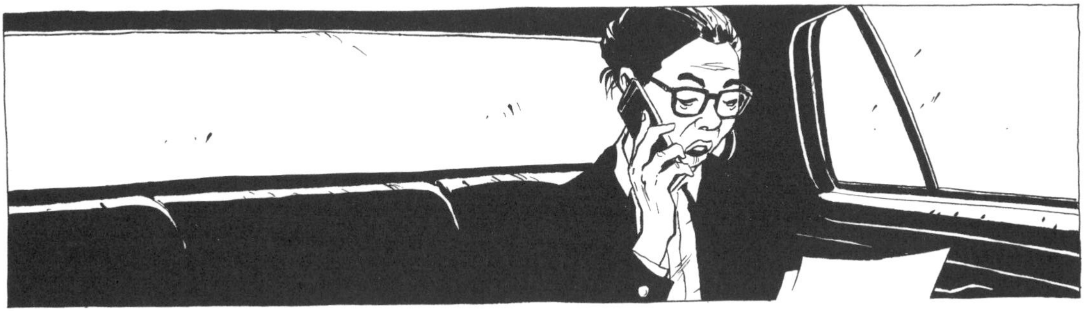

BROADWAY AND EXCHANGE PLACE

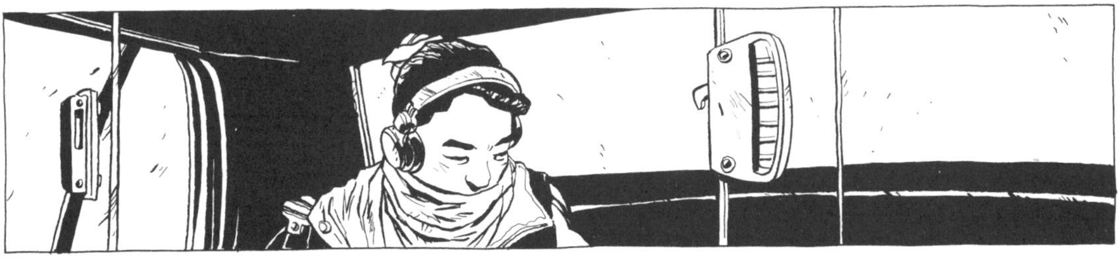

CHAMBERS STREET AND BROADWAY

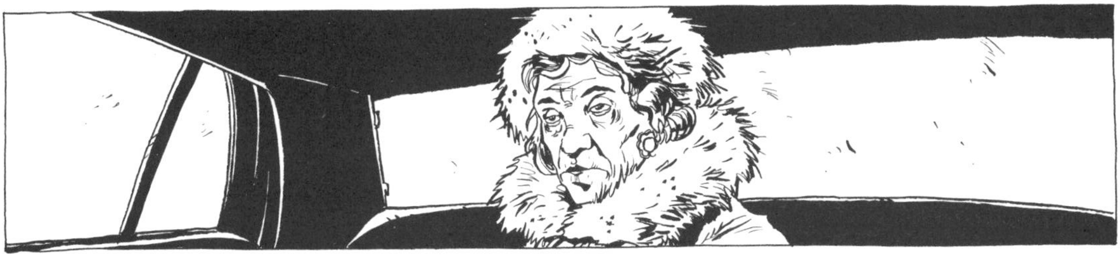

17TH STREET AND UNION SQUARE WEST

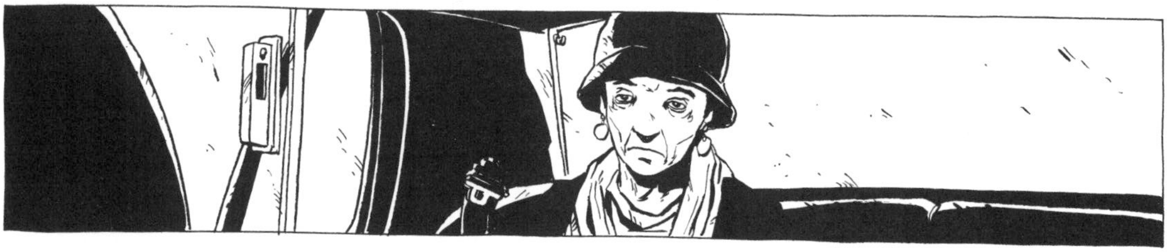

ONLY WOMEN THIS MORNING. IF I WERE A WOMAN, MAYBE THEY'D TALK TO ME, EVEN IF JUST TO EXPRESS THEIR SURPRISE AT SEEING A FEMALE CAB DRIVER. THESE ARE THE KINDS OF MOMENTS I CAN USE TO REVEAL SOME MORE PERSONAL INFORMATION ABOUT MY MAIN CHARACTER. MAYBE WOMEN PASSENGERS CAN MAKE HER OPEN UP TO THE CITY, FEEL THE FULL RUSH OF ITS ENERGY. I'M ALWAYS STRUCK BY HOW EASILY NEW YORKERS WILL START TALKING TO EACH OTHER: IN THE STREET, THE SUBWAY, STORES, EVERYWHERE. EVEN IF THEY DON'T WIND UP SAYING ANYTHING IMPORTANT, THEY TALK, AND THIS TALK IS PRECIOUS, LIFE-GIVING WHEN YOU'RE FROM SOMEWHERE ELSE AND DON'T KNOW ANYONE.

MERCER AND GRAND

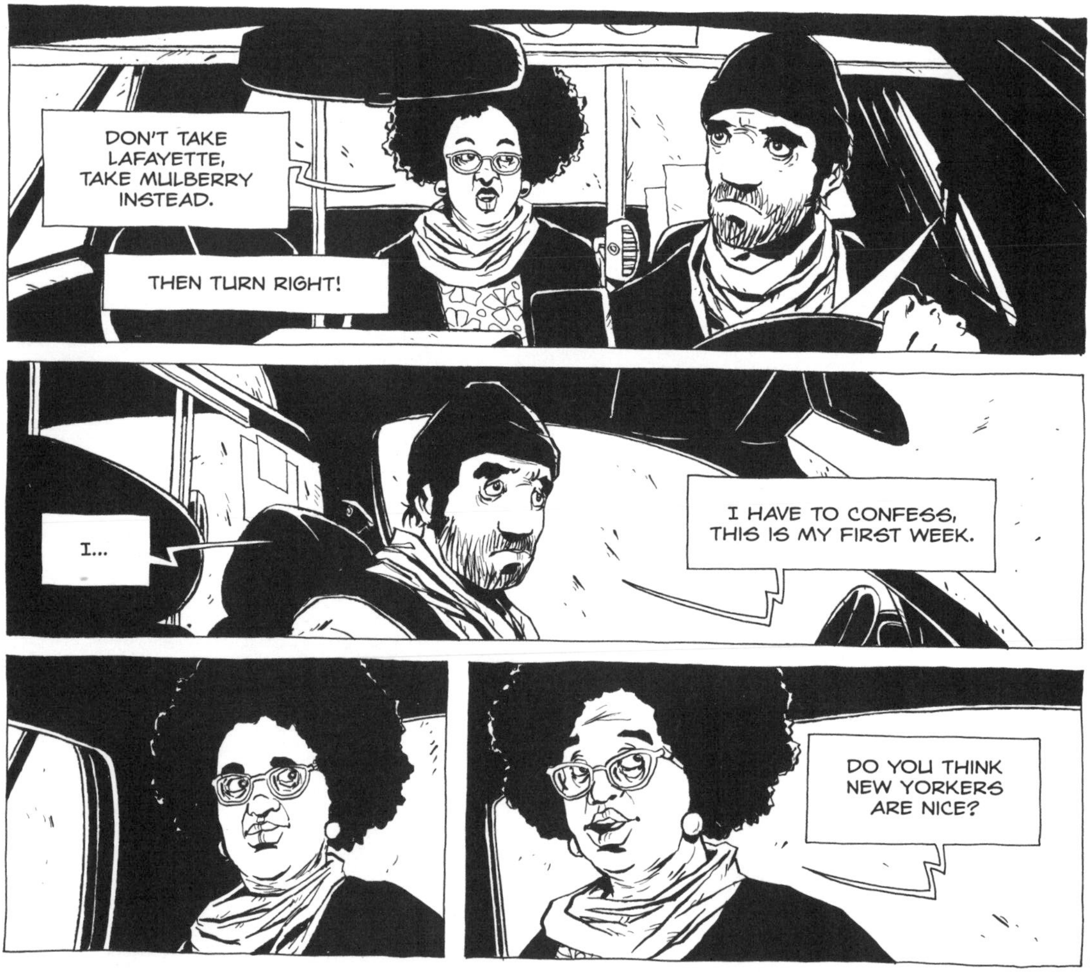
DON'T TAKE LAFAYETTE, TAKE MULBERRY INSTEAD.
THEN TURN RIGHT!
I...
I HAVE TO CONFESS, THIS IS MY FIRST WEEK.
DO YOU THINK NEW YORKERS ARE NICE?

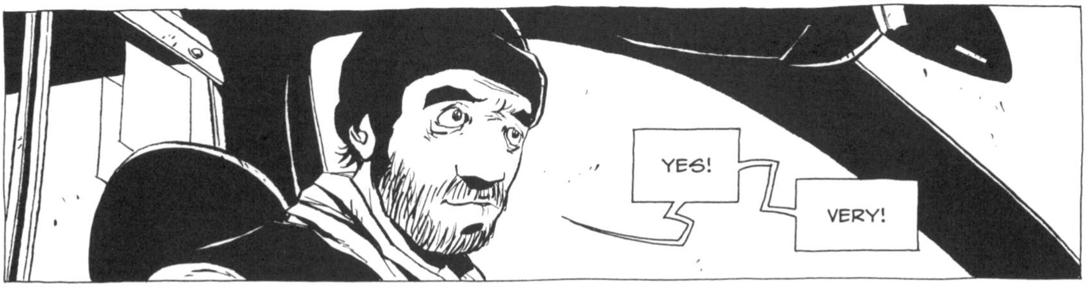
YES!
VERY!

95TH STREET AND MADISON AVENUE

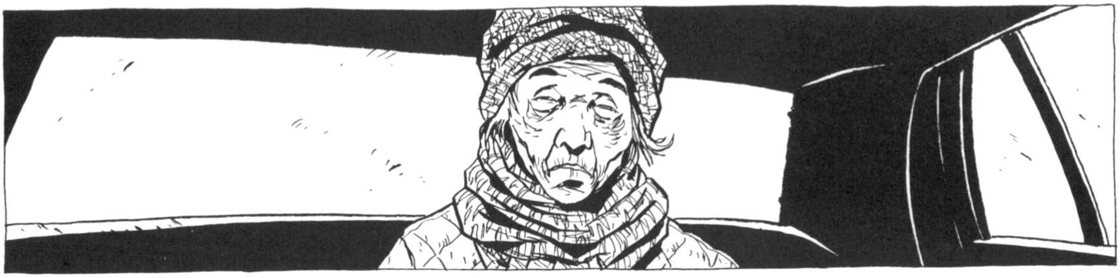

75TH STREET AND BROADWAY

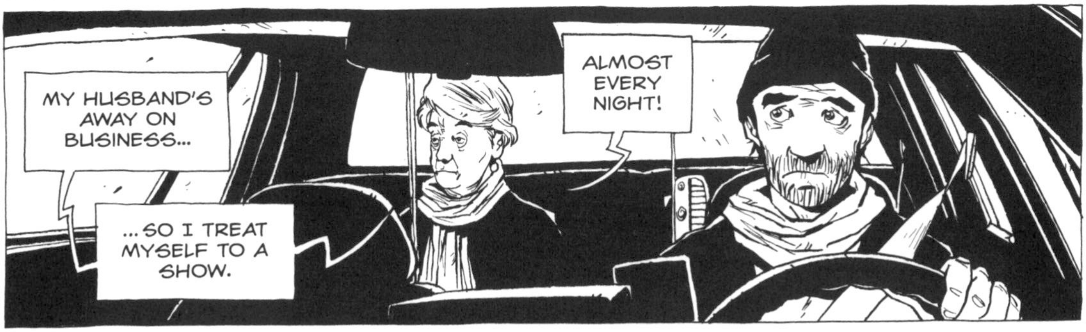
MY HUSBAND'S AWAY ON BUSINESS...
...SO I TREAT MYSELF TO A SHOW.
ALMOST EVERY NIGHT!

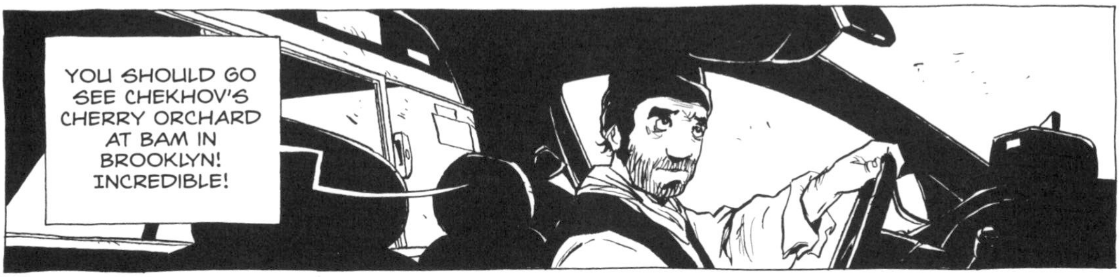
YOU SHOULD GO SEE CHEKHOV'S CHERRY ORCHARD AT BAM IN BROOKLYN! INCREDIBLE!

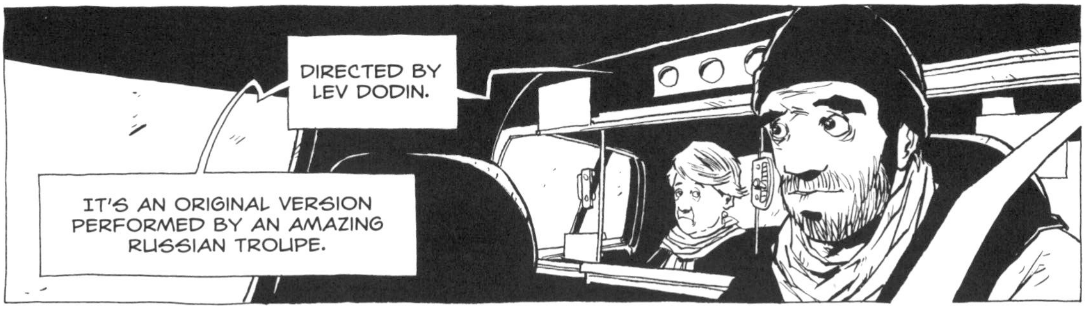
DIRECTED BY LEV DODIN.
IT'S AN ORIGINAL VERSION PERFORMED BY AN AMAZING RUSSIAN TROUPE.

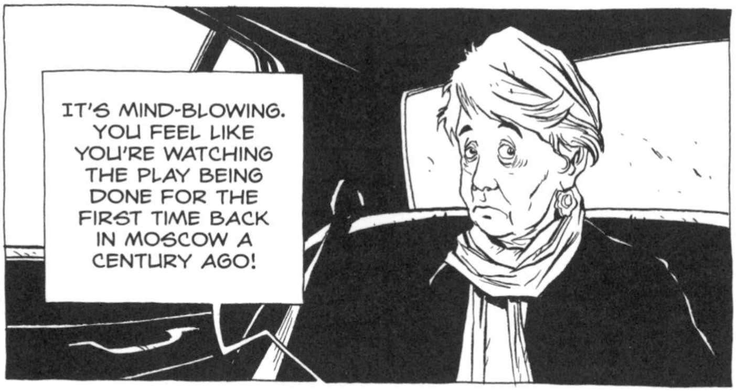
IT'S MIND-BLOWING. YOU FEEL LIKE YOU'RE WATCHING THE PLAY BEING DONE FOR THE FIRST TIME BACK IN MOSCOW A CENTURY AGO!

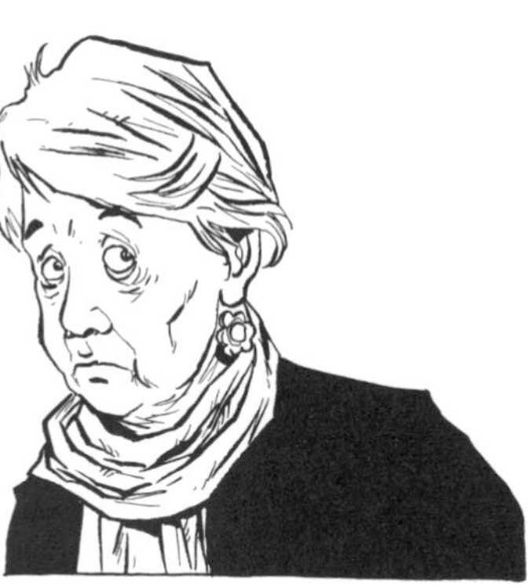

DRIVING A TAXI IS CONSIDERED A LOWER-CLASS JOB.

JUST A FEW INCHES BETWEEN YOU AND THE BACKSEAT, BUT IT MIGHT AS WELL BE A YAWNING CHASM.

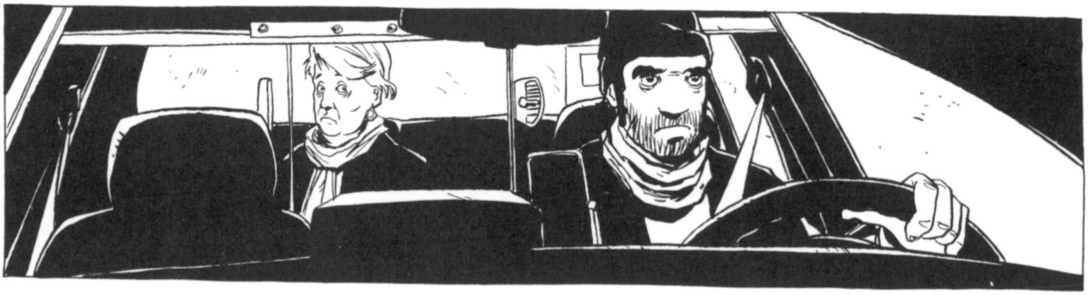

INTERESTINGLY ENOUGH, MY MAIN CHARACTER, SEIZING UPON THIS NEW COUNTRY WHERE NO ONE KNOWS HER, STARTS MAKING UP DIFFERENT LIVES, AND MUCH TO HER OWN SURPRISE TELLING PASSENGERS ABOUT THEM, AT THE SAME TIME LEADING VIEWERS DOWN THE GARDEN PATH.

WHO IS SHE? WE LEARN ABOUT HER THROUGH FLASHBACKS AS SHE DEFIES REALITY WITH THE HELP OF FICTION, FARE AFTER FARE, LIES AS A FORM OF PROTECTION, ALL THE MORE INTERESTING IN A COUNTRY WHERE LYING IS SEEN AS A SERIOUS NO-NO.

SHE USES HER ACTING TALENTS AND CREATES MULTIPLE SELVES, A NEW DIMENSION IN THIS NEW COUNTRY—ALL TO HELP HER FIND HER PLACE. BUT WHAT IS THE LINE BETWEEN ACTING AND LYING? BETWEEN LYING TO OTHER PEOPLE AND LYING TO YOURSELF?

70TH STREET AND YORK AVENUE

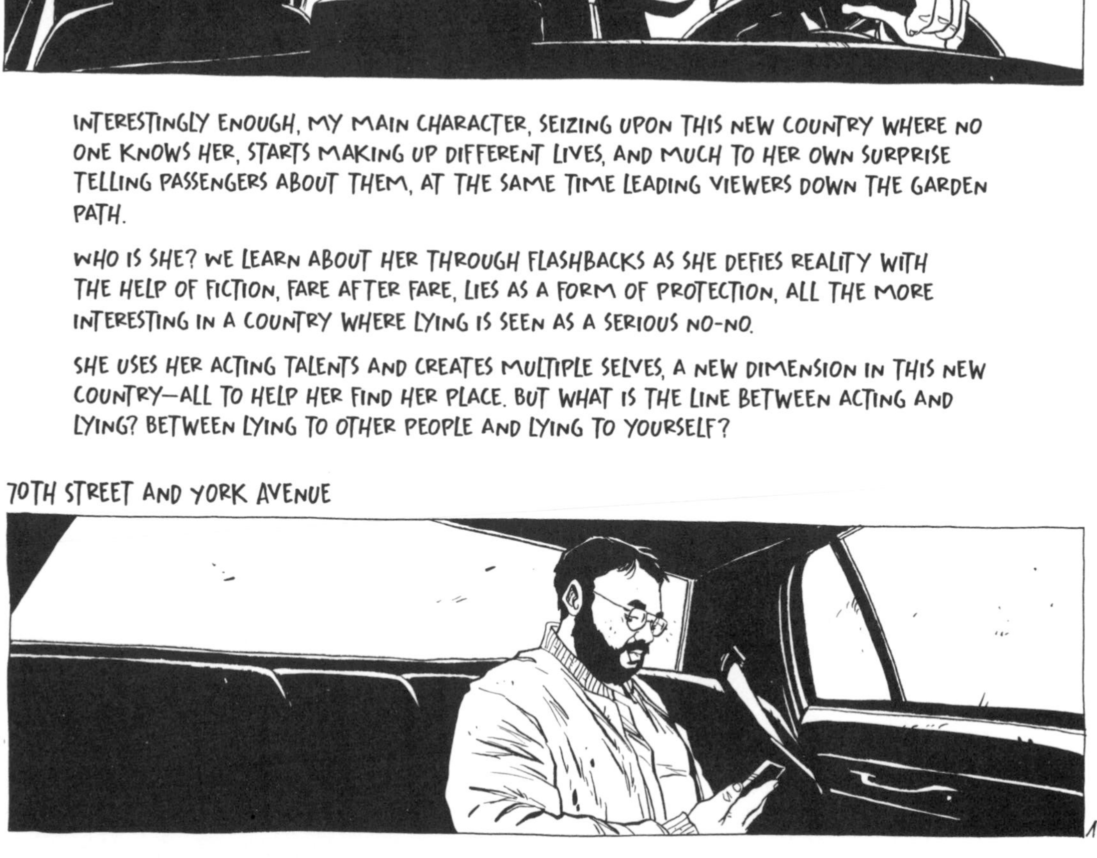

38TH STREET AND 12TH AVENUE

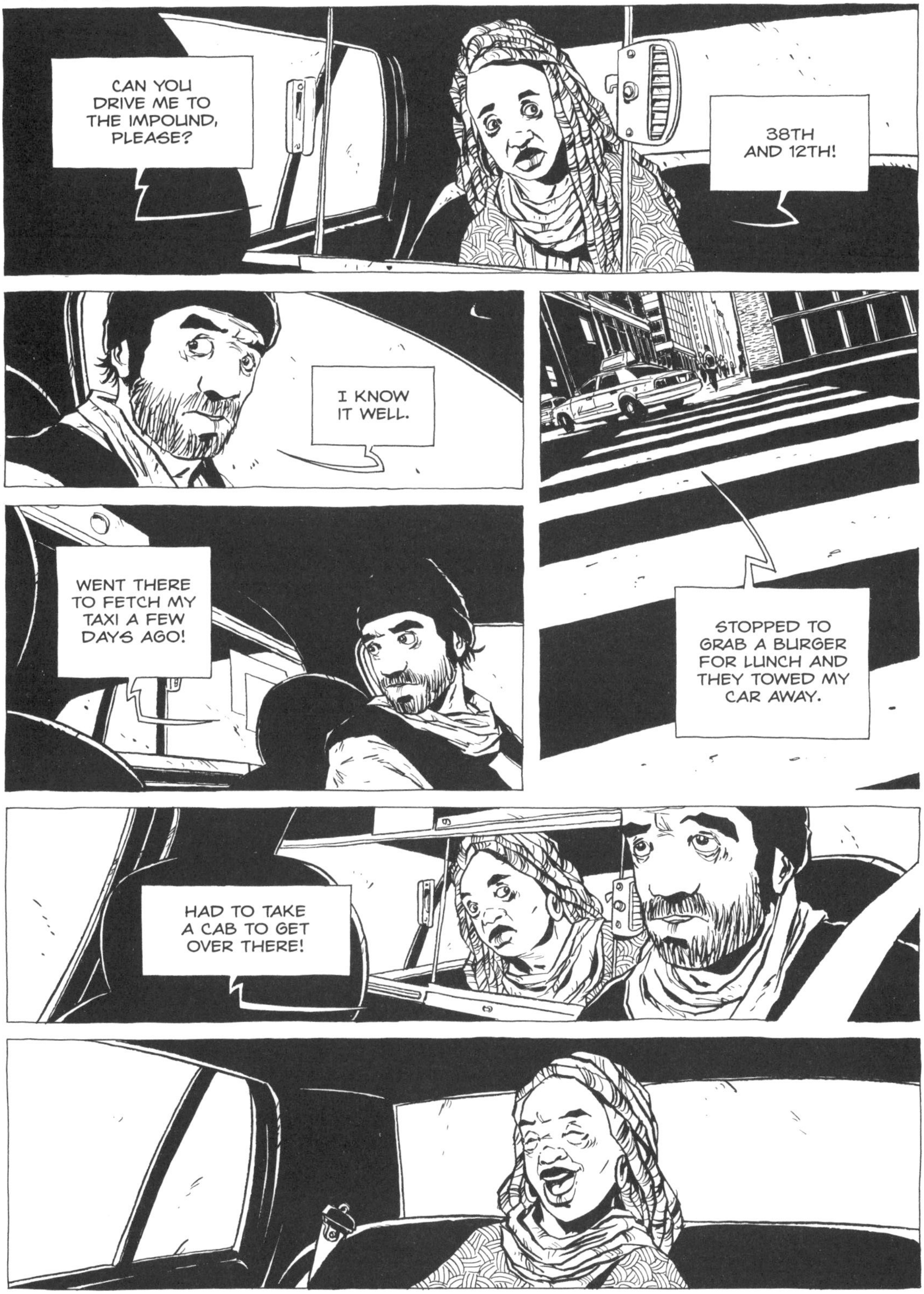

CAN YOU DRIVE ME TO THE IMPOUND, PLEASE?
38TH AND 12TH!
I KNOW IT WELL.
WENT THERE TO FETCH MY TAXI A FEW DAYS AGO!
STOPPED TO GRAB A BURGER FOR LUNCH AND THEY TOWED MY CAR AWAY.
HAD TO TAKE A CAB TO GET OVER THERE!

83RD STREET AND PARK AVENUE

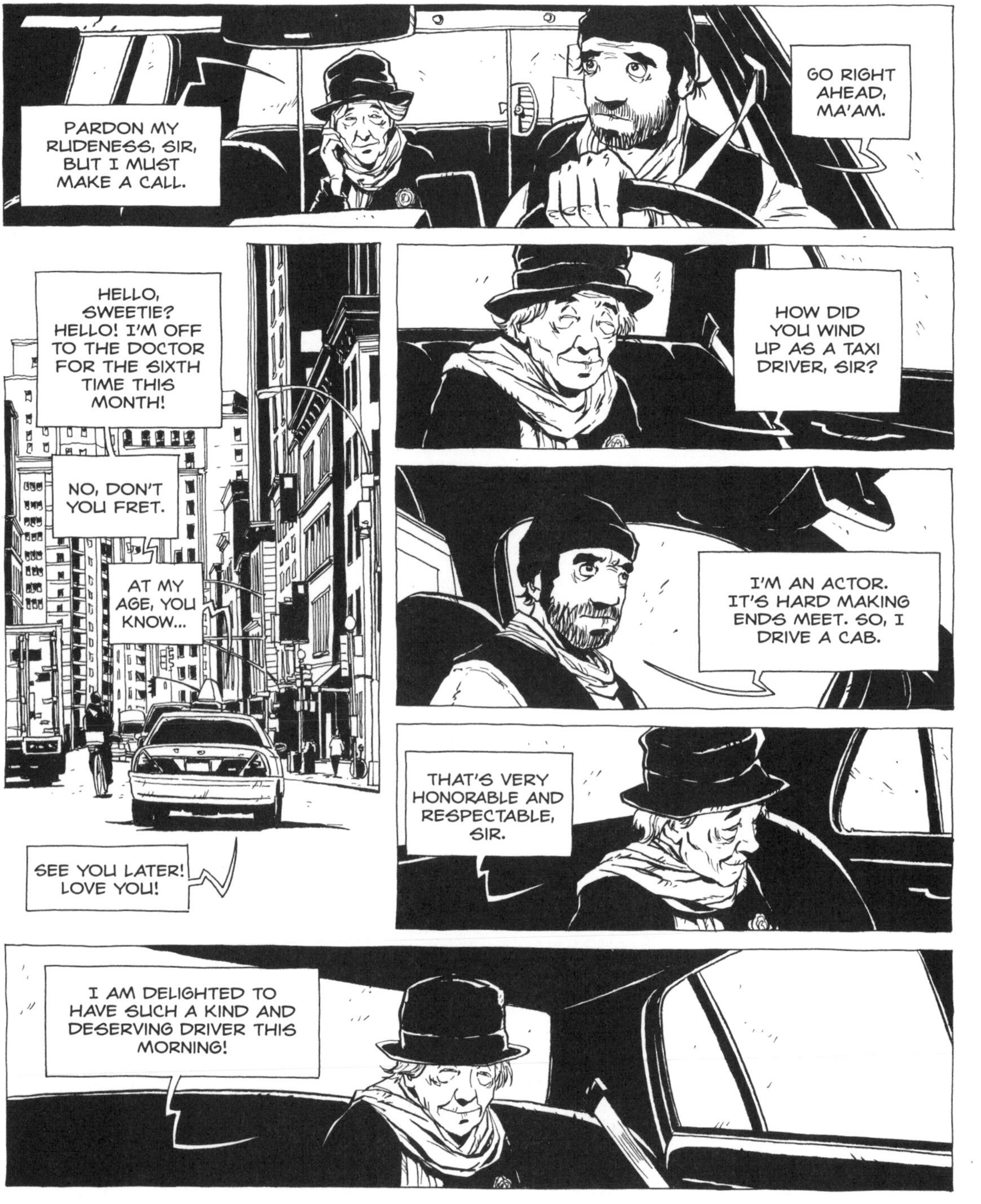
PARDON MY RUDENESS, SIR, BUT I MUST MAKE A CALL.
GO RIGHT AHEAD, MA'AM.
HELLO, SWEETIE? HELLO! I'M OFF TO THE DOCTOR FOR THE SIXTH TIME THIS MONTH!
NO, DON'T YOU FRET.
AT MY AGE, YOU KNOW...
SEE YOU LATER! LOVE YOU!
HOW DID YOU WIND UP AS A TAXI DRIVER, SIR?
I'M AN ACTOR. IT'S HARD MAKING ENDS MEET. SO, I DRIVE A CAB.
THAT'S VERY HONORABLE AND RESPECTABLE, SIR.
I AM DELIGHTED TO HAVE SUCH A KIND AND DESERVING DRIVER THIS MORNING!

A FAIRY GODMOTHER FOR MY MAIN CHARACTER: "IF YOU NEED ANYTHING AT ALL, DEAR, YOU KNOW WHERE TO FIND ME. I DON'T KNOW IF I'LL BE HERE FOR LONG, BUT SO LONG AS I AM, YOU MAY COUNT ON ME." MAYBE SOMEDAY SHE'LL COME BACK TO SEE HER. (TOO LATE?)

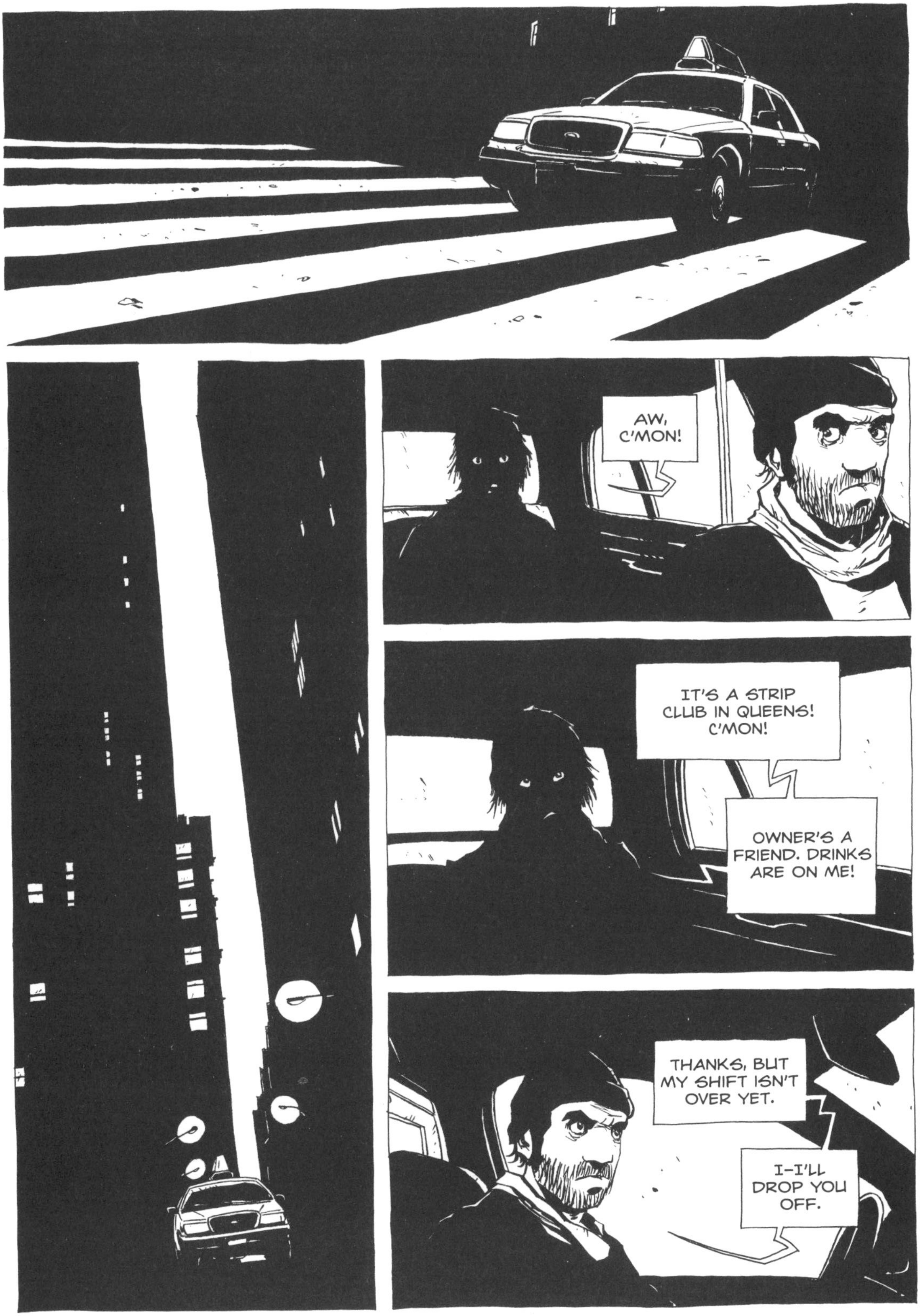
AW, C'MON!
IT'S A STRIP CLUB IN QUEENS! C'MON!
OWNER'S A FRIEND. DRINKS ARE ON ME!
THANKS, BUT MY SHIFT ISN'T OVER YET.
I-I'LL DROP YOU OFF.

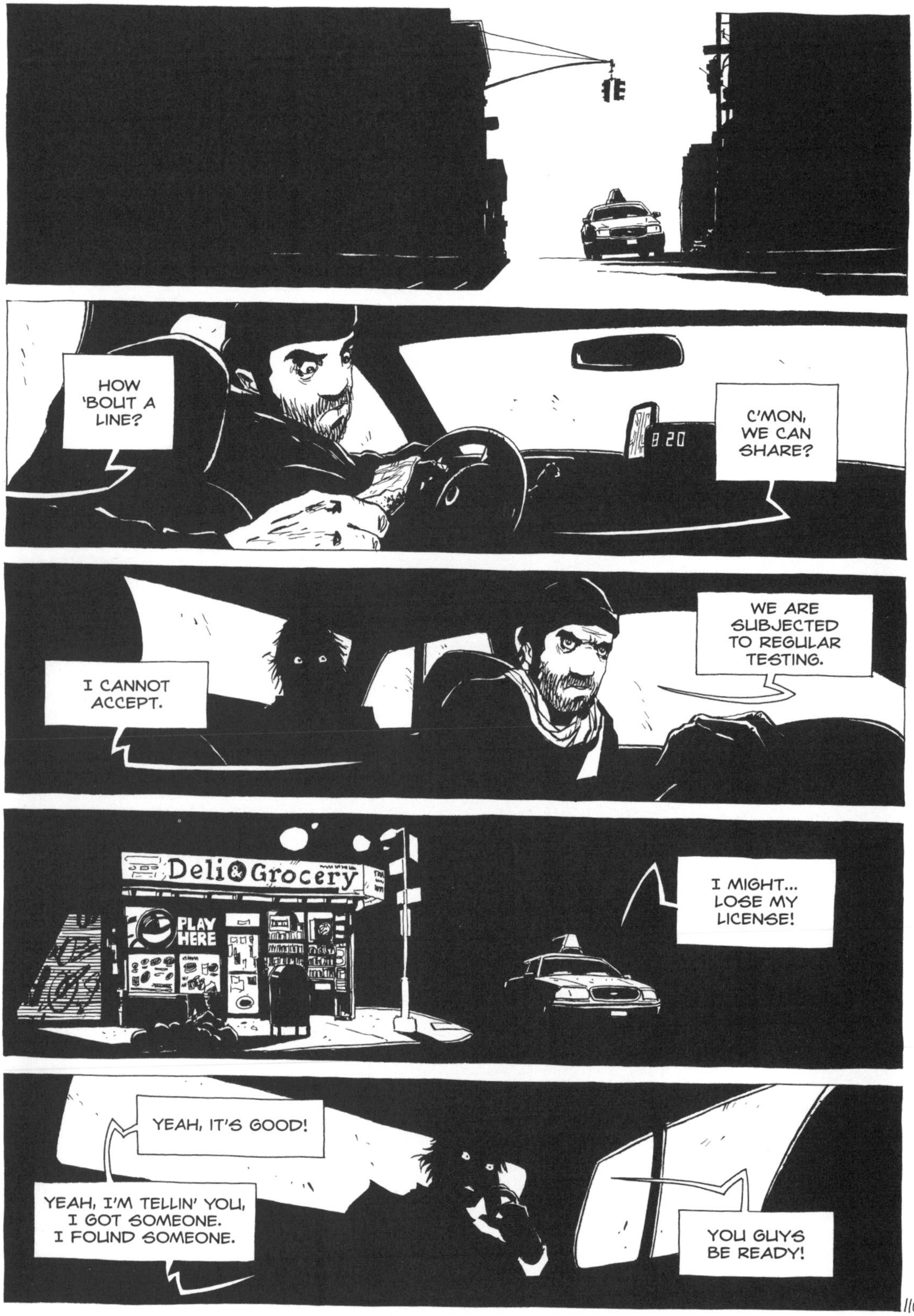
HOW 'BOUT A LINE?
8 20
C'MON, WE CAN SHARE?
I CANNOT ACCEPT.
WE ARE SUBJECTED TO REGULAR TESTING.
Deli & Grocery
PLAY HERE
I MIGHT... LOSE MY LICENSE!
YEAH, IT'S GOOD!
YEAH, I'M TELLIN' YOU, I GOT SOMEONE. I FOUND SOMEONE.
YOU GUYS BE READY!

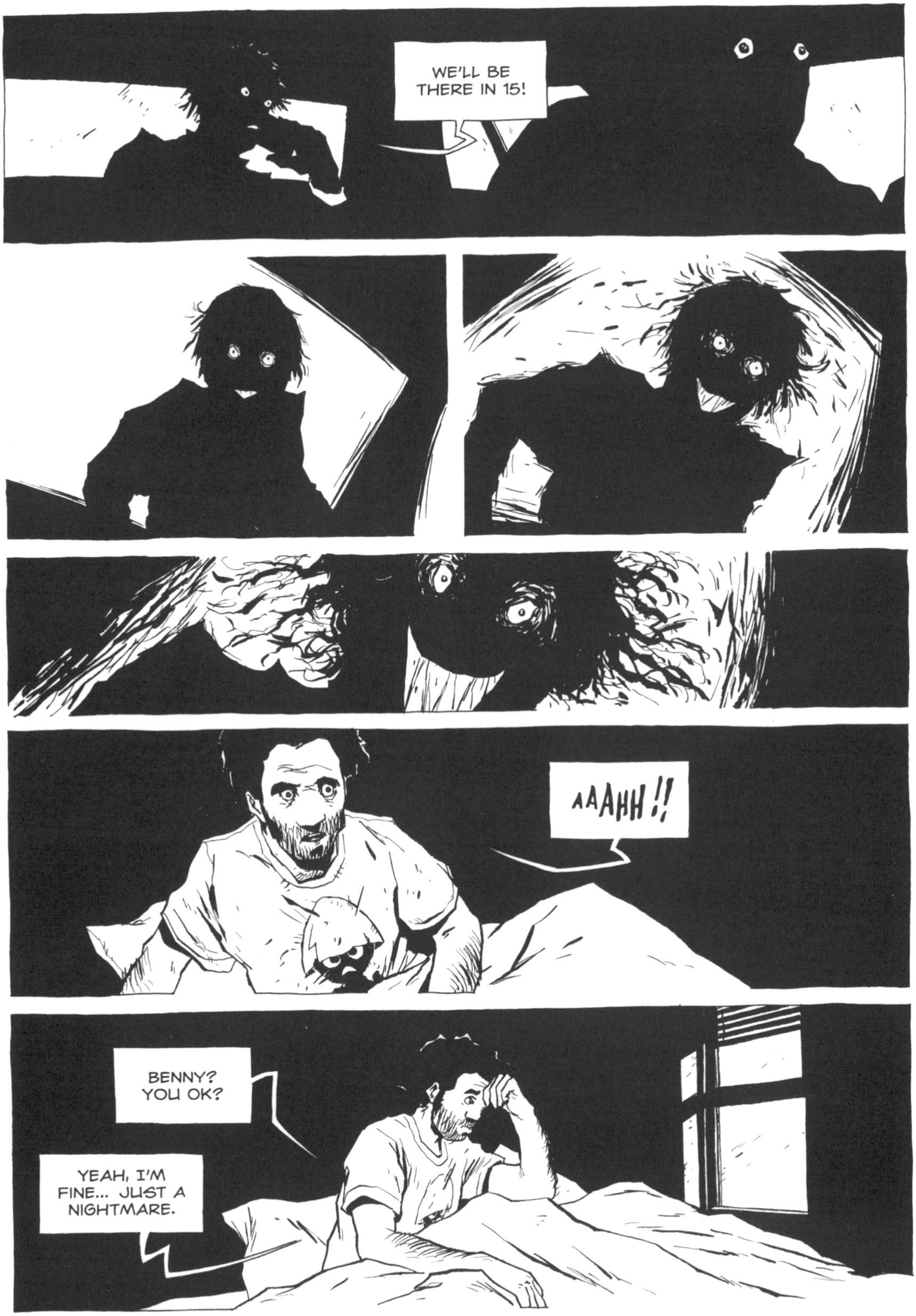
WE'LL BE THERE IN 15!
AAAHH!!
BENNY? YOU OK?
YEAH, I'M FINE... JUST A NIGHTMARE.

53RD STREET AND LEXINGTON

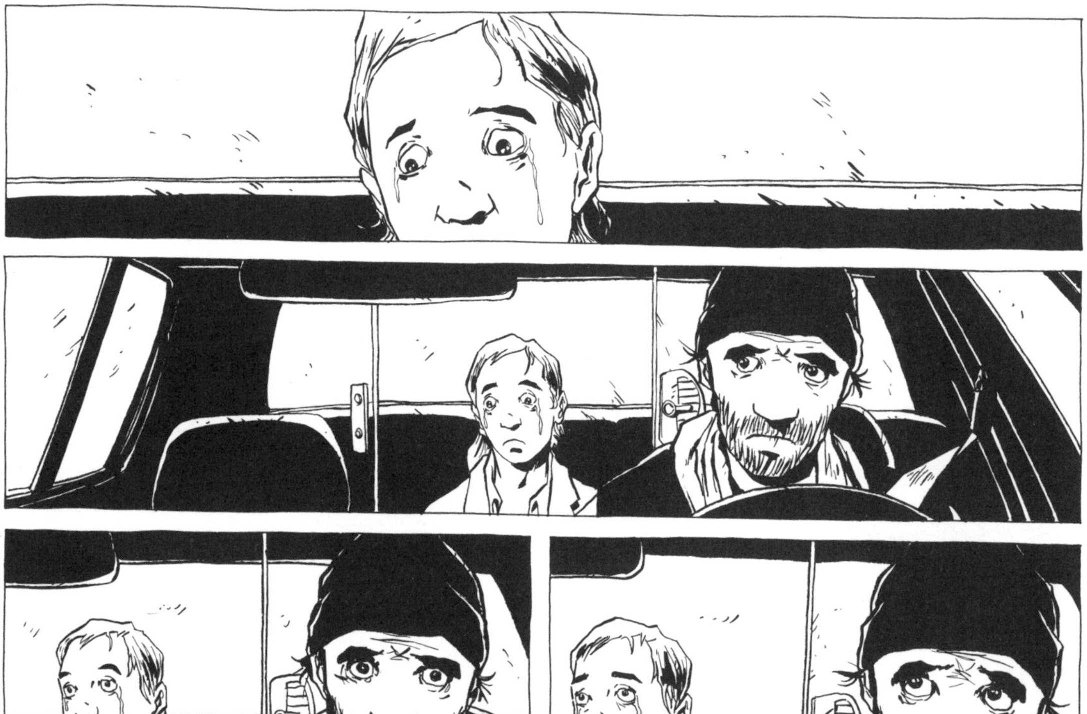

101 WEST 19TH STREET

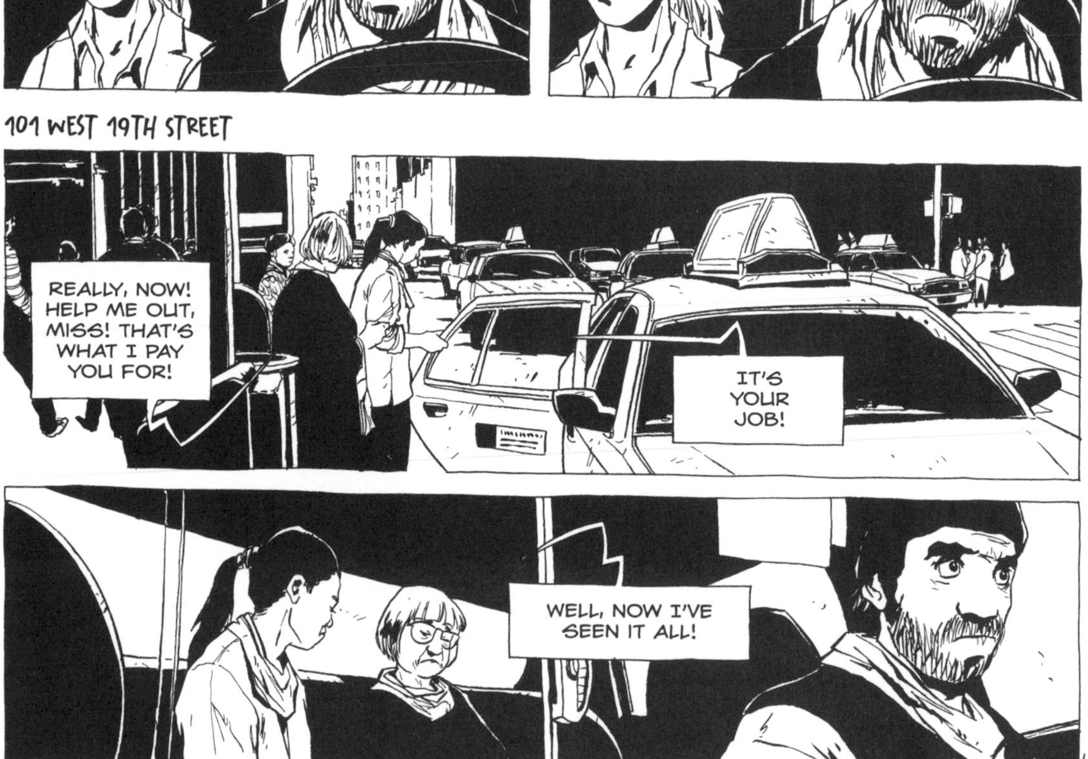
REALLY, NOW! HELP ME OUT, MISS! THAT'S WHAT I PAY YOU FOR!
IT'S YOUR JOB!
WELL, NOW I'VE SEEN IT ALL!

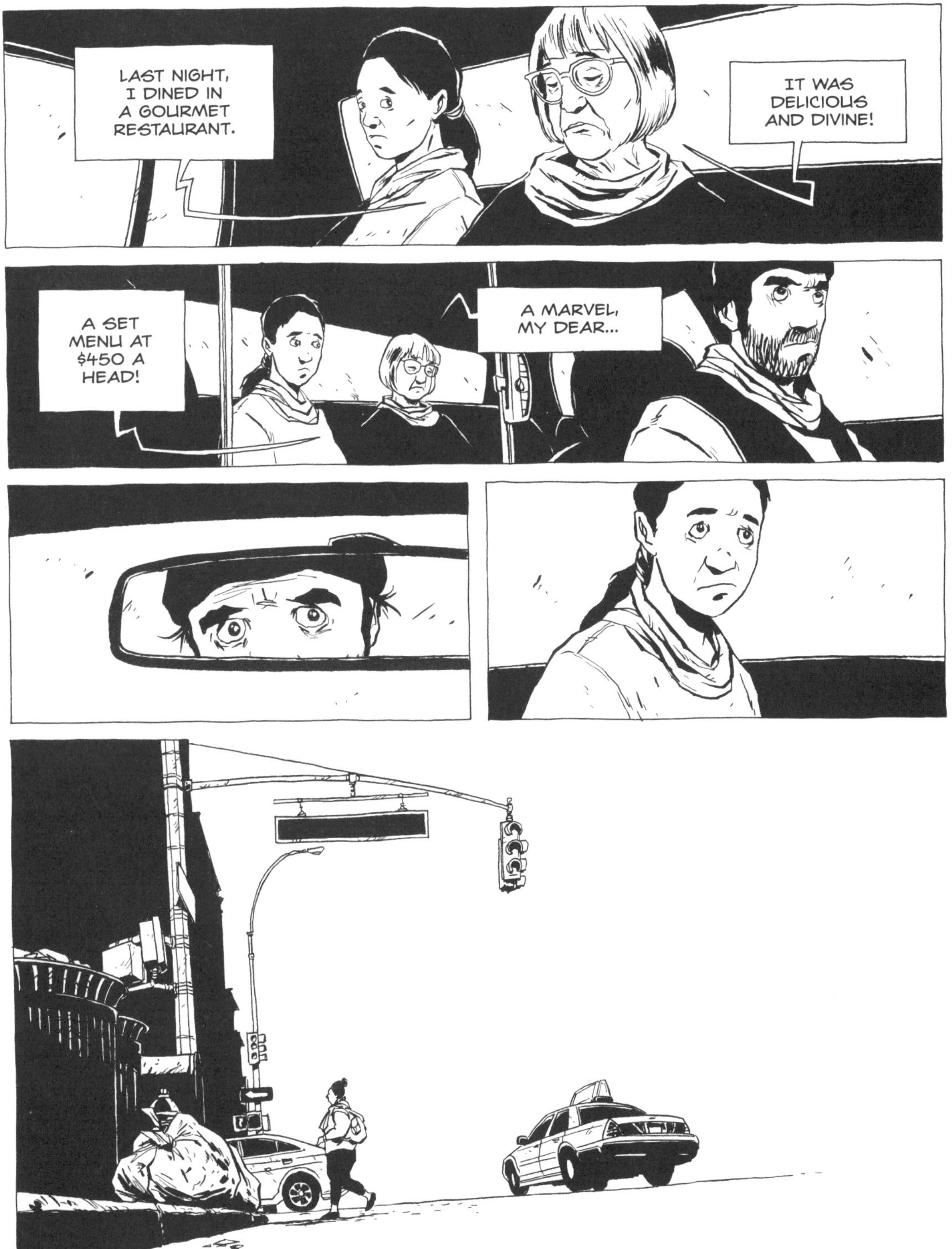
LAST NIGHT, I DINED IN A GOURMET RESTAURANT.
IT WAS DELICIOUS AND DIVINE!
A SET MENU AT $450 A HEAD!
A MARVEL, MY DEAR...

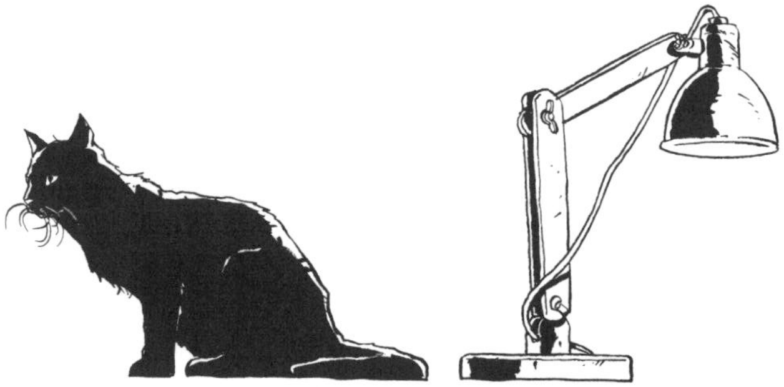

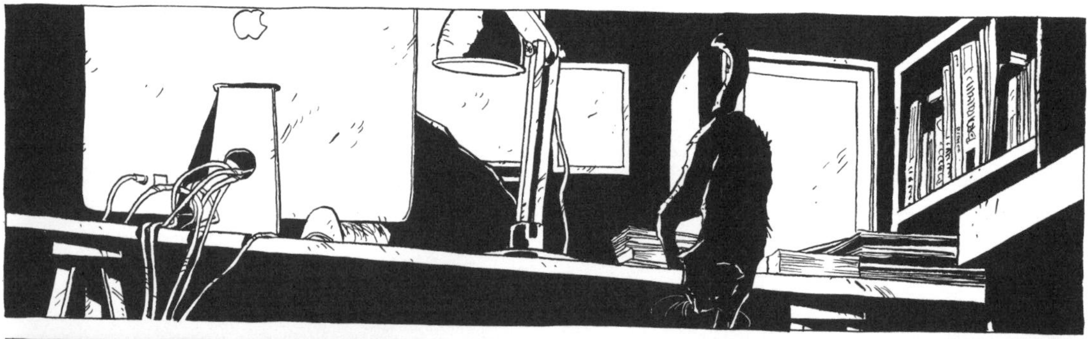

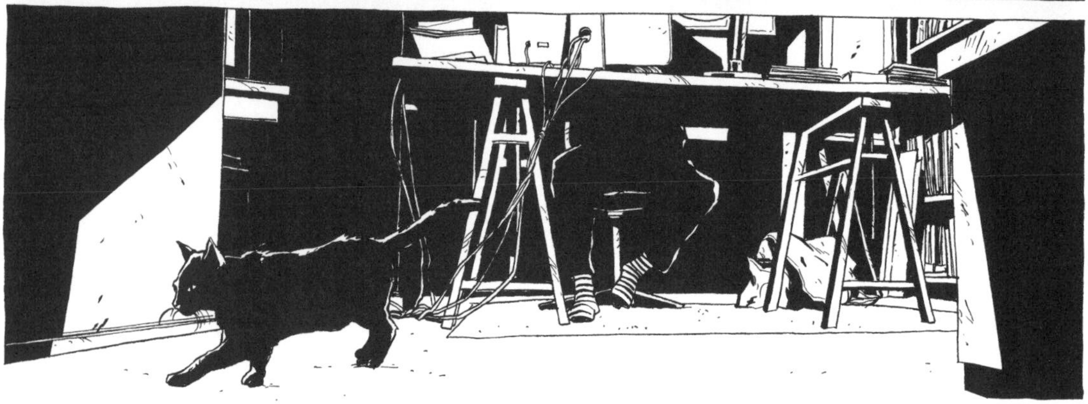

WE SPEND THE BETTER PART OF OUR LIVES SEEING PEOPLE WE KNOW.

YESTERDAY MORNING, I HAD AN ASIAN CLIENT, THEN A DUTCHMAN, THEN A MAN FROM GUINEA, AND LAST OF ALL, A SLOVAK. AROUND THE WORLD IN FOUR FARES.

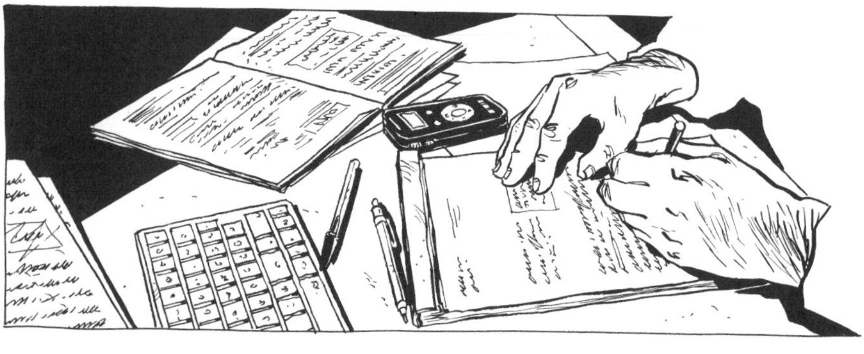

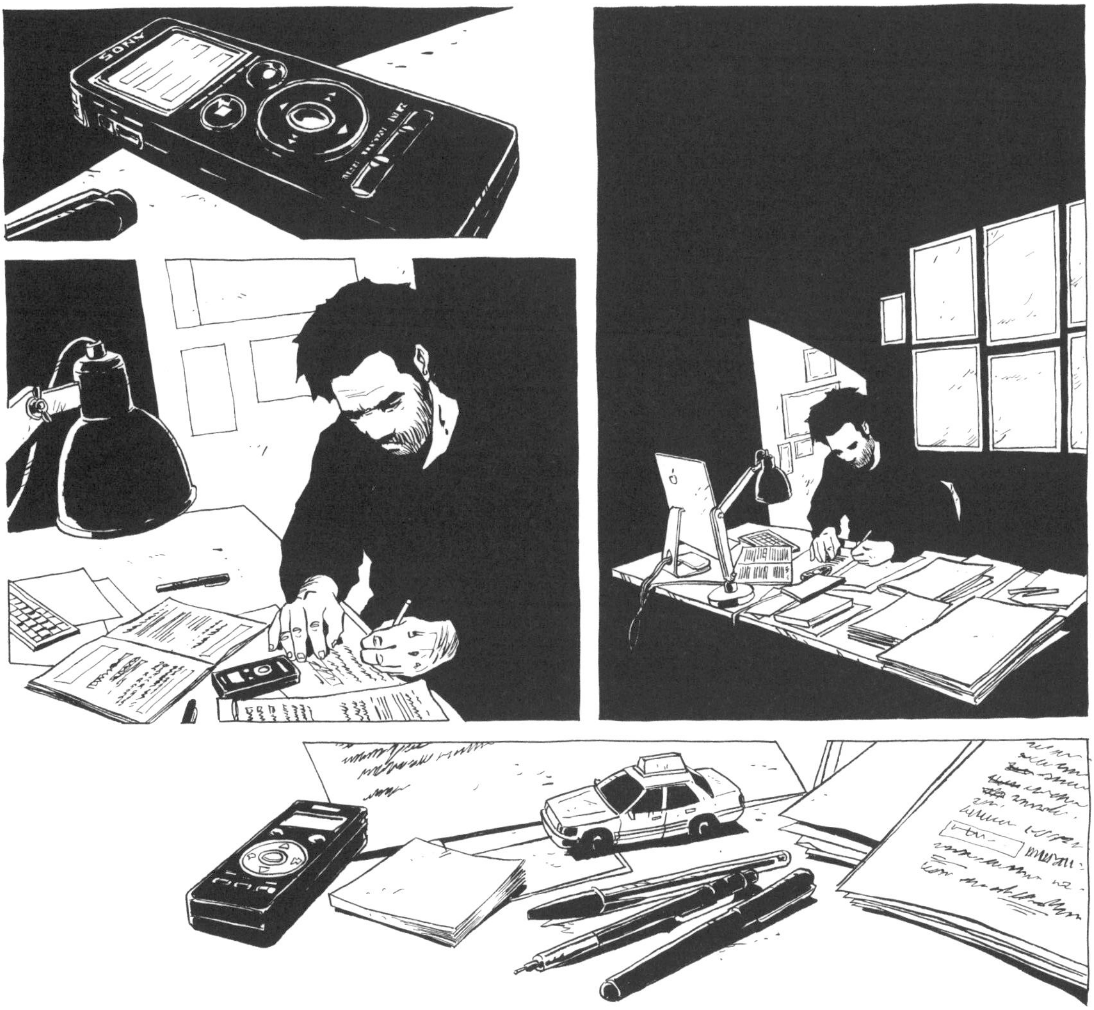

MY ADVENTURE GREATLY INTRIGUES PEOPLE WHO KNOW ME. WHAT'S THIS EXPERIENCE LIKE, LIVED DAY-TO-DAY? HOW MUCH LONGER WILL THE EXPERIMENT GO ON, AND WILL I GROW TO LIKE IT SO MUCH I'LL WANT TO KEEP GOING?

EVEN I FIND MYSELF WONDERING IF I DON'T GET MORE OUT OF RUBBING ELBOWS WITH STRANGERS ALL DAY RATHER THAN SPENDING HOURS WRITING, ALONE IN FRONT OF MY COMPUTER?

WHAT IF THIS SCREENPLAY WAS JUST AN EXCUSE?

16TH AND BROADWAY

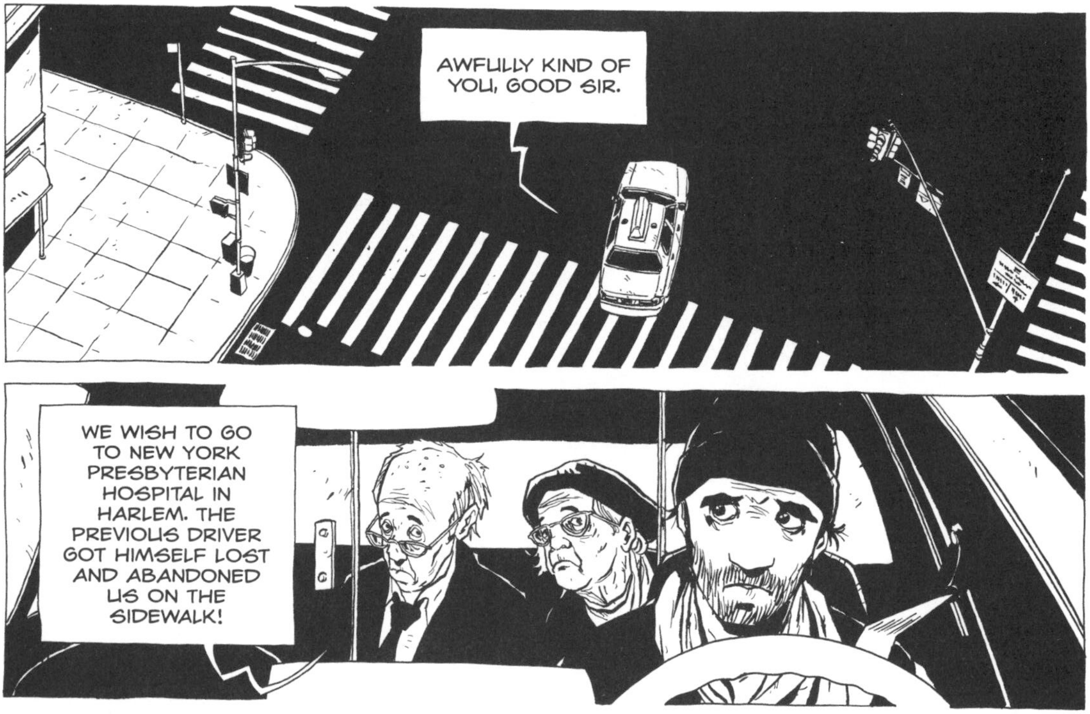
AWFULLY KIND OF YOU, GOOD SIR.
WE WISH TO GO TO NEW YORK PRESBYTERIAN HOSPITAL IN HARLEM. THE PREVIOUS DRIVER GOT HIMSELF LOST AND ABANDONED US ON THE SIDEWALK!

CANAL AND HUDSON

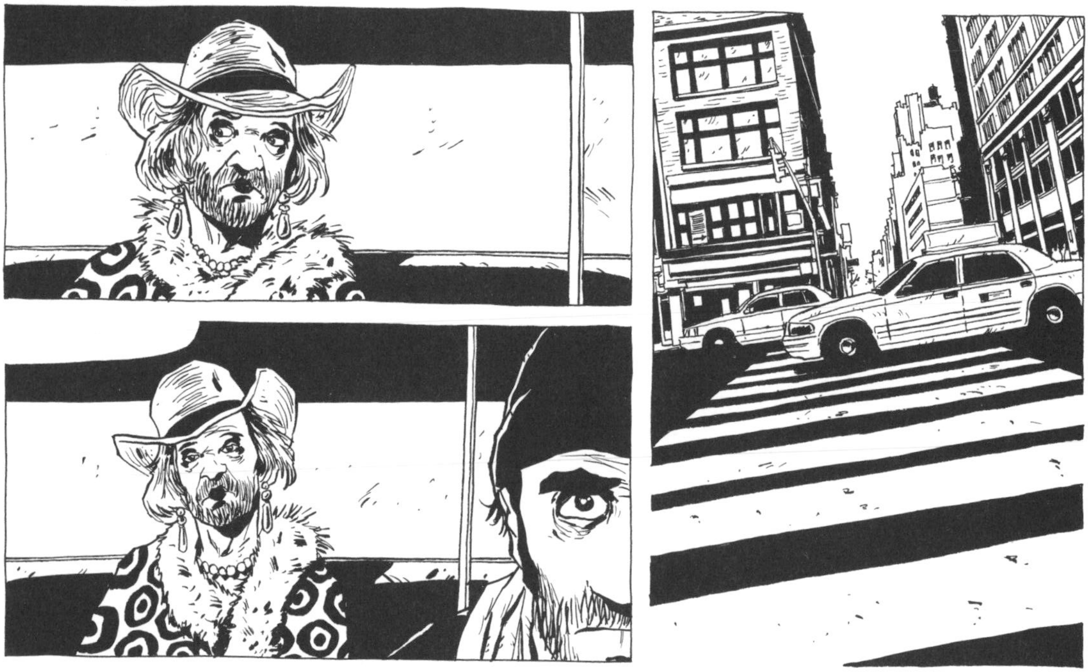

MY PROTAGONIST, THE LADY CAB DRIVER, WILL BECOME LIKE ME: SERVING A SOCIETAL FUNCTION, NOTHING MORE OR LESS, A WAY FOR PEOPLE TO GET AROUND THE CITY.

NO NAME, NO STORY, NO PAST, NO FUTURE. SHE SHOWS UP, ANONYMOUS, FOR THE LENGTH OF A RIDE. MY MOVIE COULD DEPICT THIS ERASURE IN AN ALMOST DOCUMENTARY-LIKE WAY. AN ACTRESS, WHOSE PROFESSION HAS ACCUSTOMED HER TO BEING THE CENTER OF ATTENTION, SEES HERSELF STEPPING ASIDE, THE BETTER TO REVEAL OTHERS: NEW YORKERS, ALL THOSE STRANGERS STEALING HER SPOTLIGHT. THEY'RE THE ONES DOING THE TALKING, TELLING THEIR STORIES, SHOWING THEIR TRUE SELVES ON THE WAY FROM POINT A TO POINT B, DOORSTEP TO JOB, HOSPITAL TO PARENTS' APARTMENT, LIKE SO MANY FICTIONS COMING INTO BEING...

GREENWICH AND WEST 12TH

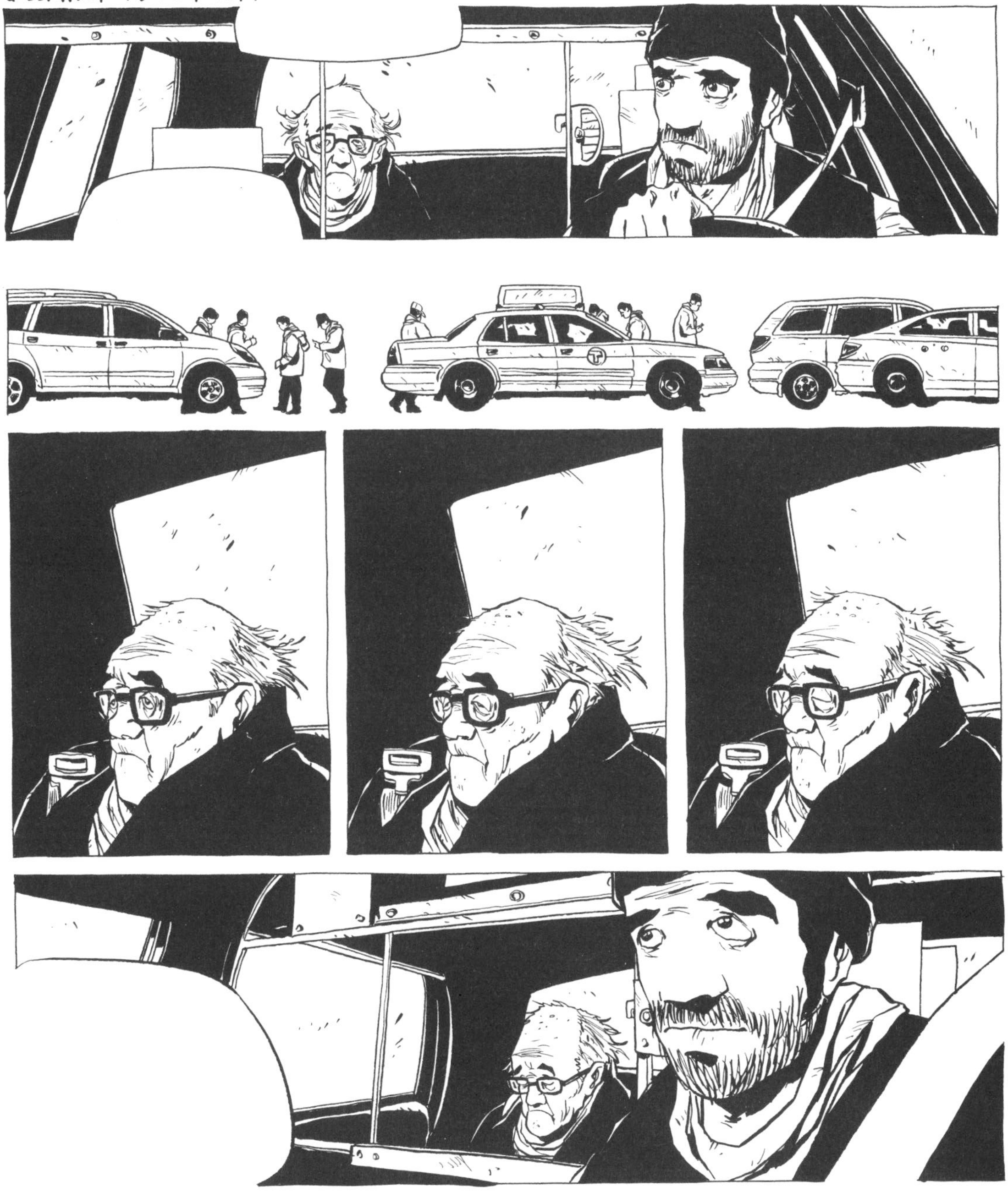

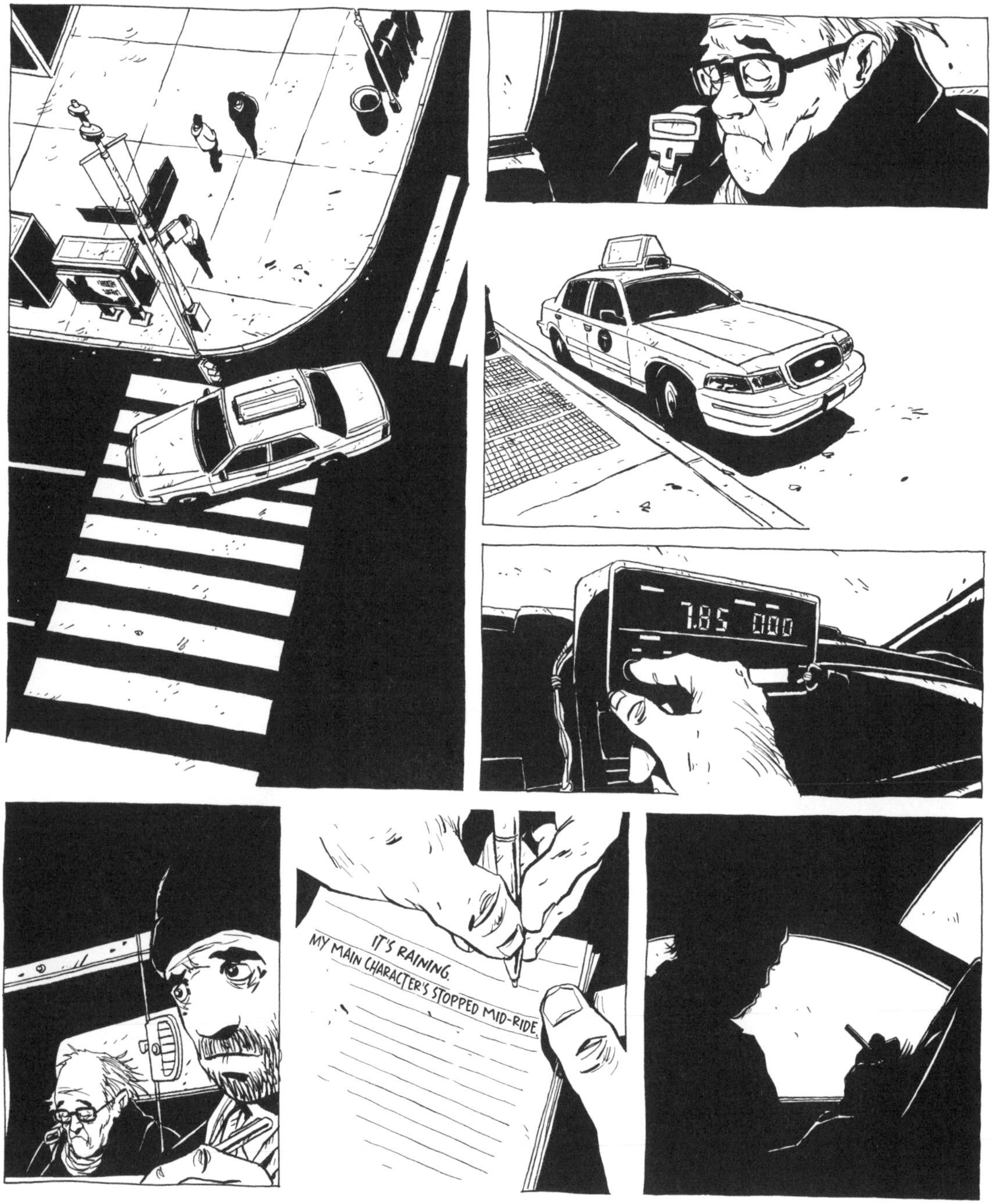
7.85 0.00
IT'S RAINING.
MY MAIN CHARACTER'S STOPPED MID-RIDE.

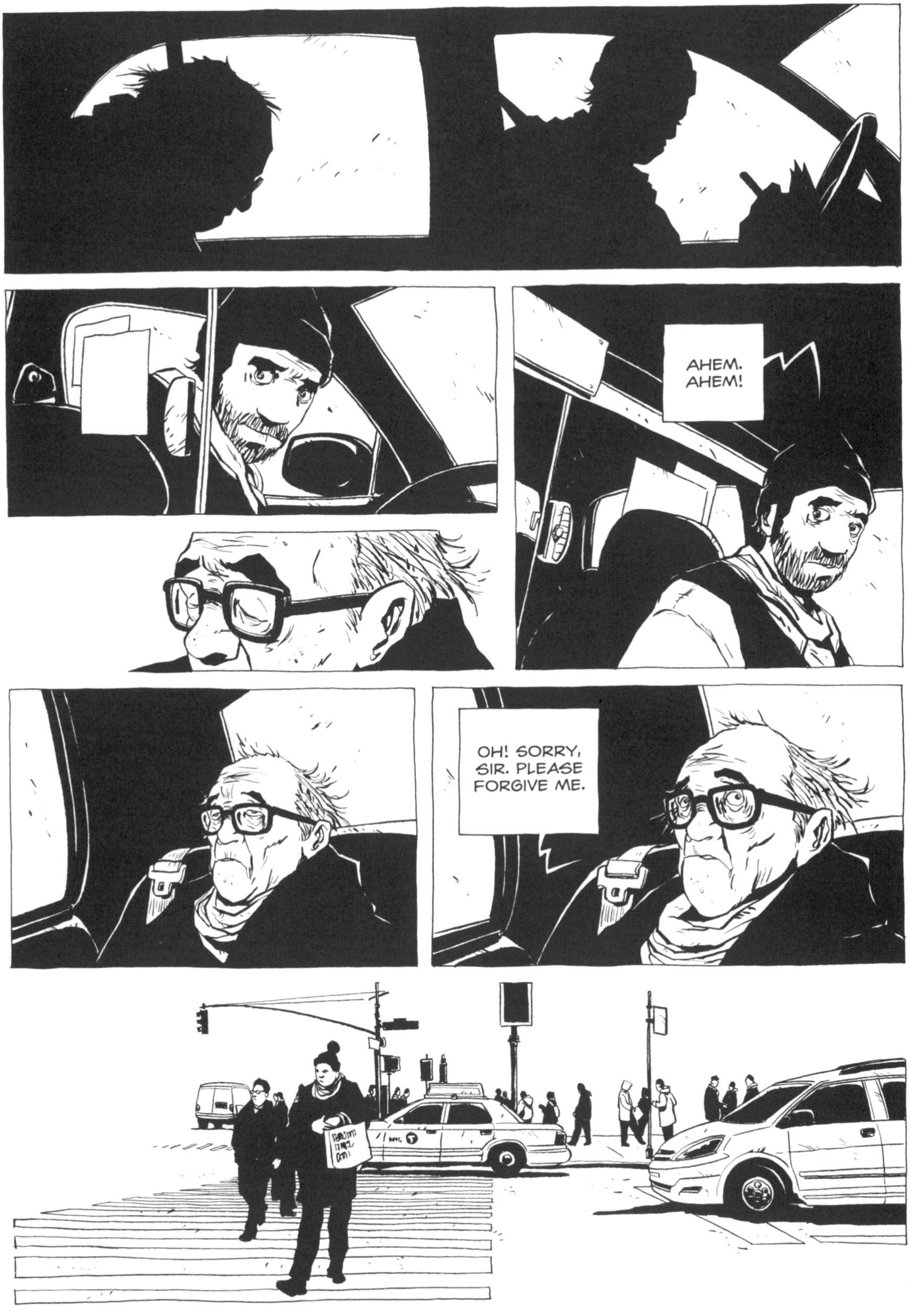
AHEM. AHEM!
OH! SORRY, SIR. PLEASE FORGIVE ME.

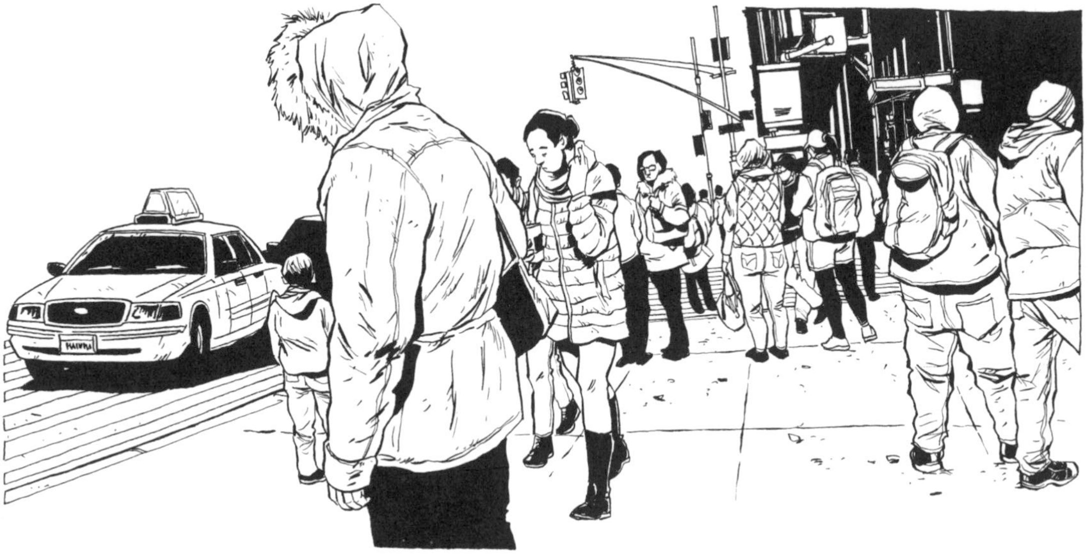

IT'S RAINING. MY MAIN CHARACTER'S STOPPED MID-RIDE AT A RED LIGHT WHEN A GUY OPENS THE BACK DOOR AND, IN A STRONG FRENCH ACCENT, TELLS HER AND HER FARE THAT HIS WIFE'S ABOUT TO HAVE A BABY, THAT SHE'S BEEN WAITING WHILE HE'S BEEN TRYING TO HAIL A CAB FOR THE LAST TWENTY MINUTES. HE'S DESPERATE. HE ASKS HER FARE IF HE'D BE WILLING TO TRADE PLACES. NATURALLY, HE'LL PAY OFF WHAT'S ON THE METER SO FAR. THE PASSENGER HESITATES FOR A MOMENT, THEN SAYS YES. THE TAXI DRIVES OFF, AND THE NEW PASSENGER BURSTS OUT LAUGHING. HE SAYS THAT'S WHAT HE DOES WHENEVER HE CAN'T FIND A CAB. SOMETIMES HE SAYS HIS MOM'S ON HER DEATHBED, OR HIS YOUNG SON'S LOCKED OUT OF THEIR BUILDING, IN TEARS. IT NEVER FAILS. MY PROTAGONIST THROWS HIM OUT OF THE CAB.

THE INCIDENT MAKES HER THINK. SHE FINDS HERSELF FACING HER OWN CONTRADICTIONS. DOESN'T SHE SPEND ALL HER TIME LYING TO HER FARES? FROM THAT MOMENT ON, SHE DECIDES TO TELL THE TRUTH AND CONFRONT HER OWN REALITY, SHOULDER THE WEIGHT OF THE PAST SHE'S ALWAYS SHRUGGED OFF TILL NOW...

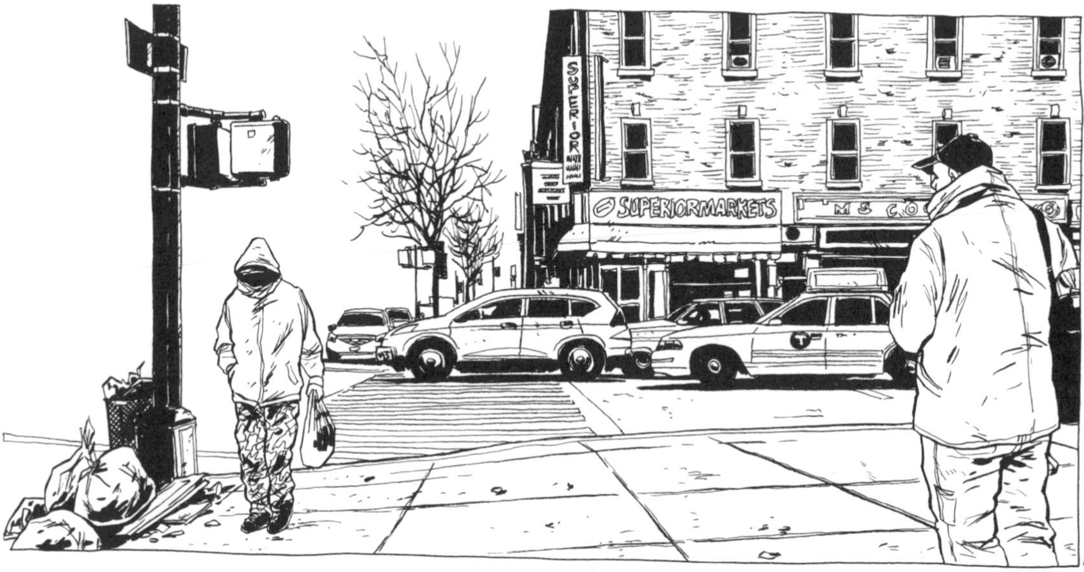
SUPERIOR
SUPERIORMARKETS

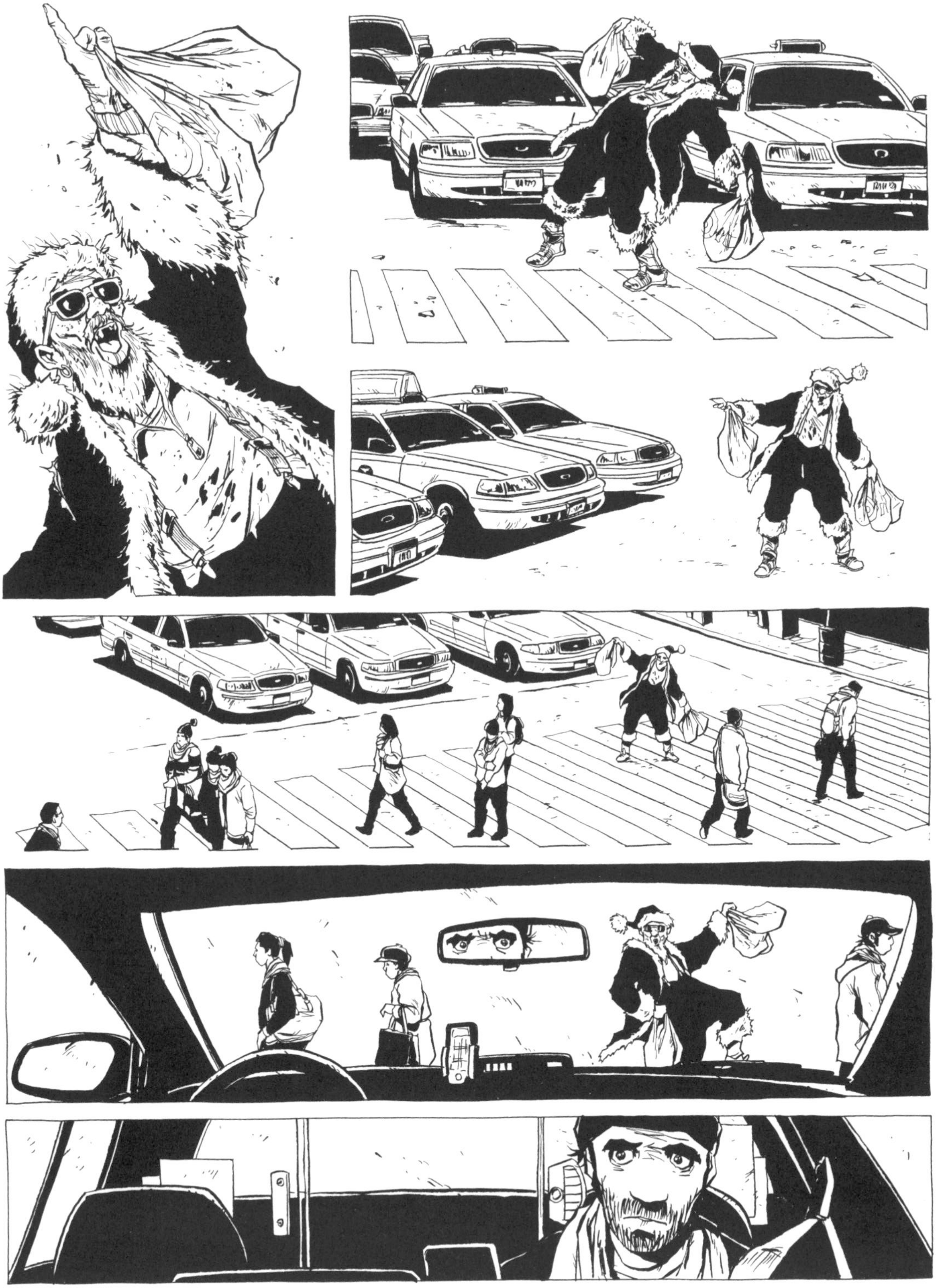

THERE'S A KEEPER FOR THE FILM!

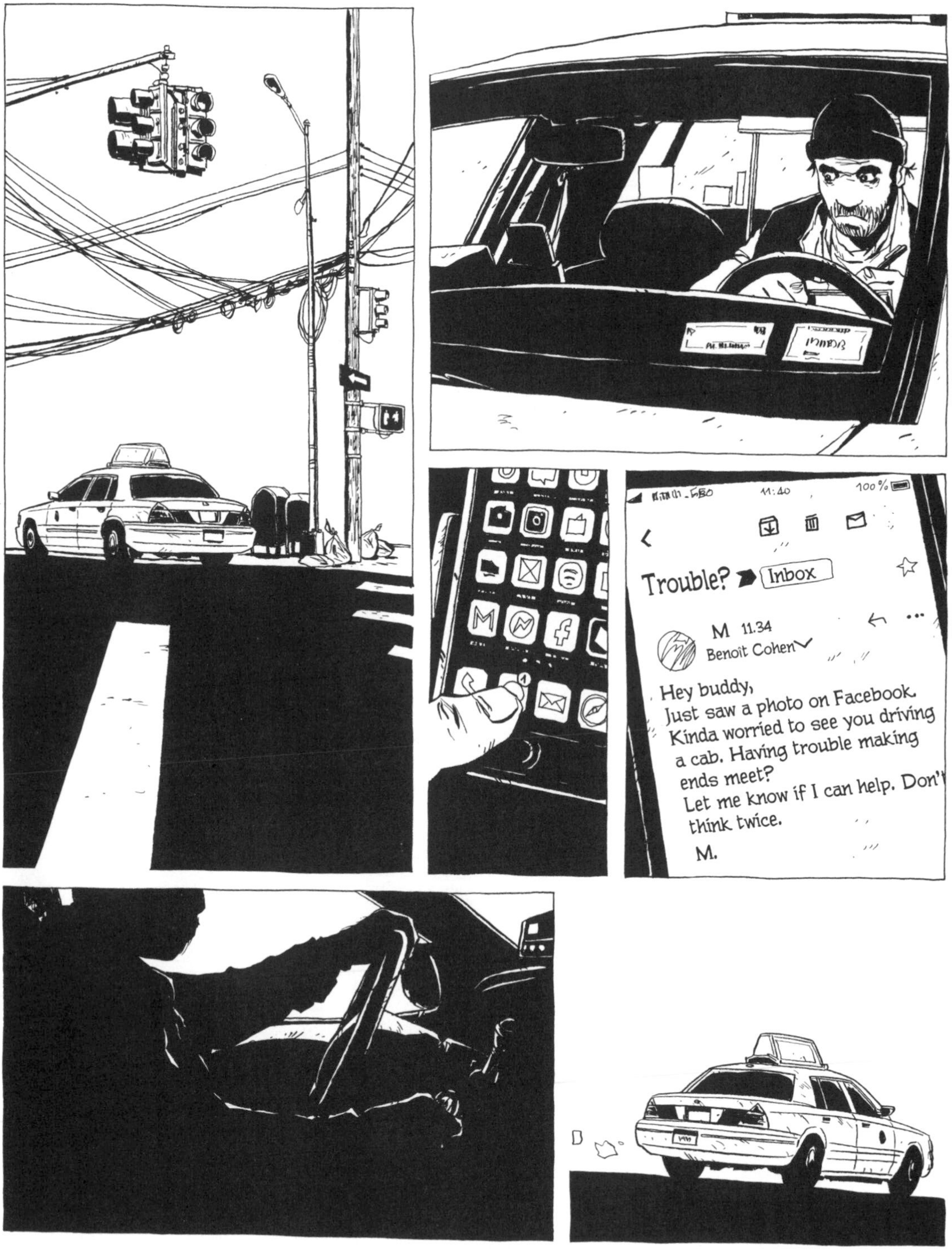
11:40
100%
Trouble? Inbox
M 11.34
Benoit Cohen
Hey buddy,
Just saw a photo on Facebook.
Kinda worried to see you driving a cab. Having trouble making ends meet?
Let me know if I can help. Don't think twice.
M.

WILL MY MAIN CHARACTER ALSO BE FOUND OUT? BY CHANCE, BY SOMEONE FROM HER OLD LIFE? WILL SHE CLAIM IT'S ALL FOR HER ART, LIKE I DO? OR IS SHE GOING METHOD TO PREP FOR A ROLE? IN WHAT FILM?

55TH STREET AND 5TH AVENUE

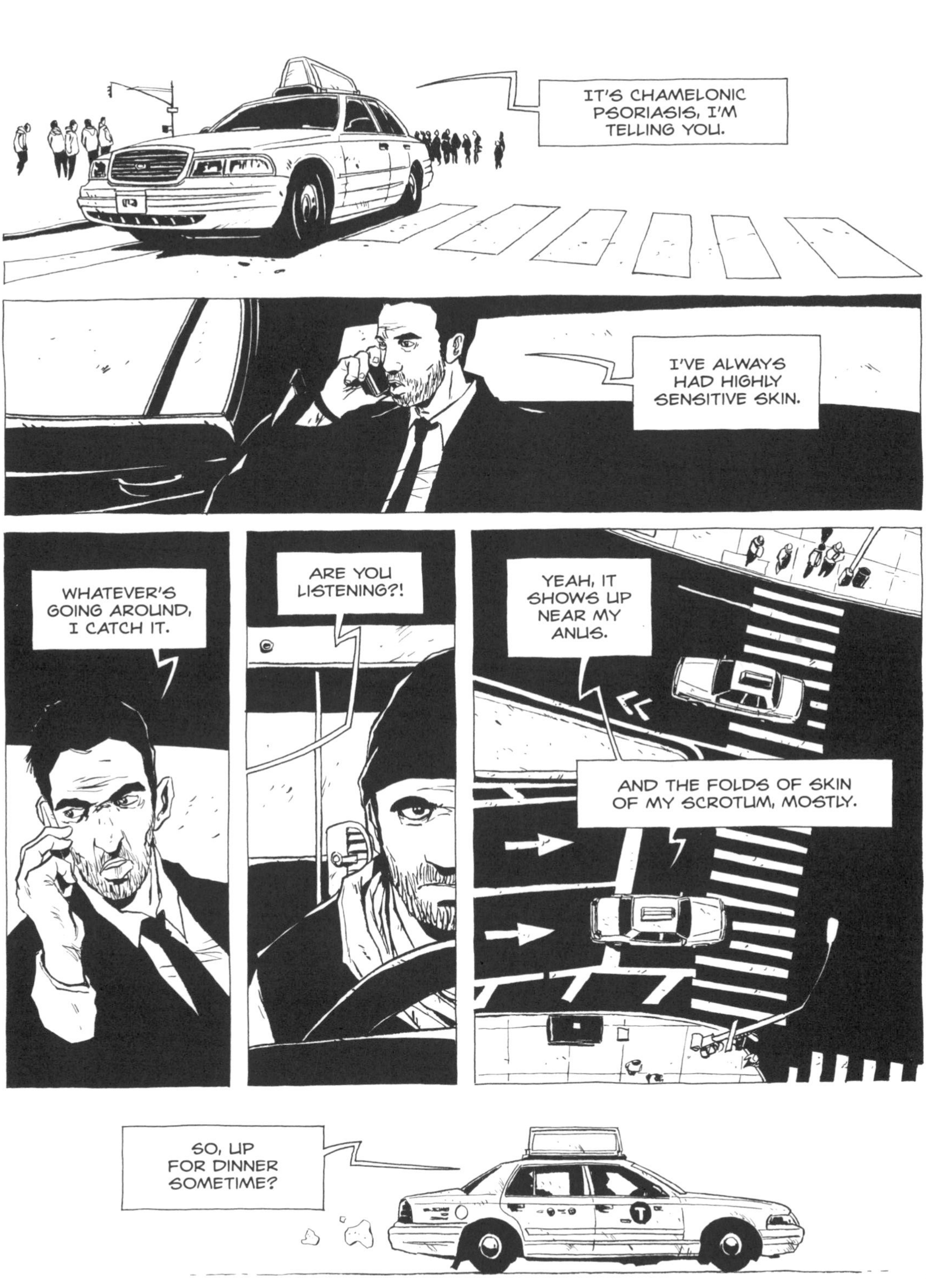
IT'S CHAMELONIC PSORIASIS, I'M TELLING YOU.
I'VE ALWAYS HAD HIGHLY SENSITIVE SKIN.
WHATEVER'S GOING AROUND, I CATCH IT.
ARE YOU LISTENING?!
YEAH, IT SHOWS UP NEAR MY ANUS.
AND THE FOLDS OF SKIN OF MY SCROTUM, MOSTLY.
SO, UP FOR DINNER SOMETIME?

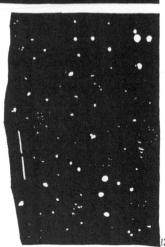

85TH STREET AND MADISON AVENUE

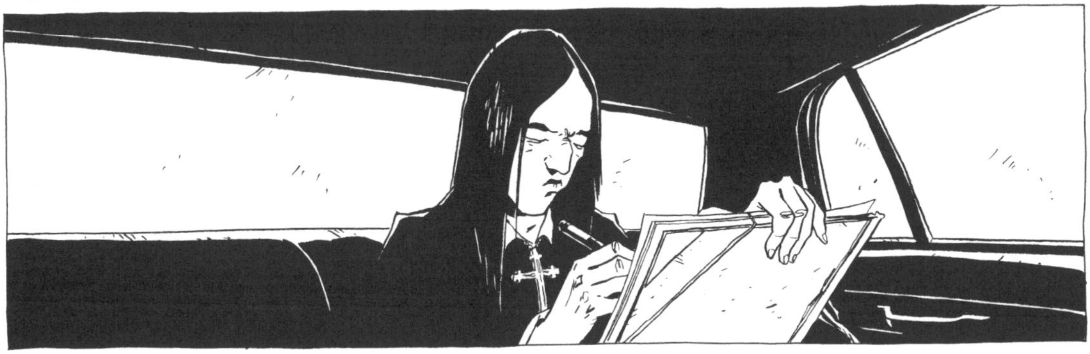

50TH STREET AND PARK AVENUE

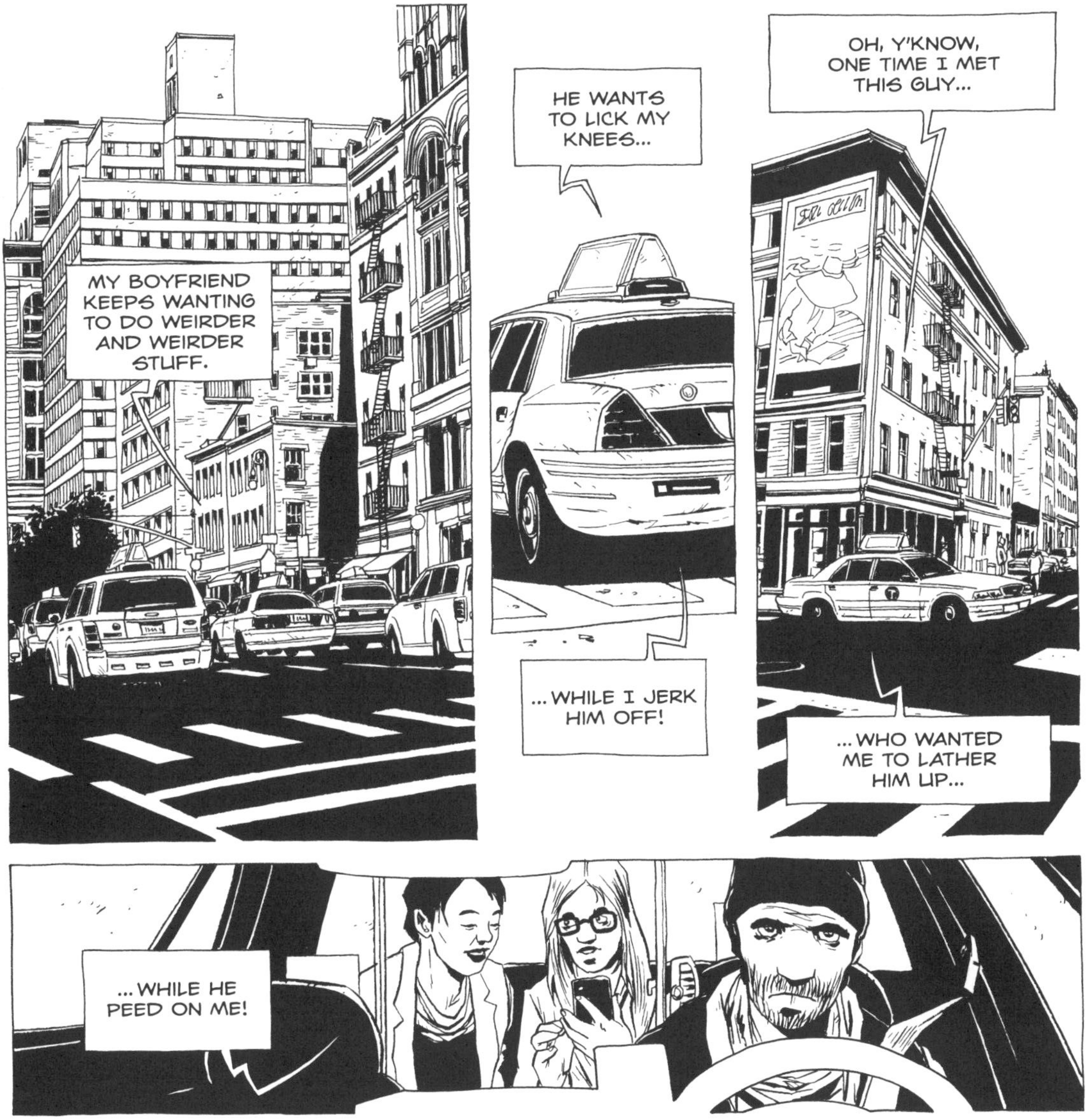
MY BOYFRIEND KEEPS WANTING TO DO WEIRDER AND WEIRDER STUFF.
HE WANTS TO LICK MY KNEES...
...WHILE I JERK HIM OFF!
OH, Y'KNOW, ONE TIME I MET THIS GUY...
...WHO WANTED ME TO LATHER HIM UP...
...WHILE HE PEED ON ME!

18TH STREET AND 6TH AVENUE

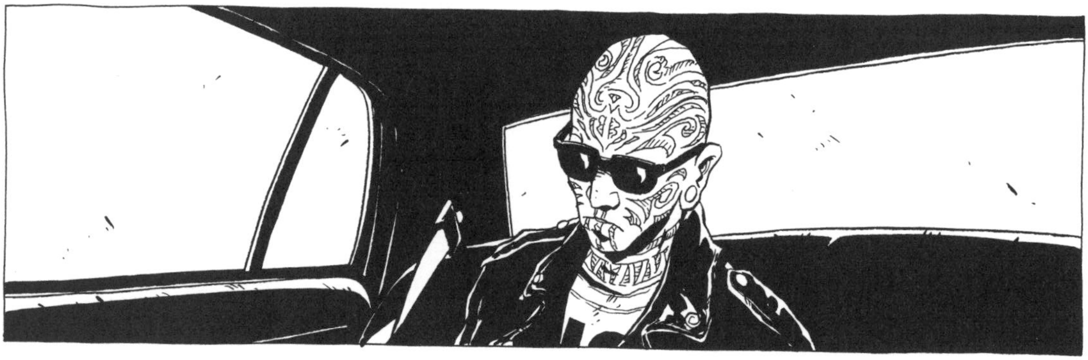

SOME DAYS, MY PROTAGONIST GETS SICK OF IT ALL. SICK OF THE TRAFFIC. SICK OF OTHER DRIVERS. SICK OF HER FARES. SICK OF DOORMEN WOLF-WHISTLING AT HER, SICK OF THE MERCILESS CITY GRINDING HER UNDERFOOT. I WANT TO SHOOT A SCENE WHERE SHE SEEKS SOLACE AT ROCKAWAY BEACH, THE LAST STOP ON THE A TRAIN.

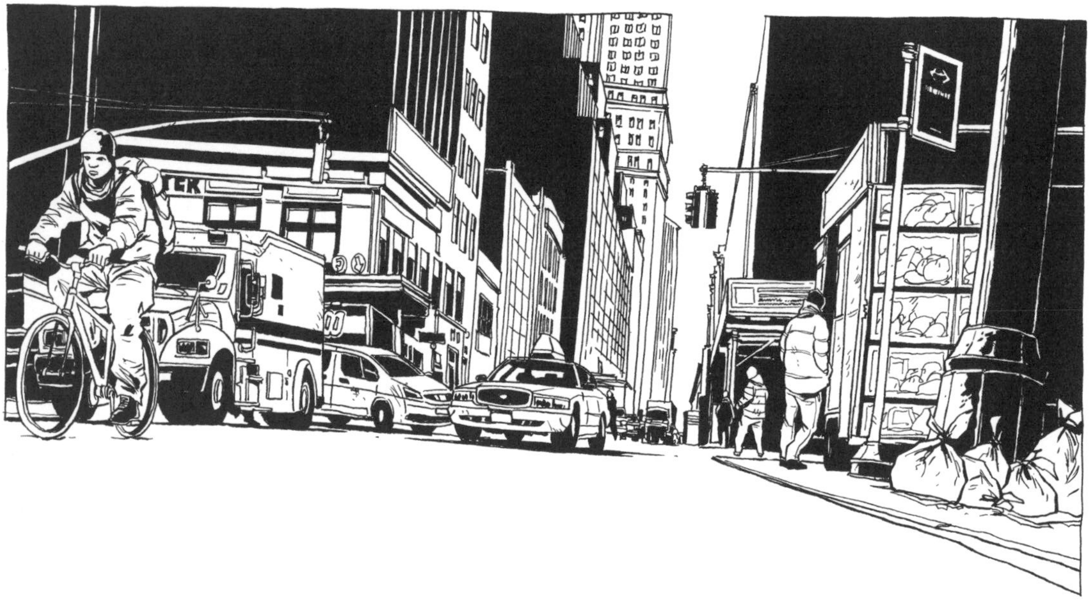

85TH STREET AND MADISON AVENUE

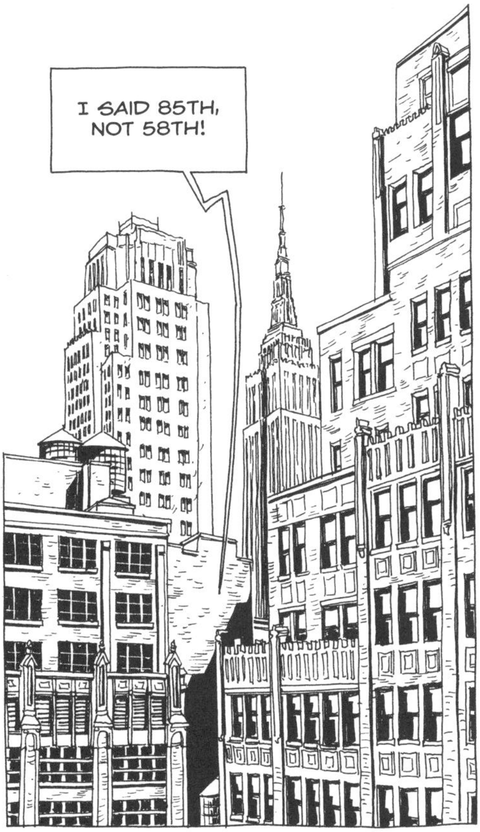
I SAID 85TH, NOT 58TH!

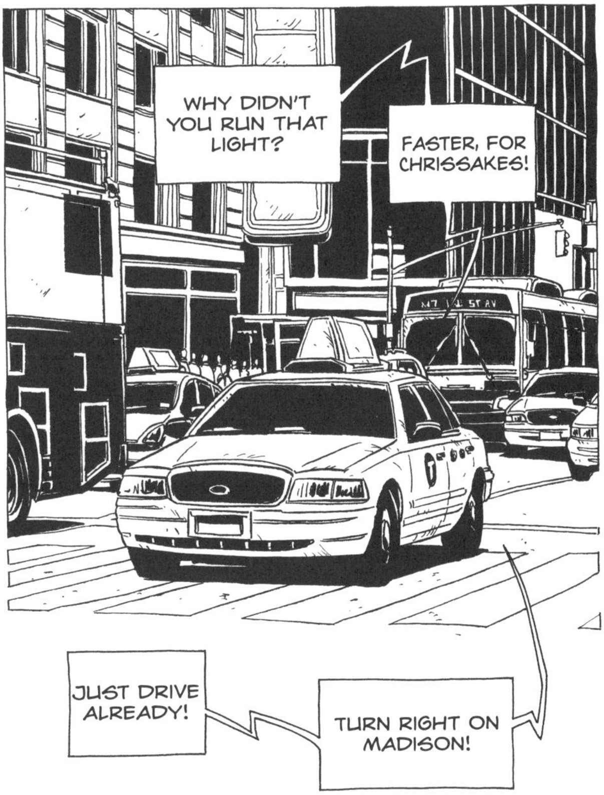
WHY DIDN'T YOU RUN THAT LIGHT?
FASTER, FOR CHRISSAKES!
JUST DRIVE ALREADY!
TURN RIGHT ON MADISON!

35TH AND BROADWAY

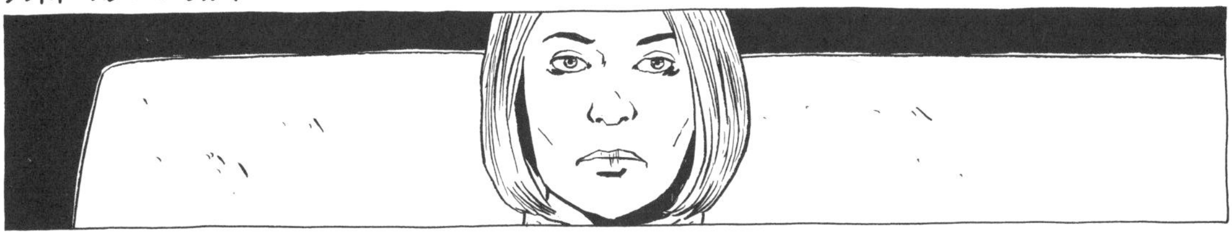

COLUMBIA HOSPITAL (165TH AND BROADWAY)

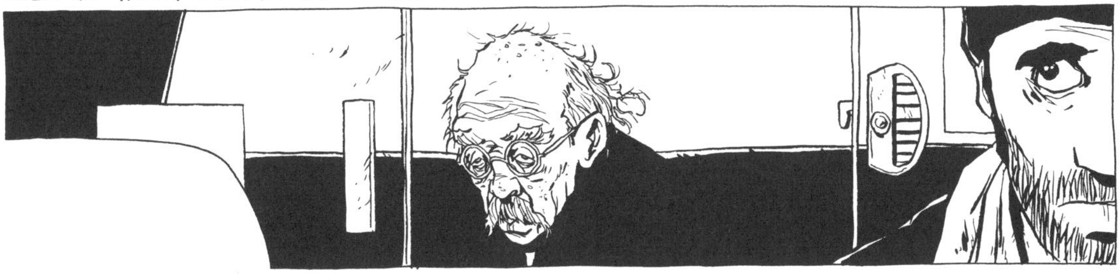

WHAT'S HE GOING TO THE HOSPITAL FOR?
POSSIBLE DIALOGUE FOR THE FILM: "HOW ARE YOU DOING TODAY?"
"NOT GREAT. I'M GOING TO DIE."

BEEKMAN STREET AND SOUTH STREET

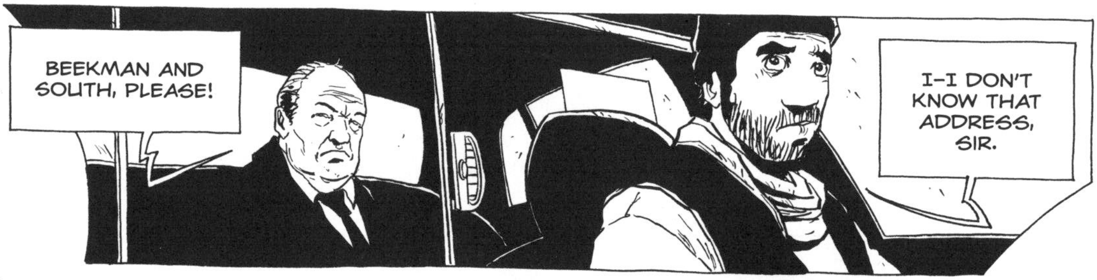
BEEKMAN AND SOUTH, PLEASE!
I-I DON'T KNOW THAT ADDRESS, SIR.

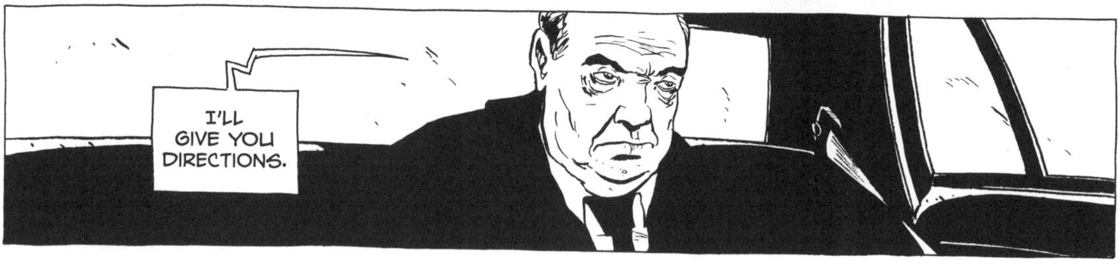
I'LL GIVE YOU DIRECTIONS.

AS I LISTEN TO THE MAN'S DIRECTIONS, I REALIZE I'M AN IMPOSTOR...

PRETENDING TO BE A TAXI DRIVER WHEN I DON'T REALLY KNOW THIS CITY AND HAVE TO RELY ON MY GPS MOST OF THE TIME TO GET MY FARES WHERE THEY WANT TO GO. BUT ISN'T THAT TRUE OF MOST DRIVERS I'VE RUN INTO ALONG THE WAY? LIKE ME, THEY SHOW UP FROM HALFWAY AROUND THE WORLD, AND AFTER A FEW HOURS OF TRAINING FIND THEMSELVES NAVIGATING THIS SPRAWLING METROPOLIS THEY KNOW ABSOLUTELY NOTHING ABOUT BECAUSE, UNLIKE ME, THEY'VE NEVER SET FOOT HERE BEFORE. SOME HAVE BEEN AT THIS FOR SEVERAL YEARS NOW AND HAVE A GOOD HANDLE ON THINGS (ESPECIALLY THOSE FROM BEFORE GPS), BUT ALL THE NEWBIES ARE IN THE SAME BOAT. THE ONLY THING THAT REALLY SETS ME APART FROM THEM IS THAT I DON'T NEED THIS JOB TO EARN A LIVING. SHOULD I FEEL GUILTY ABOUT TAKING A SPOT AWAY FROM SOMEONE WHO REALLY NEEDS IT? I NEED TO GO THROUGH THIS TO DO MY JOB AND WRITE A SCREENPLAY. IN THE END, I NEED TO EARN A LIVING TOO.

"EARN A LIVING." I'VE NEVER REALLY GIVEN THE EXPRESSION MUCH THOUGHT BEFORE, AND IT FEELS PARTICULARLY WELL-SUITED TO HOW I FEEL WHEN I'M DRIVING A CAB.

I'M EARNING A NEW LIFE, LIKE IN A VIDEO GAME.

208 CANAL STREET

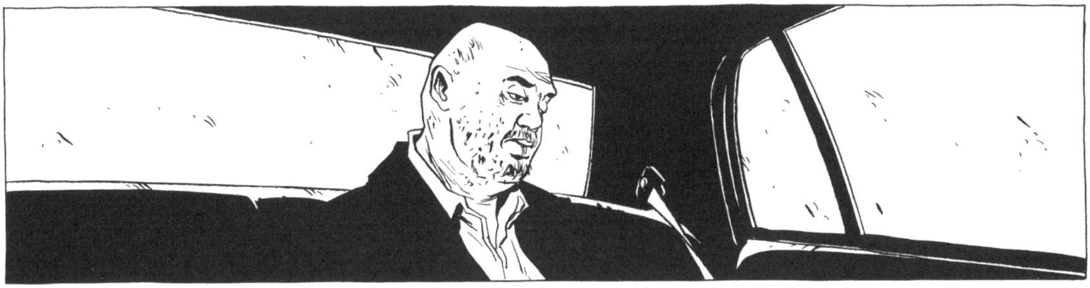

AVENUE B AND 11TH STREET

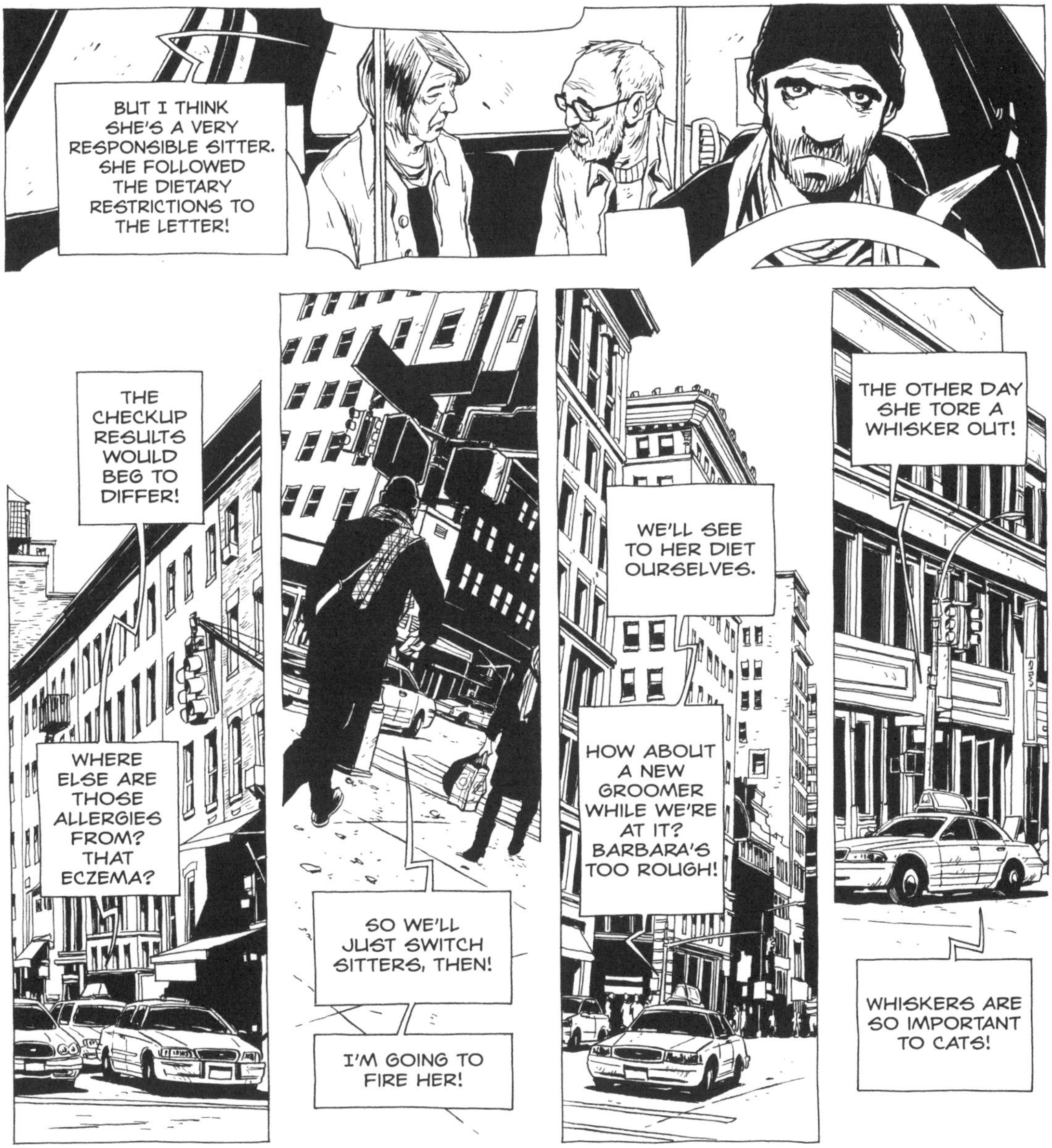
BUT I THINK SHE'S A VERY RESPONSIBLE SITTER. SHE FOLLOWED THE DIETARY RESTRICTIONS TO THE LETTER!
THE CHECKUP RESULTS WOULD BEG TO DIFFER!
WHERE ELSE ARE THOSE ALLERGIES FROM? THAT ECZEMA?
SO WE'LL JUST SWITCH SITTERS, THEN!
I'M GOING TO FIRE HER!
WE'LL SEE TO HER DIET OURSELVES.
HOW ABOUT A NEW GROOMER WHILE WE'RE AT IT? BARBARA'S TOO ROUGH!
THE OTHER DAY SHE TORE A WHISKER OUT!
WHISKERS ARE SO IMPORTANT TO CATS!

57TH STREET AND 6TH AVENUE

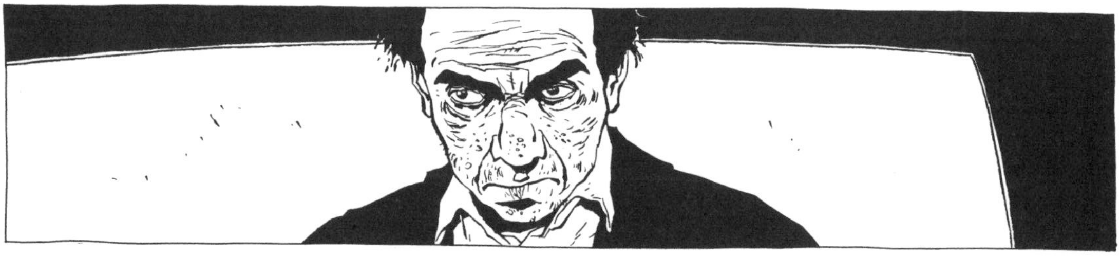

57TH STREET AND 7TH AVENUE

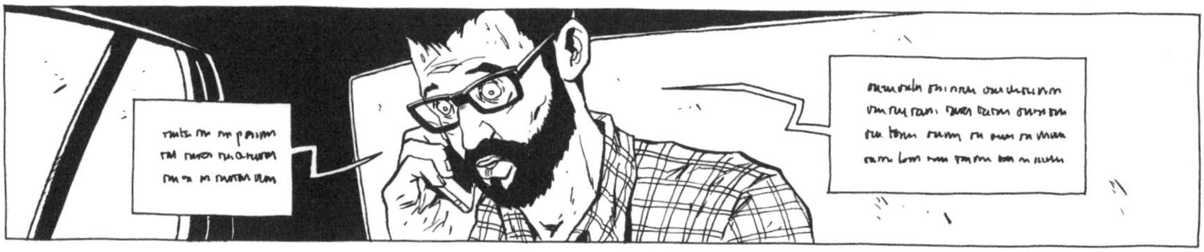

33RD STREET AND PARK AVENUE

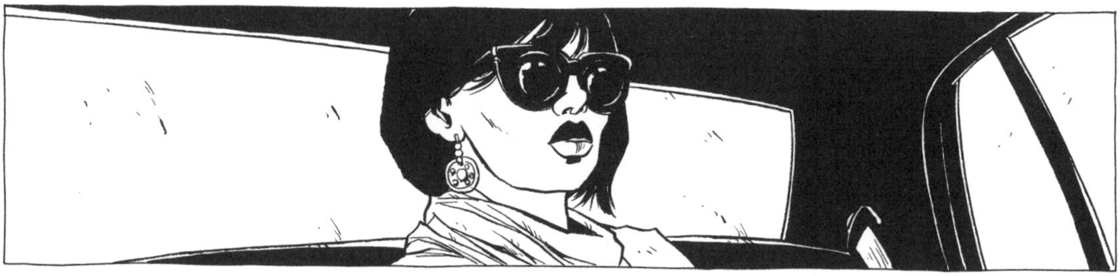

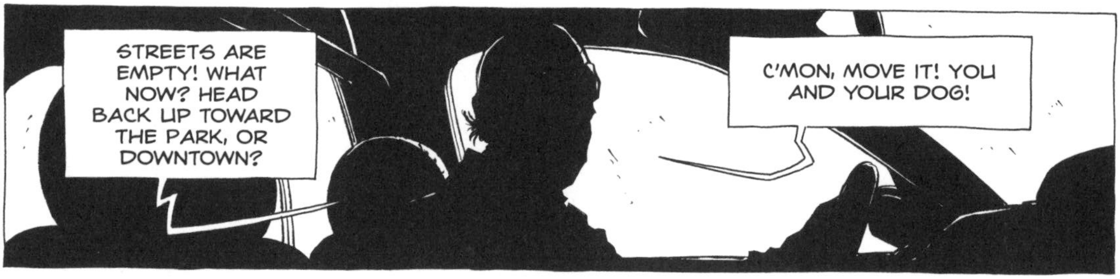
STREETS ARE EMPTY! WHAT NOW? HEAD BACK UP TOWARD THE PARK, OR DOWNTOWN?
C'MON, MOVE IT! YOU AND YOUR DOG!

TO MY SURPRISE, I OFTEN CATCH MYSELF TALKING TO MYSELF BETWEEN FARES. THIS JOB MUST BE GETTING TO ME.

I LIKE THE THOUGHT OF MY MAIN CHARACTER TALKING TO HERSELF OUT LOUD.

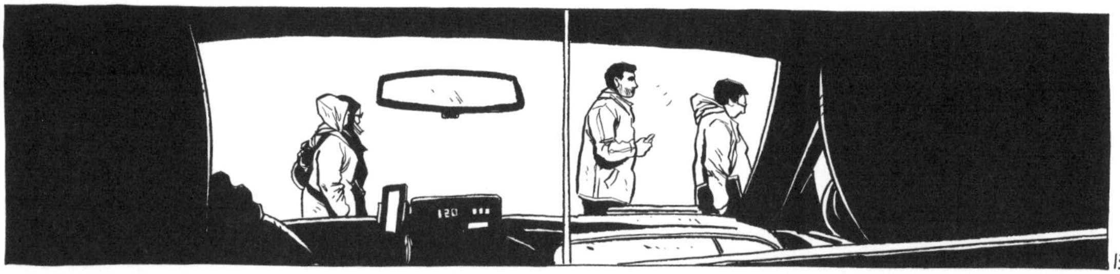

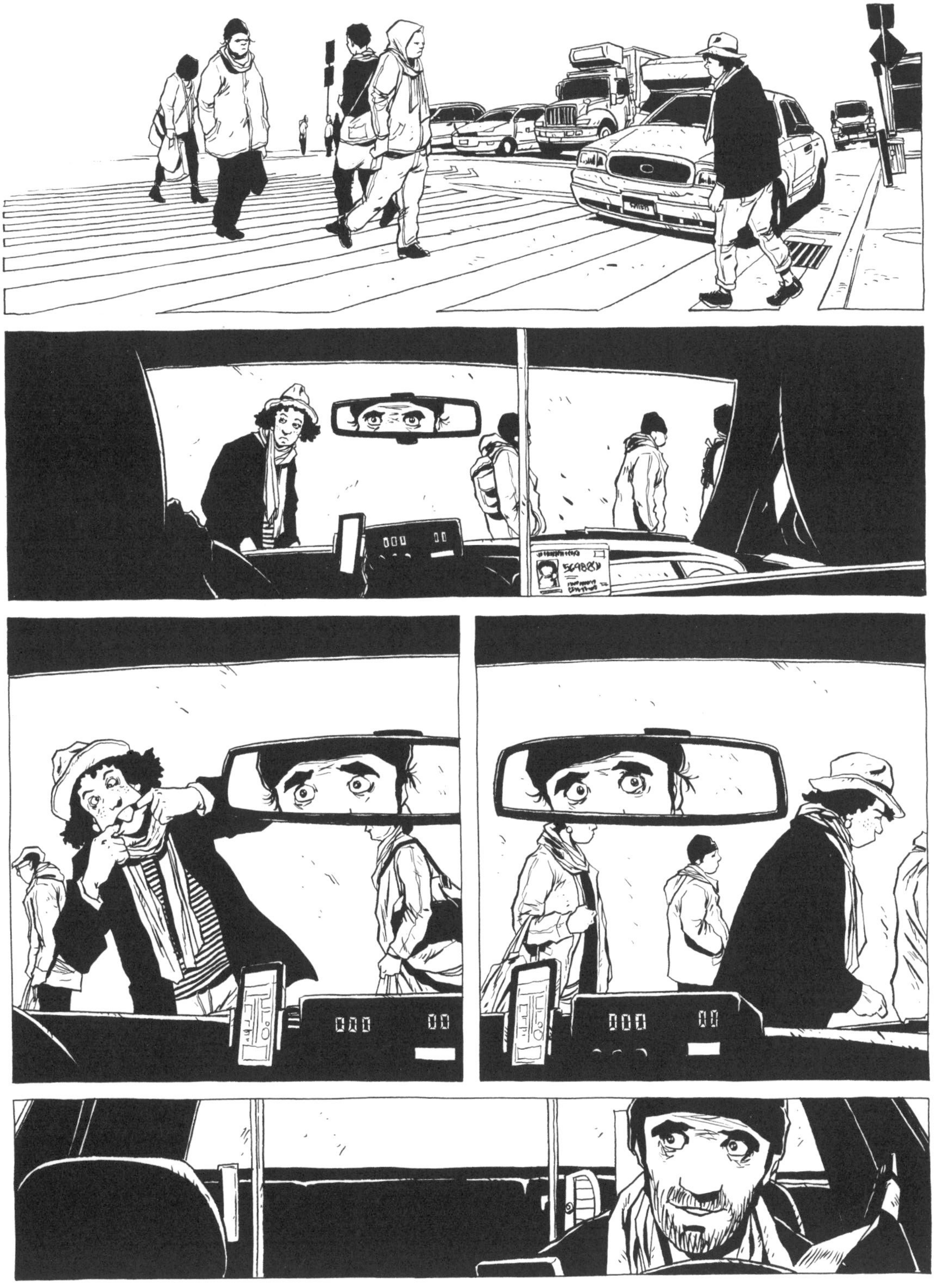

CASSAVETES SAID, "THE HOPE IS THAT PEOPLE STAY CRAZY."

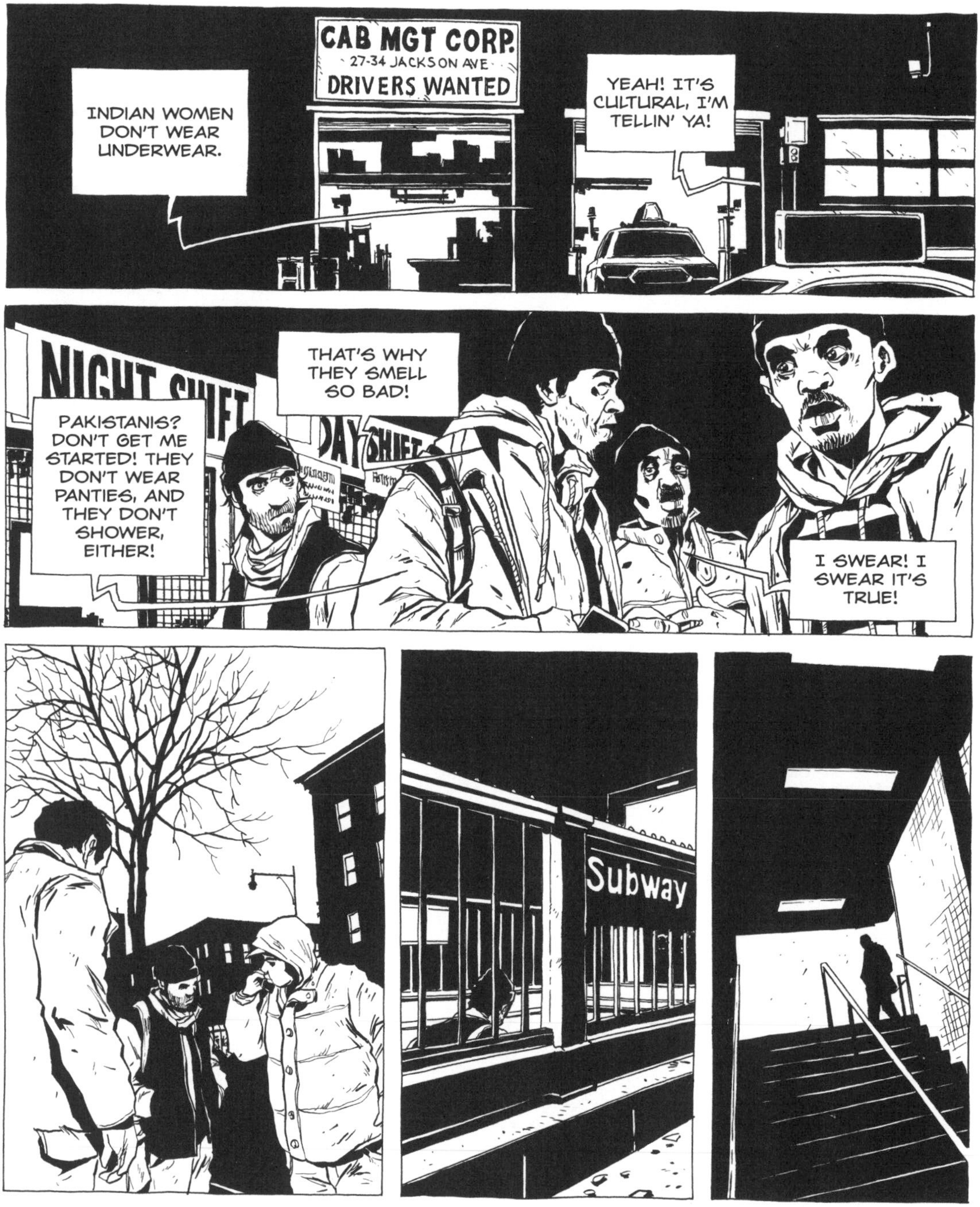
CAB MGT CORP.
27-34 JACKSON AVE
DRIVERS WANTED
INDIAN WOMEN DON'T WEAR UNDERWEAR.
YEAH! IT'S CULTURAL, I'M TELLIN' YA!
PAKISTANIS? DON'T GET ME STARTED! THEY DON'T WEAR PANTIES, AND THEY DON'T SHOWER, EITHER!
THAT'S WHY THEY SMELL SO BAD!
I SWEAR! I SWEAR IT'S TRUE!
Subway

CASUAL RACISM MAKES UP MOST OF THE CONVERSATIONS, EVEN FROM PEOPLE WHO SUFFER IT ON A DAILY BASIS.

TO KEEP AT THIS JOB, MY PROTAGONIST'S GOING TO HAVE TO FIND A NICHE, BECAUSE IT'S CLEARLY NOT THE MOST LUCRATIVE THING FOR A FAIRLY ATTRACTIVE WOMAN IN HER '40S WHO COULD BE DOING SOMETHING ELSE; A SALESGIRL, A WAITRESS, BARTENDER. HER FREEDOM AND SOLITUDE MUST BE VERY IMPORTANT TO HER.

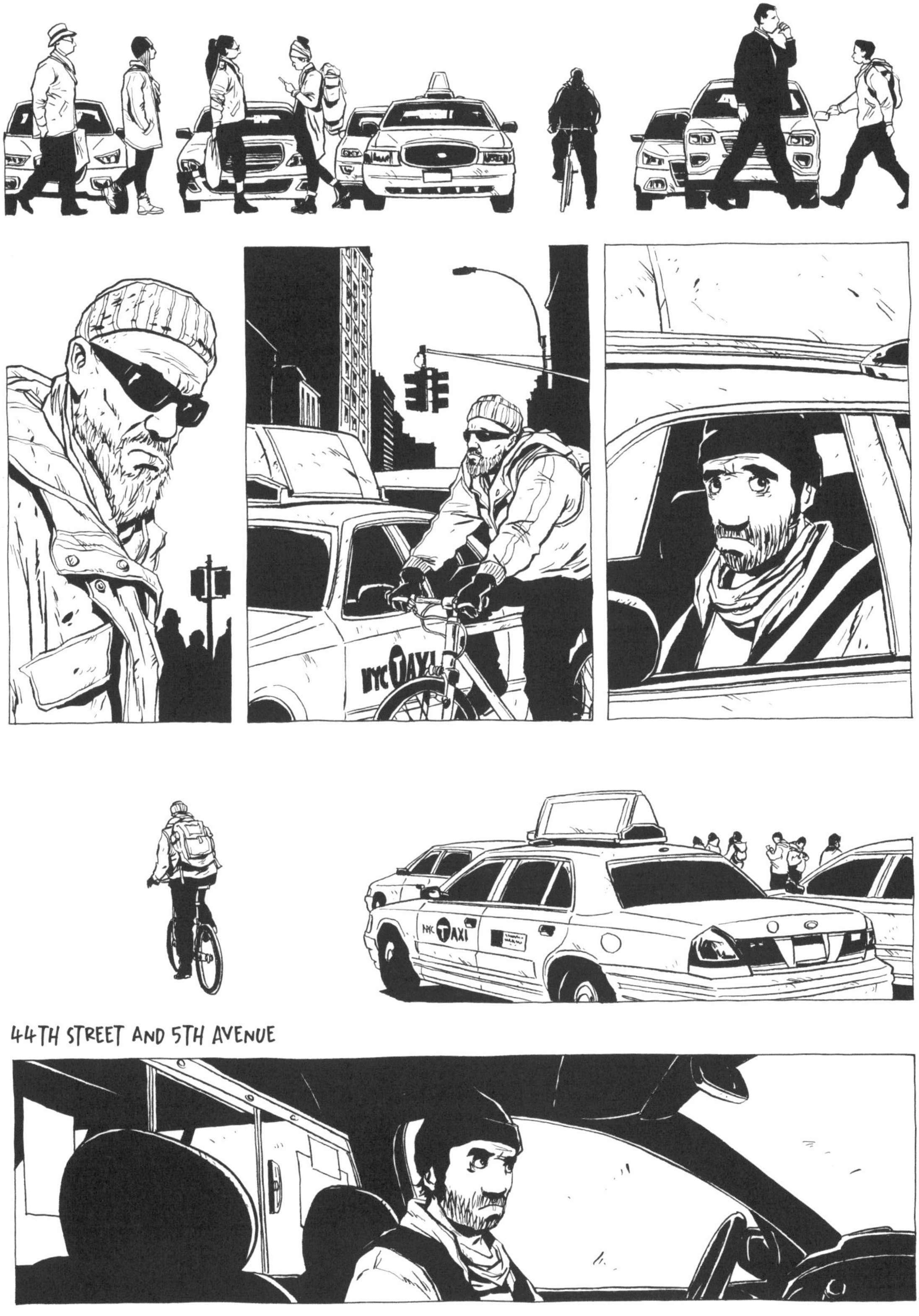
NYC TAXI
NYC TAXI
44TH STREET AND 5TH AVENUE

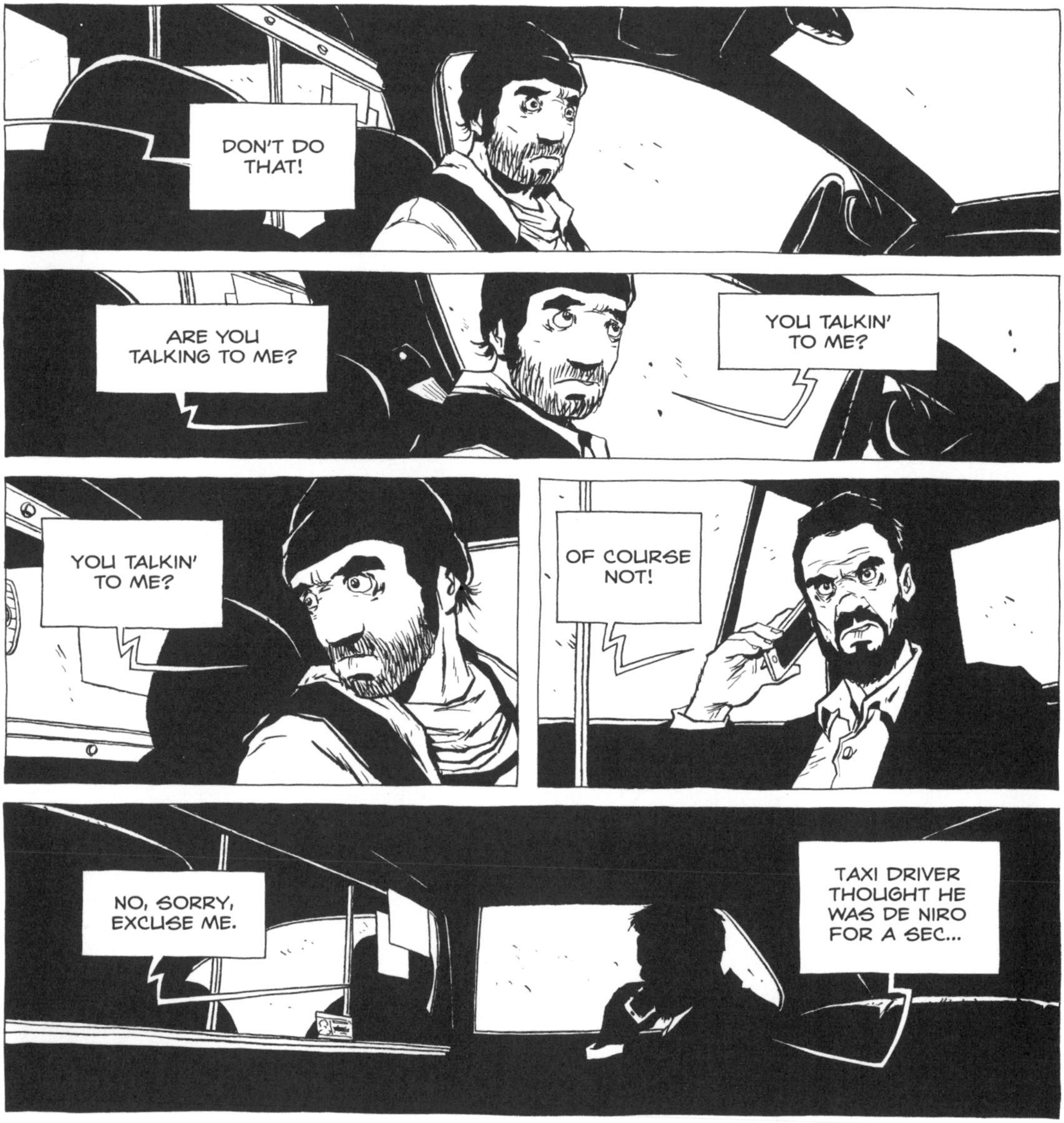
DON'T DO THAT!
ARE YOU TALKING TO ME?
YOU TALKIN' TO ME?
YOU TALKIN' TO ME?
OF COURSE NOT!
NO, SORRY, EXCUSE ME.
TAXI DRIVER THOUGHT HE WAS DE NIRO FOR A SEC...

OR MAYBE THE FILM COULD ALSO BE A SERIES OF ENCOUNTERS, PORTRAITS OF NEW YORKERS, PLACES... IN SHORT, THE CITY.

BUT HOW CAN YOU TALK ABOUT NEW YORK WITHOUT REFERENCING FICTION? EVERYTHING'S FICTIONAL HERE, LARGER THAN LIFE. EVERYTHING'S A REFERENCE. EVERY STREET CORNER IS A SET, EVERY PASSERBY A CHARACTER, AND THAT'S THE THEME OF THE MOVIE, TOO. MY MAIN CHARACTER FEEDS ON THE ENERGY OF NEW YORK IN ORDER TO UNDERTAKE HER SELF-RENEWAL AS IF SHE WERE PREPPING FOR A ROLE.

WEDNESDAY, FEBRUARY 24, 2016

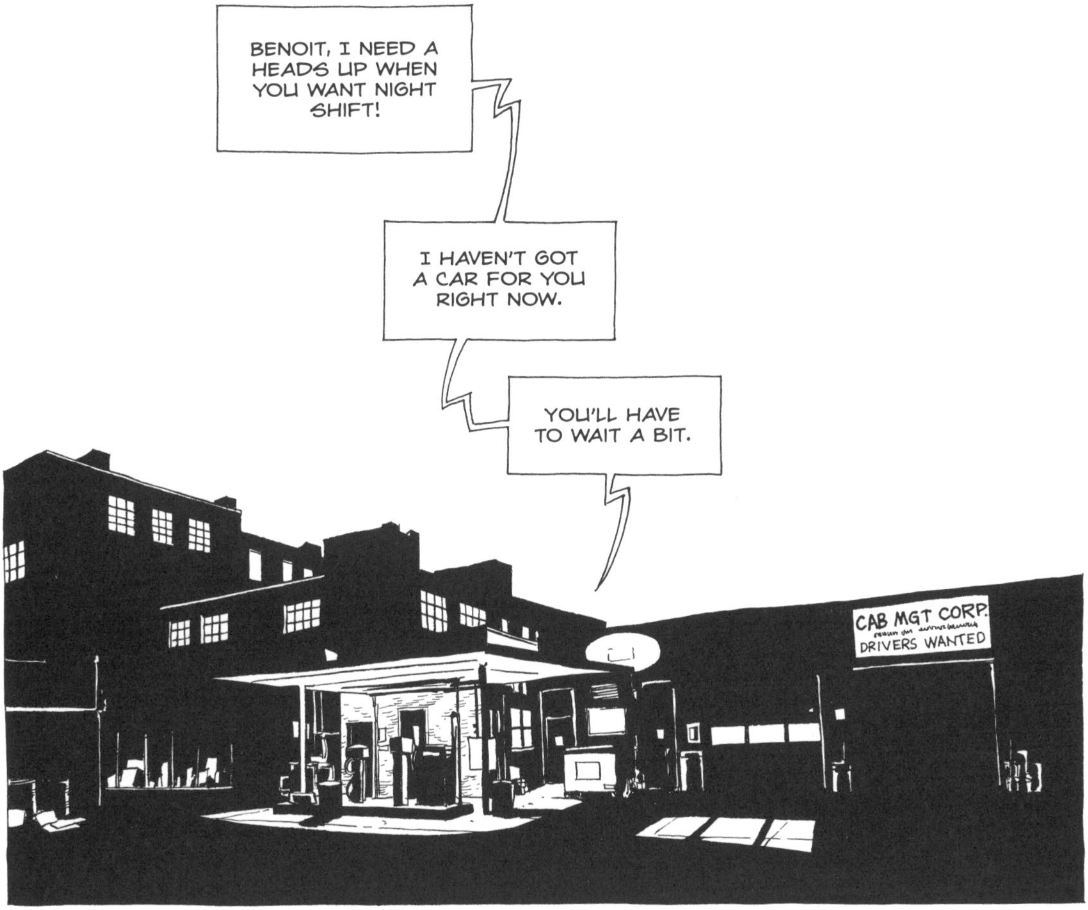
BENOIT, I NEED A HEADS UP WHEN YOU WANT NIGHT SHIFT!
I HAVEN'T GOT A CAR FOR YOU RIGHT NOW.
YOU'LL HAVE TO WAIT A BIT.
CAB MGT CORP.
DRIVERS WANTED

118TH STREET AND 15TH AVENUE

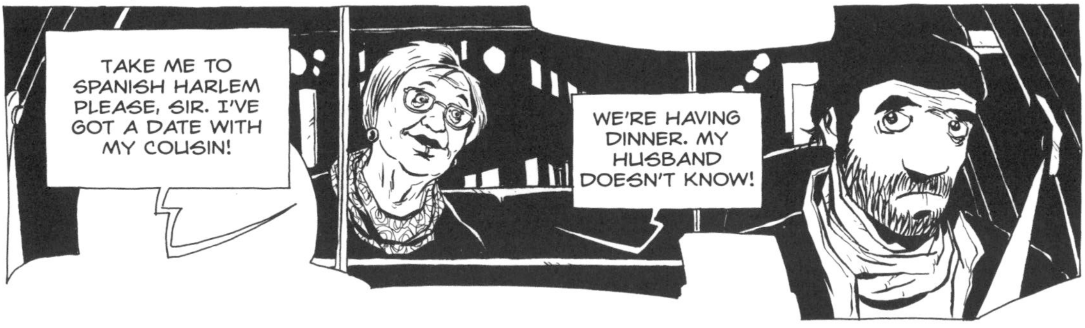
TAKE ME TO SPANISH HARLEM PLEASE, SIR. I'VE GOT A DATE WITH MY COUSIN!
WE'RE HAVING DINNER. MY HUSBAND DOESN'T KNOW!

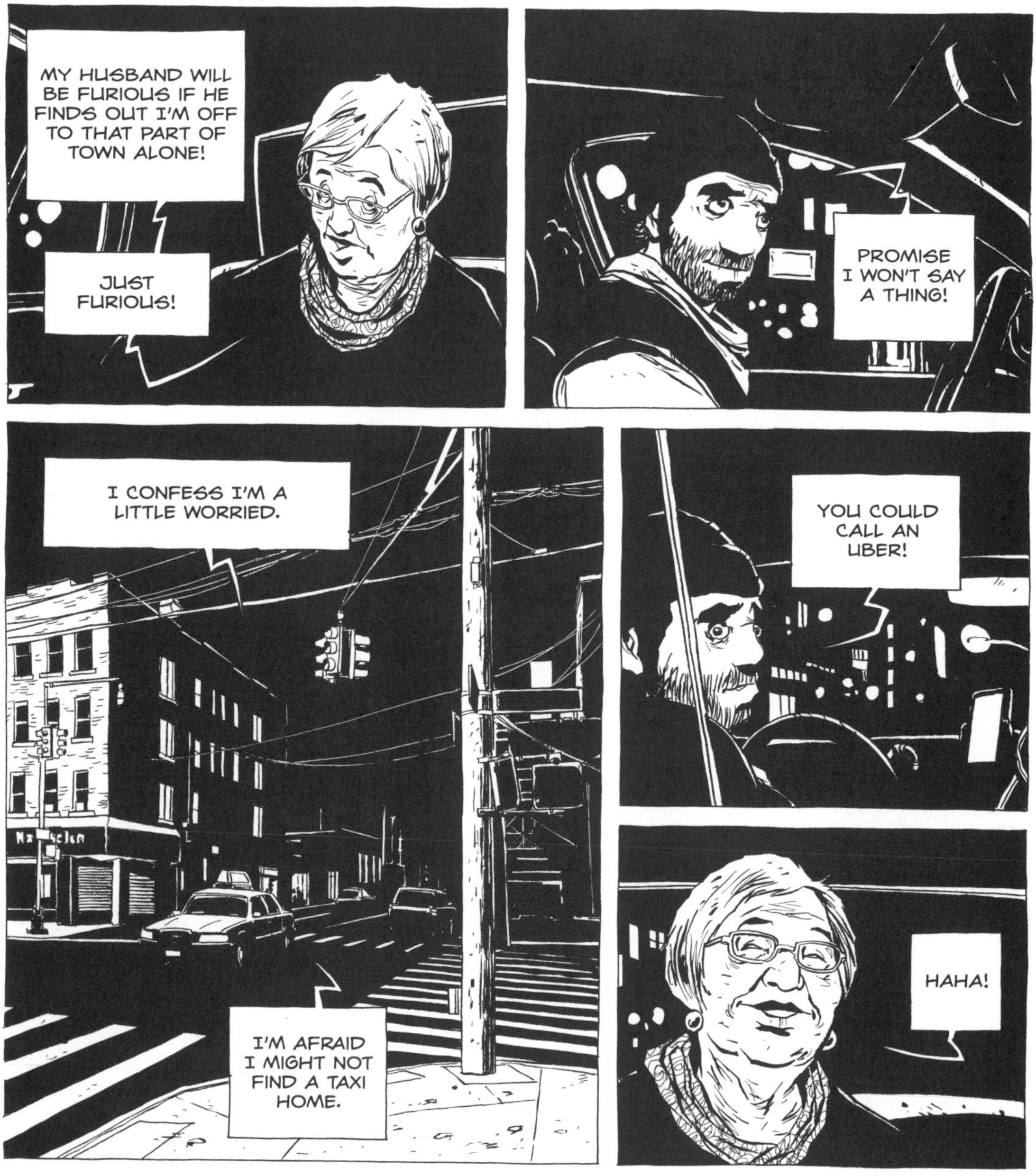
MY HUSBAND WILL BE FURIOUS IF HE FINDS OUT I'M OFF TO THAT PART OF TOWN ALONE!
JUST FURIOUS!
PROMISE I WON'T SAY A THING!
I CONFESS I'M A LITTLE WORRIED.
I'M AFRAID I MIGHT NOT FIND A TAXI HOME.
YOU COULD CALL AN UBER!
HAHA!

72ND STREET AND 2ND AVENUE

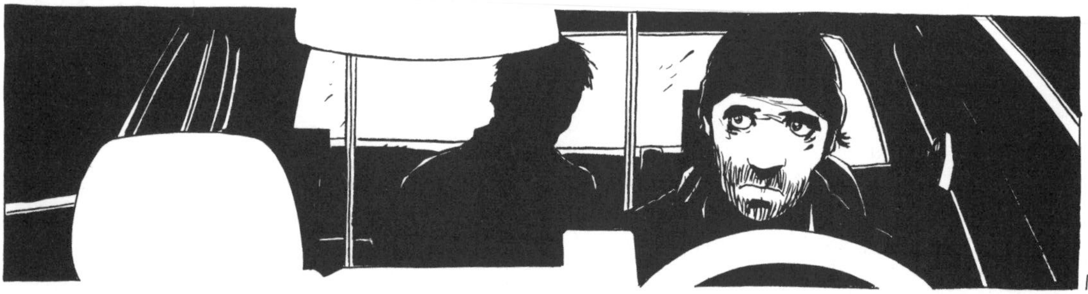

57TH STREET AND 9TH AVENUE

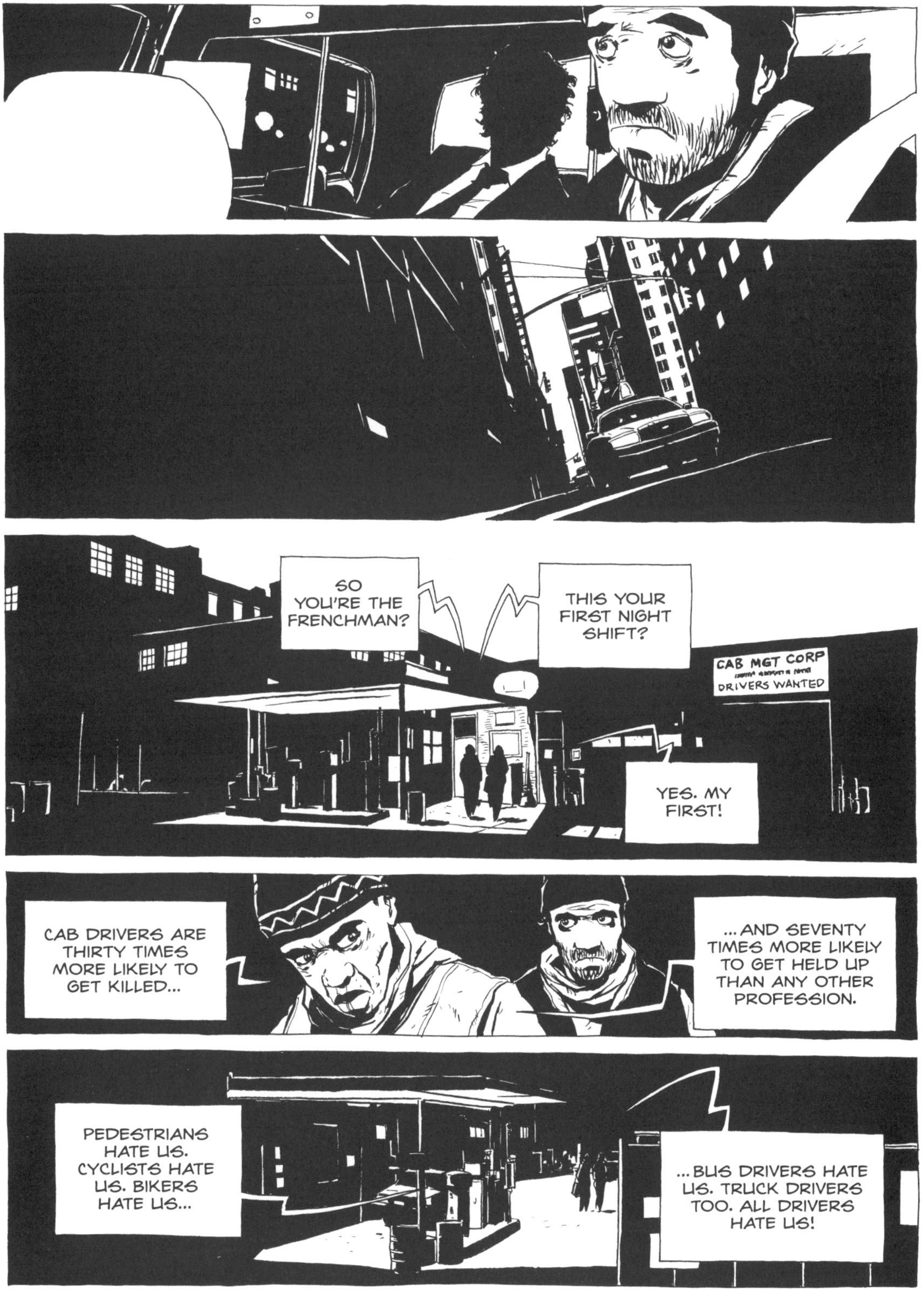
SO YOU'RE THE FRENCHMAN?
THIS YOUR FIRST NIGHT SHIFT?
CAB MGT CORP
DRIVERS WANTED
YES. MY FIRST!
CAB DRIVERS ARE THIRTY TIMES MORE LIKELY TO GET KILLED...
...AND SEVENTY TIMES MORE LIKELY TO GET HELD UP THAN ANY OTHER PROFESSION.
PEDESTRIANS HATE US. CYCLISTS HATE US. BIKERS HATE US...
...BUS DRIVERS HATE US. TRUCK DRIVERS TOO. ALL DRIVERS HATE US!

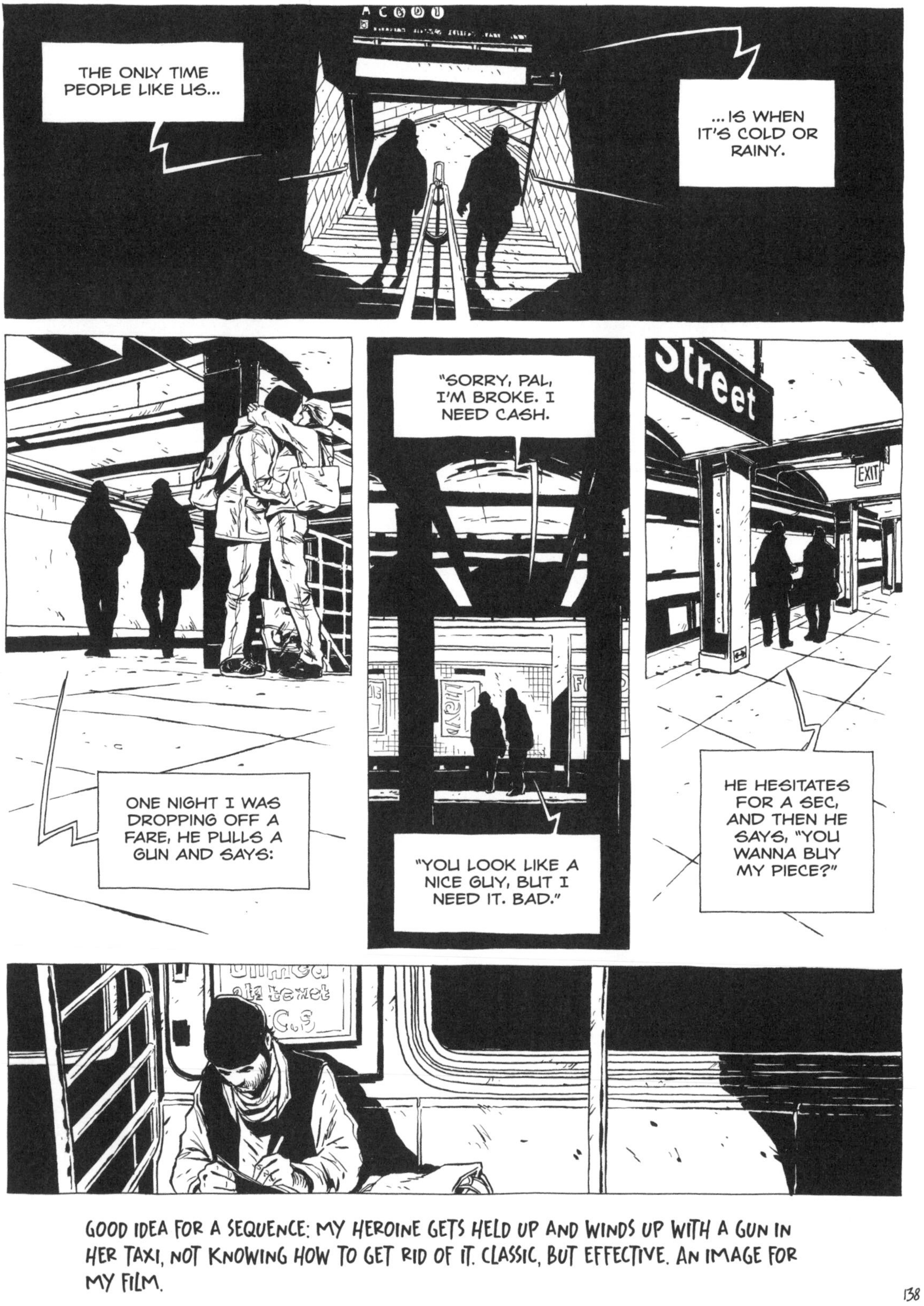
THE ONLY TIME PEOPLE LIKE US...
...IS WHEN IT'S COLD OR RAINY.
ONE NIGHT I WAS DROPPING OFF A FARE, HE PULLS A GUN AND SAYS:
"SORRY, PAL, I'M BROKE. I NEED CASH.
"YOU LOOK LIKE A NICE GUY, BUT I NEED IT. BAD."
Street
EXIT
HE HESITATES FOR A SEC, AND THEN HE SAYS, "YOU WANNA BUY MY PIECE?"

GOOD IDEA FOR A SEQUENCE: MY HEROINE GETS HELD UP AND WINDS UP WITH A GUN IN HER TAXI, NOT KNOWING HOW TO GET RID OF IT. CLASSIC, BUT EFFECTIVE. AN IMAGE FOR MY FILM.

PORT AUTHORITY

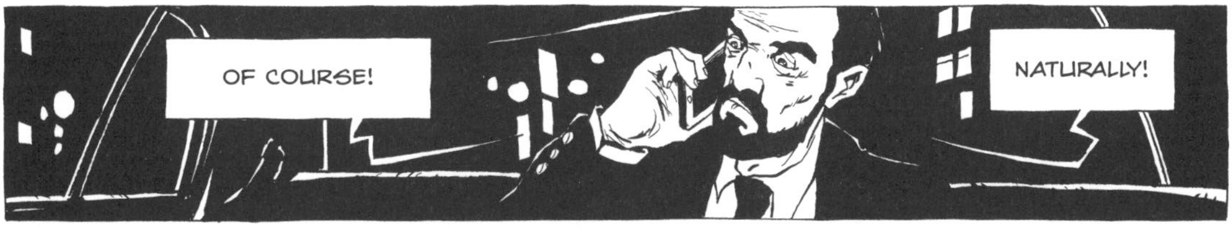
OF COURSE!
NATURALLY!

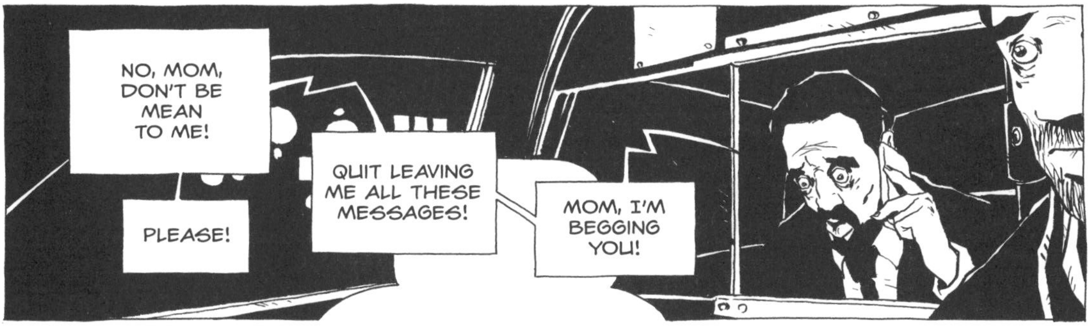
NO, MOM, DON'T BE MEAN TO ME!
PLEASE!
QUIT LEAVING ME ALL THESE MESSAGES!
MOM, I'M BEGGING YOU!

FULTON STREET AND FLUSHING AVENUE, BROOKLYN

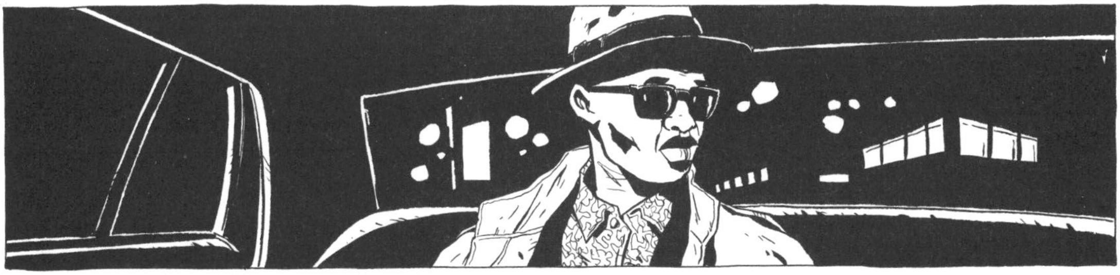

7TH STREET AND AVENUE C

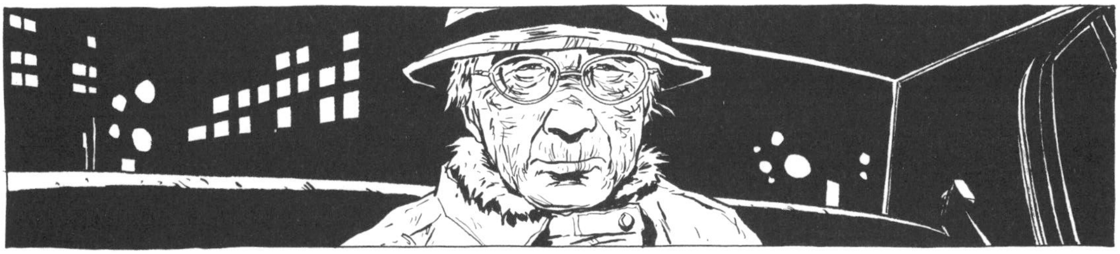

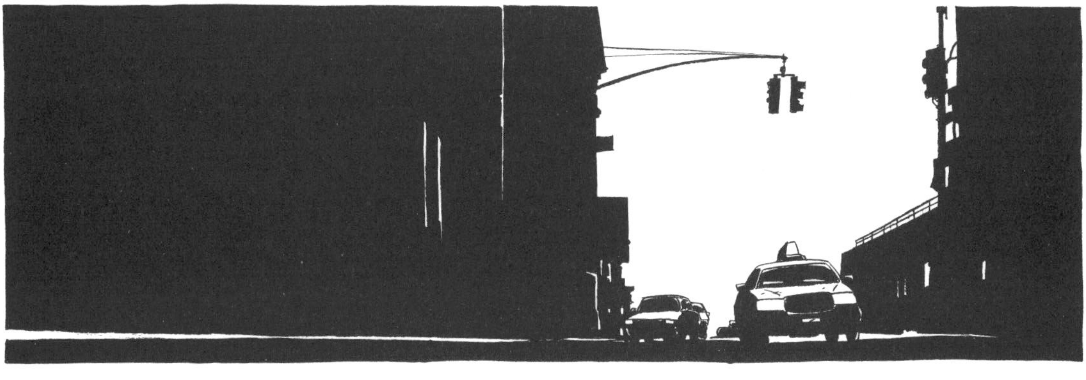

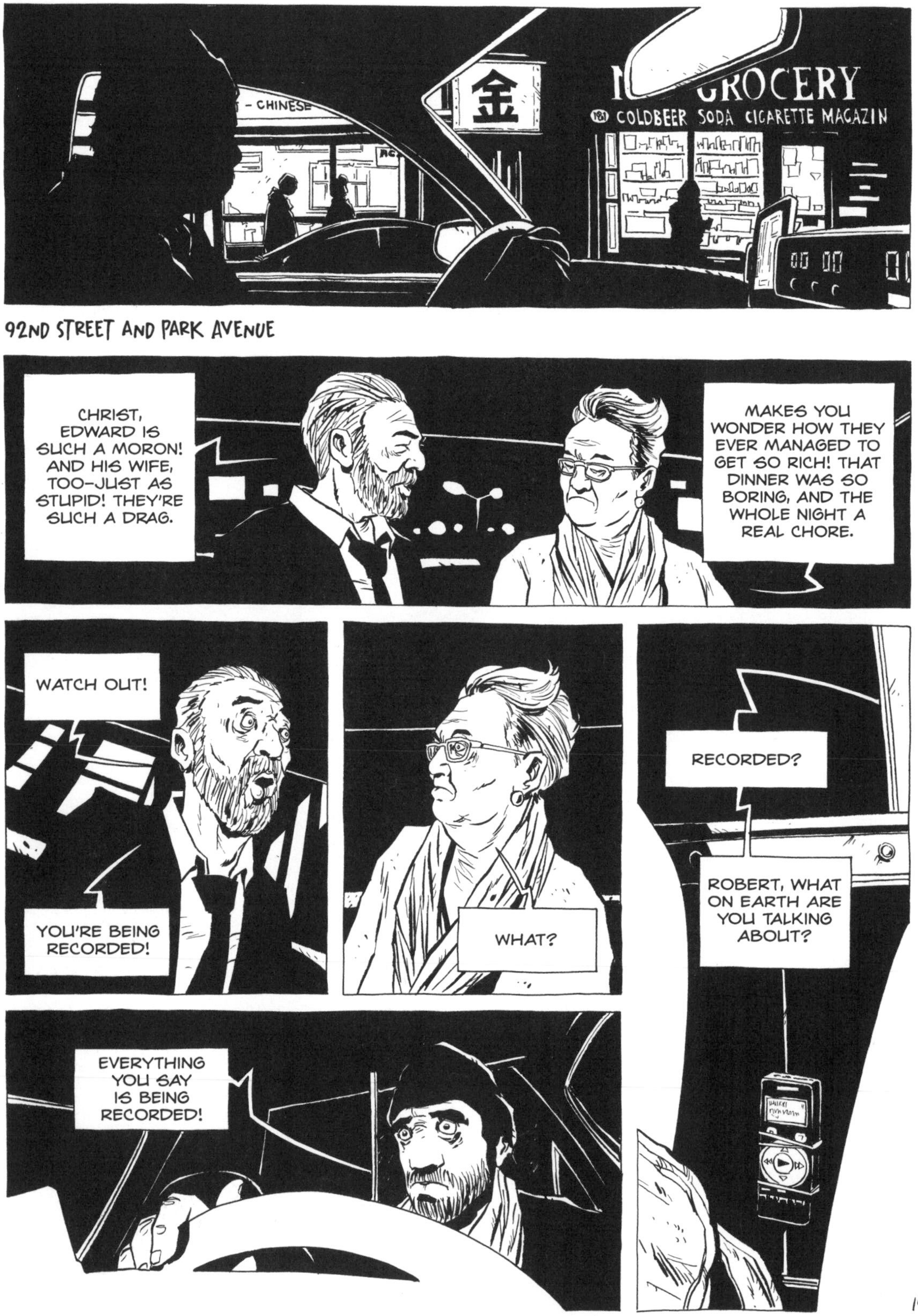
CHINESE
GROCERY
COLDBEER SODA CIGARETTE MAGAZIN
92ND STREET AND PARK AVENUE
CHRIST, EDWARD IS SUCH A MORON! AND HIS WIFE, TOO—JUST AS STUPID! THEY'RE SUCH A DRAG.
MAKES YOU WONDER HOW THEY EVER MANAGED TO GET SO RICH! THAT DINNER WAS SO BORING, AND THE WHOLE NIGHT A REAL CHORE.
WATCH OUT!
YOU'RE BEING RECORDED!
WHAT?
RECORDED?
ROBERT, WHAT ON EARTH ARE YOU TALKING ABOUT?
EVERYTHING YOU SAY IS BEING RECORDED!

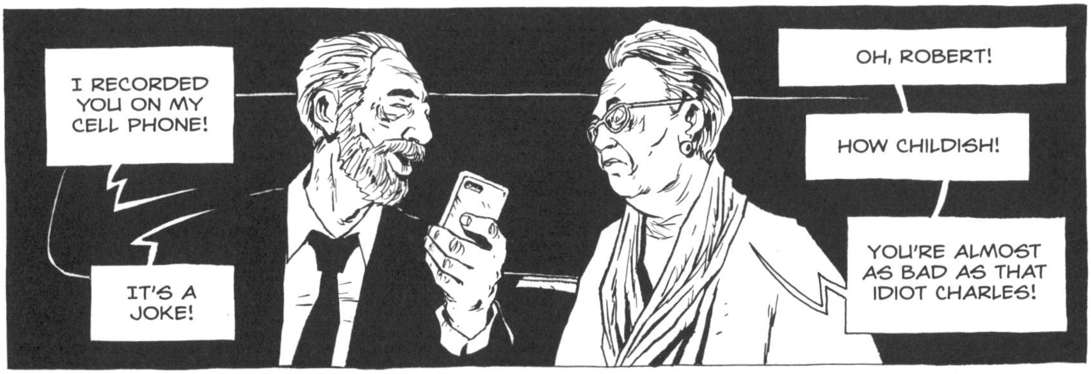
I RECORDED YOU ON MY CELL PHONE!
IT'S A JOKE!
OH, ROBERT!
HOW CHILDISH!
YOU'RE ALMOST AS BAD AS THAT IDIOT CHARLES!

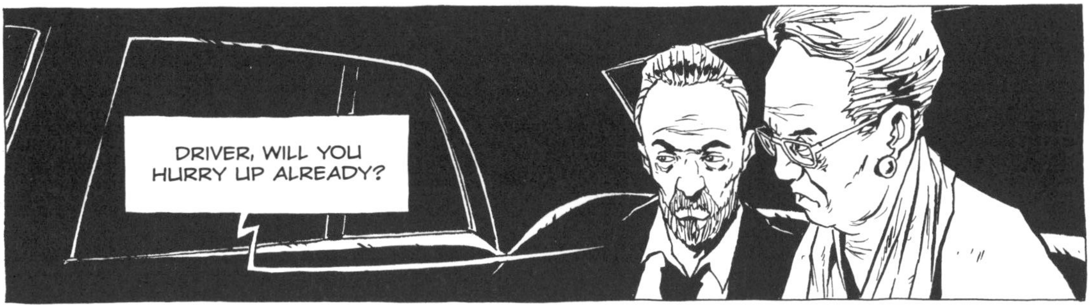
DRIVER, WILL YOU HURRY UP ALREADY?

IT MIGHT BE TIME TO GIVE MY PROTAGONIST A NAME. MINNIE: A NICE HOMAGE TO CASSAVETES, BUT IT SOUNDS A BIT LIKE A NICKNAME, AND MAKES YOU THINK OF MICKEY, TOO. WHAT'S HER REAL NAME? WHAT'S THE LAST NAME ON THAT LICENSE PASTED TO THE PLEXIGLAS DIVIDER BETWEEN DRIVER AND PASSENGER? ZOOEY... ÉLÉONORE'S ALWAYS BRINGING UP THAT NAME. IT MEANS "LIFE" IN GREEK. MY MAIN CHARACTER IS IN MOURNING. SHE LEFT FOR A FRESH START SOMEWHERE ELSE.

NOW, AS FOR HER LAST NAME...

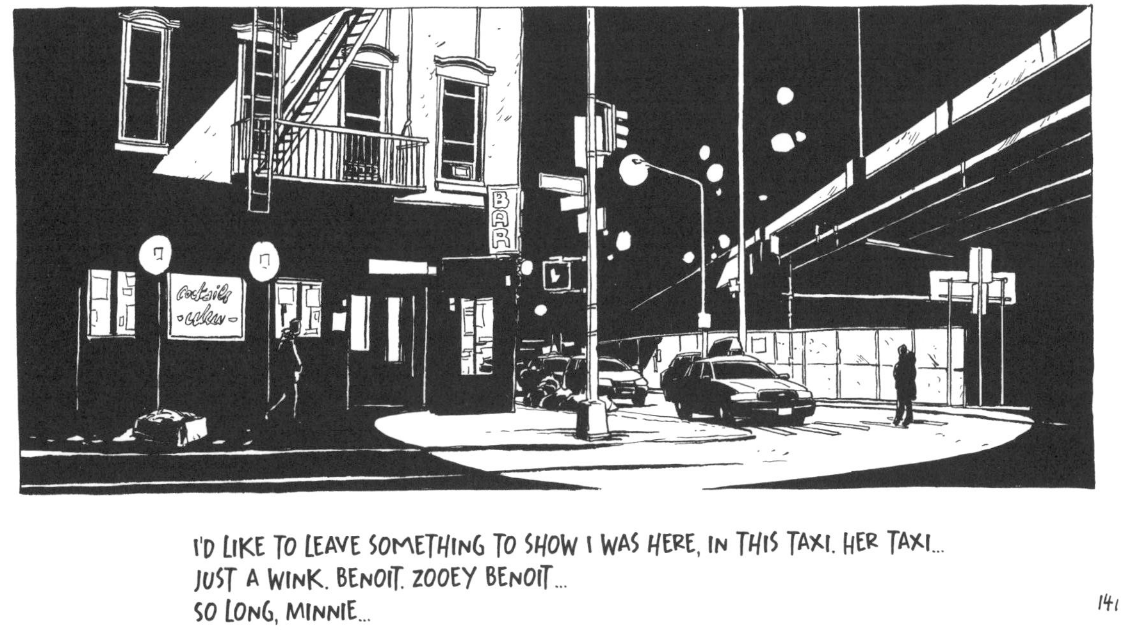
BAR

I'D LIKE TO LEAVE SOMETHING TO SHOW I WAS HERE, IN THIS TAXI. HER TAXI...
JUST A WINK. BENOIT. ZOOEY BENOIT...
SO LONG, MINNIE...

82ND STREET AND 2ND AVENUE

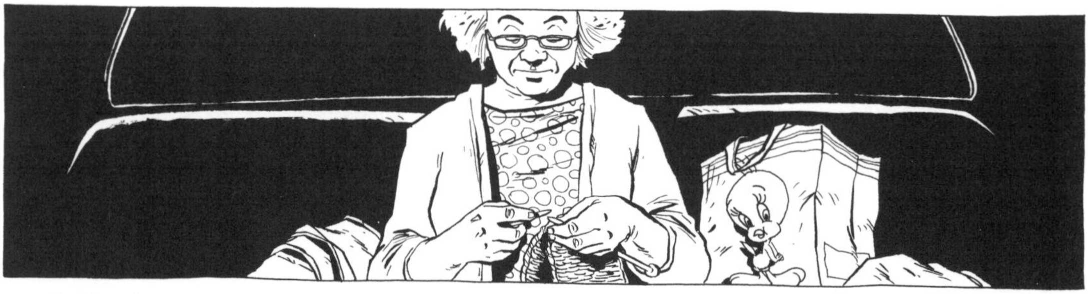

417 EAST 61ST STREET

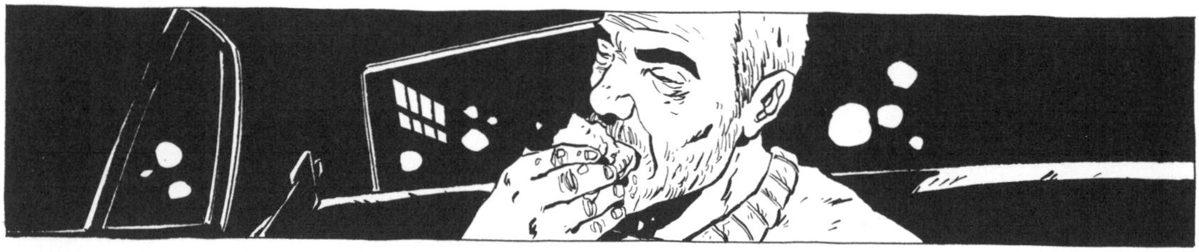

HALSEY STREET AND HOWARD AVENUE, BROOKLYN

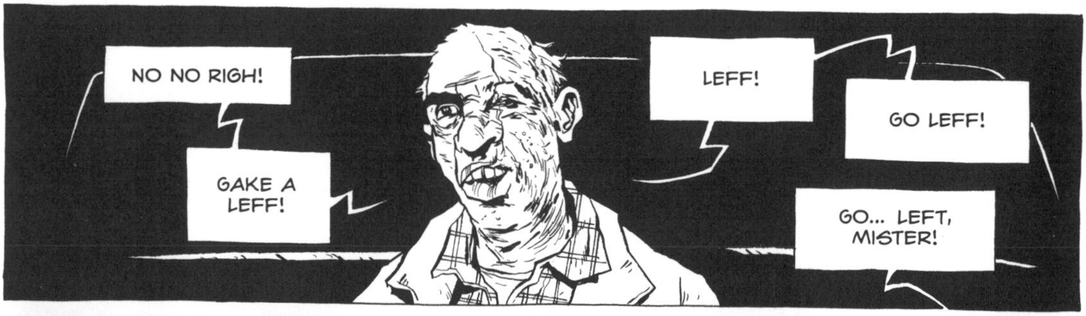
NO NO RIGH!
GAKE A LEFF!
LEFF!
GO LEFF!
GO... LEFT, MISTER!

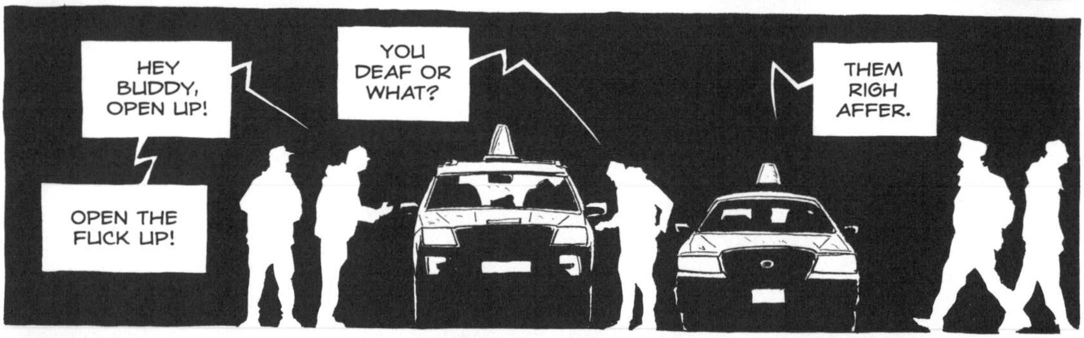
HEY BUDDY, OPEN UP!
OPEN THE FUCK UP!
YOU DEAF OR WHAT?
THEM RIGH AFFER.

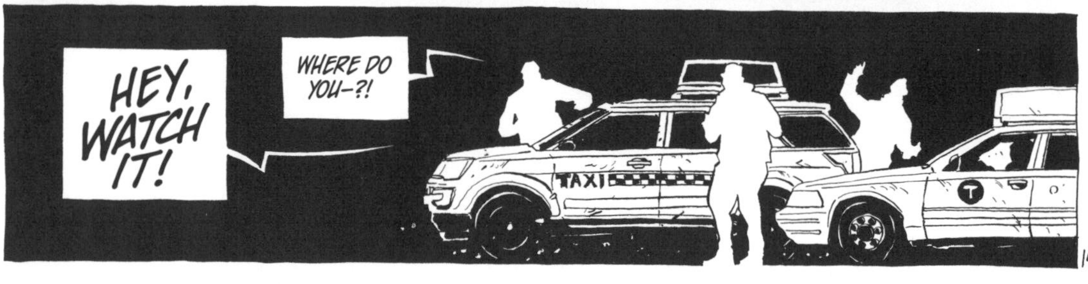
HEY, WATCH IT!
WHERE DO YOU–?!
TAXI

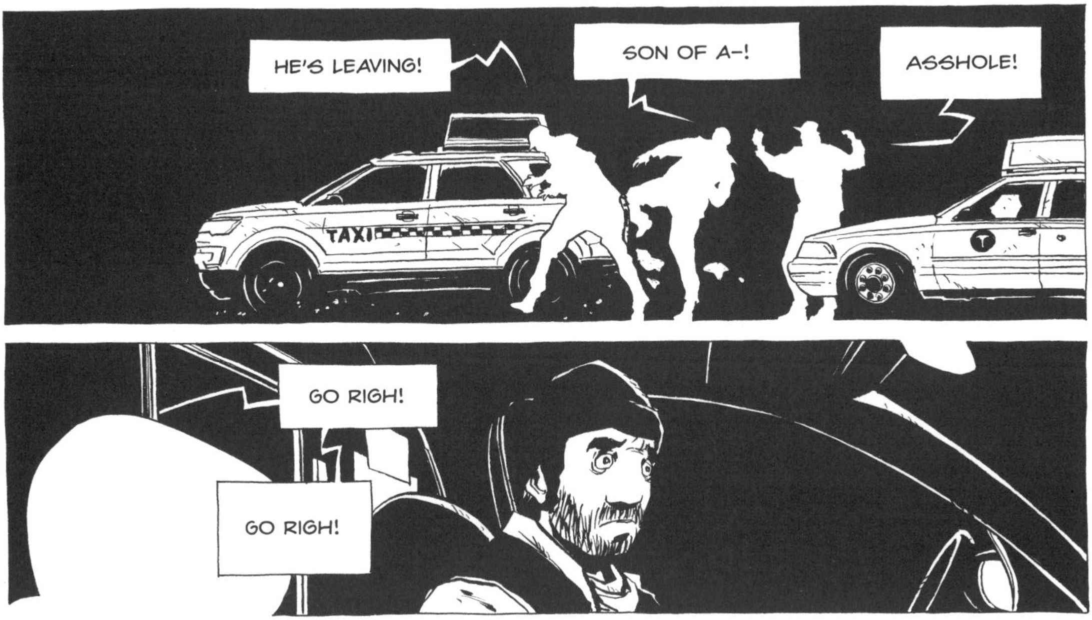
HE'S LEAVING!
SON OF A–!
ASSHOLE!
GO RIGH!
GO RIGH!

I'D TOTALLY HAVE TAKEN THEM IF I HADN'T HAD A FARE. AM I NAÏVE? OR JUST LESS RACIST?

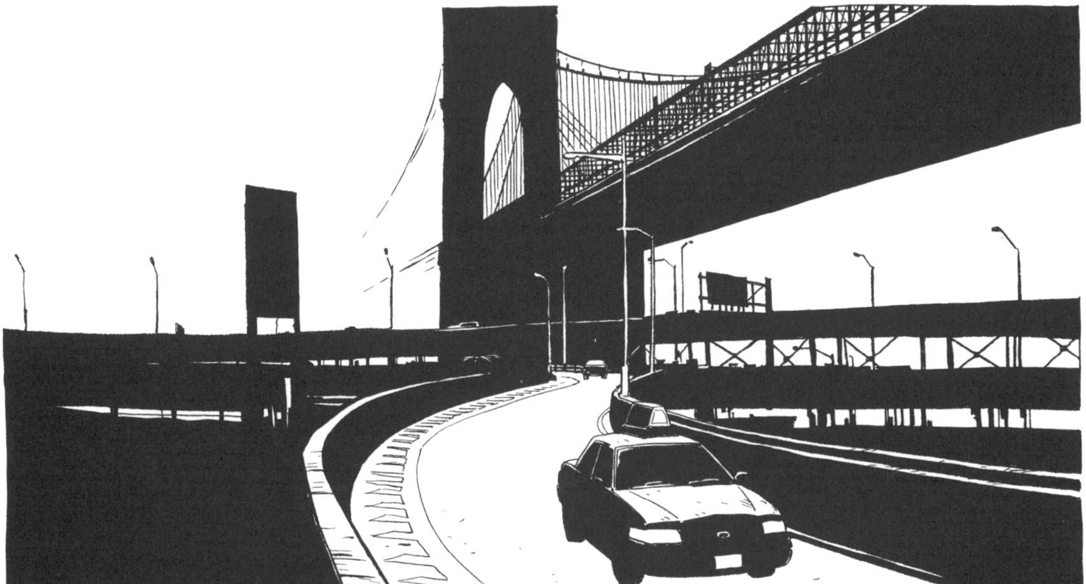

I FEEL ALMOST DIZZY. THESE LAST FEW WEEKS HAVE BEEN A HEADFIRST DIVE, FOCUSED ON A SINGLE GOAL: GETTING MY FARES SAFELY TO THEIR DESTINATION.

SOME DAYS ARE INTENSE AND FULL OF ALL SORTS OF ENCOUNTERS; I GO THE WHOLE DAY WITHOUT EVER THINKING ABOUT MY FILM. I'M HAPPY JUST PICKING PEOPLE UP ONE AFTER ANOTHER, CHATTING WITH THEM, BEING AS PROFESSIONAL AS I CAN.

NO ONE TO BLAME BUT MYSELF FOR GETTING ME INTO THIS SITUATION, WHICH SUDDENLY FEELS INCREDIBLY STRESSFUL.

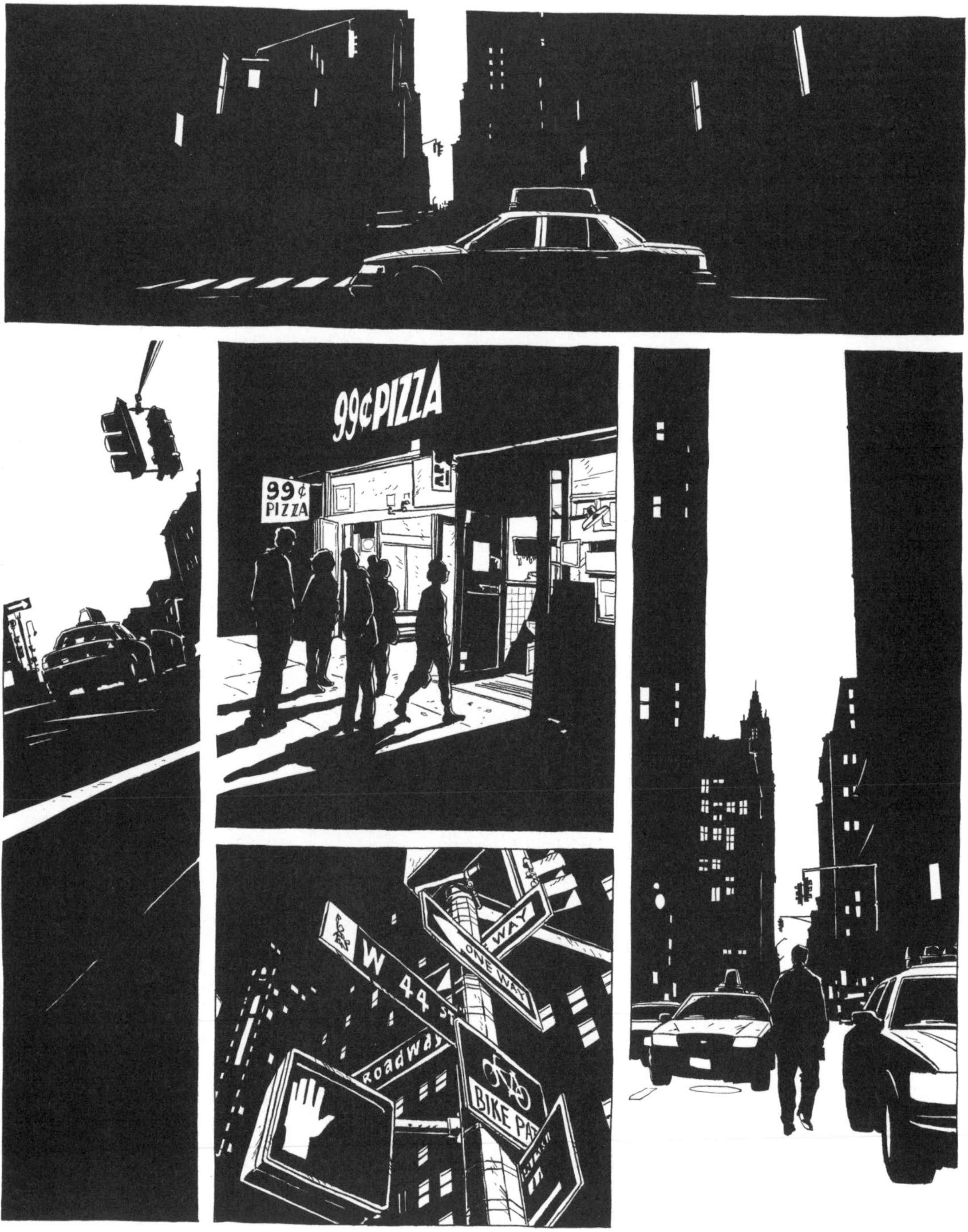
99¢PIZZA
99¢
PIZZA
W 44 ST
ONE WAY

SIMONE DE BEAUVOIR SAID: "THERE IS SOMETHING IN THE NEW YORK AIR THAT MAKES SLEEPING USELESS."

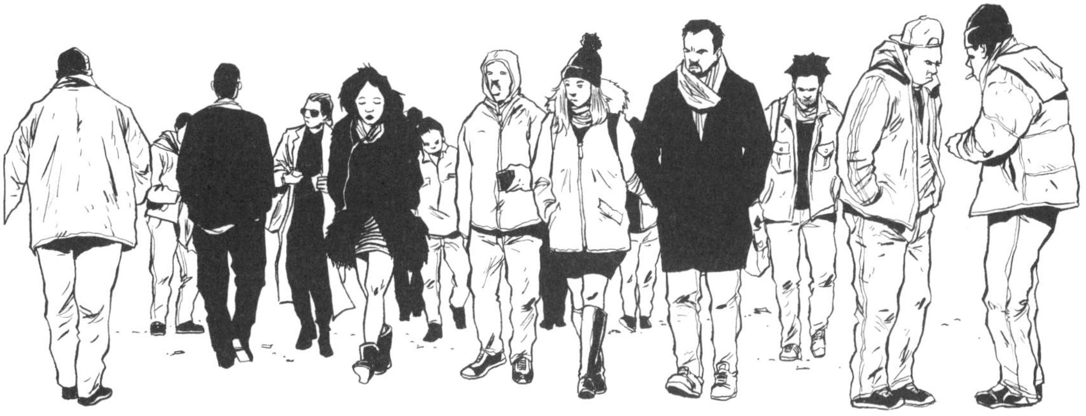

THE BLUES... DON'T FEEL LIKE DRIVING, EARNING A LIVING. FEEL LIKE GETTING DRIVEN AROUND. LOLLYGAGGING, LETTING IT ALL GO, GOING WITH THE FLOW...

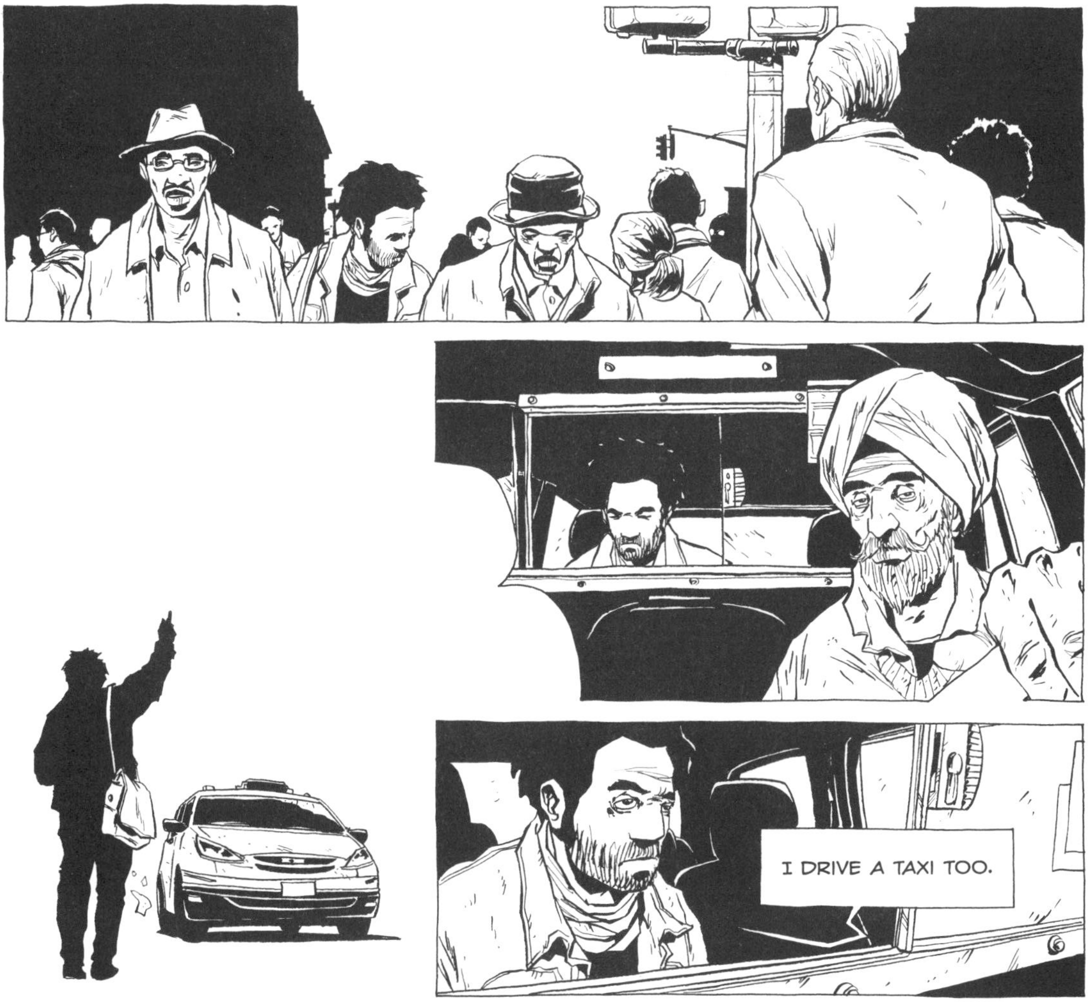
I DRIVE A TAXI TOO.

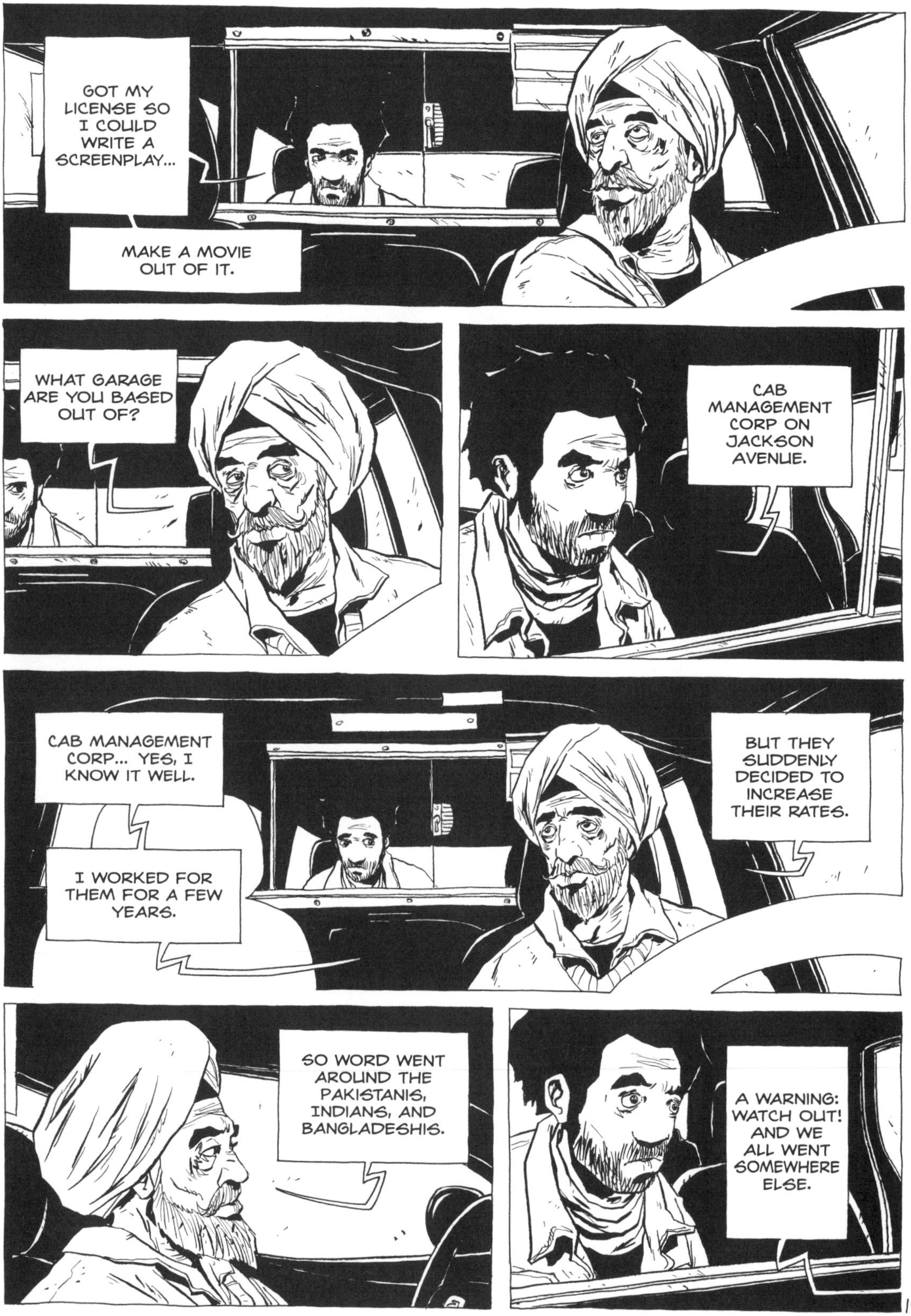
GOT MY LICENSE SO I COULD WRITE A SCREENPLAY...
MAKE A MOVIE OUT OF IT.
WHAT GARAGE ARE YOU BASED OUT OF?
CAB MANAGEMENT CORP ON JACKSON AVENUE.
CAB MANAGEMENT CORP... YES, I KNOW IT WELL.
I WORKED FOR THEM FOR A FEW YEARS.
BUT THEY SUDDENLY DECIDED TO INCREASE THEIR RATES.
SO WORD WENT AROUND THE PAKISTANIS, INDIANS, AND BANGLADESHIS.
A WARNING: WATCH OUT! AND WE ALL WENT SOMEWHERE ELSE.

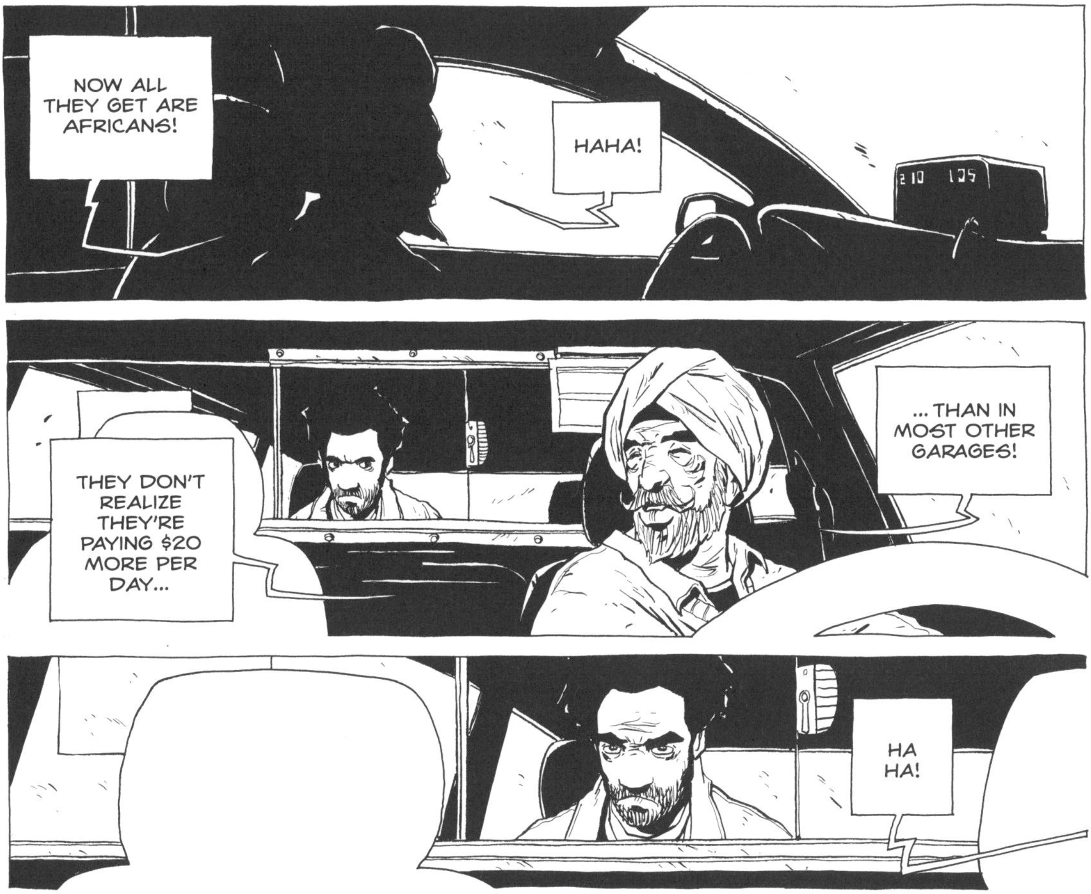
NOW ALL THEY GET ARE AFRICANS!
HAHA!
THEY DON'T REALIZE THEY'RE PAYING $20 MORE PER DAY...
...THAN IN MOST OTHER GARAGES!
HA HA!

AND ME, THE ONLY FRENCH DRIVER IN TOWN, I IMAGINE THAT THEY CALL ME THE FRENCH SUCKER BEHIND MY BACK.

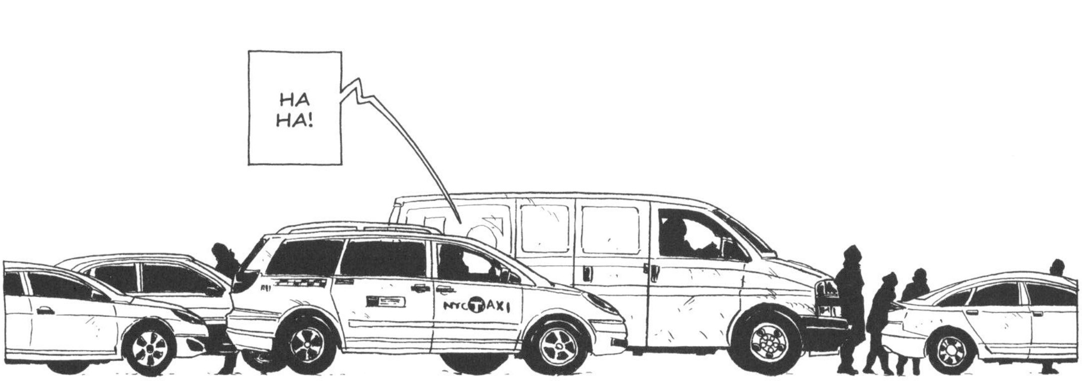
HA HA!
NYC TAXI

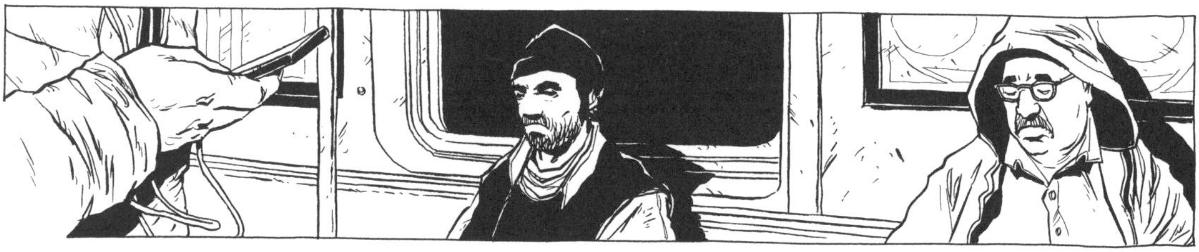

TAKING REFUGE IN THE U.S., ZOOEY TRIES TO BECOME A DIFFERENT PERSON. BY HINTING AT SNATCHES OF HER PAST, ONLY LETTING OUT EXPOSITION IN DRIBS AND DRABS, PLAYING WITH HOW SHE LIES TO FARES, I'M MAKING IT SO VIEWERS NEVER REALLY KNOW WHAT'S FICTION OR REALITY. AND IN THE END, DOES SHE EVEN KNOW HERSELF? DOESN'T SHE TAKE COMFORT IN INJECTING FICTION INTO HER REALITY? OR ELSE SHE WOULDN'T HAVE PICKED NEW YORK.

SOON IT'LL BE TIME TO HANG UP THE GLOVES AND GET DOWN TO ACTUALLY WRITING THIS THING.

THIS MIGHT BE ONE OF THE LAST TIMES I MAKE THIS RUN.

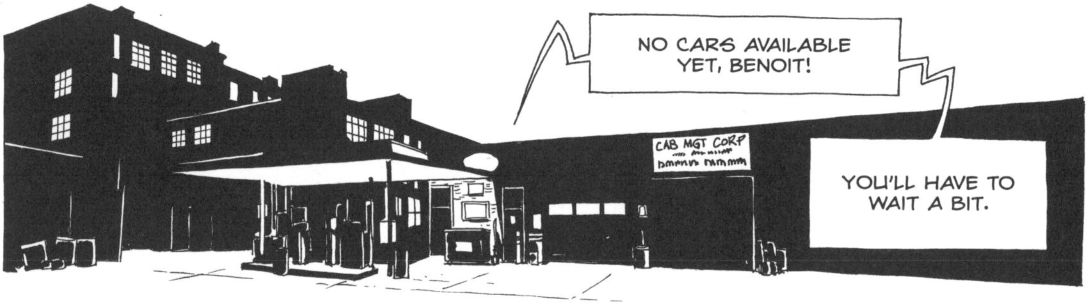
NO CARS AVAILABLE YET, BENOIT!
CAB MGT CORP
YOU'LL HAVE TO WAIT A BIT.

328 WEST 61ST, AT MADISON AVENUE

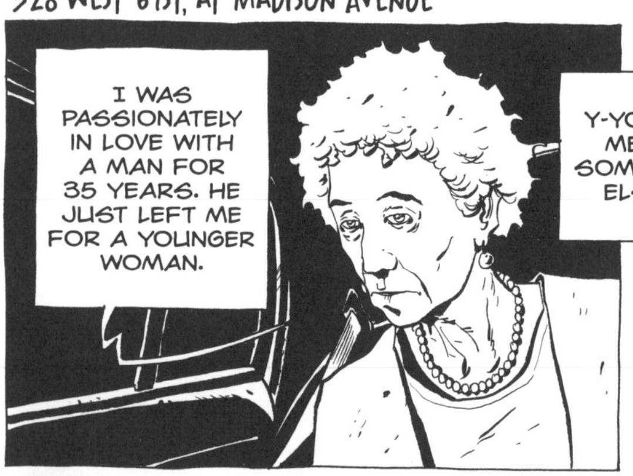
I WAS PASSIONATELY IN LOVE WITH A MAN FOR 35 YEARS. HE JUST LEFT ME FOR A YOUNGER WOMAN.

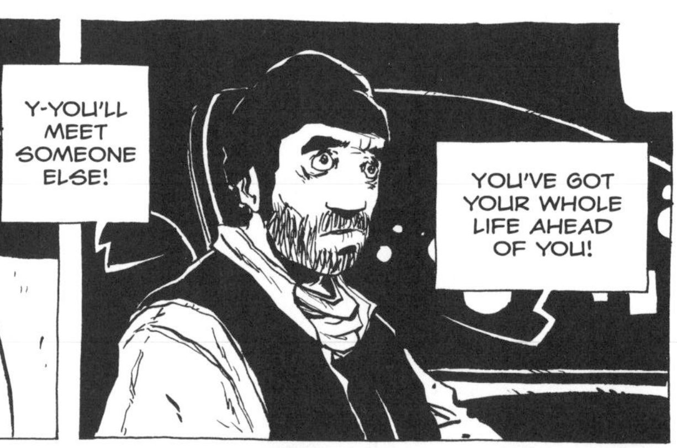
Y-YOU'LL MEET SOMEONE ELSE!
YOU'VE GOT YOUR WHOLE LIFE AHEAD OF YOU!

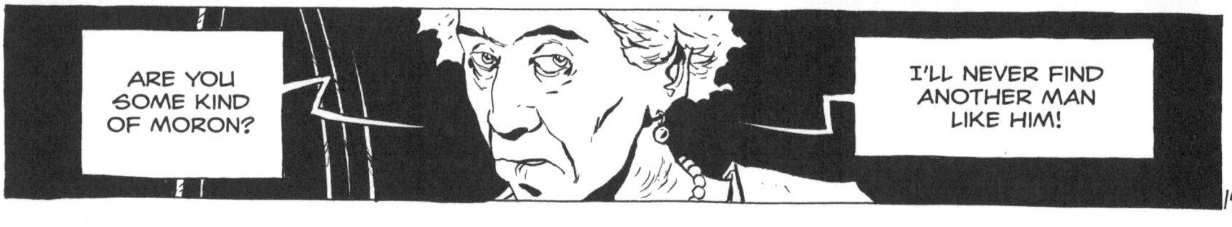
ARE YOU SOME KIND OF MORON?
I'LL NEVER FIND ANOTHER MAN LIKE HIM!

77TH STREET AND MADISON AVENUE

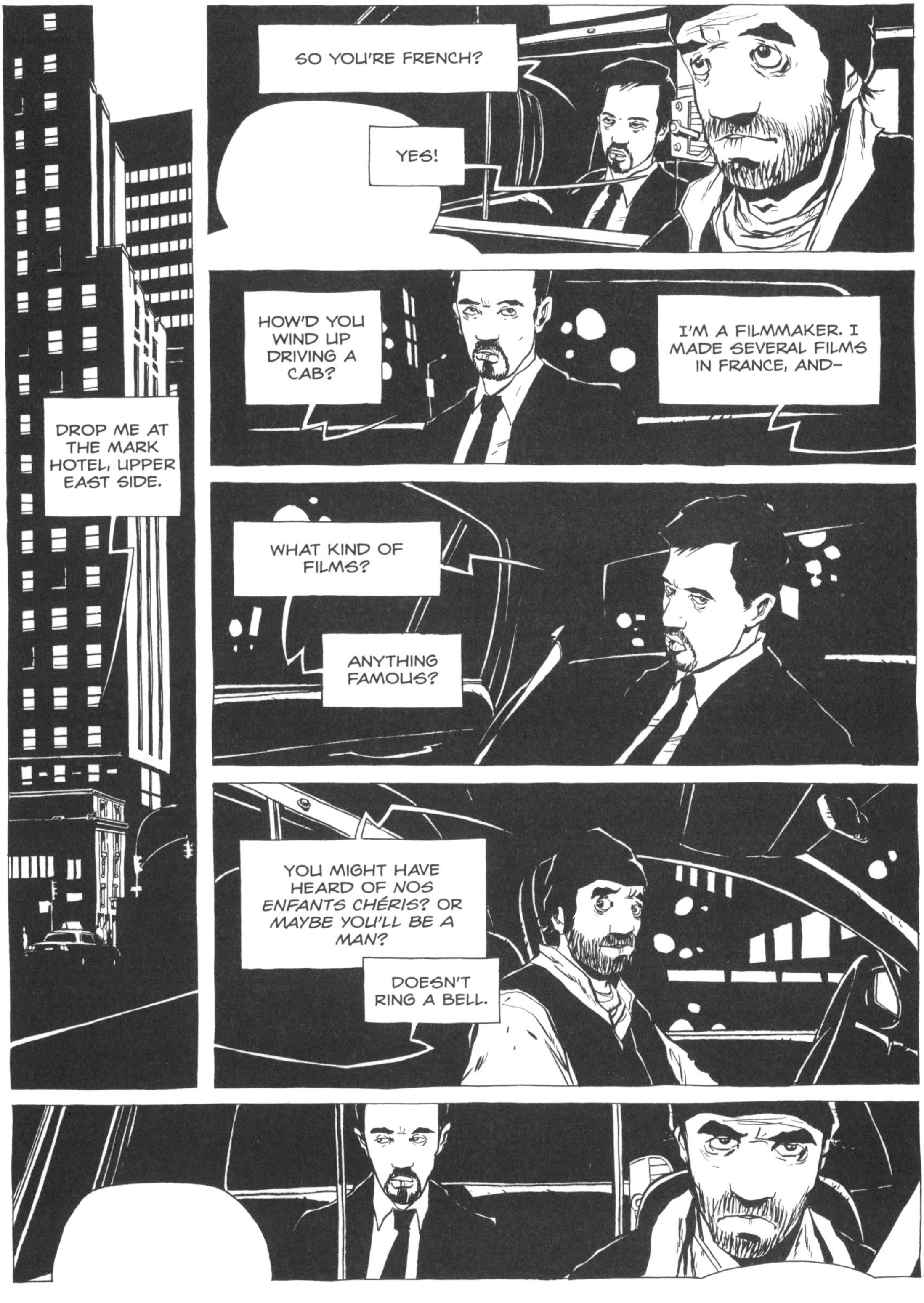

DROP ME AT THE MARK HOTEL, UPPER EAST SIDE.
SO YOU'RE FRENCH?
YES!
HOW'D YOU WIND UP DRIVING A CAB?
I'M A FILMMAKER. I MADE SEVERAL FILMS IN FRANCE, AND–
WHAT KIND OF FILMS?
ANYTHING FAMOUS?
YOU MIGHT HAVE HEARD OF NOS ENFANTS CHÉRIS? OR MAYBE YOU'LL BE A MAN?
DOESN'T RING A BELL.

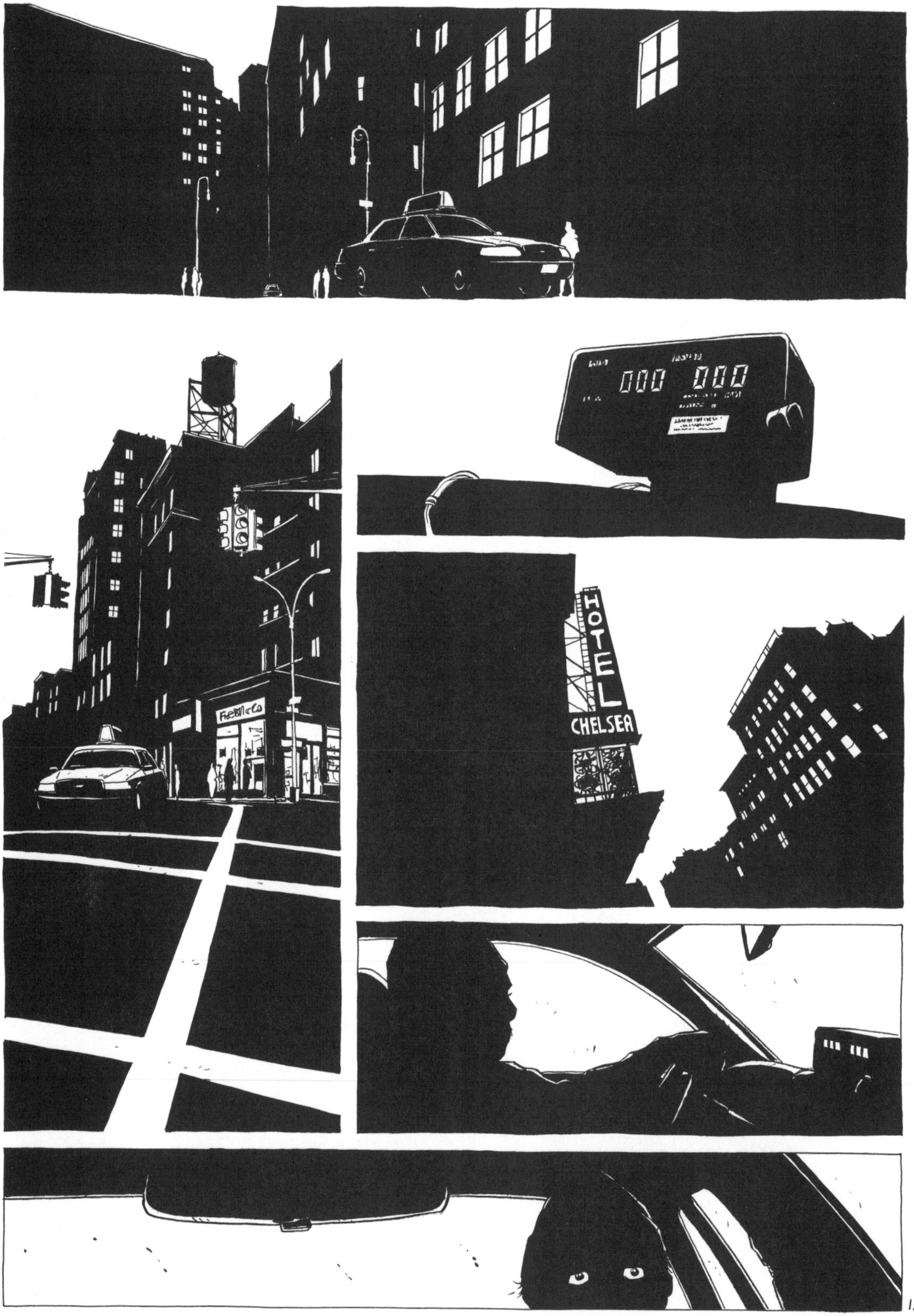
000 000
HOTEL
CHELSEA

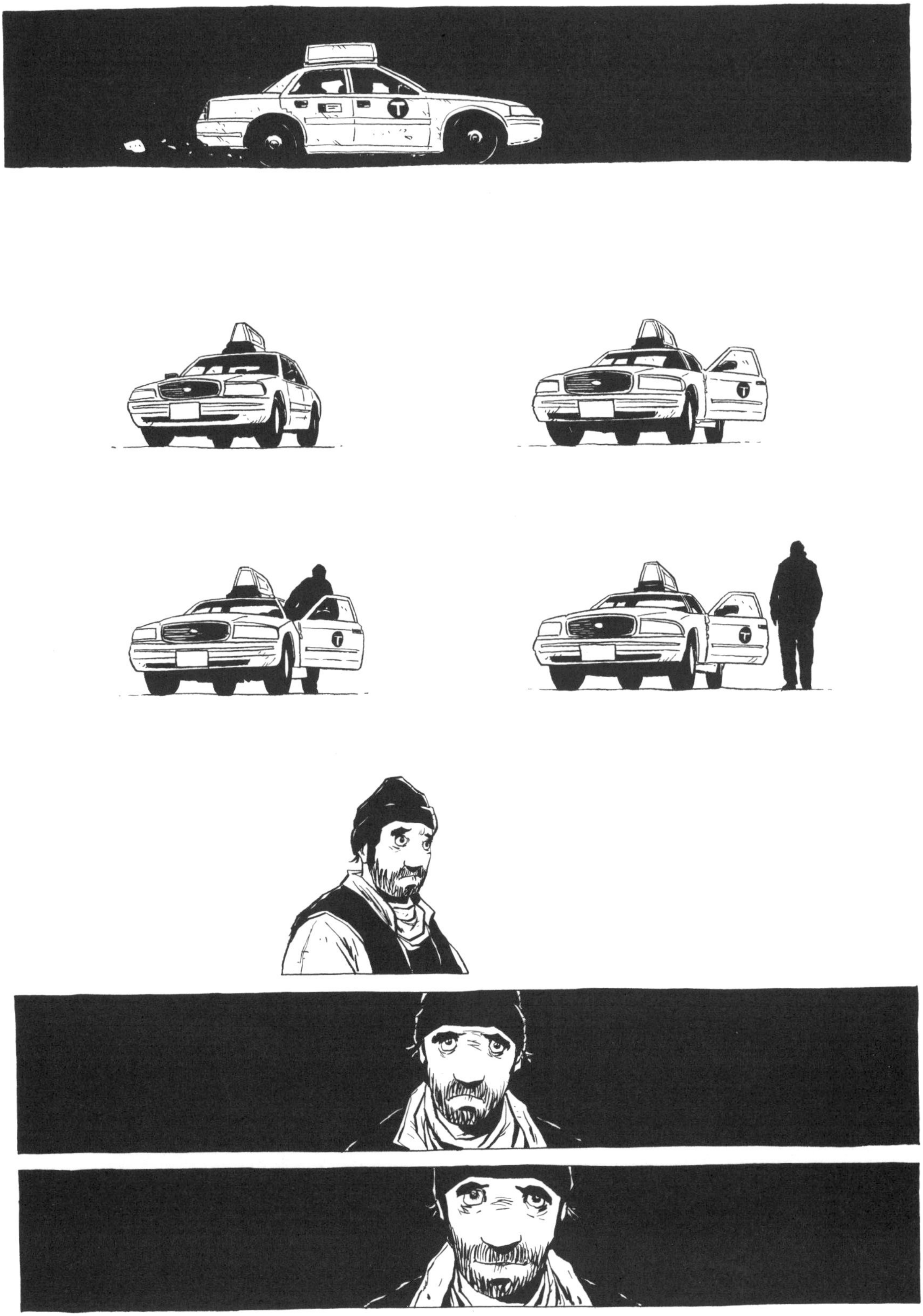

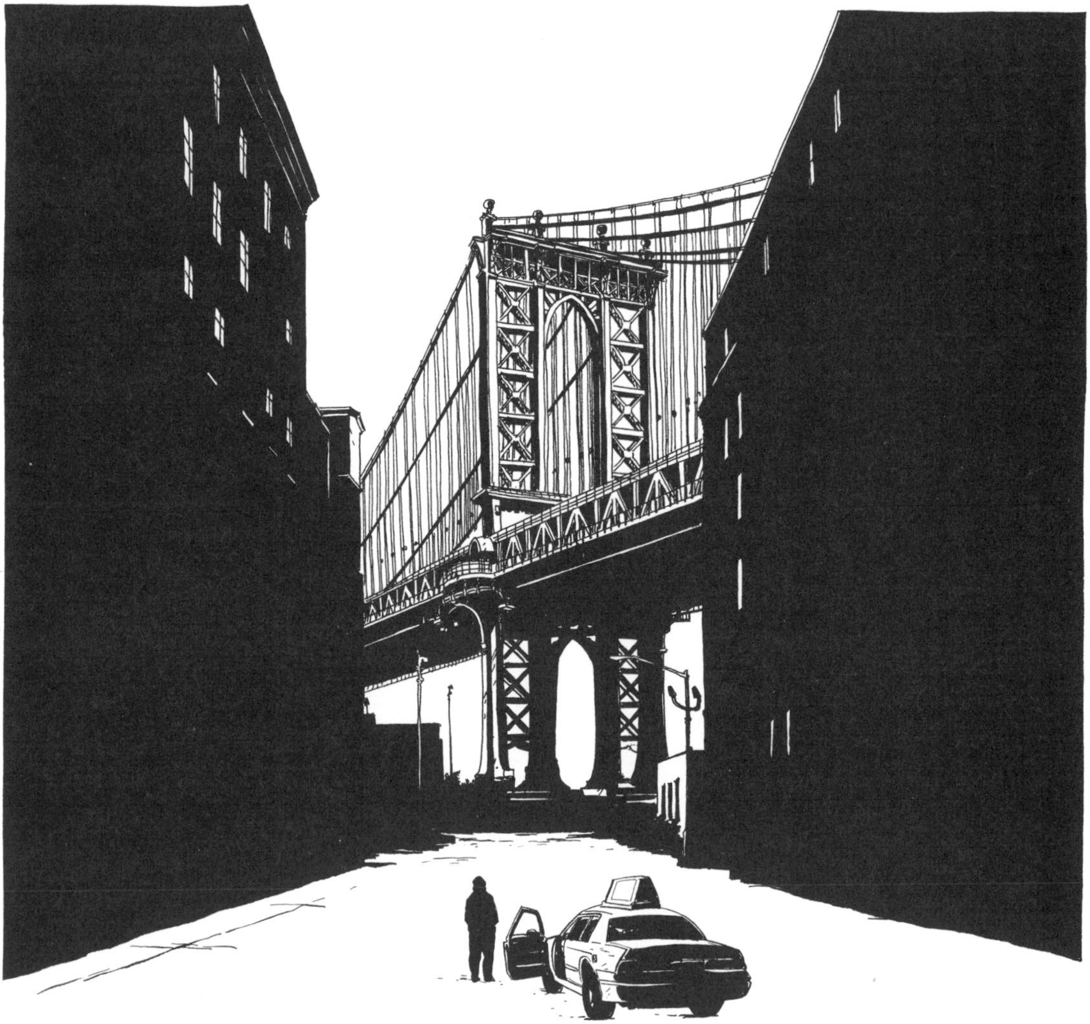

I COULD SPEND MORE DAYS, WEEKS, OR EVEN MONTHS DRIVING MY TAXI, INTERVIEWING OTHER DRIVERS, READING FIRSTHAND ACCOUNTS, GATHERING ANECDOTES, BUT I FEEL LIKE THE TIME IS NOW. OVER THE COURSE OF THESE MILES, THESE MEETINGS, THESE DAYS SPENT ALONE IN THE DRIVER'S SEAT OF MY CAB, MY FILM HAS BEEN GROWING INSIDE ME. I KNOW WHAT STORY I WANT TO TELL NOW, HOW TO TELL IT. AND I'VE GOT A WEALTH OF MATERIAL LIKE NEVER BEFORE, TO BE MINED FOR SITUATIONS, CHARACTERS, EVEN DIALOGUE.

THE TIME HAS DEFINITELY COME TO SHUT MYSELF AWAY IN MY OFFICE AND SIT DOWN IN FRONT OF MY COMPUTER.

AND IF I EVER FIND MYSELF SHORT ON INSPIRATION, OR JONESING FOR IT SOMEDAY, I COULD ALWAYS GET BACK BEHIND THE WHEEL.

FRIDAY, MAY 20, 2016

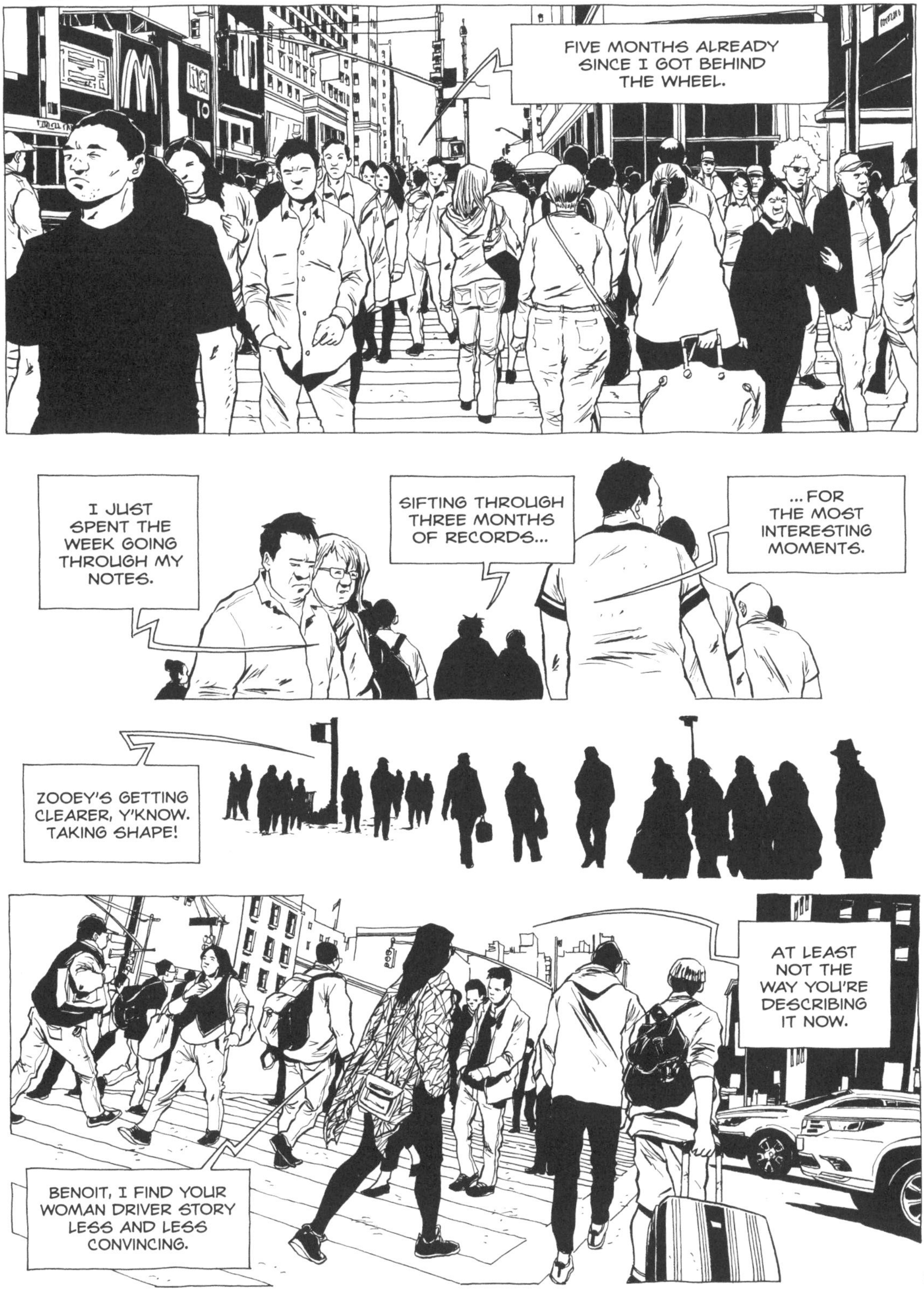
FIVE MONTHS ALREADY SINCE I GOT BEHIND THE WHEEL.
I JUST SPENT THE WEEK GOING THROUGH MY NOTES.
SIFTING THROUGH THREE MONTHS OF RECORDS...
...FOR THE MOST INTERESTING MOMENTS.
ZOOEY'S GETTING CLEARER, Y'KNOW. TAKING SHAPE!
BENOIT, I FIND YOUR WOMAN DRIVER STORY LESS AND LESS CONVINCING.
AT LEAST NOT THE WAY YOU'RE DESCRIBING IT NOW.

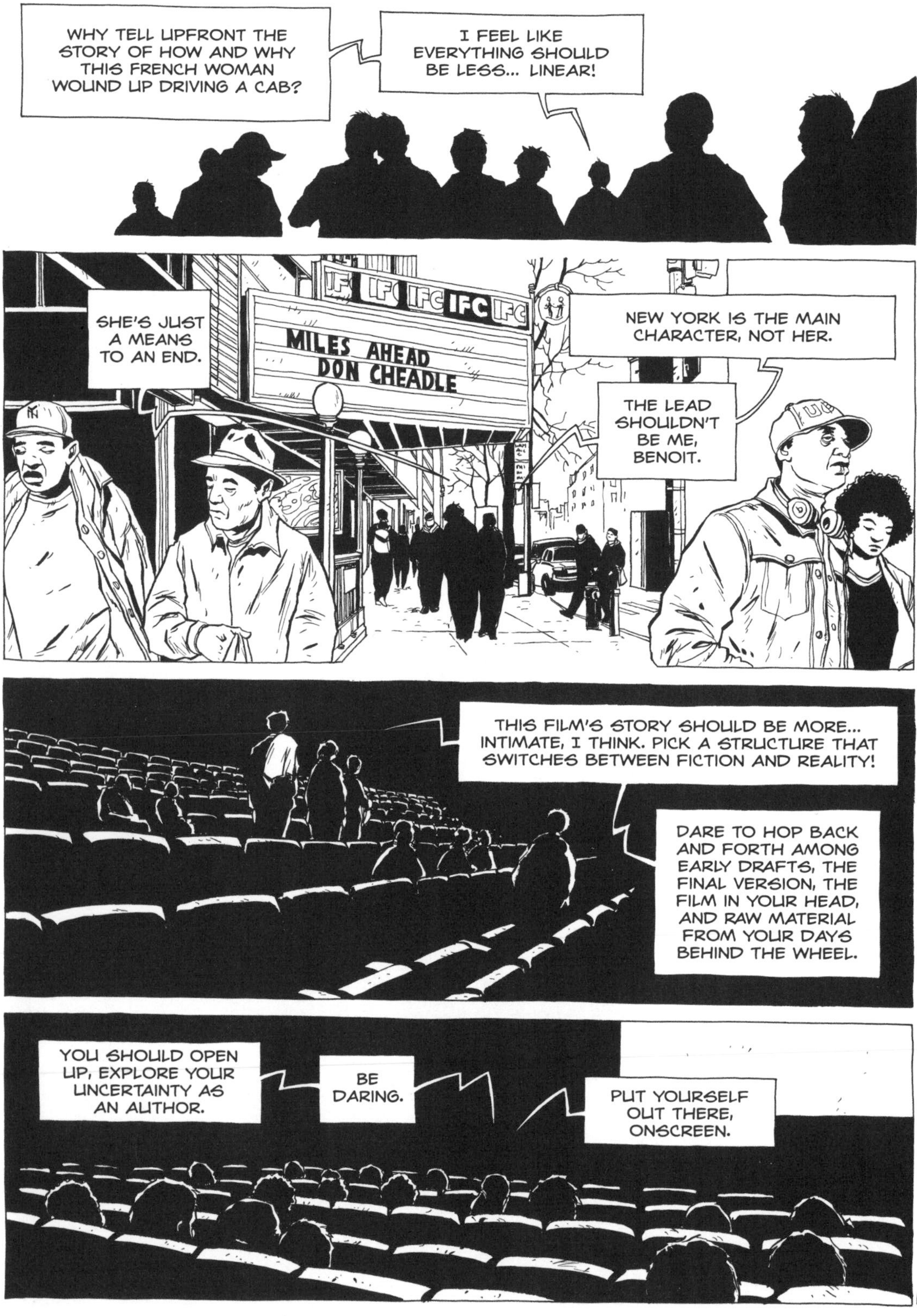
WHY TELL UPFRONT THE STORY OF HOW AND WHY THIS FRENCH WOMAN WOUND UP DRIVING A CAB?
I FEEL LIKE EVERYTHING SHOULD BE LESS... LINEAR!
IFC IFC IFC IFC IFC
MILES AHEAD
DON CHEADLE
SHE'S JUST A MEANS TO AN END.
NEW YORK IS THE MAIN CHARACTER, NOT HER.
THE LEAD SHOULDN'T BE ME, BENOIT.
THIS FILM'S STORY SHOULD BE MORE... INTIMATE, I THINK. PICK A STRUCTURE THAT SWITCHES BETWEEN FICTION AND REALITY!
DARE TO HOP BACK AND FORTH AMONG EARLY DRAFTS, THE FINAL VERSION, THE FILM IN YOUR HEAD, AND RAW MATERIAL FROM YOUR DAYS BEHIND THE WHEEL.
YOU SHOULD OPEN UP, EXPLORE YOUR UNCERTAINTY AS AN AUTHOR.
BE DARING.
PUT YOURSELF OUT THERE, ONSCREEN.

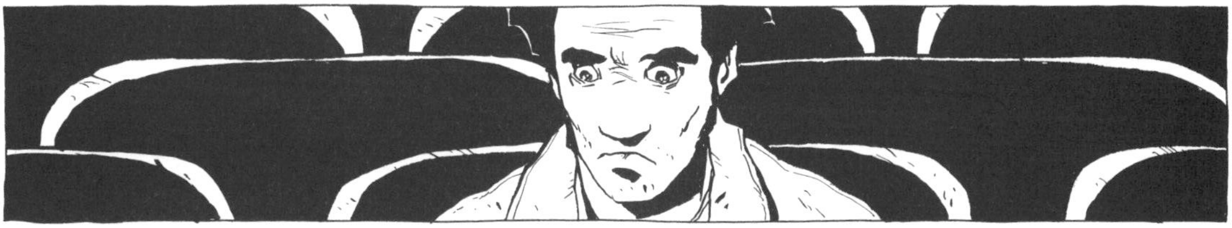

THE GAP IS GLARING BETWEEN THE POWER OF WHAT I EXPERIENCED ON A DAILY BASIS AND THE STORY I'M TRYING TO MAKE UP FROM SCRATCH.

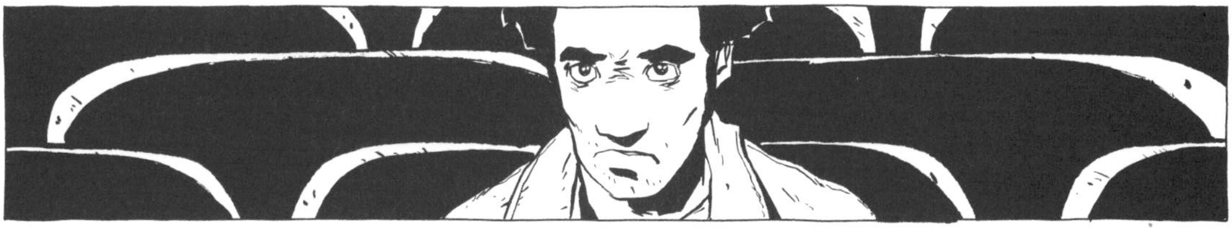

SHE'S RIGHT, OF COURSE. SO RIGHT. I WAS SO OBSESSED WITH TRYING TO WRITE A FICTIONAL STORY. I HAVE TO STOP HIDING BEHIND MY CHARACTER ZOOEY AND TRY TO TELL MY OWN STORY. IT'S SO OBVIOUS!

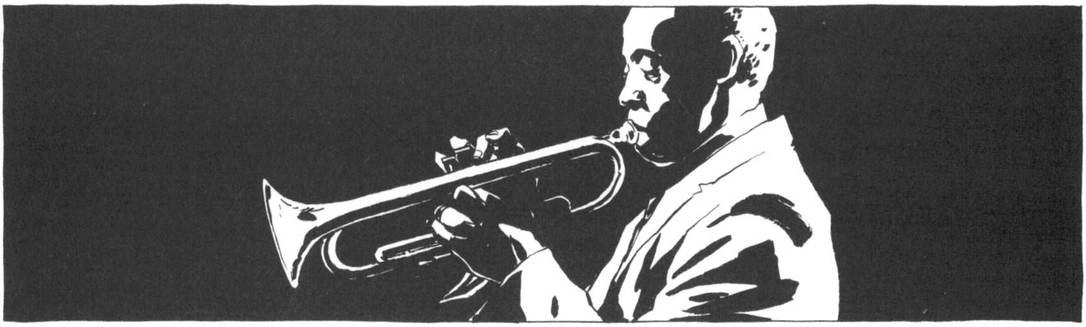

THANKS, ÉLÉONORE.

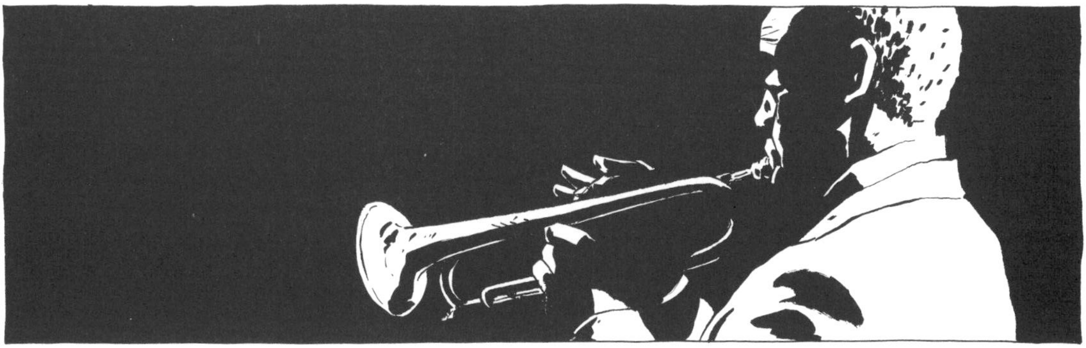

FOR OVER 20 YEARS, I TRIED TO MAKE UP STORIES. I DON'T KNOW IF I REALLY SUCCEEDED; THAT'S NOT FOR ME TO SAY. BUT I LIKED DOING IT.

WHEN I GOT HERE, I FELT THE NEED FOR SOMETHING ELSE.

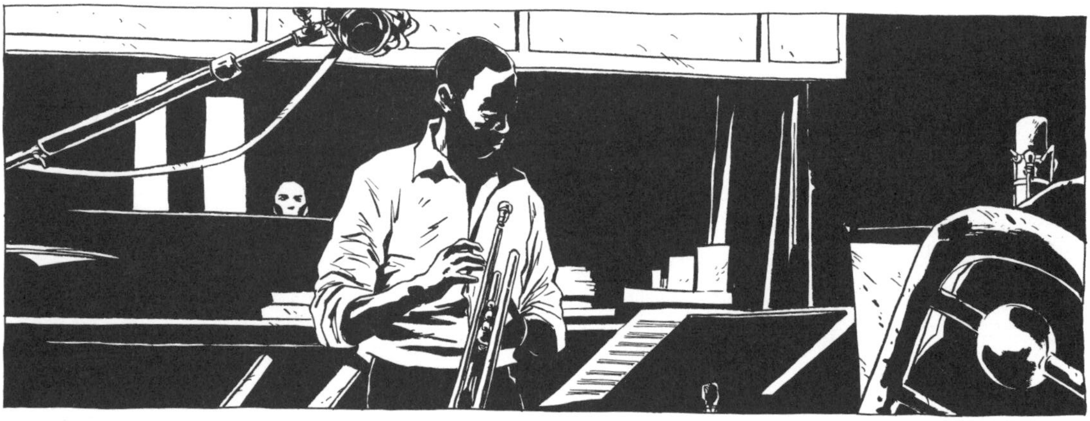

I WOUND UP IN A NEW POSITION. THAT OF AN IMMIGRANT.

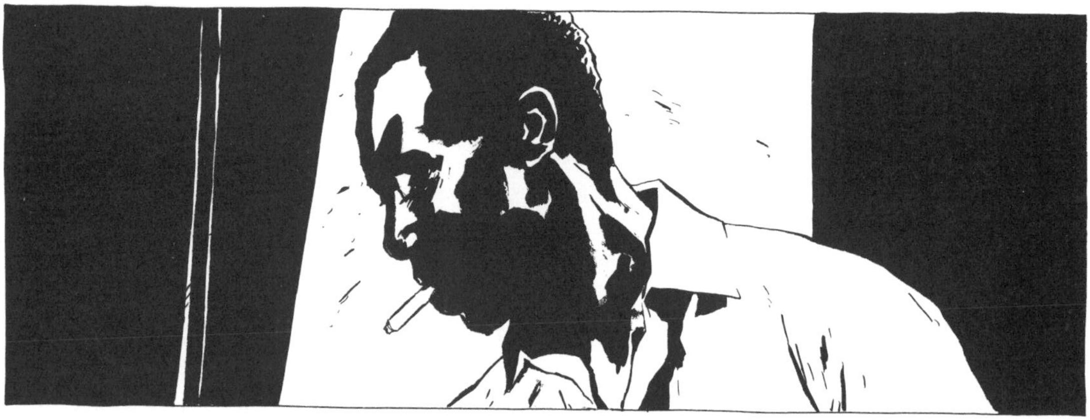

A WELL-OFF IMMIGRANT, SURE, BUT I EXPERIENCED WHAT IT WAS LIKE TO BE AN IMMIGRANT JUST THE SAME. THERE'S SOMETHING UNIVERSAL ABOUT WHAT TAXI DRIVERS FROM ABROAD GO THROUGH WHEN THEY'RE DUMPED OUT OF THE FRYING PAN AND INTO THE FIRE OF A METROPOLIS LIKE NEW YORK.

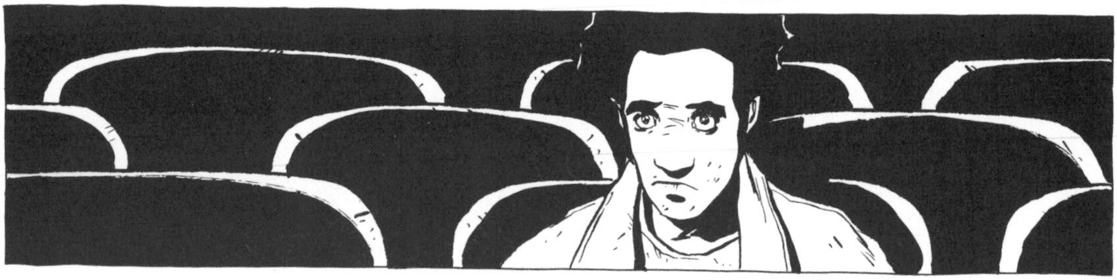

FOR A FEW MONTHS, I GOT A PEEK BEHIND THE SCENES, THE UNDERSIDE OF THE AMERICAN DREAM. CLASS STRUGGLE, IMMIGRATION, HOMESICKNESS, FORTITUDE, HUMILITY, TOLERANCE, INJUSTICE, EXILE, FEAR, VIOLENCE, SOLIDARITY, MADNESS, PLENTY, POVERTY, BEAUTY, EXHILARATION, BOREDOM, THE MIND-BLOWING VITALITY OF THIS CITY.

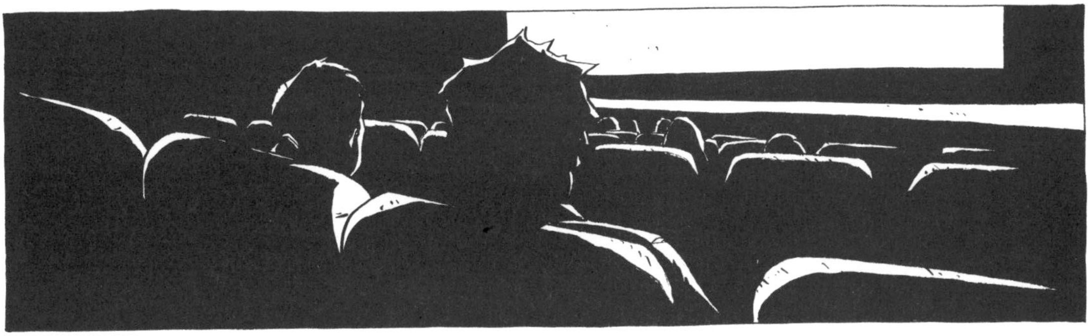

THAT'S WHAT I REALLY WANT TO TALK ABOUT.

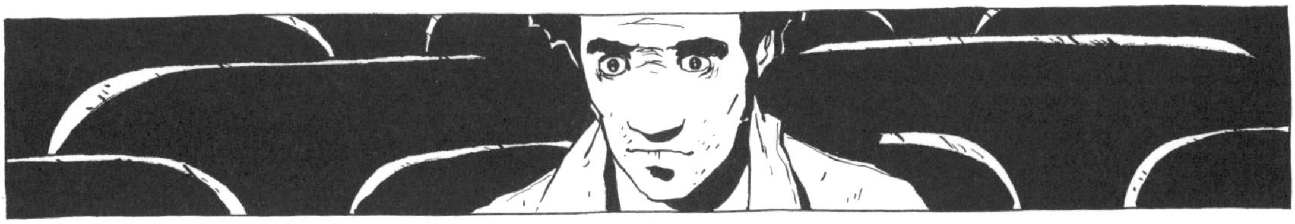

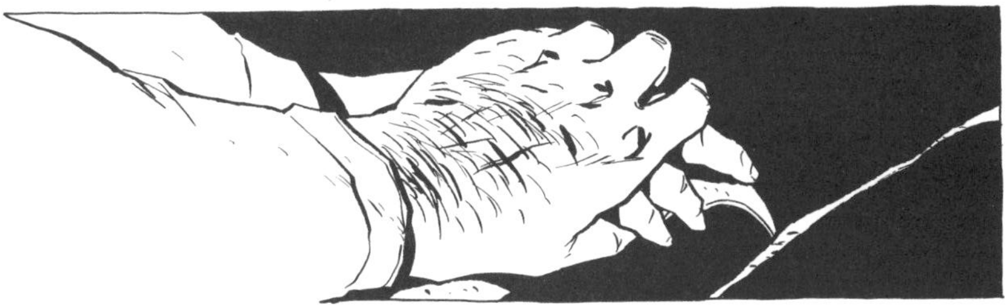

THAT'S THE STORY I HAVE TO TELL...

SATURDAY, JUNE 4, 2016

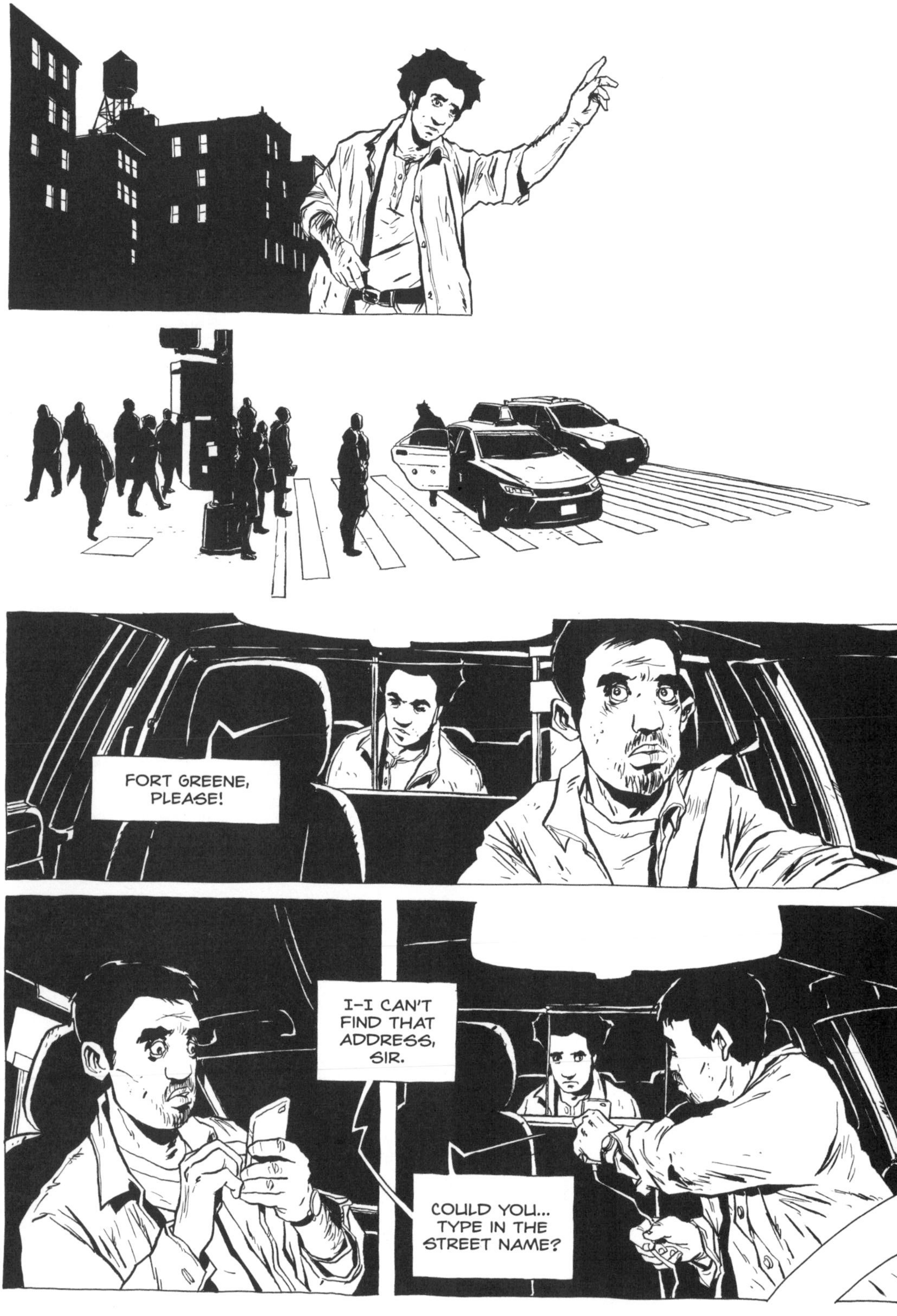
FORT GREENE, PLEASE!
I-I CAN'T FIND THAT ADDRESS, SIR.
COULD YOU... TYPE IN THE STREET NAME?

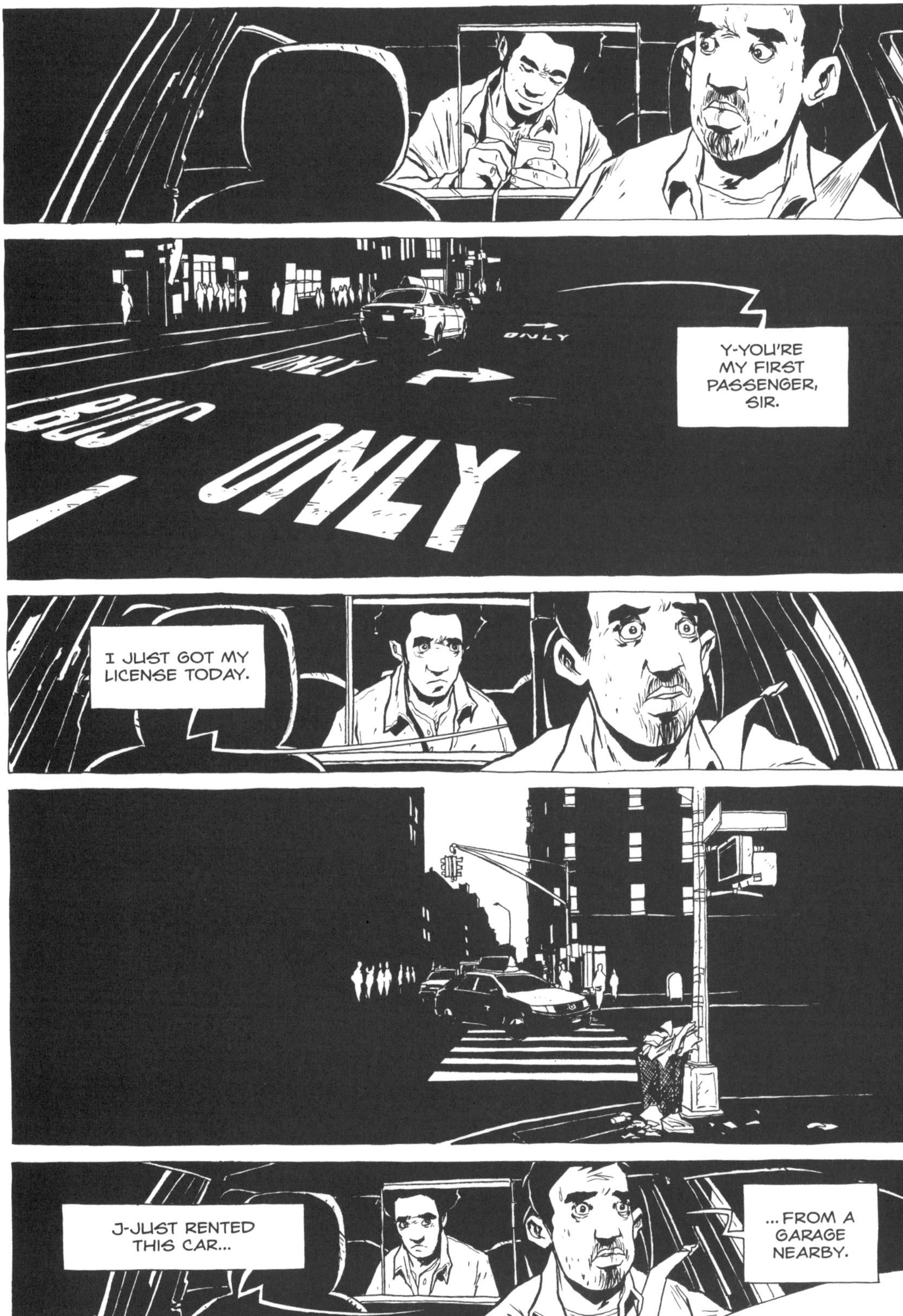
Y-YOU'RE MY FIRST PASSENGER, SIR.
ONLY
BUS ONLY
ONLY
I JUST GOT MY LICENSE TODAY.
J-JUST RENTED THIS CAR...
...FROM A GARAGE NEARBY.

H-HERE WE ARE, SIR.

EIGHT DOLLARS AND FIF—

N-NINE...

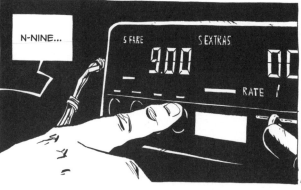

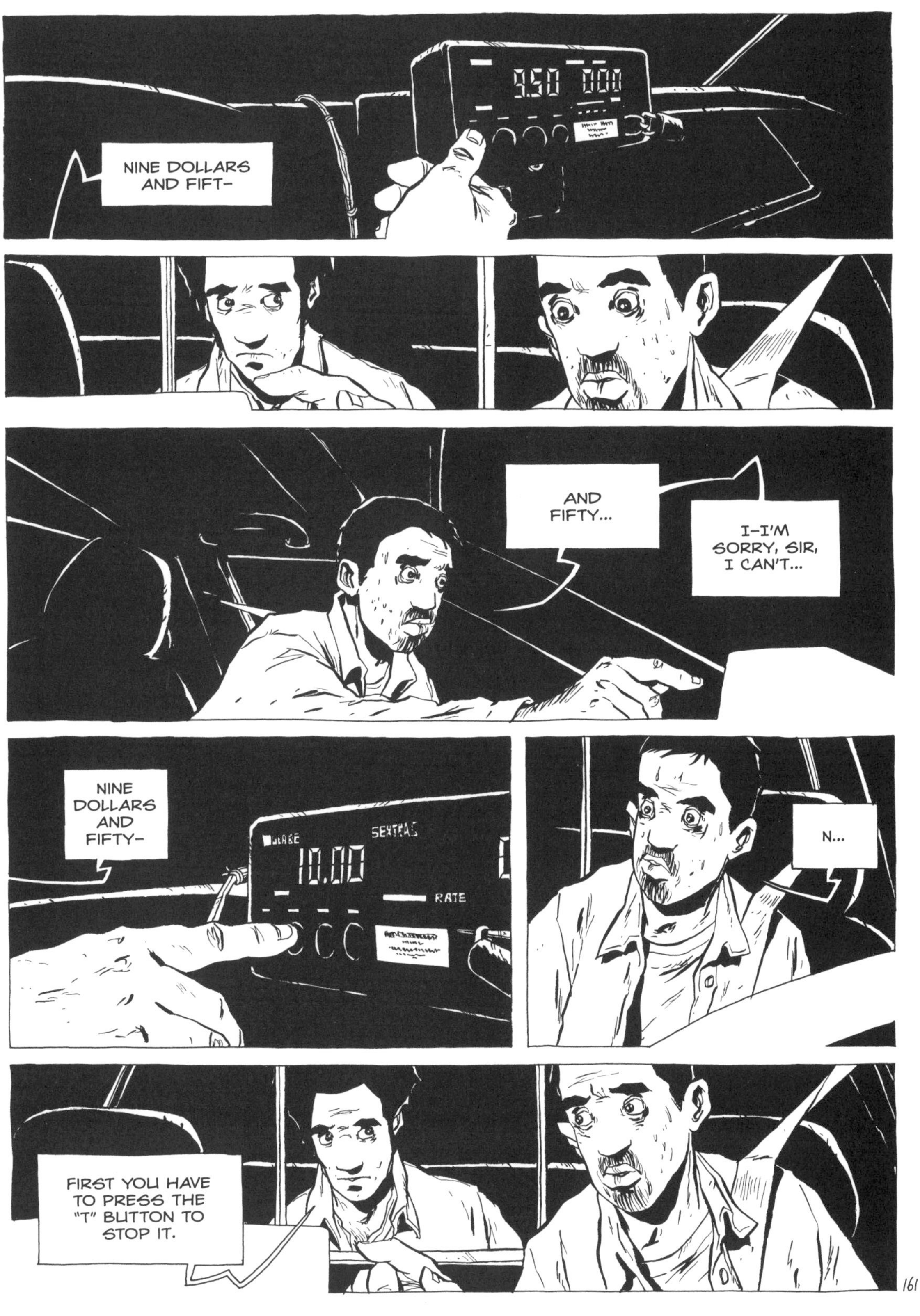

9.50 0.00
NINE DOLLARS AND FIFT-
AND FIFTY...
I-I'M SORRY, SIR, I CAN'T...
NINE DOLLARS AND FIFTY-
10.00
RATE
N...
FIRST YOU HAVE TO PRESS THE "T" BUTTON TO STOP IT.

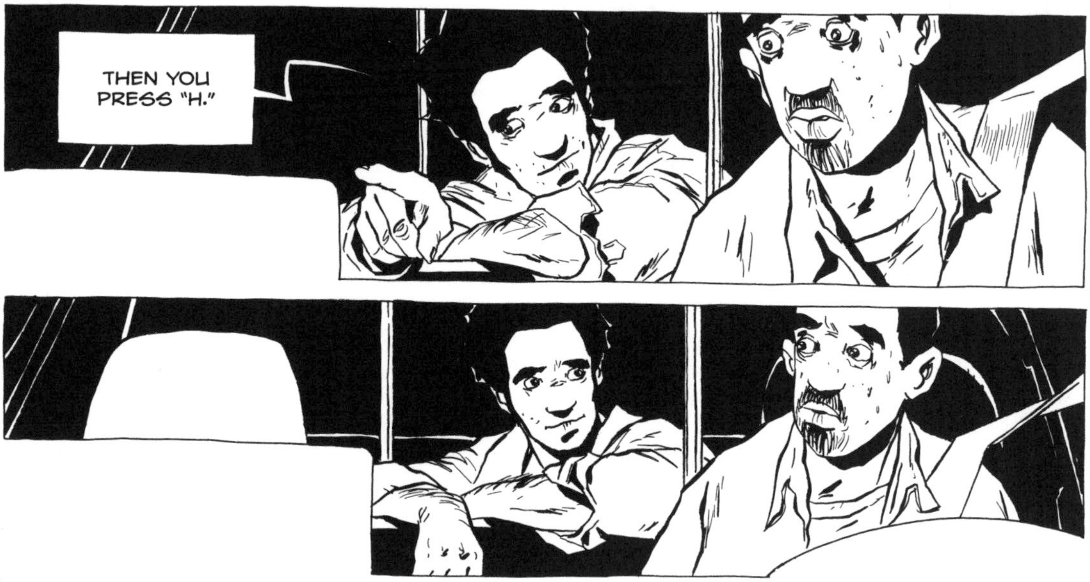
THEN YOU
PRESS "H."

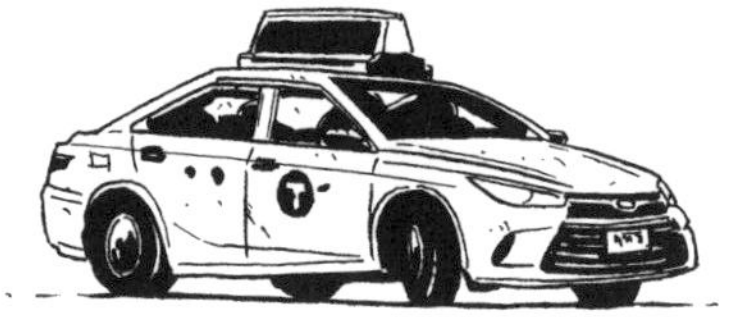

I'VE NEVER DRIVEN A TAXI IN NEW YORK...
FAR TOO CHICKEN FOR THAT.
BUT JUST LIKE YOU,
I'M ALWAYS ON THE LOOKOUT, SEARCHING,
CARRIED OFF AND CARRIED AWAY BY A NEED TO TELL STORIES...
EMOTIONAL TRANSPORT...

THANK YOU, BENOÎT.

—CHABOUTÉ